Play Therapy for Very Young Children

Play Therapy for Very Young Children

Edited by
Charles E. Schaefer, Sophronia Kelly-Zion,
Judith McCormick, and Akiko Ohnogi

JASON ARONSON
Lanham • Boulder • New York • Toronto • Plymouth, UK

Published in the United States of America
by Jason Aronson
An imprint of Rowman & Littlefield Publishers, Inc.

A wholly owned subsidiary of
The Rowman & Littlefield Publishing Group, Inc.
4501 Forbes Boulevard, Suite 200, Lanham, Maryland 20706
www.rowmanlittlefield.com

Estover Road
Plymouth PL6 7PY
United Kingdom

5/11 Gift

British Library Cataloguing in Publication Information Available

Library of Congress Cataloging-in-Publication Data

Play therapy for very young children / edited by Charles E. Schaefer . . . [et al.].
    p. cm.
  ISBN-13: 978-0-7657-0519-8 (cloth : alk. paper)
  ISBN-10: 0-7657-0519-2 (cloth : alk. paper)
  ISBN-13: 978-0-7657-0520-4 (pbk. : alk. paper)
  ISBN-10: 0-7657-0520-6 (pbk. : alk. paper)
  ISBN-13: 978-0-7657-0611-9 (electronic)
  ISBN-10: 0-7657-0611-3 (electronic)
  1. Play therapy. 2. Child psychotherapy. I. Schaefer, Charles E.

  RJ505.P6P535 2008
  618.92'891653—dc22   2008004851

Printed in the United States of America

∞™ The paper used in this publication meets the minimum requirements of
American National Standard for Information Sciences—Permanence of Paper
for Printed Library Materials, ANSI/NISO Z39.48-1992.

Contents

Part II: Applications to Specific Populations

Preface

For a person to be healthy and successful in life, how his or her childhood is spent makes all the difference. Ages zero to three years are an extremely important time in children's lives and can greatly influence the rest of their growth and development. Research and subsequent practical and clinical adaptation of these findings have shown the importance of the effect that children's very early experiences have on the rest of their life.

Neuropsychological research states that the brain of infants and toddlers is much more responsive to their social and environmental cues and responses. This brain research has shown that brain development and the ability to integrate experiences and emotions are highly dependent on children's experience from infancy and toddlerhood. The neural connections for language, emotions, impulse control, logical reasoning, social attachment, cognitive functioning, and so on, are formed during these early years. It has been shown that the most effective way to support children's success in life, socially and academically, is to enhance their development in various areas of cognition, language, physical ability, social relationships, emotional responses, self-image, confidence, et cetera, from a very early stage of infancy and toddlerhood.

Despite this research, it is only recently that the importance of infant mental health has been recognized. Intervention with infants and toddlers is still a relatively new, evolving field. The findings of various research in the past two to three decades, on the importance of early intervention on how experiences early in children's lives influence their development, show that intervention at this stage of a life has a positive impact on various aspects of development, including cognitive, social, academic, emotional, and physical growth.

The current consensus of early intervention is that if an infant or toddler has been identified with difficulties or is known to have experienced a trauma, work with the child and the parents or caretakers as early as possible is optimal. Findings in the past two decades have concluded that early intervention makes a difference to those children who receive it. The job of early intervention is to support, facilitate, identify, and build on strengths that exist in and for each child and family.

If no one understands or intervenes in the issues that an infant or toddler faces at an early stage, he or she may develop secondary emotional or cognitive difficulties. By the time the child is in preschool or kindergarten, he or she may already have been influenced by these issues long enough to be behind peers in social, emotional, cognitive, physical, academic, and other abilities. Early intervention can help foster mental health development and future healthy relationships in children with or without difficulties.

One of the key factors that decide whether children who have experienced a trauma or faced difficulties are able to lead a fairly emotionally and socially stable life as a child and adult is the experiences they have had with adults. Neuroscientists have demonstrated that appropriate, caring interactions with infants and toddlers positively influence development of parts of the brain that affects their behaviors throughout childhood and adulthood. If children have been able to form a positive, trusting relationship with a caring adult, the chance that they will be more competent and happier later in life increases. Research shows that this quality of attachment starts from infancy, and will influence the children's self-image and relationship with others, as well as social and academic competence. Playing with children has been known to enhance the quality of positive attachment to others.

The past several decades have shown an exciting increase in the use of play in treatment with children worldwide. The understanding of play as the natural mode of communication and self-expression for children has become the norm. Despite this, the use of play in treatment of infants and toddlers is a fairly new concept. Perhaps this is because play therapy is recognized worldwide as being an effective method of treating children four to eleven years old. This age specification seems to be based on assumptions that spoken language is a requirement to effectively participate in psychotherapy, including play therapy with children. And yet, if it is current "common knowledge" amongst child mental health professionals that play is used with children as their way of "talking" with or without accompanying verbalizations, it would make sense to conduct play therapy with nonverbal populations that use play to communicate. Infants and toddlers, who are much less developed in verbal expression and communication than preschool or elementary school children, should highly benefit from use of play in treating any difficulties that they may be experiencing.

Use of play in treatment can assist in dealing with the multiple obstacles that interfere with the optimal development of an infant or toddler. The opportunity for an infant or toddler to play with a variety of materials under the guidance of a caring, trusted adult has been shown to have a direct link to later academic success. In play therapy, the infant or toddler masters the environment. It is never too soon to provide the appropriate play-based intervention to young children to help them adapt successfully to their environment and family.

For those professionals who are dedicated to helping infants and toddlers, their future as older children, adolescents, and adults, and their parents, this book is an excellent resource. It is a compilation of state-of-the-art approaches, with an emphasis on the vital importance of early intervention, especially the use of play in helping young children from birth to three years of age. It is a very comprehensively edited collection of chapters on a wide spectrum of play therapy with infants and toddlers, written by child development experts and leading authorities in the field of early intervention, targeting play therapist professionals and other professionals working with children.

Regardless of the theoretical orientation of the play therapist, this book can help the clinician in conceptualizing an infant's or toddler's world and the specific play therapy interventions that can be effectively utilized with these children that would benefit from professional support. The book weaves together play therapy and infant mental health, which seems to be a natural marriage of two disciplines. It is exciting to see two fields come together to share expertise with each other.

A further goal is to provide a comprehensive guideline of the most beneficial effects of play therapy and play for the very young. These chapters are based on current research and practice, and on the solid foundation of knowledge that each author has, related to what is important for infants and toddlers and their families in the field of play therapy as an optimal form of early intervention.

The book includes extensive discussions of developmental play therapy, attachment-based caregiver-toddler play therapy, filial play therapy, mother-infant play, behaviorally oriented play-based parent training, Theraplay, play-based interventions with young children with disabilities, child-centered play therapy, Ecosystemic Play Therapy, Dynamic Play, play therapy with children in care settings, issue-specific guided play, Psychodynamic Play Therapy, play therapy with the young homeless, and play-based interventions with young children with autism. Professionals in the field of mental health, especially play therapists, will find this book useful for increase of knowledge, as well as for clinical intervention.

Multiple leading professionals in the field of early intervention and play therapy have contributed the various chapters. Although many are based in the United States, some are from other countries, and the client populations vary. Thus, this book should have helpful play therapy interventions that can be adapted for use with very young children from different cultures around the world.

Charles E. Schaefer, PhD
Sophronia Kelly-Zion, MSW, RPT-S
Judith McCormick, MEd, RPT-S
Akiko Ohnogi, PsyD

I

MAJOR THEORETICAL APPROACHES

1

Dynamic Play with Very Young Children

Steve Harvey

During an informal outdoor concert in a park, several young children were playing close to the stage in an open area while their parents were sitting nearby in the grass listening to the lively guitar music. The children's ages ranged from under two to around five. All were dancing freely, with the toddlers running after the preschool-aged children. As the music became livelier, the children added more turning and jumping and were clearly expressing an excitement that was contagious. The children were reacting easily to each other's bodies. They were all clearly sharing happiness in their facial expressions as well as their full body movement. Their expressions invited their younger watchers to join them and the adults to show expressions of positive feelings.

One three-year-old boy was able to swing his body around a cable and find just the right spot to fall into the grass for a perfect landing, exerting just the right amount of control of his body to accomplish the action to achieve maximum physical pleasure. Another younger boy began copying this movement after having watched it done once. Both boys smiled and began to laugh with each other during this exchange. The two then began taking turns, adding slightly more complexity to the movement in a complete improvisation whose only goal appeared to be to share the thrill and enjoyment of the immediate moment with each other.

When one of the boys saw his father walking over to him, he smiled and began running through the gathering of adults, clearly signaling a challenge to his parent to join in a game of chase. Both father and son were laughing with each other during the chase while running through the audience. This shared glee reached a crescendo when the father was able to pick the boy up and swing him onto his shoulders to carry him off to the mother, who then helped them sit for a snack.

The movement of this scene was choreographed in a way in which all the participants wanted to and were able to participate freely and fully. Turns were taken and allowed, movement quickened and slowed to allow the various emotional states to be expressed and shared instantaneously, all expressions were included and responded to, and a play state was created and shared by all the children or parents who involved themselves. Even those who merely watched were captivated by the shared feeling. One interaction led to another effortlessly. The clear overall feeling among all the players was of enjoyment expressed in a natural and physical manner. The nonverbal language shared among the participants and watchers was clear, as were the nonverbal invitations and acceptance to play. Once in the shared play state, each player knew exactly what to do spontaneously and how to join this complex series of interactions at just the right time and with just the right style of physical expression. The resulting web of actions was so complicated that it could have not been planned, yet the children, the father, and then the mother executed their parts freely to perfection with complete enjoyment and engagement.

A central theme of this chapter is that such seemingly effortless and natural playful interactions are cocreated and mutually learned by parents and their very young children from their earliest spontaneous physical interactions onward. The initial face games between a mother and her young infant are a good example of such a "dance," in which both infant and parent teach each other about the reciprocal turn taking, mutual gaze, and a matching of the "contours" and vitality affects (Stern 1985) of their physical expression of positive feeling. This same learning of the dance of physical matching of expressions becomes more advanced with the child's developing physical, emotional, and psychological ability. The importance of this experience of mutual expressiveness has been discussed for attachment (Bowlby 1972), psychological development (Garvey 1990), and socialization (Stern 2004). Clearly such benefits are important in any parent-child therapy (Harvey 2003).

These early experiences are also very important for the play therapist. As young children and their parents share positive expression, they are experientially learning how to signal, join, share, and then develop a play state from the child's earliest days. Such early nonverbal exchanges can be seen as the development of the implicit language of play. As this language is developed through spontaneous improvisations with a willing partner, it is very hard to learn it in a more structured or planned way should difficulties with play occur. Another implication of this early development of play is that when children and/or children and their families experience problems, this play language is likewise disrupted. The focus of this chapter is on how the disturbances in early play language can be recognized so that the work of therapy can become guiding natural mutual play toward the development of more positive playful exchanges. One of the main assumptions is that the experience of shared play has curative factors (Schaefer 1993) that can be applied to help families develop more positively. In this chapter, applications of Dynamic Play for infants, toddlers, and preschoolers will be discussed.

PLAY EPISODES

Examples of play interactions with parents and young children who are normally developing and those with clear problems will be presented to describe the difference in such play. Examples of the children with problems are taken from my long-time practice with infants and toddlers who have experienced maltreatment (abuse/neglect), domestic violence, and are in foster or adoptive placement. All of these children could be described as showing behaviors that indicate psychological trauma, disruption in their basic attachments, and difficulties with nonverbal communication. Examples of normally developing children present here are from families with no known problems. Such comparison is used to highlight differences between styles of interactive play more specifically.

Normally Developing Toddler and His Mother

Julie and her 20-month-old son Sean were invited into a playroom filled with large soft pillows, stuffed animals, colorful scarves, and several puppets. She was asked to play "Follow the leader" with him. Sean immediately went over to the large bears and hugged one while Julie followed, verbalizing about the friendliness of the stuffed bear. Sean had little interest and soon rapidly moved over to some large soft pillows in the middle of the room and fell into them. Julie followed after and fell beside him. Her movement had the same rhythmic quality that Sean had used. Their movements were so well choreographed that the mutual falling could be predicted by anyone watching this movement before it occurred.

Julie and Sean smiled at each other in a way that encouraged more pleasurable interaction. Sean lifted himself and fell in the same way a few more times while Julie again followed using matching rhythms in her voice and body. Sean then left to investigate the bear, again leading Julie to accompany him. After a brief hug, Sean then left to fall into the pillows once again, with Julie falling with him. Julie began to smile with Sean as an acknowledgment that the two had discovered a new game. Sean and Julie spent the next several minutes improvising different falls into the pillows, while adding sound that extended the rhythm of their falls. The game ended with both Julie and Sean laughing together face-to-face into pillows. During the next period of free play, Sean introduced his newly created "falling dance" with Julie between other play ideas he pursued.

The central feeling state created from this episode was one of joy and glee. Both Julie and Sean were totally immersed in the game. What started as a following, turn-taking activity turned into a joint play state in which mother and son could thoroughly enjoy each other in a very physical way. Because of the emotional sharing, the physical activity of falling together was transformed into an expressive dance that had a perfect choreography improvised to express a shared emotional feeling state in a full-body experience. This state was signaled to each participant in an instant, and both partners entered this special experience together. It ended with mutual laughter.

Their movement together could not have been planned, as the improvisation created a play language that informed each player how to respond in the moment. Positive socialization was achieved. Secure attachment between Julie and Sean was forwarded, and Sean was able to continue creating experiences that helped him in his developmental tasks of enjoying a trusting relationship with Julie and internalizing positive expectations about his being cared for. Intimacy was shared. This kind of playful attunement of a positive emotional state could be thought of as the magical "it" of relationships.

Toddler and Her Mother with a History of Domestic Violence

Another toddler, Janet, was led into the playroom by her mother, Carol, for an observation to help determine the attachment status between mother and daughter. Janet had been removed from Carol and her partner's care by a child protective agency almost nine months previous due to ongoing threats to her safety. Carol and her partner were quite violent with each other and often hit Janet. The adults were also quite involved with substance use, and their aggressiveness toward their then-infant daughter was worse and more unpredictable when drugs or alcohol were present in the home. Carol's partner had moved from the area and she wished to resume parenting Janet. This observation was a part of a larger evaluation to help the child protective workers in the decision making.

Carol and Janet entered the same playroom as Sean and Julie. Carol was asked to follow her daughter. Carol moved to the large soft pillows and sat down. She stayed in this position throughout the next 45 minutes of observation. Janet moved toward a pile of large pillows at the edge of the room about five feet from Carol and began touching them. Carol spoke to her daughter by naming the objects that she touched and said her name.

Janet did not respond verbally or nonverbally to her birth mother's statements. After several minutes, Janet picked a plastic tube and pointed in her mother's direction but dropped it after Carol did not respond to her. Janet then moved to another part of the playroom where several markers, crayons, and large pieces of paper were laid out. She sat down and began to take the caps of the markers off and on for the rest of the interaction.

Other observations revealed that Janet had developed an insecure-avoidant attachment style with Carol and showed her to have cognitive developmental delays. Observations of visits and the time Carol spent with Janet in her home were similar to those in the playroom. A review of her interactive play also revealed that Janet and Carol showed virtually no attunement (Stern 1985) in their nonverbal communication with each other. Janet and Carol showed no mutual play in their interactions. There was no nonverbal signaling to join play, no shift into a play state, and no development of enjoyable activity.

While other developmental concerns were present, the absence of playful exchanges between Carol and Janet, such as those that occurred with the other children described at the opening of this chapter, is significant to the play therapist. This lack of conjoint play is a disruption of the normal development of play. Such breaks in the natural play process between parents and children are the focus of intervention in Dynamic Play Therapy with young children. Other emotional tasks such as developing trust and intimacy with others were also not occurring in the observations. In an intervention, efforts would need to be focused on guiding Carol to recognize and respond to Janet's invitations to enter the play state and then coaching the elaboration of their play interactions.

The central play mode used in Dynamic Play with this age group involves developing movement interactions that are playful and enjoyable for both parent and child; art, music, dramatic and occasional video making are also incorporated to facilitate mutual expression. This style of intervention is best used in conjunction with other social work and early intervention practices (education and psychology), as most children and their families who require interventions at this age typically have significant problems in other areas.

BACKGROUND

Dynamic Play Therapy draws on the attachment theory (Bowlby 1972, 1973, 1980), intersubjectivity and affective attunement (Stern 1985, 1990, 2004), and developmental-oriented play therapy (Harvey 1994a, 1994b; Greenspan and Wieder 2003; Ryan 2004). Attachment refers to the style of parent-child interaction that develops to address basic emotional security.

Stern (2004) describes intersubjectivity as another basic motivational system, which leads parents and their children to develop and share intimacy particularly from their earliest nonverbal exchanges onward throughout their life together. Intersubjectivity, like attachment, is thought to be an innate communication system especially in families and addresses a basic human need to share intrapersonal experience and be included in relationship rather than experience profound isolation. Intersubjectivity develops through mutual experiences of a series of "now moments," in which a parent and child share attuned nonverbal communication. While attachment and intersubjectivity can occur separately such that attachment communication can lack intimacy, most often the development of attunement between a parent and child can lead to a more secure attachment style. Shared play moments offer fertile times for attunement and intimacy between parents and children to occur.

Several play therapists (Wilson and Ryan 2005; Ryan 2004; Brody 1997; Jernberg 1979; Harvey 1995, 2006) have described using play therapy as a way to facilitate the development of attachment through an adult's sensitive responding to the child's play initiatives. Such responding builds intersubjectivity, and then over time these experiences can be used to facilitate more secure attachment. Harvey (1994a, 1994b, 1994c) and Schwartzenberger (2004) suggest having parents participate in the play. Jernberg (1979) reports on using a structured approach in which the therapist directs parents to become involved in interactions with their children that are both nurturing and pleasurable. Brody (1997) reports using touch to promote intimate interactions that facilitate experiences rich with positive sensory experience. Greenspan and Wieder (2003) have developed a form of interventions that specifically address children with developmental disorders who lack appropriate relationships with others. In an aspect of this approach called "floortime," parents are encouraged to find ways to join their children using any interaction that fits their child's unique communicative needs. Parents are encouraged to use this relationship to help the child address various developmental delays.

Schwartzenberger (2004) describes another form of parent-child interactive play approaches that he has called guided interaction. In this approach, the therapist begins conducting individual sessions with the child while consulting and forming a therapeutic alliance with the parent(s) or other caregiver. Parents are then integrated within selected aspects of their children's play. As parents become more responsive, they are helped to play more completely with their children using the therapist's guidance.

Dynamic Play Therapy (Harvey 1994a, 1994b, 1994c, 2003, 2006) draws on the practice of dance therapy in addition to the approaches mentioned above. Unfortunately, much of this literature is not familiar to play therapy, especially in relation to applications with very young children where nonverbal approaches are so important. Tortora (2006) describes an approach in which the therapist follows the young child's movement specifically to develop a matching and then "dances" (or moves) with episodes of matched nonverbal communication. Tortora uses a systematic form of observation to help the therapist and the parents notice the particular quality of emotional communication the child prefers. These movement qualities are then incorporated in further movement episodes between therapist/ parent/child that can match each other.

Dynamic Play Therapy (Harvey 1994a, 1994b, 1994c) builds on both the play and the dance therapy approaches noted above. However, the style differs from other approaches in the combination of three significant dimensions:

- a much enlarged use of physical engagement for both parents and children
- use of several expressive mediums such as drawing, story, and occasional video
- an emphasis on spontaneous creativity in moment-to-moment playful expression

While most, if not all, parent-infant intervention utilizes the concept of a parent being able to follow or mirror the young child's nonverbal gestures and expressions, the expressive arts approach used in Dynamic Play Therapy emphasizes the use of a parent or child's whole-body expression, whether in following or in turn-taking activities, as well as helping both the parent and child recognize their mutual invitations to play. Therapists who use Dynamic Play approaches also make use of several media (e.g., drawing) even with younger children. Importantly, in this approach, therapists also stress the importance of guiding parents and children to not only develop shared communication but to experience the positive emotions that come from joint play. While Dynamic Play Therapy has been applied for children of all ages (Harvey 1995, 2003, 2006), this chapter will present how this work has been adapted for intervention with infants and children under three.

METHODS

The main goal of Dynamic Play with very young children (infancy through three years) is to increase positive interactive play between parents and their very young child in a naturalistic manner similar to the activities described in the beginning of this chapter. The majority of the time is spent with a parent(s) (or support person) in the playroom attempting to recognize and then respond to the child's invitations to play. With children this age, such invitations are mostly nonverbal. Often the therapist begins with informal conversations with the parent(s) or caregiver about the everyday family events involving the child, while observing the interactions between child and parents. These conversations then move gradually to include the present immediate interactions between parent and child. Such spontaneous interaction coupled with how such communication is viewed by the adults becomes the initial raw material or focus of the intervention. It is essential that the therapist maintain focus on the positive aspects of such interaction to keep the intent of parents and children as wanting to be with each other central in nonverbal as well as verbal communications. After the discussion/observation portion of the session, the therapist then guides the parent to engage with more physical play or other modes of expression in longer interactions, using freely improvised expressions or more structured play activity (see below).

A basic assumption is that mutual playful exchanges are natural and spontaneously communicate this mutual desire to be with each other in a reciprocal manner. As such, the primary activity of the therapy occurs between the parent(s) and their children, while the therapist is more of a guide or coach. Most if not all of the play (especially physical play involving touch) is between the parents and children, with the therapist providing encouragement, suggestions, and only sometimes being a willing play partner. While the therapist may occasionally take the role as a lead player, especially to emphasize the need to respond to the child's play, parents are helped to become the child's main play partner. More adult-oriented discussions, counseling or mental health interventions, and psycho education around parenting issues occurs in appointments with adults only, and often with other clinicians if possible. This is so that the main focus of Dynamic Play can be to identify child-initiated play communication and then to develop these in full enjoyable interactions that have attunement.

The essential steps involved in developing a Dynamic Play intervention include creating an overall warm and welcoming environment in which the play initiatives of young children are more likely to occur in a natural and spontaneous way; helping parents recognize the child's invitations to play (however tentative such invitations may be); and then helping to elaborate and extend playful exchanges using physical, artistic, video, and story/dramatic expression cocreated in a moment-to-moment fashion. It is important that parent(s) and children discover an intrinsic enjoyment. The methods of Dynamic Play follow from these general goals.

The specific practices of this method are flexible, to include the family circumstances. However, I have found some overall guidelines helpful to consider when setting up an intervention: creating an informal, positive atmosphere in which the therapist's qualities are considered; the playroom and play props; the use of semistructured to free play episodes; adaptations to fit important adults and other family members within the play; use of verbalization and discussions; and integrating the play therapy with other types of interventions (child protective services, foster caregivers, and other early intervention services).

Therapeutic Environment

The therapeutic relationship with the parent(s) is especially important in Dynamic Play, as the therapist's relationship with the adult becomes a model for the parent–very young child relationship. Many adults find engaging in spontaneous play interaction with their young child intimate, which can lead to a heightened sense of vulnerability. Some parents who require attachment-related interventions have had histories of disrupted attachments themselves and find that play can be quite emotionally challenging, especially play in response to their infant or toddler. As such, it is important for the therapist to approach the parent (quite often the mother) with acceptance, positive regard, patience, and responsiveness while guiding play to be in response to the child's attempts at communication. Attention is paid almost exclusively to when the parent is successful in engaging the child, rather than pointing out play failures.

Additionally, the therapist needs to expect and create an atmosphere that accepts infants, toddlers, and young preschoolers. Young children can show behaviors that are quite different from children even slightly older. They may spit up, need to eat or snack, show high-intensity emotions, fall asleep, and even need to have their diapers changed at times during play episodes. Parents of young children can likewise have significant frustrations, including feelings of low self-esteem and helplessness as a parent, in addition to the more day-to-day frustrations and exhaustion that comes from the demands of caring for children this age. Often parents who are referred to improve their interactions may have been marginalized through poverty, domestic violence, cultural differences, or age (young mothers).

The personal qualities of the therapist have particular importance in creating an appropriate positive environment when working with very young children. It is essential that the therapist be playful, know about and enjoy infants and toddlers, and appreciate the demands of parenting children this age. At times the gender and cultural background of the therapist facilitates a family's more positive engagement in the process. I (an older male) often work with women as cotherapists in sessions to help with the challenge of creating a more accepting atmosphere. For example, when working in New Zealand with Maori families, therapy can be improved by directly involving the "auntie," an older woman who often has a respected primary caretaking and supportive role for the extended family, in sessions when appropriate.

The therapist also needs to be highly flexible in creating positive engagements with the caregiver/family, as intrinsic motivation and ability to engage in shared positive experiences with children can vary widely. Referrals for interactive interventions can range from single mothers (and even some single fathers) who because of developmental (e.g., teenage parent), psychological, or social factors seem to have little initial interest in developing intimate relationships with their children, to older foster/adoptive parents who can be quite motivated and knowledgeable about developing an attachment with very damaged children.

A young single mother was referred to me because of her young twin boys' problems in focusing and gaining weight. The referrer was a child psychiatrist, an older woman who had been a single mother to now-adult children. The boys' mother had a long history with domestic violence herself. She was socially isolated and initially refused to play at all, saying that it was irrelevant—despite the clear change in her children's mood and attempts to seek her after even very brief episodes of her participation in therapist-coached play. She particularly did not want to be seen playing with her children by this older male psychologist. The mother did continue to see a child psychiatrist, however, for more medical consultations. The psychiatrist was able to begin to model more playful interactions with the mother and her boys, using consultation from me.

After several months the mother did return to the playroom with her children for a few sessions. The psychiatrist and I were able to coach her to recognize her boys' ideas and how they were able to communicate their enjoyment of being with her in their animated play after she was able to join. However, it was important to keep this mother's case open far longer than is typical in a mental health agency, despite her not keeping regularly set appointments, and to work with the psychiatrist in a more flexible manner than was typical in clinical procedures. Without such adjustments it was likely that this mother and her two boys would have been a "treatment failure."

An example of a very different approach involved a couple who were referred to me from a child protective service. The couple wanted to adopt an 18-month-old girl who was taken from her birth mother due to extensive physical abuse and neglect. The couple willingly came to treatment and participated in every session in a highly motivated manner. No other mental health person was involved. When conducting play activities, I approached the couple more as a coach or cotherapist to help find play activities that they could attune to, and to extrapolate from their daughter's frenzied activity, which included almost no eye contact. This couple required significant support, as they became emotionally exhausted by their daughter's apparent rejection of their ongoing approaches to her. However, such support was provided within a more traditional outpatient setting using regular appointments.

Playroom

There should be a range of toys appropriate for infants and toddlers and the parents should be encouraged to bring their own child's favorites as well. In general, the setting needs to have a large open area so that children, parents, and the therapist can move freely with full-body physical activities, ranging from running through space and falling to wiggling fingers and toes together. The room is also filled with (1) large foam pillows covered with bright material that is soft to the touch; (2) large soft stuffed animals of several sizes, including some as large as parents and children (stuffed bears and dogs are good choices); (3) several large scarves made of light transparent material of several colors, and elastic stretchy blankets and bags or parachutes; (4) several washable markers next to large sheets of paper; and (5) a video camera and monitor close by, as well as a tape or CD player.

Pillows, large animals, scarves, and the like, are materials that have multiple uses, in order to accommodate the moment-to-moment activities the parent and child develop through their improvisations. The pillows, for example, at one moment can be used as a place for the adult and child to run to and fall on safely, and the next moment can become walls of a house or be set up as a tunnel to crawl through. Likewise, the large stuffed bears or dogs can be part of a general pile of props to crawl over, only later to become part of a simple dramatic enactment of a family of bear parents and children. The scarves can be used as a way to play a peek-a-boo game in one instant, and the next instant become colorful objects to be thrown in the air in response to a child's gaze. The transparent nature of the material helps in developing a sense of constancy and security, especially with younger or more frightened children as the parent can remain in view as game interactions develop. The large elastic blankets can be used as a fun way to contain very energetic movement, then used later in the session as a place to slowly rock and calm the child as a final session activity.

The markers and large newsprint become part of expressive activity, as children are able to produce scribbles and other marks. This is usually in the later part of the child's second year or early in the third year. By having this material close to the props used for more physical activity, expression can be easily redirected back and forth from movement to art/mark making. The tape or CD player adds the ability to use recorded music to help support activity when appropriate. I have found classical music as well as selections from the more typical children's music to be helpful in developing the expressions during selected parts of the play. The camera is used to capture parts of the interactions and used to replay for view either during the session or by the parent at a later time. It is important especially to capture positive moments of play interactions to review with parents during the initial sessions.

Use of Structured and Unstructured Play Interactions

Much of the play between parents and young children is improvised free play, with the therapist guiding and coaching the interactions in order in help the parent's response to match and elaborate the child's initiative. For example, as a toddler runs and jumps in a pillow, the therapist might encourage the parent to excitedly verbalize about the action while jumping in a pillow close by in a similar manner. A therapist might also use a video to capture an interaction that expressed a moment of shared positive feeling that occurred spontaneously. However, some of the following interactive games are useful tools to provide structure to encourage more attunement naturally, especially in the beginning of the interventions.

Games with Infants

Such games include parent and child face-to-face play, games of peek-a-boo with eye contact; using the transparent scarves to cover the parent's face while encouraging the child to pull the scarves away; using touch to a limb to develop movements initiated by the child; having the parent hold the child and move in different rhythms to find the child's favorite; rolling and crawling interactions (e.g., rolling or crawling toward and away from the child); and as the infant is developing these abilities, using music and props (large pillows and colorful scarves) to elaborate each activity.

Running and Falling Games with Toddlers

Such games include encouraging and following toddlers when they run though space. Using piles of soft pillows, have both parent and child fall into them. The pillows can be spread throughout the room. Different rhythms and types of falls can be used.

Swinging the Child into the Pillows

The parent is asked to swing the child into a pile of pillows. To accomplish this activity with a sense of shared pleasure, the parent will have to match his or her rhythm to the child's physical tension and excitement. This activity is a good way to encourage nonverbal attunement. As the parent and child learn to enjoy this activity, the parent can be asked to increase the intensity of the swinging so that the child experiences the maximum excitement, and then to use a slower swing to calm the child down. A good way to end sessions is to have both the parent and another adult (the therapist or other caregiver) rock the child slowly in a stretchy blanket several times.

Pillow Houses

The pillows can be used to build a house around children of toddler years and older. This activity can then be extended by having the adults reach though the gaps in the pillows to try to catch the child, having the parent join the child in the house, and having the child break out by pushing the pillows down. This can lead to making the house and having it broken down several times. These activities can be extended to included mark-making of a house. Any scribbles that have a shape can represent a house.

Hide-and-Seek

Versions of this game can be played with all children in this age range by matching the demands of the game to the skill and developmental level of the child involved. Both parent and child can take the role of the hider or seeker. With younger toddlers, the parent is asked to use the transparent scarves and a hiding place in full view of the child to help with the finding (the big moment of the episode). As children get older and more able to tolerate separation, the pillows can be used to make more elaborate hiding places, and the adults can have less direct involvement in the setup of the hiding place to increase the tension leading up to the "finding." The complexity of the game can be increased until the caregiver can leave the room briefly as part of the game, while the child is helped to hide by the other adults (the therapist or other parent).

Stories with Stuffed Animals

Simple family stories with stuffed animals can be introduced as children are developmentally able to enter into dramatic play. Story themes can include separations and reunions of the child and parent figures, and normal, everyday events such as going to bed and eating. Playing hide-and-seek with the animals after playing the "real" game helps with the transition from physical interaction to a more representational mode.

Mark-Making

When children are old enough (during the end of toddlerhood) and they are able to use markers or crayons to make scribbles, parents and children can be asked to engage in scribble conversations. In this activity, large pieces of newsprint are placed on the floor and the parents are encouraged to scribble in response to their children's mark-making. Such exchanges are intended to produce conversations and turn taking. One variation is to have the parent leave the paper after such a scribble conversation has begun while the child continues his mark-making. The parent is then asked to rejoin the conversation after a short time. Comparisons of the initial joint drawing, the child's solo marks, and the return of the parent and child drawing together again can lead to discussions about how the child's scribbles might be expressions of feelings about being with or separate from and then with the parent again.

Strategies for Verbal Interventions with the Caretakers

The central goal of the verbal comments during the intervention is to help parents recognize that their children's nonverbal attempts have the intent to engage them in play, which is enjoyable and has communicative value. The types of comments toward this end made during the play action include the therapist speaking for the child using simple emotional phrases; having the parent interpret the child's nonverbal interactions; and having the parents tell stories about their children's everyday events, including their child's immediate nonverbal play as observed in the session in these stories; and having the parents retell very important events directly to their children in the moment, such as what happened at the child's birth or when they came to live with them (in the case of adoptions). The therapist's intent in this verbalization is to emphasize that the child is wanted and that the child's needs and emotional responses are important, and that both the parent and the child have strong positive feelings for each other, usually communicated in the process of their play interactions.

Other verbal strategies are coaching play interaction and reinforcing positive interactive moments, no matter how brief. Some ways to help keep a caregiver's interest is to frame any overall play episode as an experiment to see what they can do to increase their child's invitations for interactive play. The therapist may ask questions like: Can you see if changing the kind of smile or level of your voice might increase her looking at you? See what her legs or arms do after you stop rocking her in her favorite way? What would happen if you made your scribble move into his? What do you suppose he wants when he looks (or scribbles) away from you? Can you find a way to invite him back?

Both parents and children can develop overwhelming feelings of helplessness when their efforts to initiate play are unsuccessful. It is therefore very important for the therapist to notice and make positive comments about whenever such initial moments occur. Comments and questions similar to those above, which help verbalize the positive aspect of the playful connections especially when they are first starting to occur, can elaborate these moments—especially if they have been captured on tape.

Involvement with Other Agencies

Typically children and families who require intervention so early in the child's life have other agencies involved. These agencies include child protective agencies who are working with children who have been abused and/or neglected, early intervention teams with children who are showing significant developmental delays, mental health agencies who work with parents with mental illness, or medical providers who recognize medical conditions that may threaten early parent/child interactions. It is important to establish good working relationships with these other professions, as several decisions directly involving the family often need to be made, such as: When or should a child return to the birth parents? What style of intervention is best to improve a developmental delay? Is a parent too impaired to continue caring for the child? In general, the play therapist needs to respect the decisions of other professionals (e.g., a child protective worker's concerns about child safety). Typically, the play therapist should attempt to keep therapy observations and more formal evaluations used in child protective decisions separate.

CASE EXAMPLES

Infant and Adoptive Parents

Graham was referred to me when he was four months old because a child protective worker had concerns for his physical safety. Graham had been adopted at birth by John and Pam. He was born with a medical condition that required surgery and X-rays throughout his first year. An X-ray completed as part of a medical procedure when he was three months old suggested that Graham had a broken bone of unexplained origin. At the time of the referral, the protective worker had placed Graham in a foster home, as she determined that his adoptive father had somehow physically abused him. However, as Graham might have needed to be in a series of foster homes before new adoptive parents could be found, the worker asked me initially for an opinion related to (1) Graham's ability to attach to John and Pam; and (2) if parent-infant intervention could be used to help reestablish a positive family atmosphere.

I conducted parent-child observations with Graham and interviews with both John and Pam. John and Pam reported that they were very excited to adopt Graham and were present at his birth. They had supported his mother throughout her pregnancy. They had a four-year-old birth daughter who was developing normally and was securely attached. Graham's medical condition led him to be quite colicky when he initially began living in

Steve Harvey

their home, to the point of being inconsolable quite often. Neither John nor Pam had been able to sleep much at all. They were both exhausted and feeling very helpless as parents, despite their very genuine desire to provide for Graham. The allegation of physical abuse was devastating to their sense of themselves as parents, particularly to John.

During the initial observations, as John attempted to play with Graham it became clear that he had a limited repertoire of ways to hold him. Both he and Graham quickly became stressed. Graham kept turning away and crying, while John tried to use his voice in a calm way. However, Graham would not settle. Pam and Graham were somewhat more able to establish face-to-face contact that did lead to brief moments of calm, though Graham would look away quite often. In a discussion with John later, John reported that the observations did make him realize just how stressed he had become while trying to calm Graham during nights when Graham could not sleep. He stated that he could have squeezed too hard while he was lifting Graham over his head in an effort to get his attention while Graham was crying. The bone injury seen in the X-ray suggested this explanation was certainly possible. Pam reported she could never really develop extended face-to-face play episodes with Graham as he was always so hard to soothe. Both John and Pam stated they really wanted to continue to parent Graham despite everything that had happened, and they were motivated to engage in interactive therapy.

The child protective worker decided that parent-child play therapy would present a good treatment option. I requested that I be in the role of a family play therapist only and that all evaluation leading to Graham's placement be made by other mental health professionals. Pam and John were seen by psychologists specializing in adult mental health and were evaluated and provided with brief psychotherapy addressing stress, anger, and couples communication. The Dynamic Play Therapy was set up to help Graham develop more attunement and intimacy with John and Pam. The infant was returned home in gradual steps under close supervision directed by the child protective worker. John and Pam set up a series of play-oriented sessions, which lasted until he was seven months old. Graham was seen again with his then-adoptive parents for a few sessions when he was thirteen months old.

During the initial play sessions, John and Pam were asked to talk about their early family memories while they were also interacting with Graham. While John was describing something with emotional themes, Pam would be engaging Graham and then they exchanged roles naturally. Both adults told of events in which they had been left out and then included by their parents. I directed both parents to imagine how it might be for Graham to be included or isolated while their conversations were ongoing, and left out or included during his first months with them. This focus heightened the meaning of their nonverbal exchanges with Graham. Both John and Pam could begin to speak for Graham while the other was playing with him. Both John and Pam then were asked to observe the interactions between the other parent and Graham and to identify when the infant made small steps to engage them and when his mood lightened, however slight these shifts were. Such coaching between the couple continued at home as well.

I asked John and Pam if they would like to learn infant massage, as touch appeared to offer an avenue of communication that could be more developed. They both agreed, as Graham continued to remain somewhat tense when he was with them. A certified trainer in infant massage was found. The initial massage sessions were conducted as part of the Dynamic Play. These sessions were quite emotional especially for John, as he felt quite guilty for having harmed Graham and was hesitant to begin touching him again. Again, John was able to speak for Graham while Pam began the massage. John could later vocalize Graham's feeling while massaging him as well. Later John began to pick up Graham and began to identify changes in his body tension using touch. He was able to use these changes to guide the way he held Graham and later how he moved with him. After some practice, John and Graham began to work out several physical exchanges that had communicative value for them both and led to Graham's smiling and laughing.

Pam used her massage sessions to identify how Graham began to move his legs and later his arms slightly while she was touching him. She began to develop mutual movements allowing her hands and arms to be guided as Graham moved her. When Graham moved his leg, for example, Pam allowed herself to be pulled along by Graham's rhythm and direction. After a while, Graham sensed that he and Pam were moving in sync as he had done with John. The infant then showed clear enjoyment. Later, Pam began to use changes in face-to-face play with Graham to lead her face and later her body through the room. As Graham noticed Pam's movements, he again laughed and began to seek her face out. As Graham began to roll over during the series of sessions, Pam was able to extend her following games and roll beside him and later with him. Such joint movements gained a life of their own, as both Pam and Graham passed in and out of a shared play state quite naturally. The intervention was suspended with this development of spontaneous mutual play. Graham was seven months and he had been returned to live with Pam and John on a full-time basis.

John, Pam, and Graham returned for two final sessions when he was 13 months old, during the legal adoption process. John and Graham participated for one episode and Pam and Graham the other. Both sessions consisted of free play. Graham crawled/walked to and from John easily, and John was able to pick him up easily in several improvised ways that they both enjoyed. During the conversations with the therapist, John described several

enjoyable moments of play between Graham, his four-year-old daughter, and himself in which the infant was able to actively join the mutual activity and communicate as if he were directing his family with his gestures and nonverbal vocalizations. While John was relaying these play events, he constantly referred to and joined Graham's immediate physical play activities as they were occurring in the moment in very congruent manner. The themes of both the verbal descriptions of the family events as well as the immediate improvised nonverbal exchanges (dances) were of the shared pleasure of inclusion. During these episodes, Graham showed several invitations to John to play. John was able to recognize such moments and use them to pace the mutual play effortlessly.

Pam and Graham played together while Pam also reported on several spontaneous positive events in the home. During this interview, Pam would stop and improvise a game of "motor car," in which Graham would initiate a movement with his arm or leg while Pam was holding him, and then Pam would extend this movement as if she were driving a car (Graham), making car-like vocalizations in sync with their mutual activity. Both participants laughed together after the short "drive" together. This game was repeated several times during the conversation. The adoption was finalized a short time later.

A shorter case with a 30-month-old boy in foster placement will be presented to illustrate techniques with an older and more mobile child.

Toddler in Foster Care (Use of Physical Play)

Ben was referred by his child protective worker, as he was having continuing high-intensity mood changes and nightmares every time he was to have supervised visits with his birth father. He had been removed from his parents' care one year earlier due to extensive physical abuse and neglect. He had become relatively settled while in his stable foster care home. Jan and Mark had been his only foster parents after his initial placement. His father, Alan, had asked the court to resume visits and he was granted supervised contact on a once-a-week basis. However, Alan's attendance was quite inconsistent. Ben's mood changed every time he was taken to the home where his visits were to take place. He would become angry and fearful and refuse any comfort his foster parents tried to provide for him. He also could not sleep and had nightmares as well.

During his initial play with Jan, Ben was unable to stay in any one place in the room or focus enough to develop an interaction of any kind with her. Mark brought Ben to his next session and the therapist suggested that he just follow Ben as he moved around the room. At one point, the therapist put a large pillow down and asked Mark to run over and fall down. Ben quickly followed this movement and then began running throughout the room with Mark right behind. Ben led Mark to pillows and fell in them as fast as the therapist could put them around the room, with Ben looking over his shoulder to be sure Mark was following. Clearly a game of chase was being developed between them, and Ben was inviting Mark to play along with his falling. Each new aspect of the game brought laughter.

After some minutes Ben began to change his focus, and the therapist asked Mark to use the pillows to make a house. Ben went in as soon as he saw the shape of walls and a roof, while Mark began reaching in between the pillows to try to catch him. The chase developed a new form while Ben continued his improvisations. Finally, Ben began to knock the pillows down and burst out of his house as Mark tried to rebuild the house. This continued until the two began throwing pillows toward each other, Mark taking care not to knock Ben over. Ben lay down on a pillow and introduced a game of "sleeping." Mark and the therapist responded by rocking Ben initially while he was on the pillow and then in a large stretchy blanket. The rocking was soothing and the session ended with Ben quite calm, yet happy and close to Mark. They left holding hands.

Much of the episode was captured on video. Mark took the tape home and showed it to Ben, who loved watching it and asked for it daily. Ben's anger, withdrawal, and nightmares were greatly reduced after three more sessions and watching the tape just after he returned from the visit time with his birth father. It appeared that Ben's emotional difficulties were related to the thought of being separated from his foster parents. His play episodes with Mark helped ease some of this fearfulness. Watching the video also seemed to help Ben internalize these positive interactions.

An example of two sessions with a 36-month-old child and her adoptive parents will illustrate interactive art and story making.

Dramatic Play with a Three-Year-Old (Use of Art and Dramatic Story)

Chloe was referred with her adoptive parents, Liz and Robert, due to her inability to sleep and general fearfulness. She had been removed from her birth parents for reasons similar to the other children described in this chapter, namely abuse and neglect. She had been placed with Liz and Robert when she was two and adopted shortly after, as her birth parents had decided not to continue to raise her. Chloe had endured severe burns and ongoing physical violence at the hands of her birth parents during her first two years. She continued to have nightmares and high-intensity emotional outbursts after she had moved into Liz and Robert's home.

Liz, Robert, and Chloe had participated in Dynamic Play Therapy for one month and had developed several physically oriented games together. The therapist then introduced a drawing activity in which Chloe and Liz were asked to create a scribble conversation with each other. Shortly after they began, the therapist asked Liz to move a short distance away from the paper. Chloe's scribbles became much more constricted into small balls of color, and she began to draw only in the area right in front of her. Soon she was drawing on her own hands. At this point Liz sat down next to her and placed scribbles on the paper directly in front of both of them. Chloe joined the mark-making, initially reluctantly. After some time, Liz and Chloe began drawing together, following each other's scribbles across the page. Robert, who had been watching up until this point, and the therapist began to make a picture of a house on another sheet of paper close by and invited Chloe and Liz to "come over and visit." After a long journey across a few other sheets of newsprint, Liz and Chloe came to the door of the home and both "knocked." Robert let them in and the family drew several activities such as going to bed and having a meal, using their scribbles to represent these actions.

In the next session, Robert and Liz were asked to make a house with the pillows and put a family of stuffed bears inside. The whole family then entered the home and began to make a story involving the animals doing everyday activities, including going to bed and sleeping close by each other. Sometimes Chloe used an animal to represent a baby, and sometimes she happily took on the role herself. To help calm the baby down, Chloe asked her adoptive parents to use the elastic blanket to rock the animal in a way similar to the rocking activity described above. At times Chloe helped rock the baby (a stuffed animal), while at other times she would lie on the blanket herself. The family had ended the previous sessions by rocking Chloe and telling her how much she was wanted in their home. Chloe talked to her animal baby in a similar way during this part of the activity. Liz and Robert began to use activities similar to the rocking and storytelling to help Chloe go to sleep at home, with good results.

REFERENCES

Bowlby, J. 1972. *Attachment and loss*, vol. 1, *Attachment*. London: Hogarth.
———. 1973. *Attachment and loss*, vol. 2, *Separation*. New York: Basic.
———. 1980. *Attachment and loss*, vol. 3, *Loss*. New York: Basic.
Brody, V. 1997. *The dialogue of touch*. New York: Basic.
Garvey, C. 1990. *Play*. Enlarged ed. Cambridge, MA: Harvard University Press.
Greenspan, S. L., and S. Wieder. 2003. *Engaging autism: The floortime approach to help-ing children relate, communicate, and think*. New York: Perseus.
Harvey, S. A. 1994a. Dynamic play therapy: Expressive play intervention with fami-lies. In *Handbook of play therapy*, vol. 2, *Advances and innovations*, ed. K. O'Connor and C. Schaefer. New York: Wiley.
———. 1994b. Dynamic play therapy: Creating attachments. In *Handbook for treatment of attachment-trauma problems in children*, ed. B. James. New York: Lexington Books.

———. 1994c. Dynamic play therapy: An integrated expressive arts approach to family treatment of infants and toddlers. *Zero to Three* 15:11–17.

———. 1995. Sandra: The case of an adopted sexually abused child. In *Dance and other expressive arts therapies: When words are not enough,* ed. F. Levy. Routledge: New York.

———. 2000. Dynamic play approaches in the observation of family relationships. In *Play diagnosis and assessment,* ed. K. Gitlin-Weiner, A. Sandgrund, and C. Schaefer 457–473. New York: Wiley.

———. 2003. Dynamic play therapy with an adoptive family struggling with issues of grief, loss, and adjustment. In *Action therapy with families and groups,* ed. D. Wiener and L. Oxford, 19–44. Washington, DC: American Psychological Association.

———. 2006. Dynamic play therapy. In *Contemporary play therapy,* ed. C. Schaefer and H. Kaduson. New York: Guilford.

Jernberg, A. 1979. *Theraplay.* San Francisco: Jossey-Bass.

Ryan, V. 2004. Adapting non-directive play therapy interventions for children with attachment disorders. *Clinical Child Psychology and Psychiatry* 15 (1): 27–29.

Schaefer, C. 1993. *The therapeutic powers of play.* Palo Alto, CA: Science and Behavior Books.

Schwartzenberger, K. 2004. Guided interaction in play therapy. *California Association for Play Therapy Newsletter* 13 (2): 4–6.

Stern, D. N. 1985. *The interpersonal world of the infant: A view from psychoanalysis and developmental psychology.* New York: Basic.

———. 1990. *The diary of a baby.* New York: Basic.

———. 2004. *The present moment in psychotherapy and everyday life.* New York: Norton.

Tortora, S. 2006. *The dancing dialogue: Using the communicative power of movement with young children.* Baltimore: Brookes.

Wilson, K., and V. Ryan. 2005. *Play therapy: A non-directive approach for children and adolescents.* London: Elsevier.

2

Child-Centered Play Therapy for Very Young Children

Virginia Ryan and Sue Bratton

This chapter adopts as its main premise that the form of child-centered (or nondirective) play therapy[1] most suited to working with very young children is filial therapy. We will argue that play therapy which involves caregivers directly as therapeutic change agents is essential for very young children. We suggest that a well-researched form of therapy that combines play therapy and family therapy, known as filial therapy (L. Guerney 2000; Landreth and Bratton 2005), in which parents are trained as the therapeutic change agents for their own children (from approximately 3 years of age through 12 years of age), can be adapted for very young children (i.e., babies and toddlers) with their parents. We note in this context that special times together have already been advocated and specified for teenage children with their parents, when their younger siblings have filial therapy play sessions. Filial therapy is an intervention for all family members, not just for the child(ren) deemed to have the most prominent problems (L. Guerney 2000; VanFleet 2005; VanFleet and Guerney 2003). However, there have been no systematic discussions in the filial therapy literature on how to adapt filial therapy for caregivers with very young children under three years of age.

We have decided in this chapter to concentrate on filial therapy for toddlers between 11 and 24 months of age. Our primary reason for concentrating on this narrower age span was that discussing the entire age range from infancy to three years of age was unwieldy for a chapter of this length. We assume, however, that the foundations for working with the entire age range of infants and children under three are laid out here. Working with children over two years of age has more similarities to working with three-year-olds, the lower age range for well-established filial therapy programs.

We do recognize that filial therapy with two-year-olds merits further exploration, as does describing the developmental considerations, adaptations for practice, and applications for filial therapy for infants.

We begin with a general discussion of the theoretical and research underpinnings for using filial therapy with very young children. First we summarize the extensive literature supporting play therapy and filial therapy, then move on to examine how filial therapy can be delivered to families with very young children. In our discussion on providing filial therapy for these families, we will discuss the important developmental considerations needed for this age group, the ways in which imaginative play is fostered, and suggestions for toy selection. We then turn to adaptations of the training phase of filial therapy for parents of toddlers and explore the adaptations of the skills and procedure taught to parents. An illustrative example of a 24-month-old child shows how children may develop the beginnings of self-control during special play sessions. We next turn to a more extended case illustration of how principles of filial therapy were used by new adoptive parents of two young twin boys. Extended attachment theory is employed to explain the dynamics of attachment and careseeking-caregiving during the introductory and early months of the adoptive placement.

Finally we turn to suggestions for future practice and research. We suggest that as well as filial therapy's usefulness for parents of late-adopted children, it also can be very effective for children with special needs and their parents. Filial therapy for toddlers and parents may also have a very effective role in prevention of future mental health and behavioral problems. All of these new applications of filial therapy, we conclude, are fruitful starts, and given the strong overall research base of filial therapy, these new practice adaptations are essential avenues for future research.

THEORETICAL RATIONALE FOR FILIAL THERAPY WITH VERY YOUNG CHILDREN

The theoretical and research rationales for a filial therapy approach to child-centered play therapy with very young children are based on a rich variety of sources, including filial and play therapy theory and research, child development, and extended attachment theory. This section discusses the theoretical basis for filial therapy, and the next section will summarize its research base.

Play, Child Development, and Child Therapy

Child development literature's theoretical justification and research findings on the importance of play for young children's development are extensive. A recent American Academy of Pediatrics' report (2006) summarizes these findings. In its broadest sense play can be viewed as a basic biological function for both humans and other species (VanFleet, 2008). The young of many species appear to use play and its night-time relative, dreaming, for promoting learning and exercising new abilities; releasing surplus energy; expressing and enhancing well-being; and, for humans and perhaps other mammals, assimilating personally meaningful experiences symbolically. But above all, play seems to function in both young children and in other species as a way to form and cement closer and more cooperative social relationships with others, first with primary caregivers within attachment relationships and then within larger social networks. Play therefore is both a self-regulating and a social-regulating activity for very young children, which begins within close family relationships (Wilson and Ryan 2005, chap. 2).

The existing play therapy literature and the child therapy literature more generally also abound with reasons for using play in developing therapeutic relationships with children (Reddy, Files-Hall, and Schaefer, 2005). Because secure attachment relationships are integral to very young children's emotional well-being and development, current mental health programs for this age group concentrate primarily on enhancing and correcting infants' and young children's attachment relationships with their main caregivers and on family therapy, rather than on programs primarily directed toward children on their own (Neander and Skott, forthcoming; Shonkoff and Meisels 2000; Vetere and Dallos 2003). Throughout this chapter, we shall be discussing and illustrating ways in which family therapy and promoting more secure attachment relationships are at the heart of filial therapy. Thus, from a theoretical perspective this approach seems highly suitable to consider when working with families and their very young children.

In this chapter we will use Heard and Lake's extension of Bowlby's original formulation of attachment theory to examine the filial therapy processes that are assumed to account for the effectiveness of the filial therapy approach (Heard and Lake 1997, 2001). Heard and Lake set out a detailed theoretical framework, described below, for understanding the emotional needs and responses of children and their caregivers. Both sides of attachment relationships (that is, careseeking and caregiving) are given weight in their theory. We will argue later that for effective filial therapy to occur, the emotional needs and responses of both children and their caregivers are essential for success. Therefore we argue that the attachment needs of both children and their parents need to be assessed at the outset and then monitored for effectiveness during and after intervention. We suggest that this monitoring can be accomplished by using the main systems posited in Heard and Lake's model as guidelines for therapeutic progress as well as for increased understanding for professionals in complex cases.

The Attachment Dynamic

Heard and Lake's theory, "the dynamics of attachment and interest sharing" (2001, 1997), is a theoretical extension of the well-known attachment theory and research of Bowlby (1980) and Ainsworth (1982). Their extension is used in the case discussion later in this chapter to provide a theoretical framework for understanding the emotional needs of very young children and their caregivers.

Attachment theory and research is a well-established framework for understanding children's normal and atypical social/emotional development. It is used extensively by clinicians to design interventions, understand interactions, and assess clinical progress. However, attachment theory can seem incomplete because it does not integrate children's developing intrapersonal systems—such as their autonomy, psychosexuality, and creativity—into their attachment system. Their interpersonal systems, particularly their social relationships with family members and peers, also lack cohesion as a developmental approach within attachment theory generally (Ryan 2004).

Heard and Lake (1997; Heard 1982, 2001) extended Bowlby's theory to bridge these theoretical gaps by specifying five interrelated behavioral systems characterized by being interpersonal and intrinsically motivated. Each system is assumed to be a goal-corrected system and is instinctive. As Bowlby originally explained, the attachment system becomes active when specific signals are registered (e.g., a physical threat) and becomes quiescent when the goal of the system is reached (e.g., protection).

The five goal-corrected systems of Heard and Lake are:

The parenting system: This system is an extension of Bowlby's theory of caregiving. It includes a "growth and development subsystem" as essential to parenting. This subsystem is posited to encompass parents' capacity to develop and sustain their children's development of autonomy and exploration.

The careseeking system: This system remains unchanged from Bowlby's definition.

The exploratory system: This system is extended here to include shared interest with others during development and adulthood.

The affectional, sexual system: This system is developed more fully during adolescence and adulthood with peers.

The personal self-defense system: This system is defined more precisely; it is activated either when caregiving is perceived as not adequately nurturing and protective or when shaming or fear of abandonment are felt, and/or when angry and dismissive care are given (Heard 2001; Ryan 2004).

Heard and Lake's system seems particularly apt for understanding and assessing interventions with toddlers and their parents. While Bowlby's and Ainsworth's seminal theory emphasized careseeking, Heard and Lake's extension attempts to examine and explain caregiving in relation to careseeking, and the ways in which each of these systems activate and deactivate in relation to one another within interpersonal relationships. In addition, their extension of attachment theory also begins to outline in a general way the developmental progression from primary attachment and exploratory relationships to adult attachment and interest sharing. Their concepts of affect attunement and empathy have recently been operationalized and tracked empirically for adult dyads within therapeutic interactions, but have not yet been empirically verified for young children and their parents (Ryan 2004).

Heard and Lake assume that an adult's caregiving system must be integrated into other interpersonal components of their self system (e.g., affectional sexuality, interest sharing with their peers, and caregiving/careseeking) in order to function harmoniously. If adults' self-defense systems seep into their interpersonal attachments to children and/or peers, insecure attachment patterns develop or are maintained. Based on these theoretical assumptions, as well as on my [Virginia's] clinical experience, we recommend the assessment of adults' attachment styles alongside their children's prior to filial therapy. This practice recommendation will be more fully discussed later in the chapter.

More specifically, Heard and Lake's attachment dynamic can be used to understand parent-child interactions in the following manner:

When very young children perceive a physical or emotional threat to their well-being, the two systems of self-defense and careseeking become highly activated in them. Their exploratory system, including interest sharing with others, is deactivated. If we now look at the attachment relationship from the parents' perspective, insecure parents whose self-defense systems are easily activated, and who have low levels of interest sharing and exploration with peers, may tend to seek care more readily themselves. Thus their own children's careseeking can be perceived by them as an emotional threat that will interfere with having their own careseeking needs met. If caregivers perceive their children's attachment needs as emotionally threatening, it is more likely that the parents' self-defense system will become more highly activated. If this occurs, it is assumed that it is only when fatigue or children's own self-defense systems take over, that the exploratory, caregiving, and careseeking systems in both children and their parents return to the prethreat levels of activation. If these interpersonal responses are maintained over time, a variety of insecure attachment relationships can develop between children and their parents. As a result, high levels of anxiety and frustration are felt within their relationship by both children and their parents.

Ryan (2004) already has illustrated ways the attachment dynamic can help in understanding a complex, unsuccessful case from the perspective of the personal, interpersonal, and systemic levels of functioning. In contrast, the case example provided in this chapter of young adopted children with their new parents is a successful one. It will be used to illustrate both the ways in which filial therapy principles can be used with toddlers and the additional understanding that can be generated in this case by applying the framework of the "attachment dynamic" and extended attachment theory.

Child-Centered Play Therapy

The skills and rationale taught to parents who are trained in filial therapy to conduct special play sessions with their own children individually are based on child-centered play therapy principles and methods. Virginia Axline (1947) was the first to apply child-centered therapeutic principles in play therapy based on her trust in children's capacity to resolve their own problems through their play. Her work and writings in the late 1940s and 1950s heralded perhaps the most significant development in the field of play therapy and popularized play therapy as a psychotherapeutic treatment modality for children. Much has been written on this method of therapy (see L. Guerney 1984; Landreth 1991; Wilson and Ryan 2005; Bratton, Ray, and Landreth, forthcoming), which is now more commonly referred to as child-centered play therapy (CCPT) in the United States.

CCPT assumes that children and young people have within themselves a drive toward better emotional functioning (e.g., Rogers's "self actualizing" principle; "adaptation" in biological theories). Another major assumption is that children possess the capacity to solve their own emotional problems satisfactorily, given the opportunity and a favorable environment. Therefore the responsibility to institute emotional change is theirs. Raskin and Rogers (2005) postulated that if the therapist is successful in conveying genuineness, unconditional positive regard, and empathy, then the child will respond with a changed personality organization. Axline (1947) described this process as one in which the child has the opportunity to play out feelings as they emerge, getting them out in the open, and either learning to appropriately control them or abandon them.

Child-centered play therapists believe that a child's experience within the play therapy relationship is the factor that is most meaningful and growth-producing. Thus, the therapist's overarching role is to develop a trusting therapeutic relationship with the child-client; to understand and respond to expressed feelings, thoughts, and actions (i.e., empathic listening, in which actions and verbal reflections are communicated in a nonthreatening way); to convey unconditional acceptance; to apply therapeutic limits, including safety limits; and to use their internal thoughts and feelings arising in their relationships with children and young people in a timely and therapeutic way (e.g., "genuineness," "transparency," and "congruence") (Ryan 2007a; Ryan and Wilson 2000; Wilson and Ryan 2005).

Within the safety and consistency of this type of relationship, children will play out their feelings, experiences, and needs. CCPT therapists believe that children's play is meaningful and significant to them—that they will reveal their inner world symbolically, and sometimes literally, through the toys and materials they choose, what they do with the materials, and the stories they act out. In this way play therapy provides the therapist with an opportunity to enter the child's world as the child lives out at the moment of play past experiences and associated feelings. Children use play to develop mastery and a sense of control over their world as they reenact their experiences directly in the safety of the therapeutic milieu (Bratton, Ray, and Landreth, 2008).

CCPT is grounded in eight basic principles identified by Axline (1947). These principles insist that the therapist (1) develop a warm, friendly relationship with the child; (2) accept the child unconditionally, without wishing the child were different in some way; (3) establish a feeling of permissiveness in the relationship so that the child feels free to express self; (4) recognize and reflect the feelings of the child to create understanding for the child; (5) respect the child's innate ability to solve his or her own problems and offers the opportunity to return responsibility to the child; (6) not attempt to direct the child's actions or conversation, but allow the child to lead the way; (7) recognize the gradual nature of the child's process and not try to rush counseling; and (8) establish only those limitations that are necessary to anchor the child's experience in counseling to the world of reality. We will discuss in more detail later in the chapter the ways in which CCPT principles and skills have been distilled into skills used to train parents in filial therapy.

Empirical Support for Filial Therapy with Very Young Children

There is not as yet a body of evidence to support filial therapy with very young children. However, there is a body of research on early preventive interventions with very young children and their parents. The meta-analyses of 70 early childhood research studies investigating sensitivity and attachment interventions (Bakersmans-Kranenburg, van IJzendoorn, and Juffer 2003), for example, found that interventions offering an educational component for parents and a moderate number of sessions were most effective in enhancing parents' sensitivity to their children. They also found that the programs increasing parental sensitivity also increased the children's attachment security. The filial therapy program outlined below has both these features. Filial therapy can be conducted in groups or with individual families, and usually lasts between 10 and 20 weeks. The main focus in filial therapy training before the last, generalizing stage is on parents learning and practicing child-centered play therapy skills directly with their own children, usually under supervision with immediate feedback. Furthermore, clinicians practicing filial therapy professionally have started to make use of this method of intervention with very young children for certain referred families and within their own families as well, as our case illustrations below show.

The general research support for play therapy and filial therapy with children and families will be summarized next.

Empirical Support for Play Therapy and Filial Therapy

Play therapy, including filial therapy, has one of the longest histories of research of any psychological intervention, with research dating back to the 1940s. Since that time approximately 140 outcome studies have been published in professional journals and another 42 remain in dissertation format. Filial therapy, in particular, is a well-researched play therapy modality with an approximate count of 37 controlled studies, 27 of which were published in professional journals. The majority of filial therapy outcome studies ($N = 27$) have been published since the 1990s and utilized the 10-session filial therapy protocol, Child-Parent Relationship Therapy (CPRT) (Landreth and Bratton 2005), originally introduced by Landreth (1991).

Meta-analytic Findings for Play Therapy and Filial Therapy

A recent meta-analysis of over five decades of play therapy outcome research revealed a large treatment effect (ES = .80) across the 93 controlled studies and concluded that play therapy was an effective treatment across a variety of presenting issues (Bratton et al. 2005). On average, children receiving play therapy interventions performed more than three-fourths of a standard deviation better on given outcome measures when compared to children who did not receive play therapy. The meta-analysis further revealed that humanistic approaches to play therapy, primarily child-centered play therapy and nondirective play therapy, demonstrated an even larger treatment effect (ES = .92) compared to nonhumanistic approaches (ES = .72). Treatment duration was also a factor in the success of play therapy. Optimal treatment effects were obtained in 35 to 40 sessions, although many studies with fewer than 14 sessions also produced medium and large-effect sizes. Play therapy appeared to be equally effective across age and gender. In addressing presenting problems, the researchers encountered difficulty distinguishing specific diagnoses and symptoms. However, 24 studies were calculated as investigating internalizing problems with an effect size of .81. Seventeen studies were calculated as examining the effects of play therapy on externalizing problems with an effect size of .78. Sixteen studies addressed a combination of internalizing and externalizing problems with an effect size of .93. These results indicated that play therapy had a moderate to large beneficial effect for internalizing, externalizing, and combined problem types.

Of the 93 outcome studies included in the meta-analysis, 26 studies were coded as using filial therapy training methodology (with parents, teachers, and mentors). Interestingly, results showed stronger evidence of treatment effectiveness for filial therapy (ES = 1.05) and in fewer sessions, compared to play therapy provided by a mental health professional (ES = 0.72). All but four filial therapy studies used parents to provide treatment; thus in order to further investigate the impact of involving parents fully in their child's therapy, we coded and statistically analyzed filial therapy as a treatment modality apart from play therapy. The parent-only filial studies revealed an even stronger treatment effect of 1.15. These results indicate the importance of involving parents in their children's treatment through filial therapy training to maximize treatment effects. LeBlanc and Ritchie (2001) also found parent involvement to be a predictor of play therapy outcome. Bratton et al. (2005) concluded that filial therapy was an effective modality for intervening in young children's problems and provided the added benefit of potentially preventing the onset of more costly and serious problems that can arise across a child's lifespan, when initial problems are not treated. Landreth and Bratton (2005) further analyzed data from Bratton et al. (2005) to examine CPRT studies (1990–2000) in which individual researchers were trained and supervised directly by the CPRT authors and found an effect size of 1.25. These findings support the notion that training, supervision, and adherence to a well-developed protocol may impact treatment outcomes and further validate the importance of treatment integrity in research.

Empirical Support for Filial Therapy

Early research by the Guerneys and their protégées demonstrated that parents were capable of learning essential CCPT skills and were effective therapeutic agents with their children (B. Guerney and Stover 1971; Stover and B. Guerney 1967; Oxman 1972). The Guerneys were committed to researching their basic assumptions and methods as they developed their innovative approach.

In what can be considered the landmark study on filial therapy, B. Guerney and Stover (1971) supported their earlier results (Stover and Guerney 1967) with a more robust study of 51 mother-child pairs, funded through the National Institutes of Health (NIH). Results from live observations showed that the mothers demonstrated significant gains in empathic interactions

with their children. In addition, all 51 children demonstrated improvement
in psychosocial adjustment and symptoms, with 28 of the children rated
significantly improved. Because the above study did not utilize a control
group, Oxman (1972) studied a matched sample of mother-child pairs who
received no treatment and found that the filial-trained mothers reported a
statistically significant improvement in their children's behavior over the
matched sample. A longitudinal investigation of the B. Guerney and Stover
(1971) study was conducted by L. Guerney (1975), with 42 of the original
51 mothers responding. Thirty-two of the respondents reported that their
children showed continued improvement one to three years after treatment.
Although as noted below, the majority of filial therapy research has been
conducted on the 10-session CPRT model (Landreth and Bratton 2005) over
the past decade, the Guerneys' groundbreaking research laid the foundation.
For a more in-depth historical account of the research that influenced the
development of the Guerneys' model, refer to L. Guerney (2003).

Child-Parent Relationship Therapy (CPRT) is a 10-session filial therapy
model that has been widely researched, with a total of 34 studies, including
27 controlled outcome studies involving more than 1,000 subjects. CPRT
has been studied with varied and diverse populations and a broad array
of presenting issues. For example, CPRT's effects have been demonstrated
with single and divorced parents whose children were exhibiting behavioral
problems (Bratton and Landreth 1995), parents of children with learning
disabilities (Kale and Landreth 1999), mother-child pairs in a domestic
violence shelter (Smith and Landreth 2003), nonoffending parents of sexually abused children (Costas and Landreth 1999), chronically ill children
(Glazer-Waldman 1991; Tew et al. 2002), and incarcerated parents (Harris
and Landreth 1997; Landreth and Lobaugh 1998). The 10-session model
has also been demonstrated effective with diverse cultural groups within
the United States and abroad, including Native American (Glover and Landreth 2000), Korean (Jang 2003), Israeli (Kidron, 2004), immigrant Chinese (Chau and Landreth, 1997; Yuen, Landreth, and Baggerly 2002), and
immigrant Korean (Lee and Landreth 2003). Several CPRT studies have also
shown the effectiveness of the CPRT model with teachers and mentors in
the school setting (Brown 2003; Baggerly and Landreth 2001; Jones, Rhine,
and Bratton 2002; Morrison 2006). Additionally, the CPRT protocol was
recently manualized by Bratton, Landreth, Kellam, and Blackard (2006),
allowing for easier replication of the model. A detailed account of the body
of CPRT research can be found in Landreth and Bratton (2005).

The above-referenced controlled filial therapy research studies consistently show statistical gains in increasing parental acceptance, decreasing
parental stress, and decreasing children's problematic behaviors in as few
as 10 sessions. Additional benefits have been described in qualitative and
case study research. Although not generally accepted by the scientific com-

munity as evidence of a treatment's efficacy, qualitative and case study research has contributed to the support for the impact of filial therapy on a wide variety of presenting issues. VanFleet and Guerney have provided an invaluable sourcebook of case studies (2003), many of which focus on attachment-related problems and other systemic issues; I [Virginia Ryan] have also published case illustrations of children who have had attachment disruptions and social work involvement (Ryan 2007b).

In conclusion, filial therapy has a long and rich history of research, dating from its earliest days. A substantial body of outcome research provides support for the efficacy of this approach and its applicability to a broad array of issues and to varied and diverse populations. Although at first glance findings suggest that therapists and managed care–service providers should advocate the use of filial training over play therapy, clinical rationale would prohibit the use of filial therapy with all parents and children. There are many cases when play therapy conducted by a professional should be chosen over a filial therapy training intervention. (Note however that we argue here that filial therapy with caregivers is a more suitable intervention for babies and very young children than play therapy.) Parents who are experiencing a significant amount of emotional stress often have difficulty focusing on the needs of their children. In this case, many parents need to undertake their own therapy before they are capable of learning and facilitating the skills of therapeutic play with their children.

In addition to parental issues that prohibit participation in filial play therapy training, a child may not be best suited for this approach. On occasion, a child's emotional issues might extend beyond the capability of the parent. In a case where a child is significantly emotionally disturbed, a parent may not be able to provide a child with an effective therapeutic experience. Yet, the results of this research indicate that if a child and a parent are both firm candidates, particularly in such cases when the parent-child relationship is the source of the child's problems, or where children have social/emotional disabilities (e.g., on the autism spectrum), or in cases such as adoption where the parent-child relationship must be nurtured, filial therapy would be the most effective intervention. We discuss these special circumstances in more detail later in this chapter.

FILIAL THERAPY FOR VERY YOUNG CHILDREN: OVERVIEW AND PROCEDURES

Assessing and Supporting Caregivers

The child-centered play therapy literature traditionally did not emphasize assessment (e.g., Axline 1947; Landreth 1991). Instead it was assumed that most children were able to be helped by this method of therapy and that children themselves would determine their goals and therapeutic needs. More recently child therapy in general, and child-centered play therapy as well, usually advocate an assessment process that includes children's developmental histories and may include behavior checklists (e.g., the Child Behavior Checklist, CBCL). In current play therapy practice, parents also play a more prominent role than previously. In addition to practitioners' recognition that play therapy is unworkable without therapeutic alliances with children's parents, the direct roles parents may play in their children's play therapy interventions have been expanded and emphasized (McGuire and McGuire 2000; Ryan 2007b; Wilson and Ryan 2005). As stated above, filial therapy is a form of play therapy that places parents at the center—parents offer play therapy sessions to their own children in lieu of professional therapists and receive support and supervision themselves from qualified practitioners.

Therefore in initial assessments where families appear to have more complex relational difficulties, following Heard and Lake's formulation of the interrelationships of children's and parents' motivational systems with one another, I [Virginia] recommend assessing parents' attachment needs and styles more fully. This is in order to inform therapists and the parents themselves of their attachment needs, as well as those of their children. I [Virginia] use a reliable and clinically sensitive assessment measure: the Attachment Style Interview (ASI) (Bifulco 2002). This measure already is well researched and increasingly used in UK social services contexts to assess caregivers' support needs when adopting and fostering vulnerable children. I [Virginia] use it as part of an overall assessment of parents' and children's attachments to one another for the courts, as well as prior to filial therapy in complex cases. This clinical interview, unlike the well-established Adult Attachment Interview (AAI), has good face validity with users, is quick to administer, and is an effective clinical tool for beginning to build therapeutic relationships with parents. However in other families who have less complex needs, the Parental Stress Index (PSI), the Filial Problem Checklist (FPC), and other parenting measures may be more appropriate.

An Overview of Filial Therapy

The concept of training parents to become primary change agents in their children's therapy can be traced to the early 1900s when Freud effectively utilized a father in treating his five-year-old son's phobia. Freud (1909) was convinced that the child's progress would have been impossible without the father's involvement. Jacobs (1949), Bonnard (1950), Fuchs (1957), and Moustakas (1959), among others, were some of the earliest pioneers in advocating for training parents to intervene in their child's problems.

However, Bernard Guerney (1964), a child-centered play therapist, was the first to propose a structured program for training parents to become therapeutic agents in their child's life. He coined the term *filial therapy*, to reflect the importance of the parent-child bond to the success of this new approach, based on the belief that a parent/caregiver holds more emotional significance to a child than a therapist does. Louise Guerney worked with her husband in the early research and development of filial therapy, and she continues to be one of the leading proponents of this approach to helping children and families (L. Guerney 2000, 2003).

Filial therapy, grounded in the principles and procedures of child-centered play therapy (Axline 1947), was originally developed by the Guerneys as a treatment for children with social, emotional, and behavioral problems. As in play therapy, play is viewed as the vehicle children use to express themselves and is used as the developmentally responsive means of fostering interactions between children and parents. Their revolutionary approach to child therapy was founded on the then-novel belief that parents could be trained to be effective primary therapeutic agents for children with clinical levels of behavior problems. The Guerneys further theorized that training parents in basic child-centered play therapy skills to be used in structured, weekly parent-child play sessions could effectively reduce their children's problems.

Since the late 1980s the recognition of filial therapy by practitioners and researchers as an effective treatment for a wide variety of presenting issues has grown tremendously (Bratton et al. 2005). L. Guerney (2000) credited this growth, in part, to the efforts of Landreth (1991) and his protégés. Building on the work of the Guerneys, Landreth developed a more condensed 10-session parent training format based on his experience that time and financial constraints often hindered parents' participation. Landreth and Bratton (2005) formalized the 10-session training format in a text, *Child-Parent Relationship Therapy (CPRT): A 10-Session Filial Therapy Model*. Grounded in philosophy and procedures similar to the Guerneys' model, the CPRT parent training model emphasizes a balance of didactic and supervision experiences in a two-hour weekly supportive group format and requires parents to conduct weekly, videotaped, or live play sessions under supervision of a trained filial therapist. Parents are taught the core filial skills of empathy and allowing the child to lead, as well as the importance of structuring and appropriate limit setting. The CPRT protocol was recently manualized by Bratton, Landreth, Kellam, and Blackard (2006) allowing for replication of the model. Although originally conceived as a group model for training parents, filial therapy has also been successfully adapted with individual parents and couples. VanFleet (1994) follows the Guerney model of including all family members where possible in interventions and has developed intensive training programs for professionals, helping them to learn to adapt the time scale and training phase of filial therapy to each family's needs. Her well-developed training programs have increased the recognition and implementation of filial therapy worldwide, particularly in the United Kingdom and Ireland. Filial therapy also is used for training teachers, mentors and other paraprofessionals who play a significant role in children's lives (Jones, Rhine, and Bratton 2002; Morrison 2006; White, Flynt, and Draper 1997).

Because the term *filial therapy* was not a familiar term to most parents, this approach has been referred to by various names over the years, including Child Relationship Enhancement Therapy (CRET) (L. Guerney and B. Guerney, 1989), Filial Family Therapy (FFT) (L. Guerney, 2003), Filial/Family Play Therapy (FFPT) (Bratton 1998), and more recently, Child-Parent Relationship Therapy (CPRT) (Landreth and Bratton 2005). Regardless of the difficulty in finding a suitable name for this approach, it appears that the term filial "is here to stay" (Guerney 2003, 14).

In addition to being a proven method of treatment for children and their families, filial therapy serves a preventive function as parents learn attitudes and skills that they will continue to use throughout their child's life. Thus this approach offers the potential for long-term benefits for the entire family. In addition to being an effective means of strengthening parent-child relationships, filial therapy provides an economical and efficient method of providing treatment, showing effects in as little as 10 sessions—an attractive feature for third-party payers and other funders.

Filial Therapy for Caregivers of Young Children

The overarching goal of filial therapy is to help parents learn the attitudes and skills necessary to develop a closer emotional relationship with their children, where children experience acceptance and understanding from their parents within the boundaries of clear and consistent limits. Children who experience this type of relationship, as attachment research has demonstrated repeatedly, internalize a sense of self as worthwhile, lovable, capable, and competent.

The primary objective of strengthening the attachment relationship between parent and child is accomplished by helping parents

1. Become more sensitive to their child's emotional world.
2. Understand their child's needs and how to respond appropriately.
3. Gain insight into themselves in relation to their child.
4. Learn to encourage their child's self-direction, autonomy and self-responsibility.
5. Change negative perceptions of their child that hinder expression of unconditional acceptance. (Landreth and Bratton 2005)

These objectives are fulfilled through training and supervising caregivers in child-centered play therapy skills and principles. Through didactic instruction, demonstration play sessions, role-playing, and direct supervision of caregivers' play sessions with their child, their sensitivity to their child's needs is enhanced. Caregivers learn how to create a nonjudgmental understanding and accepting environment in which their children feel safe and secure enough to explore ways of relating to their parents, as well as to learn about themselves. While filial therapy was designed to build on an already established parent-child relationship, we argue that it also offers a viable means of helping adoptive children and their caregivers form secure attachments as they begin their life together as a family. We are grateful to have been given permission to write in more detail about one family's story later in this chapter.[2]

Training caregivers of very young children to practice filial therapy offers the significant advantage of providing a viable means for early intervention rather than waiting until children are displaying significant symptomology, which often does not occur until children enter school. Early intervention can diminish unnecessary suffering and prevent the development of more serious impairment across the lifespan, thus providing a more cost-effective intervention. Another distinct advantage of this approach for this population of children and parents is the primary focus on the quality of the parent-child relationship and the emphasis on facilitating children's emotional development. Growing research supports the notion that the quality of the parent-child relationship in the earliest years significantly impacts brain development and optimal emotional and cognitive growth (Greenspan and Wieder 2006; Lipari 2000) and that emotional development is the foundation for intelligence and learning (Greenspan and Greenspan 1989).

The first two years of life are critical in building children's mental foundation, including social, emotional, language, and cognitive capacities as well as the ability to regulate behavior, impulses, and mood. Most vital to the development of this foundation are high-quality interactions with caregivers, characterized by an exchange of emotions and a fundamental sense of relatedness (Greenspan and Wieder 2006). Studies have shown that secure attachment in the first two years of life is highly related to more desirable cognitive and social characteristics in later preschool years (Rosenblith 1992). Thus, providing filial therapy training for parents of children under three who are at risk for attachment difficulties seems imperative to ensure their optimal growth and development.

Delivering Filial Therapy to Families with Very Young Children

In our discussion of how filial therapy works with very young children and their caregivers, we assume that typically families likely to be seeking or mandated to receive mental health services would require direct training and supervision by a trained filial therapist (unlike the parents in the case illustration below). Similarly to traditional filial therapy programs, training for parents of very young children can be conducted with individuals and couples (VanFleet 2005) or with small groups of parents (L. Guerney 2003; Landreth and Bratton 2005), depending on parent and child needs. When delivering group filial therapy for parents of this age group, we believe that it is important to form homogenous groups of parents based on their children's ages. This stipulation is due to the significant differences in developmental needs of toddlers compared to older children and very young infants.

The format for training caregivers of young children would be similar to the traditional filial therapy formats (L. Guerney 2003; Landreth and Bratton 2005; VanFleet 2005), with modifications of playtime structure, toys, and parent responses to accommodate for the developmental needs of toddlers. In general, we propose four phases for filial therapy training with this population: (1) supporting and training parents in CCPT principles and procedures (two to three sessions); (2) parent-child play sessions directly supervised by a filial therapist, along with continued training and parent support (approximately four to six sessions); (3) weekly home play sessions supervised by filial therapist via videotape, along with continued parent support and reinforcement of filial skills and attitudes (minimum of six sessions); and (4) generalization of filial skills to everyday situations (two or three sessions). The length of each phase is dependent on the training format (group versus individual, length of sessions, number of sessions per week) and the specific needs of both parent and child. For example, higher-functioning adoptive parents such as those in the longer case illustration would need less training and could move directly from the initial training phase to at-home play sessions supervised via videotape. Similarly to traditional filial training, longer training sessions (two hours) will be needed for small group formats, whereas individual parents can be trained in one-hour sessions.

Developmental Considerations

It is important that therapists be familiar with typical cognitive, social, and emotional developmental milestones for this age group in order to help parents develop realistic expectations for their children (Berk 2003; Schaefer and DiGeronimo 2000). Children at this age often engage parents briefly and then quickly disengage and focus completely on a toy (Schaefer 1984, 1989). At times, it may seem that the child is more interested in the toys than the parent. It is important to help parents understand that children will experience their parents' closeness and full attention even when not directly interacting with their parent. The theoretical and research underpinnings of these social interaction patterns in young children are discussed in more detail by Ryan and Wilson (1995). They describe infants' and toddlers' developmental limitations when attending to objects and people simultaneously, the scaffolding role of caregivers, and ways that play therapists create optimal conditions for the development of more advanced socialization patterns.

Toddlers who are newly adopted, as in our case illustration below, may need time to feel safe in engaging their parent directly. One important role for the filial therapist, which parallels the parent's new role with the child, is to monitor the child's needs and help the caregiver to avoid overwhelming the child. At the same time it is important for filial therapists to understand and support caregivers' need to connect with their new baby or toddler and help minimize adults' possible feelings of rejection and activation of their defensive responses. In these and other ways, filial therapists serve the very important function of providing caregiving to parents, thus enabling them in turn to meet their new children's emotional needs.

As we stated above, understanding normal social-emotional development is crucial for filial therapists who plan to work with parents of toddlers. According to Erikson (1950), children's emotional development during their second year of life is characterized by the development of a sense of autonomy—a prerequisite for self-control and self-confidence—without developing an overwhelming sense of doubt and shame. Autonomy is fostered by caregivers who understand children's need to choose and decide for themselves, and provide plenty of opportunities for freedom to explore their environment. Children who have a history of insecure attachments must first experience consistent, responsive care in order to gain a sense of trust in others and the world before they feel secure enough to begin their quest for autonomy. Toddlers need a balance of healthy dependence on adults, along with the freedom to discover their own capabilities. A strong sense of trust in primary caregivers and a developing sense of autonomy provide a basis for healthy self-esteem (Wilson and Ryan 2005, chap. 3).

Another important concept for parents of toddlers to understand is their children's development of self-control. The ability to control responses, beginning with compliance and delay of gratification, emerges in the second year of life as children develop the cognitive ability to internalize and recall a rule or limit expressed by their caregivers. Self-control, therefore, emerges within primary attachment relationships and may or may not develop in an optimal manner. In order to control themselves, toddlers must have achieved a degree of autonomy, that is, they must possess a sense of self as separate from their caregiver. Children who have been provided more opportunities to direct their own activities are then more prepared to begin to control their actions (Berk 2003). On the other hand, children who have insecure attachments with their caregivers, or who have developmental difficulties, often remain less able to develop adequate patterns of self-control (Vondra et al. 2001). Special play sessions during filial therapy provide optimal conditions for this developmental task and may be useful for prevention of future difficulties as well as for advancing children's development of self-control. And finally, children's capacity for emotional self-regulation is closely tied to the ability to control themselves. Babies and toddlers who have had their emotional needs met by caregivers can more easily regulate their emotions and calm themselves. A caregiver's empathic responses to the infant's emotional cues, particularly distress, powerfully affects the child's ability to self-regulate emotions, a prerequisite for self-control (Bakersmans-Kranenburg et al. 2003).

Finally, before turning to the topic of toy selection for special play sessions with toddlers, filial therapists will need to be familiar with conditions that seem most conducive for young children to engage in imaginative play. This area of their development is at a rudimentary stage for normally developing toddlers, and may need additional opportunities and conditions for children who are developmentally delayed or who have special needs, as we discuss later in the chapter. I [Virginia] have proposed several conditions that seem essential to the development of imaginary play in children (Josefi and Ryan 2004; Ryan 1999; Wilson and Ryan 2005). Along with providing opportunities for messy play in young children's environments, she proposed the following essential conditions, based on both developmental research and on clinical case material, that seem required for children to develop independent, imaginative play routines:

1. Opportunities for children to participate in caregiver-child social routines based on reciprocal roles, with these routines becoming simple, social games during early development (e.g., pretending to feed themselves and their caregivers with a spoon).
2. Opportunities for children to use play objects during playful social routines that have close resemblances to real-life objects with which they are familiar (e.g., the caregiver playfully pretending to have a suck at the infant's bottle).
3. Ensuring that children are highly motivated and emotionally involved in play activities (e.g., that children have already directed their attention and interests toward a particular person or object).
4. Children having access to a more advanced play partner who follows the child's lead and modulates their own social interactions to suit the child's capacities.
5. Children being relaxed mentally and physically because their basic physical and security needs have already been met.

6. Children having the cognitive capacity to allow one object to represent another. It is important to note in the context of this chapter's topic of filial therapy with toddlers that this cognitive capacity emerges in rudimentary fashion at 12 to 18 months of age.

7. Helping children to learn the distinction between "pretend" and "real" in social situations, including the use of social signals by the more advanced play partner to convey the playful nature of the social interaction (e.g., smiling, a lighter tone of voice, etc.).

Many of these features are present in the play examples we have used in this chapter to illustrate parent-child social interactions involving imaginative play. We invite the reader to note these features, as in the example of Mark with his adoptive father when engaged in rudimentary imaginative play. Filial therapists help parents set up the ideal conditions for imaginative play at a rudimentary level. With parents who have not experienced playful exchanges with children, or whose own development was marred by emotional neglect or trauma, filial therapists may need to spend a longer time training these parents to learn to be playful with their toddlers. In general, the conditions under which filial therapy takes place—no interruptions, play times at a point in the day where the toddler is able to have alert attention (e.g., not hungry, tired, or in need of a diaper change!), following the child's lead, having a "play space" and toys that are closely associated with playful times—all help parents to create these ideal conditions for imaginative play to emerge in their toddlers.

Toy Selection

By two to two-and-a-half years of age, children can benefit from the standard list of play session toys suggested by Landreth and Bratton (2005) and VanFleet (1994), with only slight modification. For children under two years of age, the symbolic value of toys is not yet well developed; therefore the variety of toys suggested for traditional filial therapy is not as relevant. Unlike filial therapy with older children, toys and play objects can be selected from those already owned. Instead, consideration should be given to which real-life objects used within a child's social routines may be useful as triggers to scaffold rudimentary, imaginative play (see more suggestions below). Parents may occasionally add a new toy or two to whet their child's interest or to provide a new challenge as current toys are mastered.

As is true for toys suggested for traditional filial therapy, toys selected for toddlers should be developmentally appropriate, as well as a few toys that the child has already mastered and a few toys that are slightly above the child's developmental mastery. Providing some toys and experiences below the toddler's chronological age is particularly important when using filial therapy with newly adoptive parents where there have been disruptions in the formation of a secure attachment. With this population, filial therapists will need to educate parents about the likelihood of regression of their children's developmental needs in some areas. Parents of children who have special needs also require more guidance in what to select. To help parents normalize their expectations of their children, it is helpful to inform them that children generally do not have smooth progression in their overall development and help them to apply this concept to their own children's development. Parents will need to understand that their children require opportunities to revisit successful experiences from earlier phases in their development, in order to consolidate and rework these experiences into their current mental functioning (Wilson and Ryan 2005). Toddlers also need opportunities to "coast" in some areas of their development, especially when they are being persistent in the face of regular frustrations when trying to master other new areas in their development.

Safety is always a primary consideration—toys selected should be non-toxic, have no sharp edges, not be easily breakable, and be large enough to prevent accidental swallowing. A general rule is to select toys that require parents to set minimal limits during the special play times. For example, select a foam ball the child cannot take bites out of instead of a hard rubber ball—a foam ball thrown by a child is not likely to cause damage.

Appropriate toys for this age group can be classified into two broad categories: toys that facilitate mastery and real-life toys. Toys that facilitate mastery include manipulative toys and toys that respond to the child's touch. Examples of mastery toys include stacking toys/blocks, pop-up toys, cash registers, toys that make noise (musical-type toy or rattle), shape sorters, and so on. Examples of real-life toys include plastic dishes and spoons, play telephones (one cell phone and one cordless-type phone to allow for interaction between parent and child); a few realistic animal figures the child is familiar with (e.g., dog, cat, cow, horse, etc.); toys that can be used for nurturing, such as a baby doll (brush for hair, toy bottle, etc.), a few stuffed toys, and a few larger cars and trucks. Alongside real-life toys, it is important to include real objects that immediately cue young children into familiar everyday routines, such as a feeding bottle or cup, a small bib of the kind used by the toddlers themselves, a face cloth, a real wooden/metal/plastic spoon, and empty packets of food. As early as 12 to 15 months, children's capacity for imaginative play begins to be expressed, but typically when using toys that represent the real object. Caregivers will be able to follow their toddlers' lead and expand on the rudimentary imaginative play routines they instigate. For example, an 18-month-old will use a play phone and pretend to talk, or at least hold it up to their ear, but they generally do not use a block and pretend it is a phone until after two years of age. The parent may use the block themselves, or hold the cell phone up to a teddy's ear and have a conversation with their toddler, thus using objects in more imaginative ways themselves, but all the while following their child's lead. (See our discussion later on meeting the imaginative play needs of children with developmental difficulties and delays.)

For toddlers around 12 months old and older, and depending on their parents' tolerance of mess, an appropriate addition to filial therapy materials would be those that provide sensory experiences for toddlers. For example, a small amount of water in a rubber dishpan, cooked pasta shapes, or a small amount of pudding on a baking sheet or tray that can be used for smearing—as long as a plastic sheet is spread to protect the living area used in the house—may be very beneficial to include. Toddlers can be directed toward this "messy play" area, which always should include wipes for quick cleanups of messy hands and faces! Selecting items that the child can safely eat is also important at this age, because children will be likely to want to put these items in their mouth. Filial therapists with parents of toddlers, similarly to parents of children at other ages, will need to explore the limits and tolerances each parent has in this respect, as well as in other areas. It will be important to discuss ahead of time with parents if they will allow their child to feed them the smashed pasta shapes or smeared pudding, so they are prepared for that eventuality and can respond appropriately. As parents master the skills of empathy and allowing the child to lead, and as their toddlers mature, it may be helpful to add a few materials that allow the parent to respond to situations of which they may be less tolerant. However instituting changes to materials should be done with caution and by consultation with experienced filial therapists, rather than done on an ad hoc basis by parents. Providing certain parents with these types of experiences while they are under the direct supervision of the filial therapist helps parents begin to use their empathy skills in more challenging situations. It also prepares them for generalization of skills to outside the special playtimes.

Adaptations for Toddlers in Structuring Playtimes

Initial training and direct supervision of play sessions may be done in a clinic setting or in the family's home. Regardless of location, therapists are initially responsible for establishing the structure and setting the stage for successful parent-child play sessions, including selection of developmentally appropriate toys. Therapists can gradually give parents more responsibility for setting up the play area in preparation for transitioning to the next phase of conducting play sessions without the therapist present. Unlike traditional filial play sessions where parents are instructed to be consistent, with a set time for length of play sessions (typically 30 minutes for three years and up), the length of special playtimes with toddlers depends on their interest level and attention span and can vary somewhat from week to week. Ideally, play sessions would be held for briefer periods (10–15 minutes) at least twice per week. Because of managed care considerations, it may not be possible to hold more than one play session per week under the direct supervision of the filial therapist. An alternative, depending on parental readiness, would be for parents to conduct one play session per week under direct therapist supervision and conduct a second home play session that is videotaped. (We have found that most parents of children this age own a video camera; however, it is helpful for therapists to have video equipment for checkout to parents who cannot afford their own.)

Special considerations for the play area (clinic or home) include safety, ease of cleanup, and low level of distraction. A small area that is free from distractions such as a phone ringing is preferable. An old blanket can be placed on the floor to protect the surface and serve as a visual designation of the play area, with a plastic sheet or vinyl tablecloth placed alongside for messy play. If possible, a room that has a door that can be closed will keep the child from wandering off from the established play area. Again, safety is of prime concern in selecting a play area. The area should be free from unsafe or off-limit items (e.g., items valuable to parent or therapist, depending on where play sessions are held). The room should be toddler-friendly to encourage exploration and expression of autonomy, and one that keeps limit setting to a minimum. Therapists and then caregivers at home need to be aware of potential dangers such as outlets, power cords, and items easily pulled over by young toddlers whose balance may be unsure.

Parents are instructed to play on their child's level, in order to allow for plenty of eye contact and to allow the child to easily engage the parent. Parents are also directed to play close to their child, but to allow the child to lead the play, being sensitive to their child's need for space to explore and to take the initiative in approaching their parent. As our case illustration below shows, with children who have experienced disrupted attachments or more serious trauma and show signs of fearfulness, taking the child's lead is essential in order for parents to attune to their children's emotional needs.

Adaptation of Skills for Toddlers

For the purpose of this chapter, we will focus on what we consider the core skills in filial therapy: (1) empathy and following the child's lead and (2) structuring and limit setting. For a detailed description of filial therapy procedures and skills, refer to Bratton, Landreth, Kellam, and Blackard (2006) and VanFleet (2005).

Empathy and Following the Child's Lead

During playtimes, the primary task for parents is to demonstrate keen interest in their child and their child's play and to communicate their interest in, understanding, and acceptance of their child's feelings, thoughts, and needs through their words and actions, including full attention on their child (Landreth and Bratton 2005). Thus the skill of empathy includes both carefully listening with eyes and ears and accurately responding to what is "heard." Empathic listening and responding skills allow children to begin to see themselves as unconditionally acceptable and lovable as they experience feeling accepted by their parents. Parents are taught by filial therapists to reflect their child's feelings, wants, and wishes, as well as their play behavior. Children, in turn, begin to learn to label their feelings and express their feelings in constructive ways. Parents are taught to respond and enter into their child's play without dominating or leading—to play close by, but not intrude, always showing full attention.

Allowing the child to lead during playtimes helps parents better understand their child's needs and helps their child develop problem-solving skills, while furthering the development of autonomy. Parents of even very young children can convey their willingness to lead by saying such things as, "You want me to hold the baby." Parents are taught to be sensitive to their child's emerging use of imaginative play. Unlike with older children who may invite the parent to play by telling them to pretend to "talk to grandpa" on the phone, parents of toddlers will need to be taught to help facilitate and join in imaginative play more fully with their child. For example, if the child picked up the phone and put it to her ear, the parent could pick up the second phone and pretend to talk to the child. As explained above, one of the essential roles for parents in helping their young children to develop imaginative play is for them to scaffold their children's rudimentary attempts at play, adding stylized features of play routines, learned during their own childhoods. They may respond, "Hello, Daniel!" in a high-pitched, exaggerated tone of voice to indicate its playful nature, and then talk about what "Daniel" is doing, if this engages the toddler's interest.

It is important to stress that it is parents' underlying attitude and intent that is vital in these playful exchanges, rather than the words spoken. What is most important is the parent's full attention, including a genuine attitude of wanting to enter into the child's world—to see the world through the child's eyes—and simply "be with" the child. When parents give their child this type of full attention and prizing, they communicate the four important messages described by Landreth and Bratton (2005): I am here, I hear you, I understand, and I care. Particularly with very young children, parents are encouraged to pay close attention to their child's facial expressions as clues to understanding their child's feelings, thoughts, and needs. Similarly, for toddlers, parents' nonverbal communication and facial expressions are powerful communicators of the parents' intent and interest.

Parents are taught to reflect what they see and what they hear, using simple language and using their voice to match their child's level of affect and interest: "You want baby to have a bath," or if feelings are obvious, ". . . It's fun! Baby's having a bath!" If the child startles in response to a sudden loud noise, the parent would respond, "That scared you!" As noted above, the parents' matching of facial expressions, voice tone, and inflection are critical to their child's feeling understood and fosters emotional self-regulation. For children this age, language development is an important developmental task. Although in traditional filial therapy, parents are instructed to avoid naming all toys in order to allow the child to use toys symbolically, for children this age, naming objects is appropriate and desirable.

Structuring and Limit-Setting Skill

Although some flexibility is important, the therapist should establish a consistent time and length for play sessions in order to provide consistency for parents and children. We encourage parents to provide children with a reminder when there are five minutes and one minute left to play, not because children this age can tell time, but rather to help parents begin to establish a consistent structure that they can generalize to other settings. In this way, parents learn to consistently provide children with a familiar phrase they can use to help the child prepare for transitions in their daily lives. (The case illustration below gives an example of this method of helping children to understand and respond to everyday routines.)

The skill of limit setting is one that parents are generally eager to learn. In helping parents use limit setting with children under two years of age, therapists will need to assess the child's ability to internalize a limit and respond, in order to guide parents through appropriate responses. (Again, both case illustrations below provide examples of the ways in which young children move from being familiar with the limit to becoming more autonomous in their responses.) Although the overall goal of limit setting with toddlers is consistent with the methods outlined by VanFleet (2005) and Landreth and Bratton (2005), an abbreviated version including more simple language may be needed to accommodate to the child's developmental level. During their second year of life, children are beginning to develop self-control as they learn to live within their significant relationships, internalizing what is acceptable and what is not (Wilson and Ryan 2005). By two years of age, we have seen children who are able to bring themselves under control using the child-centered approach to limit setting (Guerney in VanFleet, 2005; Landreth 1991; and Wilson and Ryan, 2005). At this young age children will need more time to bring themselves under control, so patience is the order of the day. Limits may need to be restated several times to allow children to hear the limit, internalize the message, and bring their behavior under control. A note of caution: the skill of effective limit setting cannot be developed without a well-developed level of parental empathy. We have seen many parents fail at effectively setting limits when their goal was to control their child, rather than to provide an opportunity for their child to practice self-control.

The following example illustrates the self-control of a 24-month-old whose mother (a play therapist) had, on her own, been conducting modified filial play sessions at home for approximately six months prior to the time of this example. This excerpt is from a second filial play session conducted in my [Sue Bratton's] play therapy room. It is important to note that this was a fully equipped playroom with sand and water and a host of potentially messy materials that had not been part of the home play sessions. In response to 24-month-old Sarah's delight in putting water in the sandbox during their first session in the playroom, Sarah's mother had arbitrarily set a limit that she could put three cups of water in the sand. Sarah had trouble complying with the limit during her first time in the playroom, but eventually had been able to bring herself under control. During the last five minutes of their second session in the playroom, Sarah went over to the sandbox, looked in, and said, "Three cups." She immediately retrieved a cup from the play kitchen, filled it with water, and dumped it in the sand. Sarah's mother was amazed that she had remembered the rule and reflected, "You know you can put three cups of water in the sandbox." Sarah stopped briefly and looked at her mom before she filled the second cup at the sink and quickly poured it in the sand, quietly stating, "Two," as if counting to herself. Sarah went back for a third cup and as she poured it she looked at her mother and said, "Three." Her mother nodded and said, "You know that's three." This interaction allowed the mother to observe that her child was understanding the limit, a new advance in Sarah's development that she had not been able to do a few months before. However, Sarah was enjoying the sand and water so much that she went back to the sink for a fourth cup. Her mother responded, "Sarah, I know you want more water in the sand. But that's all the water the sandbox can have for today." By then Sarah was back at the sandbox holding the cup and ready to pour. Her mother calmly, yet firmly, restated the limit two more times, with Sarah looking at her mother and looking at the sand and dribbling a little water in the sand. The third time Sarah's mother stated the limit, she pointed to the sink and added, "You can pour the water in the sink." (Note that for a two-year-old, providing a concrete alternative for meeting her needs is developmentally necessary and appropriate.) Sarah looked at the sink and proceeded to go to the sink. She filled and poured several more cups of water. After the play session Sarah's mother reported that she was surprised that Sarah was able to stop herself from pouring the fourth cup of water, literally in the midst of pouring. Because the mother had been practicing the filial skill of empathy and to a lesser degree the limit-setting skill with Sarah for several months, Sarah had the opportunity to begin to learn to accept responsibility for her own behavior and experience what it feels like to exercise self-control.

Younger children will need more assistance in bringing their actions under their own control, thus the play area and type of toys should be chosen to minimize the need for limits. Most limit setting for toddlers and babies arise out of the child's interest in something that is unsafe, valuable to the parents, or messy, not because the child has an intent to break a rule or cause damage or harm. As stated previously, children in this age range are just developing the capacity for self-regulation and need plenty of practice (and patience on the part of the parent) in order to bring themselves under control. For younger toddlers, parents will first need to simply state the limit while they physically remove the child from an unsafe or undesirable situation or behavior and redirect to a desirable behavior. Most parents require support and guidance in how to respond appropriately and adapt their responses as their child matures. The case example that follows illustrates how filial limit setting was adapted for use with younger toddlers (13 months) and then how their increased maturity changed the way in which limit setting was practiced by their adoptive parents at 21 months of age.

THERAPIST REQUIREMENTS

As all of our comments above have implied, training and supervision in child-centered play therapy as well as filial therapy are prerequisites for becoming a filial therapist. Additional requirements for working with this population of toddlers and their parents include a keen understanding of the developmental needs of toddlers, as well as an understanding of parent and child needs relative to attachment issues.

We turn now to our longer case illustration of two young children who were forming new attachment relationships with their adoptive parents and describe filial therapy principles emerging in their interactions.

CASE ILLUSTRATION

The case study below will illustrate the usefulness of a filial therapy approach for very young children who have experienced disrupted attachments. We will analyze the principles of filial therapy displayed by the parents as their story unfolds, and we also will link the interactions among family members with the components of the attachment dynamic outlined earlier in the chapter. We hope to show how extended attachment theory helps filial therapists understand and monitor the progress of all participants in the complex social interactions that occur in such cases over an extended period of time.

Daniel and Mark are fraternal twins who were placed for adoption with a gay couple, Robert and Patrick, when they were 13 months old. They were both healthy boys at birth, although some developmental concerns had been raised with Mark due to his initial dysmorphic features. They are the youngest of their birth mother's nine children. Daniel and Mark had remained with her for two days in the hospital under full care orders by the local authority before going into a planned local authority temporary foster placement with an older married couple. Daniel and Mark were the only children currently being cared for by their devoted foster caregivers until they were placed for adoption with Robert and Patrick, who had been a couple for 18 years and had no other children. At the time of writing this chapter, Daniel and Mark are 21 months old.

Robert is a skilled and experienced filial therapist, as well as a play therapist and family therapist. His partner Patrick is an experienced social worker who is familiar with attachment concepts and the adoption process from his own work. Robert was interviewed by me [Virginia] about the ways in which he used his clinical experience to help him establish new parental relationships with his children and to strengthen his altered relationship with his partner Patrick. Robert and Patrick both read and approved my [Virginia's] draft write-ups. Robert also made welcome suggestions and corrections to the information being presented.

Robert described both his children as being different from the description given by their foster caregivers prior to introductions. They had viewed Daniel as more anxious, while Mark was described as easy-going and often smiling. However, Robert noticed from the start that Mark, while smiling frequently, seemed more anxious and cautious than his older (by 13 minutes!) brother Daniel. In terms of the attachment dynamic, Mark's self-defense system seemed to be preset at a higher level than that of his brother, in Robert's view.

The Matching Week

Robert described the week prior to placement as "one of the most stressful parts of the entire adoption process" for himself and Patrick. He stated that his own training in child-centered play therapy was drawn on frequently during this week. Robert also found that his training in filial therapy was of help to Patrick, who was not a trained therapist, in understanding their own and their children's reactions. Robert emphasized that while other play therapy skills were important, the most important was his ability to empathize with his children. Another important source of support for Robert and Patrick was the children's foster caregivers. The caregivers were asked for reassurance at times by the couple at the beginning of the matching week, and then became adept at spontaneously offering Robert and Patrick reassurance when the caregivers assessed that the couple would benefit from positive feedback on their new parenting skills.

Applying the attachment dynamic to this phase in the adoption process, both Robert and Patrick recognized that their self-defense systems were activated at a much higher level than usual during this week. Both had their parenting systems activated at a high level too, but because Robert was more experienced in forming new, close relationships with children, Patrick turned to him for emotional support (careseeking system), and Robert in turn gave Patrick reassurance (the caregiving subsystem of the parenting system) in order to lower Patrick's and his own anxieties (self-defense systems) and join together (affectional sexual system) in exploring their new relationships with Daniel and Mark (exploratory system). Robert described how his own exploratory system was more highly activated in most situations, including this one, and his self-defense system less highly activated than Patrick's. Robert more easily took the lead in exploring their new relationships with their children initially than his partner. Patrick also provided caregiving to Robert during this stressful period, but perhaps not as often as Robert did for Patrick.

The foster caregivers also had a vital role for Robert and Patrick during this phase in the adoption process. The caregivers quickly were used as attachment figures, not just by the children, but by Robert and Patrick as well. As new parents, they instigated careseeking from the foster caregivers, who became sensitively attuned to their attachment needs quickly. The caregivers soon were able to initiate caregiving toward Robert and Patrick spontaneously, without being asked for it, once their caregiving relationship with them had been established.

Because both Daniel and Mark appeared anxious at their first meeting, their new parents' ability to empathize and to contain and manage their own adult anxieties was essential. Robert described their first encounter with 13-month-old Daniel and Mark at their foster home:

> They had their favorite toys in the sitting room. I decided to get onto the floor, to be at their level. Instead of too eagerly picking up their toys and starting to play with them, I let Daniel and Mark initiate all the interactions between us. I noticed that Daniel was braver—Mark sat and watched his brother from a distance and did not venture nearer. After a relatively short time, Daniel moved a truck he liked across the room, starting to get closer to me . . . There were lots of times during this matching week, and especially this first time, that it was important to follow our children's lead and not rush them. It seemed right to

let them come close to us when they wanted and not to pick them up and hold them too soon just because we desperately wanted to.

Robert stated that it was very important in general to remain in the foster home and then start playing together in their new home, with the children's foster caregivers nearby, during this matching week. Robert summarized his feelings: "It was a short, but *very* intensive, week in our lives."

Again applying the attachment dynamic, this time to the children themselves, both Daniel's and Mark's self-defense systems were highly activated initially when meeting their new parents. Robert and Patrick took pains to ensure that the children's self-defense systems did not remain highly activated by allowing the twins to approach them at their own pace, and by having their foster caregivers remain nearby for potential comforting if the children became overly distressed. This approach allowed Daniel to activate his exploratory system more easily without being hampered by highly self-defensive responses, and it allowed Mark to lower his own self-defensive responses somewhat. But Mark was unable initially to activate his exploratory system with his new parents. As discussed more below, it seems likely that Mark was depending on his brother Daniel to provide the rudimentary security he needed to begin to explore these new relationships. (Note that the attachment literature's understanding of the attachment properties of sibling relationships and the ways siblings use these relationships as primary or substitute attachment relationships seems underdeveloped and warrants more research.)

The Core Skills in Filial Therapy:
Empathy and Following Children's Lead

Robert's description of his way of first developing relationships with his own children underlines several important concepts in filial therapy practice. First and foremost, he was able to contain his own anxiety and help Patrick contain his, by knowing that the filial/play therapy principle of allowing children to lead and not rushing them into new relationships and activities is a highly effective method of relationship building. Daniel and Mark were able to come close and move away at their own individual paces. Second, Robert's play therapy experience enabled him to appreciate that his children were communicating fully with them nonverbally, through their toys and actions. He saw meaning and significance in Daniel using a favorite toy to move toward him, knowing that Daniel felt more secure when a ("transitional") object was used, rather than moving himself forward. And Robert also understood that Mark was more cautious than Daniel, not choosing to move toward either Robert or Patrick himself until Daniel had begun to feel comfortable with them.

Early Months in the Adoptive Placement

At the outset of his placement Mark sat back most of the time and did not participate; he watched and closely tracked Daniel's play with Robert and Patrick. Daniel seemed to be Mark's "safe base" and his most important attachment figure during these early days. Mark did not want to be too involved with his new parents for two to three months and often played on his own near the others. Robert felt he was able to understand and accept Mark's need to regulate his contact with them more easily than Patrick was. Currently 21-month-old Mark is still more cautious, using a toy or a book to initiate contact, but becoming increasingly secure. His brother Daniel is now very relaxed and initiates big hugs with both Robert and Patrick. Robert finds Mark's behavior understandable, given Mark's strong anxieties initially with them. He has been able to help his partner, Patrick, whose temperament is more similar to Mark's, realize that their son's reactions are a defense against anxiety, rather than a rejection of them as his parents.

Applying the attachment dynamic to this phase in the parents' and children's developing relationships with one another, the activation level of Daniel's self-defense system lowered considerably in a relatively short time. Daniel soon became able to interact with his new parents and easily activated his exploratory and careseeking systems with them. However, Mark's self-defense system remained highly activated in the early months of his placement and he was unable to highly activate his careseeking and exploratory systems with his new parents. Mark viewed Daniel as his main source of emotional security, even though Daniel was obviously unable to provide caregiving to Mark due to his young age. In recent months Mark's self-defense system's activation is lowering and he is able to activate his exploratory and careseeking systems more with his parents. Turning to the parents themselves, Robert's self-defense system was not highly activated in his relationship with his children after placement. He was able to help (e.g., the caregiving subsystem of the parenting system became activated) Patrick lower the activation of his self-defense system, which was likely to be preset at a higher level than Robert's already, in relation to Mark. Neither parent had his self-defense system raised in relation to Daniel after placement. They were able to have their parenting and exploratory systems easily activated, without raising their defensive responses, with Daniel.

Engaging in Imaginative Play

At this point in the interview, Virginia and Robert discussed the ways in which play was understood and used by the family once the children had moved to their new home. Robert described how excited he was to see from the outset that both children at 13 months of age were taking part in developmentally appropriate play. He stated that both he and Patrick naturally play with their children, and that it was important to both parents at their first meeting that their children showed that they already had the foundations for building relationships through play. When Daniel and Mark first were placed with them, both children were able to enjoy turning pages of books over while looking at them with their parents, crashing towers built with bricks that made a noise as they crashed, and having their parents wind up and send a crab scuttling back and forth between them and their new parents. Daniel's and Mark's play has expanded in numerous ways by now, at 21 months of age. Mark's favorite, often-repeated activity with Robert and Patrick at the beginning of his placement was "peek-a-boo," which Robert understood as a reaction to losing his foster caregivers and trying to develop new relationships with him and Patrick. Now both Daniel and Mark take part in construction play, such as building towers, doing shape sorting, and puzzles, and in early forms of symbolic play, for example, having horses in their farm set engage in running, eating, and drinking.

Robert described his partner Patrick as better at organizing and doing structured play with their sons, and being better at one-on-one interactions with each boy, possibly partly due to his hearing disability. Robert, on the other hand, is more spontaneous in his play and takes opportunities to include imaginative play in many of their interactions. For example, when Mark went to bed with his teddy as usual one night recently, he started to duck teddy's head down onto the bed sheet, reminding Robert of their family dog, who often eats in that way. Robert suggested that teddy was hungry and Mark looked delighted, then began to "feed" his teddy. The twins are now more reciprocal in their relationships with one another, again in a developmentally appropriate way. For example, at bath time they now squirt one another vigorously with water, and Daniel sometimes rubs Mark's head when he cries a bit. Their spontaneity and imaginative play is most apparent at home with Robert and Patrick, even though they visit relatives regularly. The children both are quieter at their grandparents' houses, even though each set of grandparents have an enticing toy box to engage their interest.

Applying the attachment dynamic to the situations described above, it is evident that both parents' exploration and interest-sharing systems were highly activated during play both with one another and with each of their children. Robert described how much his interest-sharing system and the growth and development subsystem of his parenting system were activated during his early meetings with their children when he saw that they were able to play. Patrick is described as having the growth and development component of his parenting system highly raised during one-on-one play times with their children. And all four members of the family are described by Robert as having their self-defense systems' activation levels lowered during play and their exploratory systems' activation levels raised, the usual response humans have when playing freely. Finally, it is interesting to note that Daniel is beginning to develop his own parenting/caregiving system with Mark, affectionately rubbing his brother's head when he cries at times, a typical response of a more securely attached two-year-old.

Structuring

Robert mentioned that one of the key pieces of general advice to new adopters[3] is to maintain the children's routines that already have been established in their foster placements. He and Patrick found it highly beneficial for their children to stick closely to the foster caregivers' daily routines (e.g., bedtime, nap time, mealtime, etc.). Robert commented, "This certainly worked wonders!" He also speculated that by sticking to these familiar routines, their children were able to derive comfort from this continuity in their care and seemed to more rapidly increase their trust in their new parents. This trust in turn enabled Daniel and Mark to explore their environment more readily.

Robert described how structuring has been changed and adapted to the ongoing developmental needs of their children. The parents have new expectations and responses in keeping with their children's current capacities. At bedtime, for example, Daniel and Mark are told "Five more minutes"— not because they are precocious and tell the time, but because this serves as a familiar phrase to announce that the next part of the evening will soon arrive for them!

Robert's comments about limit setting illustrate well the ways in which the growth and development subsystem of Robert's and Patrick's parenting system was highly activated at these times, with both parents working cooperatively to increase and sustain their children's development of autonomy, exploration, and compliance.

As outlined earlier when we discussed the filial therapy skills to be taught to toddlers' parents, establishing the structure of beginning and ending play sessions, for example, and helping parents then to generalize this learning to everyday life, is an important aspect of the intervention. This is because children's exploratory systems are most highly activated when their care-seeking and insecurity are reduced.

Limit Setting

Robert observed that both he and Patrick were confident as parents in setting clear limits to their children's behavior in a firm but gentle way, and without becoming overly upset or distant from either of them. Robert gave an illustration of one of the limits that they set and how they carry it out, now that their children are 21 months of age. He stated that it is important to both Patrick and him that their children do not damage their music system. Therefore they have always tried to enforce the limit in an age-appropriate way that there is no playing with or on the stereo. Very simple limit setting had been introduced when their children began playing freely, after they had become relaxed in their new environment. When Mark and Daniel were younger, the limit setting was mostly in the minds of their parents. Robert and Patrick would say "No playing" and help their children move the toy they were using to the floor or to an area near their parents.

At this stage in their lives, however, the children seem to know the rule, because sometimes they try several times in succession to play on the stereo, glancing at their parents as they do so. Robert's and Patrick's limit setting has changed accordingly. This is because their children seem to have moved away from exploration of the possibilities of play and finding out what their parents' responses to this behavior will be. The children now seem to have assimilated the "house rule" and are testing their own autonomy, a normal developmental task at their age. The parents use the filial therapy limit-setting approach more fully at this stage, when either child begins to run a car along the top of the music system. First, they state the rule in a firm, nonplayful tone of voice, "The stereo is for daddies" and then wait for a positive response. If the children's play behavior continues, they give another reminder. If this reminder does not suffice, they take another car and run it along the floor themselves, stating firmly that the children's cars go there, too. There are very few times that this limit setting is not effective, Robert adds, as long as the parents are emotionally and physically available to their children. However, very recently, as Mark and Daniel move toward increased autonomy, very occasionally they will smile mischievously and continue to run their cars and trucks along the stereo, refusing to move. Their parents, after repeating the rule and actions described above a few times, have then moved on to the next stage of limit setting. They acknowledge their children's feelings: "You want to play there. Come and play here." Then, if there is no response, they firmly state the rule: "The stereo is for daddies." They follow this by saying in a confident and nonconfrontational tone of voice, "Your truck will be put away." If Mark and Daniel do not respond to this warning, the parents follow through and remove the toy (but leave the other ones on the floor!), again acknowledging their children's feelings, this time of anger or upset.

(Note that this limit setting is an abbreviated form of filial therapy limit setting. When used with older children the rule is stated, the child's feelings acknowledged, and the child redirected—"You can do most other things in your special play time." On the second statement of the rule, the consequence is introduced.)

The Family's Hopes and Plans

Robert stressed how pleased they are with their children's relationships with them and with their own progress in parenting them. He feels his filial therapy and play therapy training have enhanced both his own and his partner's ability to form close and meaningful relationships with "their boys." And the interest both Robert and Patrick share in taking time every day to play with their children has been very important in consolidating and deepening their family as a whole. However, Robert also feels that they are still learning a lot about how to be parents together. There are particular challenges their family faces because it is still very uncommon in the United Kingdom for gay couples to adopt young children. Robert is confident that they have and will continue to work well as a couple, with both of them being able to provide nurturing as well as playful times for one another so far. But Robert and Patrick are realistic and recognize that their parenting tasks may prove more challenging in the future. For now, Daniel and Mark seem confident to play on their own, to play in parallel with one another, and to play with one or both parents. But Daniel and Mark, as twins, do spend almost all their time with one another. Given the hesitancy Mark still feels with his parents, and especially with Patrick, it may be helpful for Patrick and Mark to have individual, filial play sessions together at a set time every week for a few months. This plan also may increase Mark's confidence, which his brother Daniel already shows, by spending time away from Daniel and with each of his parents.

FURTHER AVENUES FOR PRACTICE AND RESEARCH

Implications for Parents of Late-Adopted Children

This case illustration shows that new parents are able to develop closer attachment relationships with their adoptive children when filial therapy principles are used. However, it also highlights a difficulty for an adoptive couple when one parent is highly trained in filial therapy and the other is not—it is then more difficult for the untrained parent to feel competent, especially when adopting a child or children with disrupted attachment histories and other vulnerabilities. Therefore, in general we would recommend that *both* parents be trained together as a couple, if at all possible, in order to help couples maintain a balance between themselves of parenting competencies.

Second, if new adoptive parents have playful interactions available to them, this in turn is likely to help them enhance their relationships with their children more quickly (VanFleet 1994). Heard and Lake's extended attachment theory helps explain the added dimensions within attachment relationships that children and their caregivers develop in their early years together. Interest sharing and education are two essentials that are most easily accessed through play with very young children. Another suggestion that Robert had is that filial therapy for adoptive parents ideally would begin before the matching process, for both very young and older children. This form of relationship therapy would enhance adopters' skills with their children and enable all family members to make new attachments with one another.

Applications for Children with Special Needs and Their Parents

Another practice and research area that shows promise is using filial therapy with families where very young children have developmental difficulties and delays. These difficulties may be apparent in the population discussed above, namely late-adopted children, but more widely may include young children with autistic spectrum difficulties and children with other types of developmental delays (e.g., learning impairments, genetic disorders, very low birth weight children). Filial therapy for families of these children addresses one of the intervention difficulties raised in the literature concerning intensive interventions for very young children with special needs and their families. That is, when interventions concentrate on the relationships of these children with their parent(s), other relationships in the family may become less prioritized and problematic. The potential unmet needs of siblings and other family members of children with learning disabilities and autistic spectrum difficulties have been discussed elsewhere (e.g., Vetere 1996; Furman 1993). This recognition of family systems concerns has led, for example, to group and individual programs for siblings of children with life-threatening illnesses and disabilities (Hitcham 1995; Meyer and Vadasy 1994; Wilkins 1992).

One of the major advantages of filial therapy for these families is that the entire family is included in interventions. In fact, this systemic thinking is one of the motivations for writing our chapter. Including very young children in filial therapy seems both possible and necessary in order to work toward family change. In two-parent families, ideally both adults would train and conduct filial therapy play sessions with each of their children. In one-parent families and families from cultures where extended family members form close attachment relationships with children, another significant adult (e.g., partner, grandparent, aunt, uncle) may be included in filial therapy (for examples, see VanFleet and L. Guerney 2003). As we mentioned in the introduction to this chapter, filial therapy is intended for all of the children in the family, not just for the child(ren) deemed to have problems. It also enables parents and caregivers to develop more supportive relationships and higher levels of interest sharing with each other as parents, as they train and carry out filial therapy with their children. Indeed, one of the tasks of parenting, outlined above by Heard and Lake, is for parents to meet children's needs to develop their language, emotional understanding, cognition, and play. Therefore a very positive feature is that attachment relationships in the family as a whole are strengthened when filial therapy is successful.

A case illustration using both qualitative and quantitative analysis of child-centered play therapy with a child severely impaired by autism and functioning overall on the level of a very young child has been discussed elsewhere (see Josefi and Ryan 2004). Josefi and Ryan concluded that this type of child therapy may have the potential to increase the emotional/social development of children with autism, including the development of their imaginative play, when all of the essential features for this type of play to emerge are emphasized by their play therapists. Ways in which play therapy and filial therapy create conditions in which children are able to experience highly sensitive caregiving on an intensive level, led by children's own interests, also have been examined (e.g., Ryan 2007b, 2004, 1999; Wilson and Ryan, 2005). While systematic research is not yet available, clinical case analysis shows that where the essential features for the development of symbolic play are consciously employed during therapy, child-centered play therapy appears effective in helping children with Asperger's syndrome and other autistic spectrum difficulties, as well as helping children, young people, and adults with serious learning disabilities, to develop emotionally, particularly in the areas of autonomy and imaginative play.

Play therapists have reported training parents of disabled children informally, at the end of play therapy interventions, to carry on with special play sessions with their children afterward (e.g., Josefi and Ryan 2004). However, there are no examples in the filial therapy literature of training parents of very young children with disabilities to conduct filial therapy sessions with them and their siblings. Hopefully, this chapter will inspire clinicians and researchers to undertake this important task in the future.

Prevention for Higher Risk Groups

Filial therapy has the added benefit of intervening in family dynamics and providing parents with skills and resources that can serve to prevent future problems. We have selected a few populations that seem vulnerable to future difficulties, in addition to needing more intensive ongoing support, in order to illustrate ways in which filial therapy can be employed to ameliorate emotional distress and future emotional difficulties. It is our belief that play therapists and filial therapists have a responsibility to use filial therapy findings and new practice advances in an advocacy role, to not only educate managed care companies and other service providers, but also to educate and work with parents, government, schools, and the medical and legal communities to ensure that children and their families receive the most beneficial and cost-effective treatments. As discussed earlier, filial therapy provides a viable means for early intervention, rather than waiting until children are displaying significant symptomology, often first noticed when children enter school. Early intervention can diminish unnecessary suffering. It also prevents the development of more serious impairment throughout the lifespan, another strong argument for filial therapy as a cost-effective intervention.

CONCLUSIONS AND FUTURE DIRECTIONS

We hope this chapter has been persuasive in presenting the case for using filial therapy with toddlers and their parents. As stated earlier, it can be used as a stand-alone treatment for individual or groups of families with very young children. It also can be used when working with individual families whose children cover the age range from babies to teens, and very young children can be given the important place in their families that they rightfully require. Their developmental and mental health needs can be met early, alongside their older siblings' needs, with the hope that serious future problems will be ameliorated.

Having explored many issues involved in working with very young children in filial therapy here, the next important step is for clinicians to implement these procedures and fine-tune filial therapy practice with babies, toddlers and their parents. Alongside this clinical program, a well-orchestrated research program is essential. We suggest that the special populations of children we outlined above—very young children with disrupted attachments, and those with special needs in particular—would benefit from filial therapy that is well supported by research findings. This type of research would make a major contribution to the resiliency and early intervention literatures. Ultimately the hope is that working with the very youngest and most vulnerable children will give families and very young children increased ability to cope with the further challenges that life inevitably brings.

NOTES

1. This method of play therapy is often labeled "child-centered" in the United States and "nondirective "in the United Kingdom and Ireland. The term "nondirective" was retained in the United Kingdom and Ireland to distinguish it from

"child-centered play therapy," a term that is used more generically. (See the British Association of Play Therapists website at www.bapt.info for details.) In this chapter, since this book is published in the United States, we will use the term child-centered play therapy throughout.

2. We thank the family for permission to describe their new relationships with their adopted children in order to illustrate the ways in which filial therapy principles can be applied to developing attachment relationships between very young children and their new parents. All names and certain identifying background details have been changed for confidentiality purposes.

3. Exploration of the ways in which social workers involved in the adoption process serve as caregivers to adoptive parents is another feature to analyze using extended attachment theory, but is beyond the scope of this chapter.

REFERENCES

Ainsworth, M. D. S. 1982. Attachment: Retrospect and prospect. In _The place of attachment in human behaviour_, ed. C. M. Parkes and J. Stevenson-Hinde, 3–30. New York: Basic.

American Academy of Pediatrics. 2006. _Clinical report: the importance of play in promoting healthy child development and maintaining strong parent-child bonds._ Elk Grove Village, IL: American Academy of Pediatrics.

Axline, V. M. 1947. _Play therapy._ London: Churchill Livingstone, 1989.

Baggerly, J., and G. Landreth. 2001. Training children to help children: A new dimension in play therapy. _Peer Facilitator Quarterly_ 18 (1): 6–14.

Bakersmans-Kranenburg, M. J., M. H. van IJzendoorn, and F. Juffer. 2003. Less is more: Meta-analyses of sensitivity and attachment interventions in early childhood. _Psychological Bulletin_ 129 (2): 195–215.

Berk, L. 2003. _Child development._ Boston: Allyn & Bacon.

Bifulco, A. 2002. Attachment style measurement: A clinical and epidemiological perspective. _Attachment and Human Development_ 4:180–188.

Bonnard, A. 1950. The mother as therapist in a case of obsessional neurosis. _Psychoanalytic Study of the Child_ 5:391–408.

Bowlby, J. 1980. _Attachment and loss._ 3 vols. London: Hogarth.

Bratton, S. 1998. Training parents to facilitate their child's adjustment to divorce using the filial/family play therapy approach. In _Handbook of parent training: Parents as co-therapists for children's behavior problems._ 2nd ed. Ed. C. Schaefer and J. Breismeister, 549–572. New York: Wiley.

Bratton, S., and G. Landreth. 1995. Filial therapy with single parents: Effects on parental acceptance, empathy, and stress. _International Journal of Play Therapy_ 4 (1): 61–80.

Bratton, S., G. Landreth, T. Kellam, and S. Blackard. 2006. _Child-parent relationship therapy (CPRT) treatment manual: A 10-session filial therapy model for training parents._ New York: Routledge.

Bratton, S., and D. Ray. 2002. Humanistic play therapy. In _Humanistic psychotherapies: Handbook of research and practice_, ed. D. Cain and J. Seeman, 369–402. Washington, DC: American Psychological Association.

Bratton, S., D. Ray, and G. Landreth. 2008. Play therapy. In *Handbook of clinical psychology*, vol. 2, *Children and adolescents*, ed. A. Gross and M. Hersen. New York: Wiley.

Bratton, S., D. Ray, T. Rhine, and L. Jones. 2005. The efficacy of play therapy with children: A meta-analytic review of the outcome research. *Professional Psychology: Research and Practice* 36 (4): 376–390.

Brown, C. 2003. Filial therapy training with undergraduate teacher trainees: Child-teacher relationship training. PhD diss., University of North Texas. *Dissertation Abstracts International* A 63 (09): 3112.

Chau, I., and G. Landreth. 1997. Filial therapy with Chinese parents: Effects on parental empathic interactions, parental acceptance of child, and parental stress. *International Journal of Play Therapy* 6 (2): 75–92.

Costas, M., and G. Landreth. 1999. Filial therapy with nonoffending parents of children who have been sexually abused. *International Journal of Play Therapy* 8 (1): 43–66.

Erikson, E. 1950. *Childhood and society*. New York: Norton.

Freud, S. 1909. *Analysis of a phobia in a five-year-old boy*. London: Hogarth, 1955.

Fuchs, N. 1957. Play therapy at home. *Merrill-Palmer Quarterly* 3:89–95.

Furman, W. C. 1993. Contemporary themes in research on sibling relationships of nondisabled children. In *The effects of mental retardation, disability and illness on sibling relationships: Research issues and challenges*, ed. Z. Stoneman. Baltimore: Brookes.

Glazer-Waldman, H. 1991. Filial therapy: CPR training for families with chronically ill children. Master's thesis, University of North Texas.

Glover, G., and G. Landreth. 2000. Filial therapy with Native Americans on the Flathead reservation. *International Journal of Play Therapy* 9 (2): 57–80.

Greenspan, S., and N. Greenspan. 1989. *The essential partnership: How parents and children can meet the emotional challenges of infancy and childhood*. New York: Penguin.

Greenspan, S., and S. Wieder. 2006. *Infant and early childhood mental health: A comprehensive developmental approach to assessment and intervention*. Arlington, VA: American Psychiatric Association.

Guerney, B. 1964. Filial therapy: Description and rationale. *Journal of Consulting Psychology* 28 (4): 303–310.

Guerney, B., and Stover, L. 1971. *Filial therapy final report (MH 18264-01)*. University Park: Penn State University Press.

Guerney, L. 1975. Brief follow-up study on filial therapy. Paper presented at the Eastern Psychological Association, New York.

———. 1984. Client-centered (non-directive) play therapy. In *Handbook of play therapy*, ed. C. E. Schaefer and K. J. O'Connor, 1:21–64. New York: Wiley.

———. 2000. Filial therapy into the 21st century. *International Journal of Play Therapy* 9 (2): 1–17.

———. 2003. The history, principles, and empirical basis of filial therapy. In *Casebook of filial therapy*, ed. R. VanFleet and L. Guerney, 1–20. Boiling Springs, PA: Play Therapy.

Guerney, L., and B. Guerney. 1989. Child relationship enhancement: Family therapy and parent education. In Person-centered approaches with families, special issue, *Person-Centered Review* 4 (3): 344–357.

Harris, Z. L., and G. Landreth. 1997. Filial therapy with incarcerated mothers: A five-week model. *International Journal of Play Therapy* 6 (2): 53–73.

Heard, D. 1982. Family systems and the attachment dynamic. *Journal of Family Therapy* 4:99–116.

———. 2001. Extending attachment theory by introducing the concept of the attachment dynamic. Paper presented at the IAN introductory course.

Heard, D., and B. Lake. 1997. *The challenge of attachment for caregivers.* London: Routledge.

Hitcham, M. 1995. Direct work techniques with the siblings of children dying from cancer. In *Interventions with bereaved children,* ed. S. Smith and M. Pennells. London: Jessica Kingsley.

Jacobs, L. 1949. Methods used in the education of mothers: A contribution to the handling and treatment of developmental difficulties in children under five years of age. *Psychoanalytic Study of the Child* 4 (March): 409–422.

Jang, M. 2003. Filial therapy with Korean parents. In *Casebook of filial therapy,* ed. R. VanFleet, and L. Guerney, 441–452. Boiling Springs, PA: Play Therapy Press.

Jones, L., T. Rhine, and S. Bratton. 2002. High school students as therapeutic agents with young children experiencing school adjustment difficulties: The effectiveness of the filial therapy training model. *International Journal for Play Therapy* 11 (2): 43–62.

Josefi, O., and V. Ryan. 2004. Non-directive play therapy for young children with autism: A case study. *Clinical Child Psychology and Psychiatry* 9 (4): 533–551.

Kale, A. L., and G. Landreth. 1999. Filial therapy with parents of children experiencing learning difficulties. *International Journal of Play Therapy* 8 (2): 35–56.

Kidron, M. 2004. Filial therapy with Israeli parents. PhD diss., University of North Texas. *Dissertation Abstracts International* A 64 (12): 4372.

Landreth, G. 1991. *Play therapy: The art of the relationship.* 2nd ed. New York: Brunner-Routledge, 2002.

Landreth, G., and S. Bratton. 2005. *Child-parent relationship therapy (CPRT): A 10-session filial therapy model.* New York: Routledge.

Landreth, G., and A. Lobaugh. 1998. Filial therapy with incarcerated fathers: Effects on parental acceptance of child, parental stress, and child adjustment. *Journal of Counseling and Development* 76 (Spring): 157–165.

LeBlanc, M., and M. Ritchie. 2001. A meta-analysis of play therapy outcomes. *Counseling Psychology Quarterly* 14:149–163.

Lee, M., and G. Landreth. 2003. Filial therapy with immigrant Korean parents in the United States. *International Journal of Play Therapy* 12 (2): 67–85.

Lipari, J. 2000. Four things you need to know about raising a baby. *Psychology Today* 33 (4): 38.

McGuire, D. K., and D. E. McGuire. 2000. *Linking parents to play therapy: a practical guide with applications, interventions and case studies.* New York: Brunner-Routledge.

Meyer, D., and P. Vadasy. 1994. *Sibshops: Workshops for siblings of children with special needs.* Baltimore: Brookes.

Morrison, M. 2006. An early mental health intervention for disadvantaged preschool children with behavior problems: The effectiveness of training Head Start teachers in Child Teacher Relationship Training (CTRT). PhD diss., University of North Texas.

Moustakas, C. 1959. *Psychotherapy with children: The living relationships.* Greeley, CO: Carron.

Neander, K. and C. Skott. Forthcoming. Bridging the gap. *Journal of Qualitative Social Work.*

Oxman, L. 1972. The effectiveness of filial therapy: A controlled study. PhD diss., Rutgers. *Dissertation Abstracts International* B 32 (11): 6656.

Raskin, N. J., and C. R. Rogers. 2005. Person-centered therapy. In *Current psychotherapies.* 7th ed. Ed. R. J. Corsini and D. Wedding, 130–165. Belmont, CA: Wadsworth.

Reddy, L. A., T. M. Files-Hall, and C. E. Schaefer. 2005. *Empirically based play interventions for children.* Washington, DC: APA.

Rosenblith, J. F. 1992. *In the beginning: Development from conception to age two.* London: Sage.

Ryan, V. 1999. Developmental delay, symbolic play, and non-directive play therapy: Essentials in atypical and normal development. *Clinical Child Psychology and Psychiatry* 4 (2): 167–185.

———. 2004. Adapting non-directive play therapy interventions for children with attachment disorders. *Clinical Child Psychology and Psychiatry* 9 (1): 75–87.

———. 2007a. Filial therapy: Helping children and new caregivers to form secure attachment relationships. *British Journal of Social Work,* 34, 643–647.

———. 2007b. Non-directive play therapy with abused children and adolescents. In *The child protection handbook.* 3rd ed. Ed. K. Wilson and A. James, 414–432. London: Harcourt Brace.

Ryan, V., and K. Wilson. 1995. Non-directive play therapy as a means of recreating optimal infant socialization patterns. *Early Development and Parenting* 4: 29–38.

———. 2000. *Case studies in non-directive play therapy.* London: Jessica Kingsley.

Schaefer, C., and T. DiGeronimo. 2000. *Ages and stages.* New York: Wiley.

Schaffer, H. R. 1984. *The child's entry into a social world.* London: Academic Press.

———. 1989. Early social development. In *Infant development,* ed. A. Slater and G. Bremner. Hillsdale, NJ: Erlbaum.

Shonkoff, J. P., and S. J. Meisels, eds. 2000. *Handbook of early childhood interventions.* 2nd ed. New York: Cambridge University Press.

Smith, N., and G. Landreth. 2003. Intensive filial therapy with child witnesses of domestic violence: A comparison with individual and sibling group play therapy. *International Journal for Play Therapy* 12 (1): 67–88.

Stover, L., and B. Guerney. 1967. The efficacy of training procedures for mothers in filial therapy. *Psychotherapy: Theory, Research, and Practice* 4 (3): 110–115.

Tew, K., G. Landreth, K. D. Joiner, and M. D. Solt. 2002. Filial therapy with parents of chronically ill children. *International Journal of Play Therapy* 11 (1): 79–100.

VanFleet, R. 1994. Filial therapy for adoptive children and parents. In *Handbook of play therapy,* ed. K. J. O'Connor and C. E. Schaefer, 2:371–386. Chichester, UK: Wiley.

———. 2005. *Filial therapy: Strengthening parent-child relationships through play.* 2nd ed. Sarasota, FL: Professional Resource Press.

———. 2008. *Canine play therapy: The benefits of cross-species play for children's developmental and psychosocial health.* Sarasota, FL: Professional Resource Press.

VanFleet, R., and L. Guerney, eds. 2003. *Casebook of filial therapy.* Boiling Springs, PA: Play Therapy Press.

Vetere, A. 1996. The neglect of family systems ideas and practices in services for children and young people with learning disabilities. *Clinical Child Psychology and Psychiatry* 1:485–488.

Vetere, A., and R. Dallos. 2003. *Working systematically with families: formulation, intervention, and evaluation.* London: Karmac Press.

Vondra, J., D. S. Shaw, L. Swearingen, M. Cohen, and E. Owens. 2001. Attachment, stability and emotional and behavioral regulation from infancy to preschool age. *Development and Psychopathology* 13:13–33.

White, J., M. Flynt, and K. Draper. 1997. Kinder therapy: Teachers as therapeutic agents. *International Journal of Play Therapy* 6 (2): 33–49.

White, J., M. Flynt, and N. P. Jones. 1999. Kinder therapy: An Adlerian approach for training teachers to be therapeutic agents through play. *Journal of Individual Psychology* 55 (3): 33–49.

Wilkins, R. 1992. Psychotherapy with the siblings of mentally handicapped children. In *Psychotherapy and mental handicap*, ed. S. Waitman and S. Conboy-Hill. London: Sage.

Wilson, K., and V. Ryan. 2005. *Play therapy: A non-directive approach for children and adolescents.* 2nd ed. London: Elsevier Science.

Yuen, T., G. Landreth, and J. Baggerly. 2002. Filial therapy with immigrant Chinese families. *International Journal for Play Therapy* 11 (2): 63–90.

3

Filial Play Therapy for Infants and Toddlers

Hilda R. Glazer

BASIC RATIONALE AND THEORY

For the play therapist, a critical element is the relationship between the therapist and the child that develops in the playroom. The playroom becomes a safe place to play and to express emotions and to process events. And the therapist provides the context in which expression occurs. The relationship between the child and therapist is developed as part of the process of play therapy. The communication in the playroom is bidirectional, with both the child and the therapist responding to the interaction.

When conceptualizing the interventions for a particular child, there are a number of questions that should be asked. These include:

- What is the presenting issue?
- What are the needs of this child?
- Who is going to have the greatest impact on the child?
- Which intervention will have the greatest potential to facilitate change?
- How does the family system impact the presenting problem?

For the young child, the answer to the second question is determined through interaction with the family and child and understanding what brought them to therapy. The answer to the third question is often the parent rather than the therapist, and one intervention that should be considered in treatment planning with the young child is filial therapy. Filial therapy provides the opportunity for the parent to become the primary therapist with the child under the guidance of the play therapist. While still being child-centered, the intervention uses the attachment bond between parent and child to facilitate change and provide the context for processing. The playroom becomes a place where the parent and child will have something special.

Filial therapy, which is child-parent relationship training, is a theoretically integrative approach combining elements of psychodynamic, humanistic, behavioral, cognitive, social learning, attachment, and family systems theories. However, the primary theoretical basis is client-centered play therapy. Moustakas (1959), in describing relationship therapy, saw therapy as a unique growth experience created by one person who needs help and another person who accepts the responsibility of offering it. Two people, in this case the parent and child, participate in a genuine and fundamental way. The parallel in filial therapy is that it is based on the parent-child bond and the assumption that the parent has more emotional significance to the child than does the therapist. The parent and child are developmentally linked and the playroom becomes a place where they learn and grow together.

Theoretically, Relational-Cultural Therapy (RCT) is related to filial therapy. RCT is based on a set of core principles that include the following:

- People grow through and toward relationships throughout the lifespan.
- Movement toward mutuality rather than movement toward separation characterizes mature functioning.
- Relational differentiation and elaboration characterize growth.
- In growth-fostering relationships, all people contribute, grow, or benefit; development is not a one-way street.
- Therapeutic relationships are characterized by a special kind of mutuality. (Jordan 2000, 1007)

According to Jordan (2000), the work of RCT is the understanding of the individual patterns of connections or disconnections. In filial therapy, the relationship between the parent and the child becomes the focus, and often the restoration of that relationship is the goal of therapy. For the child experiencing trauma or loss, the parent and child use the playroom to explore the meaning of the experience for the child. Both the parent and the child learn and grow in the experience. It is the empathy and mutuality that are encouraged and reinforced in filial therapy. The construct of mutual empathy suggests that each individual in a relationship is affected by the other (Jordan 2000). This supports the role of parent in filial therapy, as the parent-child bond already exists and is strengthened in the process of the therapeutic encounter in the playroom.

The model for filial therapy is "a competence-oriented psychoeducational framework" in which parents are taught to conduct special playtimes, supervised through the skill development, and eventually helped to integrate the playtimes and parenting skills at home (VanFleet 1994, 2).

Training for filial therapy is provided through a number of training institutes and associations, and courses in filial therapy are provided at universities such as the University of North Texas. As with play therapy, one should not assume that it can simply be added to the tool kit without proper training.

Filial therapy was developed in the 1960s by Bernard and Louise Guerney at Rutgers University and Penn State University. In her 2000 article, Louise Guerney reviewed the rationale originally developed by Bernard Guerney in 1964:

- Child problems are often related to a lack of parenting knowledge and skill.
- Playing with their child in a therapeutic role should help parents and children to relate in a more positive and appropriate way.
- There was precedent in the use of play sessions in the work of earlier client-centered therapists.
- Much of the resistance to therapy on the part of parents is eliminated.
- The parent-child relationship is one of the most significant in the child's life; thus the potential for change is greater with the parent than with a therapist.

Originally applied with typical child behavior and/or emotional problems, with lower middle to middle-class, white urban and suburban intact families, variations have focused more on the interaction between parent and child. Foley, Higdon, and White (2006, 39) describe filial therapy as a "relationship-based therapy model built on the assumption that under certain conditions, a safe and secure context will be created to foster intimacy and understanding between parent and child."

The method has now been applied successfully with many ethnic and racial groups (e.g., Lee and Landreth 2003; Jang 2000); lower-income families; divorced, blended, foster, and adoptive families (e.g., Glazer and Kottman, 1994; Bratton and Landreth 1995); children with chronic illness (e.g., Glazer-Waldman, Zimmerman, Landreth, and Norton 1992); grieving children (e.g., Glazer 2006); and parent surrogates in the United States and abroad. Research demonstrates that parents learn to be more accepting of their children, allowing them more self-direction, and are more empathic. Louise Guerney summed it up:

Based on the variations in application of [filial therapy (FT)] that have proven workable across a range of populations, we think that FT is a remarkably robust approach that can be shorter or longer, used with groups or individual families (with only a single parent as well), applied in inadequate sized offices or lovely treatment rooms, and still be depended upon for bringing about desired change. (L. Guerney 2000, 13)

Filial therapy is done in a consistent, manualized approach using either the original long approach of the Guerneys, the Landreth 10-week model, or modifications of these models.

PLAY IN A DEVELOPMENTAL CONTEXT

Play is a social activity that is typically (though incorrectly) seen as having no immediate purpose. Play, however, takes place in the context of what is going on within the child, and may have consequences outside of the activity itself. Play is not always what it seems to be on the surface, because the play is inherently meaningful to the child. Through play the child can process events or solve problems. Play occurs spontaneously, and in its spontaneity is one of the ways that we know that play is important in and of itself, or in a predetermined manner, and is an opportunity to explore, experiment, and discover (Bailey and Farrow 1998).

The type of play in which children engage changes with age. Through play, the infant acquires the skills and strategies that contribute to the formation and integration of self and object representations: representational thought. Valentino et al. (2006) note that there is a predictable (and empirically supported) sequence for play development in infants, from undifferentiated exploration to sensorimotor play to decontextualized pretend play, following the cognitive development paradigm of Piaget. A critical cognitive achievement of toddlers is the ability for representational thought using symbols; the ability of toddlers for representational thought is first expressed in play (Valentino et al. 2006). Play activities may aid in social development and development of a sense of mastery and self-efficacy for the child. Social interactions during play are important to the development of friendships and social acceptance (Spinrad et al. 2004). Other benefits may include physical fitness, fighting and dominance skills, affiliative and cognitive skills (Pellegrini and Smith 1998), self-regulation (Bodrova and Leong 2003) and creativity and originality (Howard-Jones, Taylor, and Sutton 2002).

Bailey and Farrow suggest that there are a number of important functions of play in relation to problem solving and life skills. First, while playing the child is able to try out a variety of behaviors in a safe place before needing them in life. The second is that the child can try out alternative solutions. Children will also use play to find some regularity in situations where there is little. Children in the Holocaust painted pictures of flowers and butterflies while living in concentration camps (Glazer 1999). Third, repetition results in increased efficiency and simplicity (Bailey and Farrow 1998).

Alternately, Brems categorized the functions of play into three categories: self-development, maturation, and relationship. Self-development refers to developing a sense of self. The maturation function refers to the fact that play promotes a child's general growth. The relationship function is that the child can try out and learn about roles and apply what he or she has learned to relationships outside of play. Play helps children communicate. Children can also learn and practice roles through play and can learn social skills (Brems 2003).

There is some research supporting the restorative functions of play. Barnett (1998) in a study that included preschool children in the sample, concluded that there was support for the proposition that playful children may manage their environment through play to achieve a desired emotional state. Preschool children in this study were effective at using play to restore equilibrium when the environment was distressful.

McCune (1995) notes a sequential development of play. Symbolic play and language are a function of the underlying capacity for mental representation, emerging in the context of a system of related skills. Representational play develops in an orderly fashion, beginning with presymbolic acts (level 1), progressing next to single pretend acts (levels 2 and 3), then to representational sequences (level 4), and finally to hierarchical pretend (level 5) (McCune, 1995). Her research also supported the relationship between play and language development in terms of the development of representational play.

For the infant and young child, in representational play we see through the eyes of the child. The child may use objects in the playroom to represent objects related to the events in his or her life and may represent feelings symbolically. We do not have to know the meaning of the play to the child for the play to be meaningful to the child.

Play and Attachment

The positive relationship between secure attachment and exploratory play has been supported by research (Belsky, Garduque, and Hrncir 1984; Slade 1987). Slade (1987) in her review of the research on child-caregiver play noted the importance of play with the caregiver. Specifically, she noted that mother-toddler play among securely attached children resulted in increased exploration and competence and increased symbolic play. She reported the following results of her study:

> The fact that the two groups did not differ in the alone condition raises the possibility that for young children the secure base is experienced via mother's

concrete involvement rather than as a more internal presence and that active engagement is an effective way of maintaining the sense of mother's availability for the child. (Slade 1987, 84)

The Clinical Report of the American Academy of Pediatrics (2006) speaks to the importance of play developmentally but also points out the importance of parental participation in child play. Parents have the opportunity to be fully engaged with their children and through play can build enduring relationships and have an opportunity to experience and understand the views of the child.

FILIAL THERAPY INTERVENTION PROCEDURES ("HOW TO" SPECIFICS)

Why Filial?

In looking at filial therapy as an intervention, there are a number of factors that can be taken into consideration. First, child problems are often related to a lack of parenting knowledge and skill. Playing with their child in a therapeutic role should help parents and children to relate in a more positive and appropriate way. The parent-child special playtime is shared engagement. Filial therapy can also reduce much of the resistance to therapy on the part of parents. Also, the parent-child relationship is one of the most significant in the child's life; thus the potential for change is greater with the parent than with a therapist (Guerney 2000). Bowlby (1969) spoke to the importance of the attachment relationship for the growth of the child. "When a mother is perceptive of her child's signals and responds promptly and appropriately to them, her child thrives and relationship develops happily" (357). We can extrapolate from this statement that in the secure attachment relationship, the parent is the best person, with the aid of the therapist, to encourage optimal growth.

We can look at filial therapy as changing the relationship between the parent and child through play. If one of our goals with a child is restoring or strengthening the parent-child bond, then having the parent in the playroom is the best way to support this. There may be times for the grieving child that the parent is not the best person in the playroom, as the child may have developed a rule that he or she does not want to do anything to upset the parent. When this is the case, beginning the work with the therapist and moving later on to filial therapy may be the best intervention strategy.

Another consideration is the change in the family and family system that results as a natural consequence to filial therapy. The changes that occur in the relationship in the playroom, transfer or generalize to life outside the playroom, both for the parent and child engaged in special playtime and for the family.

The Toys

The toys in the playroom for filial or play therapy follow the same groupings:

- Real-life toys
- Acting-out/aggressive toys
- Toys for creative expression
- Family/nurturing toys
- Scary toys
- Pretend/fantasy toys

In the playroom, I have found that younger children use toys within reach and often pick a toy saying that they have one at home. So I make sure that some in each category are at eye level and below. The chalkboard and paper and markers are also favorite activities, as is clay and play dough.

Nurturing play is often a theme of play, with the toddlers using the kitchen and clay and paper to make the meals. Nurturing play is also when the toddlers often include me and the parent in their play. Most of the play of the toddler is solitary play. Some children start the early play sessions asking me to tell them what each thing they pick up is or what it is for. My response is that in the playroom they can decide. Often this only continues for two sessions.

Filial Therapy Model

I have modified the 10-week model developed by Garry Landreth (1991) to be flexible and meet the needs of the family and child. The rationale for the change is based on the time, rather than eliminating any skill or activity. When this is done one-on-one, less time is needed than a group. There is a consistent sequence of learning and practice following the outline developed for the original research I conducted on filial therapy (Glazer-Waldman, Zimmerman, Landreth, and Norton 1992). I use two processes. The first is when play therapy is conducted for the first three to five sessions and the second is when filial therapy begins right away.

Regardless, one of the goals of the first session with the parent is to determine what the best intervention is for the child based on the presenting problem and the child/family history. In my practice I use play therapy or filial therapy or a combination. One of the determining factors is the willingness of the parent or guardian to be part of the process. Another is the family dynamics: I look at the relationship between parent and child and in a loss or trauma situation note the ability of the parent to parent. I have found that some parents are grieving and are unable to participate in filial therapy at the present time. Others are able and want to participate in therapy for their children.

As part of the discussion, the importance of play to the child developmentally is discussed. The appropriateness of filial therapy and the process are explained to the parent. If the parent agrees to filial therapy, a schedule is set for the meetings between the parent and therapist. Parents are given a workbook with information, articles, and exercises that I developed or the handbook for parents developed by Rise VanFleet (2000).

Session 1: The goal of the first session is to introduce the parent to the goals of filial therapy and to set goals for the parent and child. Behavioral goals with observable outcomes are set so that the parent can see changes. Typical goals for filial therapy may include

- Increase the parent's understanding of his or her own child.
- Help the parent recognize the importance of play in the child's life and in the parent's (VanFleet, 1994).
- Establish an optimal relationship between parent and child.
- Improve emotional and behavioral adjustment.
- Increase the parent's warmth and trust toward the child (VanFleet, 1994).
- Provide a nonthreatening place where the parent deals with his or her own issues as they relate to the child and parenting (VanFleet, 1994).

Homework for the first week is to find something new about the child and to list three strengths that the child has. There is also a discussion of the role of play and playing.

Session 2: The objective of the second session is to introduce emotional development and practice basic skills. The homework is reviewed. There is a short review of emotional development and ways in which we communicate our feelings. Based on the interest level of the parent, readings may be suggested. The first two skills are reflective listening and tracking. The way that this is typically introduced is by going over a tape of a play therapy session so that the parent can see the skills, critique the actions, and ask questions about the process. Part of the time is spent in the playroom, demonstrating and trying the skills, with the therapist and the parent taking turns as the child. Homework for the week is to practice reflective listening and tracking for five minutes each. "Can you have a five-minute conversation with an adult without asking any questions?" Part of this session and each of the following sessions is to talk about the issues of the family system and concerns of the parent.

Session 3: The objective of the third session is to prepare the parent for the special playtimes with his or her child. The first task is to review the homework and then to practice the skills in the playroom with the therapist role-playing the child. The skill level of the parent determines the objective for the day. If the skill level is inadequate, then the third session is spent in review. If the skill level is adequate, then the next step is to review the basic tenets of client-centered play therapy following the principles set by Axline (1947). The list of toys for filial therapy is shared and the site for the play session is discussed. Presenting the sessions to the child is one of the major things to review. Presenting the special playtime as truly a time for parent and child with no interruptions and as a special time for them to be together sets a context that this is important to the parent and is important and unique. One dad told me that the time in the car alone together to and from the playroom became important to them and part of the special time that they had together. There is also a discussion of emotional development and naming emotions, leading to why we reflect emotions and practicing reflecting emotions. Homework for Week 3 is to buy the toys or collect them in a box, to tell the child about the play sessions, and to practice reflection and tracking.

Session 4: This session is the first with the child in the playroom. In my playroom, I can sit in the hall and see all of the room. Agency playrooms may have one-way mirrors with the capability to videotape and/or to communicate with the parent while the session is in progress. The parent and child play for 30 minutes, with me watching and videotaping if possible. If necessary, I can interject comments and make suggestions to ease the way for the parent.

Session 5: The objective of this session is to review the first play session and to review and practice skills as needed. The first question to the parent is: Did anything seem different this week after the play session? This usually becomes the basis of an important discussion about the parent-child relationship. At this session, limit setting is introduced, as it usually comes up in the first session review. Using some of the rules for communication between parent and child developed by Haim Ginott (1959), there is a conversation about communication. The focus is on the following:

1. If you cannot say it in 10 words or less do not say it!
2. Never ask a question to which you already know the answer.
3. Be an emotional thermostat, not a thermometer.
4. It is not what you said, but what you say after what you said.

The following sessions are play sessions in the playroom with review of tapes shortly thereafter. The parent often notices quickly how some of the skills transfer to the rest of the week and the resulting changes in the family system. The transfer from the play session to the rest of the week often seems to the parents an important change. Reviewing the original goals for filial therapy often reveals that there are other positive changes in the relationship. Often parents see their child or children as separate individuals, rather than seeing the child's issues and concerns as a reflection of their own. After there is a comfort level and adequate skill level, the play sessions are moved to the home, with the parent videotaping and reviewing the tapes with me.

The termination phase of filial therapy begins when the parent and child are conducting the sessions at home, and they begin to see it as part of the weekly routine. During the final session with the parent, the goals set at the first session are reviewed. The value of continuing the play sessions is discussed.

There are follow-up phone calls with the option for additional sessions at three and six weeks after termination. Parents are usually still doing play sessions and report that they have continued to see filial therapy as reinforcing and strengthening the relationship with their children. Some have expanded it to the other children and ask about how they can use it with older children and teens. The transfer to daily life usually occurs naturally once the parent is comfortable with the skills. And it is the new way of interacting with the child that remains even when the special play sessions end.

EMPIRICAL SUPPORT

Though a relatively new therapy, filial therapy has been heavily researched since its inception and has been adapted and applied in a variety of settings and with a variety of populations, resulting in a rich quantitative, evidence-based, and qualitative research base supporting the effectiveness of filial therapy. Guerney (2000) notes that between 1971 and 2000, there were a large number of studies that supported filial therapy with a variety of populations of children and parents. The studies by Guerney and others in the 1970s using the original protocol for filial therapy also used the same measures originally developed by Guerney, thus giving the advantage of comparison of the studies and adding support for the effectiveness of the protocol for decreasing negative behaviors such as aggression (Guerney 2000). Rennie and Landreth (2000) reviewed a number of studies of filial therapy, concluding that filial therapy did promote and enhance the parent-child relationship and parents could learn the client-centered play therapy skills necessary to become effective therapeutic agents with their children. They found that research supported filial therapy as an effective intervention for increasing parental acceptance, self-esteem empathy, making positive changes in the family system, increasing child self-esteem, and decreasing parental stress and child behavior problems. Additionally,

Landreth's 10-week variation has been extensively studied at the University of North Texas and found to be an effective intervention with different populations. Bratton, Ray, Rhine, and Jones (2005) in their meta-analysis of play and filial therapy research, concluded that their research strongly supported the adoption of filial therapy as an effective therapeutic modality in working with children.

A recent qualitative study by Foley, Higdon, and White (2006) found that the parents who participated in filial therapy attributed positive and progressive meaning to their experience. These parents also reported that they increased their self-awareness, problem-solving resources, and confidence, and improved their relationships with their children.

The age for children in most of the studies reported was 4 to 10, which is the typical ages for play therapy; Bratton et al. (2005) found a mean of 7 in their meta-analysis. I did not find any research on filial therapy with infants and toddlers. While there is strong empirical support for filial therapy, more research is needed to move filial therapy into an evidenced-based therapy. Longitudinal research is also needed to determine how long parents continue play sessions and the long-term effects of filial therapy on the family.

CASE ILLUSTRATION

The case that I will present is a family trauma that was witnessed by the two-year-old. The four-year-old brother was hit by a car in front of the home with Mom and Charlie (the two-year-old) watching. Mom had been distracted and had not seen the brother go into the street after his ball. Charlie did not go to the funeral, and during the time immediately after the death acted as if nothing had happened. When his aunts, uncles, and grandparents went home, Charlie began to have nightmares and cried easily and would not talk about his brother. The parents sought therapy for themselves and Charlie. Dad and Mom both came for the intake but were anxious, since this was the first time they had been away from Charlie since the funeral. Developmentally Charlie was reported as being in the normal range for talking and walking and was physically at the 75th percentile, according to the pediatrician.

Assessment

The first meeting was with Mom and Dad. They shared the events of the day and what had occurred since then in the family. The history and discussion of current behavior did not indicate any regressive behaviors, behavior, or eating problems. Dad said that he would be the one to bring

Charlie to the sessions and related how the boys and he did bath time and bedtime together every night. As we talked, I became convinced that filial therapy was the appropriate intervention for the family, but that while the family was so close to the incident and since the parents were also seeing a therapist I would begin with play therapy and move to filial therapy with the father as the therapist. The parents also shared the support they were receiving from the community and that they were both getting individual as well as couple therapy.

Charlie's play behavior was normal for a child of his age. The ease of establishing a relationship with me was unusual. Often the child who has experienced trauma or a significant loss will show some regressive behaviors such as clinging and wanting to know where the parents or caregivers are. Each time Charlie wanted to go in the playroom and often walked right in as soon as I opened the door to greet them. This facilitated building the relationship in play therapy. The *DSM IV-TR* (American Psychiatric Association 2000) diagnosis for Charlie was V62.82, as the insurance provider allowed the single diagnosis of the V-code in this case. The diagnosis did not change as there were no behavior issues at home or the following fall at preschool.

For the grieving child, the nondirective stance toward the grief and the loss experience is in line with the research on the adult in bereavement therapy. Mancini and Bonanno (2006) noted that the evidence on effective treatment for bereavement suggests that the therapist should take a neutral, nondirective stance with regard to the experience, providing a safe environment for disclosure and construction of the meaning of the event.

The first session was typical of many early play therapy sessions. Charlie explored the playroom and tentatively took note of me as he played. Toward the end of the session, he played with the doll family using a Mom and Dad doll and two child dolls, telling me they were he and Allie, his sister. During the second session, after playing with the dolls and dollhouse, he replayed his recollection of the accident, from his mother's screams to the blood coming from his brother's ears to Mom laying on the ground and the look on her face, and lastly to saying that it would be OK now that he was in his father's arms. Thus Charlie found the playroom a safe place and was able to use actions and a few words to replay the trauma. According to his dad, Charlie did not do that at home, but after that session Charlie was not as upset when others mentioned his brother and Charlie began to talk about him. The theme of the third session was "booboos": Barbie dolls fell off the house and were hurt but were OK. Two of the Kens had a fight and one hit the other, with Charlie telling me that Allie bit him. The fourth play therapy session included Charlie playing with the "Ken" dolls and having them take baths together and play together. This play lasted for about 10 minutes of the 45-minute sessions. The rest of the play often included sand play and nurturing play.

After the fourth session, Dad called and scheduled a consultation. At that visit, we talked about filial therapy again and Dad was anxious to begin learning about it. I shared my workbook with him and we set up two additional sessions that followed the outline noted above. We reviewed a few play therapy tapes. I gave Dad a copy of *Annie Stories* as a way that he might help all of his children.

At the fifth session, Charlie had trouble separating from Dad and had to check on him every five minutes or so. He appeared distracted and his play had no apparent themes. Toward the end of the session, Charlie told me about his brother falling down and hurting. Then he took out the fish puppet and had the puppet bite me, telling me that I was to bite the fish back. He had trouble ending the session and Dad had to come to the door of the playroom to support my statements about leaving the playroom.

At the next session with Charlie, Dad and I were in the playroom with my coaching him in reflective listening. I sit close to the door so I am in the playroom but out of the way. Charlie did the doll play again, using the Barbie pool as a tub and talking to the two dolls as he bathed them. Dad had a visible reaction to the play but as Charlie's back was to him, Charlie did not see this. The theme of play in the rest of the session was cooking for Dad. Dad's reflections included the statement that this was just like breakfast at home when Dad prepared it. The session was 30 minutes. After taking Charlie home, Dad called me and told me why he had reacted to the bath scene. Charlie had been replaying the bath ritual in the family before his brother died, even to using the words that his Dad used. For Dad this seemed like an expression of Charlie's grief; Charlie was able to let us know that he saw life as different now. We also talked about social learning and how Dad could see it in Charlie's play. This was reinforced at a later session when Charlie pretended that what was he was pretending to drink from a bottle was beer. Dad said as an aside to me that he never realized how aware of him Charlie was.

Dad quickly developed the skills and enjoyed the play sessions. We did two sessions a week. One was a play session and one was working with Dad on the filial techniques following the outline I typically use. Nurturing play continued to be a theme of the play sessions, with Charlie leading the way and telling Dad what to do. Dad became adept at letting Charlie do this and asking him what he should say or do. Dad noticed that he was beginning to use the skills at home and reported using them in conversations with his spouse—he was listening and hearing more, he said. We talked about moving the play sessions to home and taping them for us to review.

This worked well; we met each week to review tapes of the play sessions and to talk about skills. At the meeting with Dad after session 9, we reviewed the goals for therapy and where he thought that Charlie was in relation to the goals. We reviewed childhood grief issues and talked about what he might see in the future. After 10 weeks, we moved the meetings with Dad to every other week and then to monthly phone calls. Six months later, Dad called to say that Charlie wanted to come to the playroom. It was gratifying to see the change in both and fun to see the developmental spurt that Charlie had achieved. Dad said that he felt that this had changed his parenting and had allowed him to hear and see Charlie in a different way. When I heard from him six months later, Charlie was doing well and so were Mom and Dad. Dad was doing play sessions less regularly but kept the special playtime toys in a box ready to go. Charlie and Dad came for a visit this August; I had not seen them for over a year. Charlie wanted to see "My Lady" so Dad set it up. Charlie checked out what was the same and what was new in the playroom and then began a play session with Dad. There was nurturing play and sand play, with lots of inclusion of Dad and me in his play. The strong relationship between the two was evident. Charlie had a hard time leaving the playroom; he wanted to "sleep here." Dad was able to use the skills for terminating a session and choices for an easy end to the session. Dad reports that Charlie continues to talk about his brother and reminds others of things that happened. Developmentally, Charlie appears to want to develop a different understanding of the events of that day and asks questions that he did not ask when it happened nearly two years ago.

Dad's View of the Experience

In a recent conversation with Dad, I mentioned the fact that I was using the family in this chapter, and I assured him that I would disguise the family. I asked him if he would talk about his experience with filial therapy. This is what he wrote:

> The sessions that [Charlie] and I attended were amazing. Filial therapy allowed [Charlie] to express his grief in ways I didn't know were available. The fact that I could learn to see and hear [Charlie] and my other child in a more caring way has made this a life-changing experience for me. We've built a terrific relationship that continues to flourish because I'm a better listener to my kids.
>
> [Charlie] is a very nurturing and sensitive child who was protecting [his] mom and me at home by not expressing [his] own pain and loss of [his] brother. Through several sessions of filial therapy, Charlie opened himself up to me through our "special playtime" activities, expressing what made [him] happy and sad. These playtime activities allowed me to watch [Charlie] express . . . emotions through playing . . . something I didn't know was possible but made me a better listener. I became more aware of [Charlie's] emotions in our everyday life, which made me a better parent.
>
> The filial therapy program with Dr. Glazer guided me through the steps of not only helping [Charlie] sort out [his] problems in dealing with the loss of [his] brother but also allowed me to become a better parent to [Charlie] and

my other child. It allowed me to be a better listener and helped me relate to [Charlie's] needs in a more loving and caring way.

CONCLUSIONS AND FUTURE DIRECTIONS

Filial therapy has been shown to be an effective intervention with infants and toddlers. For the case presented in this chapter, filial therapy was an effective intervention. The family has continued to apply the skills since ending therapy. The comments of the father match those found by Foley, Higdon, and White (2006). I believe that the importance of restoring or enhancing the relationship between parent and child is the basis for the success of therapy. As Dad shared, this process allowed him to be part of his child's grieving and to journey with him through his grief.

The potential for filial therapy with a variety of family and child issues is unlimited. Particularly in situations of trauma, loss, and grief where the impact is on the family system, filial therapy can be effective in facilitating the healing of the family as they process the events together. In supporting the healing process, filial therapy becomes a set of skills that often continue to have a positive impact on the parent-child relationship. The relationship has been changed through play.

The child-centered approach provides the context for using filial therapy with young children. We meet the child where he or she is and work with the parent to develop the skills necessary to provide the context in which change can occur and in which the relationship between parent and child can be healed or enhanced.

However, more research should be done to verify the efficacy of filial therapy. Practitioners should be trained in filial therapy rather than assuming that this is an intervention that can be added to the tool kit.

REFERENCES

American Academy of Pediatrics. 2006. *Clinical report: The importance of play in promoting healthy child development and maintaining strong parent-child bonds.* Elk Grove Village, IL: American Academy of Pediatrics.

American Psychiatric Association. 2000. *Diagnostic criteria from DSM-IV-TR.* Arlington, VA: APA.

Axline, V. M. 1947. *Play therapy.* New York: Ballantine.

Bailey, R., and S. Farrow. 1998. Play and problem solving in a new light. *International Journal of Early Years Education* 6 (3): 265–275.

Barnett, L. A. 1998. The adaptive powers of being playful. In *Play and culture studies,* vol. 1, *Diversions and divergences in fields of play,* ed. M. C. Duncan, G. Glick, and A. Aycock, 97–119. Greenwich, CT: Ablex.

Belsky, J., L. Garduque, and E. Hrncir. 1984. Assessing performance, competence, and executive capacity in infant play: Relations to home environment and security of attachment. *Developmental Psychology* 20 (3): 406–417.

Bodrova, E., and D. J. Leong. 2003. *Educational Leadership* (April): 50–53.

Bowlby, J. 1969. *Attachment and loss*, vol. 1, *Attachment*. New York: Basic.

Bratton, S., and G. Landreth. 1995. Filial therapy with single parents: Effects on parental acceptance, empathy, and stress. *International Journal of Play Therapy* 4 (1): 61–80.

Bratton, S. C., D. Ray, T. Rhine, and L. Jones. 2005. The efficacy of play therapy with children: A meta-analytic review of treatment outcomes. *Professional Psychology: Research and Practice* 36 (4): 376–390.

Brems, C. 2003. *A comprehensive guide to child psychotherapy.* 2nd ed. Boston: Allyn & Bacon.

Brett, D. 1988. *Annie stories: A special kind of storytelling.* New York: Workman.

Foley, Y. C., L. Higdon, and J. F. White. 2006. A qualitative study of filial therapy: Parents' voices. *International Journal of Play Therapy* 15 (1): 37–64.

Ginott, H. G. 1959. *Psychotherapy with children: The living relationship.* Greeley, CO: Carron.

Glazer, H. R. 1999. Children and play in the Holocaust. *Journal of Humanistic Counseling, Education, and Development* 37 (4): 194–199.

———. 2006. Expressive therapies with grieving children. In *Creative arts therapy manual*, ed. S. Brooke, 87–94. Springfield, IL: Charles C. Thomas.

Glazer, H. R., and T. Kottman. 1994. Filial therapy: Rebuilding the relationship between parents and children of divorce. *Journal of Humanistic Education and Development* 33 (1): 4–12.

Glazer-Waldman, H. R., J. E. Zimmerman, G. L. Landreth, and D. Norton. 1992. Filial therapy: An intervention for parents of children with chronic illness. *International Journal of Play Therapy* 1 (1): 31–42.

Guerney, L. 2000. Filial therapy into the 21st century. *International Journal of Play Therapy* 9 (2): 1–17.

Howard-Jones, P. A., J. R. Taylor, and L. Sutton. 2002. The effect of play on the creativity of young children during subsequent activity. *Early Childhood Development and Care* 172 (4): 323–328.

Jang, M. 2000. Effectiveness of filial therapy for Korean parents. *International Journal of Play Therapy* 9 (2): 21–38.

Jordan, J. 2000. The role of mutual empathy in relational/cultural therapy. *Journal of Clinical Psychology* 56 (8): 1005–1016.

Landreth, G. 1991. *Play therapy: The art of the relationship.* Muncie, IN: Accelerated Press.

Lee, M., and G. L. Landreth. 2003. Filial therapy with immigrant Korean parents in the United States. *International Journal of Play Therapy* 12 (2): 49–66.

Mancini, A. D., and G. A. Bonanno. 2006. Bereavement. In *Evidence-based psychotherapy*, ed. J. E. Fisher and W. T. O'Donohue, 122–130. New York: Springer.

McCune, L. 1995. A normative study of representational play at the transition to language. *Developmental Psychology* 31 (2): 198–206.

Moustakas, C. 1959. *Psychotherapy with children: The living relationship.* New York: Harper & Row.

Pellegrini, A. D., and P. K. Smith. 1998. The development of play during childhood: Forms and possible functions. *Child Psychology and Psychiatry* 3 (2): 51–57.

Rennie, R., and G. Landreth. 2000. Effects of filial therapy on parent and child behaviors. *International Journal of Play Therapy* 9 (2): 19–37.

Slade, A. 1987. Quality of attachment and early symbolic play. *Developmental Psychology* 23 (1): 78–85.

Spinrad, T. L., N. Eisenberg, E. Harris, L. Hanish, R. A. Fabes, K. Kupanoff, S. Ringwald, and J. Holmes. 2004. The relation of children's everyday nonsocial peer play behavior to their emotionality, regulation, and social functioning. *Developmental Psychology* 40 (1): 67–80.

Valentino, K., D. Cicchetti, S. Toth, and F. Rogosch. 2006. Mother-child play and emerging social behaviors among infants from maltreating families. *Developmental Psychology* 42 (3): 474–485.

VanFleet, R. 1994. *Filial therapy: Strengthening parent-child relationships through play.* Sarasota, FL: Practitioner's Resource Press.

———. 2000. *A parent's handbook of filial play therapy.* Boiling Springs, PA: Play Therapy Press.

4

Caregiver-Toddler Play Therapy: An Attachment-Based Approach

Helen E. Benedict

The past 30 years have seen an explosion of research on attachment development and infant mental health. Both literatures have shown clearly that many infants and toddlers are in distress, showing problems with attachment relationships, affect and emotions, and self-regulatory behaviors (Kobak et al. 2006, 333–69). The mental health organization Zero to Three has even developed a downward extension of the *Diagnostic and Statistical Manual, Fourth Edition* for infants up to age three (Zero to Three 2005). This multi-axial system, *DC: 0–3: Revised*, includes anxiety and depression disorders of early childhood as well as disorders of relating and communicating, a variety of regulatory disorders (regulation disorders of sensory processing, hypersensitive, hyposensitive, and sensory stimulation–seeking), adjustment disorders, disorders of affect, eating and sleeping disorders, and both deprivation/maltreatment and posttraumatic stress disorder. Because of the importance of the caregiver-infant relationship to this developmental period of life, it also has an Axis II focused on the relationship between the infant and primary caregiver as it relates to the disorders on Axis I.

Interventions for these distressed infants and their caregivers have increasingly been recognized as essential to the infant's well-being as development proceeds. Longitudinal research following infants with secure and various insecure attachment styles shows that toddlers showing insecure avoidant or resistant styles tend to have less ego strength, resilience, and effective social skills than do securely attached toddlers (Cicchetti and Valentino 2006, 146–68). Also, infants showing disorganized attachment are high risk for significant psychopathology as they develop (Koback et al. 2006, 347–48). When these possible long-term outcomes are considered in light of the high degree of plasticity seen during the toddler period, when development is both rapid and highly responsive to environmental input, intervention during this period becomes vital to protect the mental health of our children.

Many approaches to mental health intervention with infants and toddlers have been developed in recent years. The most common approach has been to intervene primarily with the caregiver. This has been done in several ways, either by psychoeducational approaches focused on caregiving skills (Olds 2005, 217–49), by using individual therapy to modify the parents' attachment styles (Cohen 2006, 39–64), or using group approaches to help parents more accurately perceive the needs of their infant (Cooper et al. 2005, 127–51). These interventions have taken place at clinics and also through a home visit approach (Cicchetti, Rogosch, and Toth 2006, 623–49). Other approaches direct their attention to the caregiver-infant relationship, usually focusing on the mother-infant relationship (Lieberman 2004, 97–122). Both types of approaches tend to focus on interventions with the mother, and if they include the child in sessions, the inclusion is almost incidental. The infant's presence appears to be more to demonstrate various skills or to provide a setting where the mother can try her new skills or understandings with the infant. These approaches have been effective to various degrees with infants between birth and three years, with the greatest effectiveness often shown for infants up to 18 months (Cicchetti, Rogosch, and Toth 2006, 642–46).

The play therapy approach to be presented here focuses on older infants, or toddlers, between 18 months and 3 years of age. This approach combines a focus on the toddler-caregiver relationship with a focus on the toddler's play. This dual focus is based on the centrality of the caregiver-toddler relationship to development at this age and the pivotal role of play in that relationship.

THE ROLE OF PLAY IN HEALTHY INFANT AND TODDLER DEVELOPMENT

While the development of the earliest caregiver-infant attachment relationship has been extensively researched, resulting in a detailed picture of this developmental process, the importance of play both to that relationship and to the infant's cognitive, social, and language development has received much less focus (Cicchetti and Valentino 2006, 152–53). Play develops initially within the caregiver-infant relationship and begins very early in development in the first few months of life. This early play is primarily affective and social in nature, when the caregiver repeatedly engages the infant through brief playful interactions: nuzzling an ear, blowing on a tummy, singing nonsense words, bouncing, gently swinging, or kissing a neck. All of these interactions are part of the infant's intersubjectivity system (Trevarthen et al. 2006, 65–126). Trevarthen and associates (2006) argue that this emerging system is integral to the infant's capacity to show awareness of another person, which is later essential to the attuned affective states between the caregiver and infant that enable emotional regulation.

As infant development proceeds later in the first year, play continues to provide both a context for much of the infant's learning and a significant motivating force for both partners in the interaction, the infant and caregiver (Trevarthen et al. 2006, 110–11). At this point, the attachment relationship between the caregiver and infant builds out of this intersubjective awareness. Each dyad develops a unique attachment relationship, whether secure or insecure, that then creates a relational template or internal working model the toddler brings to new relationships (Trevarthen et al. 2006, 103–6). Thus play, which begins as early as the second month, is a compelling aspect of the caregiver-infant interaction from then forward.

Through play and the affective social communication that takes place in early play, three major capacities of the infant (and later toddler) emerge: the capacity for emotional regulation, the infant's basic attachment style, and the cognitive-affective neuronal networks that enable the toddler to engage the world. According to Trevarthen and his associates, play is closely associated with joy. This playful joy, by motivating the intensely intimate caregiver-child interactions necessary to the development of the three capacities outlined above, must be recreated in interventions with distressed infants and toddlers if the interventions are to be effective (Trevarthen et al. 2006, 112–13). Play is therefore an essential component of therapy directed at distressed toddlers and their caregivers.

CAREGIVER-TODDLER PLAY THERAPY

Caregiver-toddler play therapy is a play-focused intervention for the distressed caregiver-toddler relationship. The relationship between the caregiver and infant or toddler may be distressed for any number of reasons (Benedict 2005a, 2005b). The primary caregiver, most often the mother in this culture, may suffer from postpartum depression, high stress related to factors like single parenting or poverty, other forms of psychopathology such as personality disorder, psychotic disorder, substance use and abuse disorders, or a personal history of insecure attachment. All of these problems have the potential to disrupt the caregiver-child relationship in significant ways. Similarly, the child may have developmental problems such as hypersensitivity, colic, premature delivery, minor or major neuro-developmental problems, or difficult temperament, all of which may interfere with the infant's ability to engage fully in the relationship with the caregiver. In addition, the caregiver-toddler dyad may have been disrupted by illness, natural disasters, or war and reflect the effects of significant separation or trauma (Lieberman and Van Horn 2004, 111–38). Finally, the caregiver-toddler relationship may be a new relationship formed through such mechanisms as late adoption or adoptive or foster care following maltreatment of the infant (Dozier, Lindbiem, and Ackerman 2005, 178–94).

GOAL OF CAREGIVER-TODDLER PLAY THERAPY

The goal of caregiver-toddler play therapy is to enhance the relationship between the caregiver and the toddler through play. The therapist achieves this goal by forming simultaneous therapeutic relationships with each part of the dyad and intervening to improve the relationship while in the midst of play. The setting for this approach is typically a playroom equipped with toys suitable for toddlers and comfortable seating for the three participants—the therapist, the caregiver, and the toddler. Healing takes place both through the relationship of the caregiver with the therapist and through the play of the toddler both with the therapist and with the caregiver as facilitated by the therapist. This approach contains many of the elements of the caregiver-focused interventions described above, including use of the therapist-caregiver relationship to help the caregiver be more responsive to the toddler's needs, direct instruction of the caregiver in ways to be with the toddler, and feedback to the caregiver about her interactions with the toddler (Lieberman 2004, 97–122).

Three additional components make this approach unique. First, the simultaneous relationship between the therapist and the toddler enables the therapist to model ways of interacting with that toddler. Second, the therapist, by knowing the toddler and interpreting the toddler's communications, can "speak for the child" in the relationship with the caregiver and thus facilitate caregiver-toddler communication. Finally, the therapist uses his or her expertise in play to guide the play in healthy directions encompassing the relationship features, the regulatory mechanisms, and the cognitive-affective connections discussed earlier. Each of these components—the therapist-caregiver relationship, the therapist-toddler relationship, facilitating caregiver-toddler play, and ensuring play follows essential developmental lines—will be discussed in detail in the following sections.

THE THERAPIST-CAREGIVER
THERAPEUTIC RELATIONSHIP

The first component of caregiver-toddler play therapy is the relationship between the therapist and the caregiver. This relationship must be one of trust. The caregiver who is experiencing distress in the relationship with the toddler is vulnerable in many ways. First, she is not feeling competent as a caregiver, which has a negative impact on her self-esteem and life satisfaction. From an attachment theory viewpoint, her internal working model of the self has become increasingly negative (Slade, Sadler, and Mayes 2005, 152–77). She may be feeling unlovable and bad, especially as a parent. In order for the caregiver to move toward more effective parenting and a more positive sense of self, she will need to experience the therapist as a secure base (Zeanah and Smyke 2005, 195–216). The therapist needs to be perceived by the caregiver as caring, accepting of the parent, and constant. Within this trusting relationship between the therapist and caregiver, the caregiver will feel supported, comforted, and at the same time encouraged when she explores new ways of interacting with her toddler.

Creating a secure-base caregiver-therapist relationship is the first part of this intervention. The process of building this relationship begins with the first contact between the therapist and the caregiver. The first contact, or intake, involves a meeting with the primary caregiver (or caregivers, if available) and the therapist. At this time, a developmental history is obtained, the parent is given an opportunity to share her or his concerns, and some form of attachment interview is conducted to get a sense of the caregiver's current internal working models of the self, the toddler, and relationships. Examples of empirically validated attachment interviews would include the Working Model of the Child Interview, developed by Zeanah and his colleagues, and the Adult Attachment Interview (Zeanah, Smyke, and Coots 2007). By showing a genuine caring attitude coupled with a strong sense of acceptance of the caregiver, the therapist begins to build a trusting relationship with the caregiver.

Following the initial session, the parent brings the toddler and together they participate in activities designed to give a picture of their current relationship. These activities, which are preferably videotaped, may vary between formal caregiver-infant assessments such as the Marschak Interaction Method (Lindaman, Booth, and Chambers 2000, 371–400), the Strange Situation assessment (Cooper et al. 2005, 127–51), or the Crowell procedure (Zeanah et al. 1999, 222–35), and less formal interactions between the caregiver and toddler with the therapist present.

In a final session in this initial phase of treatment, the therapist meets again with the caregiver and shares both the caregiver's experiences in completing the assessment and the therapist's observations of their needs as a dyad, often illustrating the observations with video clips of the caregiver-child interaction. It is vital that this feedback session be deeply sensitive to the caregiver's concerns and convey to the caregiver the therapist's acceptance of the caregiver as well as the therapist's confidence that the caregiver-toddler relationship can be improved by working together.

Helen E. Benedict

THE THERAPIST-TODDLER RELATIONSHIP

The relationship between the toddler and the therapist is unique among roles typical for play therapists. The therapist has several goals for the toddler-therapist relationship, such as serving as a role model for the caregiver, communicating for the child, and directing the play in developmentally facilitative ways. To be effective, the therapist must be a positive, interesting, engaging, and safe person for the toddler, while not competing or interfering with the toddler's attachment to the caregiver. The therapist should approach this relationship initially through the caregiver, since the caregiver's trust and comfort with the therapist is the toddler's initial cue about the safety of this new person.

The initial session involving the therapist, caregiver(s), and toddler should occur in a playroom specifically prepared for this purpose. There should be an assortment of toys appropriate to toddlers and some comfortable seating, preferably a sofa or large stuffed chair that would easily accommodate the caregiver and toddler sitting together if they wish. Playrooms designed for older children could be adapted for this use only if the toys that are too developmentally advanced (i.e., unsafe because of small parts or too challenging for a toddler to use successfully) can be made unavailable (and unobservable) to the toddler. The therapist initially interacts casually with the caregiver while giving the toddler time to explore the room (visually and/or physically) and observing the caregiver's comfort level with the therapist. Only then should the therapist interact directly with the toddler, always taking her cues from the toddler for how close or interactive she should be. The goal is for the toddler to feel safe with the therapist and to experience the therapist as engaging and attuned to his or her needs but not a preferred person in the setting. The challenges of this therapeutic stance will be discussed further in the section on therapist roles later in this chapter.

ESSENTIAL COMPONENTS OF DEVELOPMENTAL PLAY

There are five essential components to developmentally sensitive play with toddlers that combine to create the shared pleasure or joy described by Trevarthen (2006, 104–11). These five components are joint attention on objects and events, attunement or matched affect vitality, scaffolding, maintenance of safety via limit setting, and regulation of arousal and feelings. All of these components emerge naturally from an engaged caregiver who communicates to the toddler "sympathy for what the child is feeling, genuine emotional response that is accepting and flexible, good humor in play . . . calm attentiveness in listening to the child, and firmness in setting clear boundaries" (Trevarthen et al. 2006, 113). Some or all of these components and this attuned communication is likely to be missing when there is a distressed relationship between caregiver and toddler.

The first two components, joint attention and attunement, focus on shared affect and interest between the caregiver and toddler. Joint attention is when the caregiver, through such mechanisms as pointing or verbalizations, directs the child's attention to particular objects and events and shares that focus with the child (Siegel 1999, 200). Attunement is a broad term used to describe the caregiver's constant reliance on cues from the child to adjust his or her own behavior to match the needs, affect, and interests of the child. In matching affect, the caregiver matches the vitality or intensity of the feeling rather than the content, especially if the feelings are negative. This matching gives the child the sense of both a sympathetic understanding of the feelings and an acceptance of the feelings (Trevarthen et al. 2006, 66–71).

The remaining three components focus on providing a secure base, or sense of safety, to the child in the play. Scaffolding is a term used to connote the caregiver's help to the child when the child is exploring (Cooper et al. 2005, 127–51). It means that the caregiver gives just enough help and guidance to enable the child to continue to play, being careful to avoid taking over the child's play. An example would be a child playing with a shape toy having difficulty getting a shape in the hole, and the caregiver showing the child how to turn the shape and then backing away and letting the child work again at turning it until it goes in the hole.

A second important aspect of establishing a secure base is the continuous monitoring of the physical and psychological safety of the setting. One way of doing this involves setting firm limits and boundaries. Because toddlers lack experience and judgment of possible risks in the environment, the caregiver must anticipate possible risks in the child's play and either set limits or redirect the child so that safety is maintained. Thus, the caregiver might need to say no to throwing hard objects or reach out an arm to help the child who has lost his or her balance.

The final component of play central to providing a "secure base" environment is the regulation of the toddler's arousal and feelings (Trevarthen et al. 2006, 103–8). In the course of play, the typical toddler moves from feeling to feeling—at one moment wary with a new toy, at another moment excited by some roughhousing play. In the first instance, the toddler will require some tender encouragement to explore the toy, while in second instance the child may need some calming activity to scale back the excitement before it becomes overwhelming. In the normal course of caregiver-child interactions, the caregiver routinely makes these adaptations in her or his behavior to help the child have pleasure in the play without becoming over-aroused or overly hesitant. It is often the case with distressed toddlers and their caregivers that this caregiver regulatory system does not function effectively, resulting in a dysregulated and uncomfortable state for the toddler. For play to be developmentally appropriate for toddlers, both aspects of the Circle of Security—a safe haven and a secure base—must be present (Cooper et al. 2005, 127–51).

The five components discussed here are usually present in normal caregiver-toddler play. When the toddler is distressed, it is likely that one or more of the essential components of play is not functional within the caregiver-toddler relationship, which in turn is related to interaction problems in the relationship. By addressing the caregiver-toddler relationship through play, the therapist employs developmentally naturally occurring mechanisms to repair the relationship. When, for whatever reason, the caregiver-toddler relationship is lacking these components of play, the therapist intervenes with the dyad to shape a healthier playful interaction and ultimately a more secure relationship between them.

THE ROLE OF THE THERAPIST IN ENHANCING THE CAREGIVER-TODDLER RELATIONSHIP

Four specific therapeutic interventions serve to build on the previously discussed trust-based relationship between the therapist and the caregiver and the safety-based relationship between the therapist and toddler. Each intervention facilitates the caregiver-toddler relationship by enhancing the needed components of play that are not functioning well in the caregiver-toddler relationship. These interventions are translating, or "speaking for the child," modeling play components for the caregiver, providing psycho-education for the caregiver about attachment and secure base relationships, and providing gentle feedback to the caregiver in the situation to enhance the play activities.

The translator role encompasses a variety of activities. In all of the activities, the therapist must first be able to accurately perceive the toddler's intentions and communications—whether verbal, nonverbal, or through play—and then convey those communications to the caregiver while simultaneously reassuring the toddler that he or she has been understood and accepted regardless of the content of the communication. As one might expect, this translation process may take several forms. At the simplest level, such translation might only require the therapist to engage responsively in the child's play. For example, the child might begin play with a doll by feeding it, and the therapist facilitates the attunement component of play by stating something such as "You are feeding that baby." While this seems very simple, it is often the type of attention to and acceptance of the child's play that has not been part of the caregiver's previous interactions with the toddler.

Translating for the child often is quite challenging for the therapist because it necessitates "speaking for the child." This is a very directive intervention that is sometimes uncomfortable for the therapist. This type of intervention is needed in two distinct settings: when the caregiver fails to recognize the child's signals and when the child is providing "miscues" to the caregiver (Cooper et al. 2005, 127–51).

Often when a caregiver and toddler have a distressed relationship, the caregiver either fails to perceive the child's cues about feelings or needs or makes an error in assigning meaning to the cues actually perceived. An example of the former is when a child pulls back and is hesitant in a new setting and the caregiver shows no awareness of the anxiety, continuing to push the child to play with the toys rather than giving the child a few minutes to get comfortable in the setting. An example of the second problem is seen when a child throws a toy snake that seems scary for the child and the parent reacts with annoyance at the throwing behavior, failing to perceive the child's fear or the motive behind getting the snake further away. In these and similar events, the therapist can effectively "speak for the child" in a way that shows understanding of the child and makes overt and recognizable for the caregiver the feelings or communications of the child. In the first example, the therapist might say "Mommy, I'm not so sure about this new place," cuing the caregiver to be patient while the child visually explores the room. In the second instance, the therapist may say "That snake seems scary to you" or "Get away from me, snake—I don't like you" using either direct commentary or speaking for the child to cue the caregiver about the child's reason for throwing the toy.

The Circle of Security model of attachment therapy has articulated the importance of miscues in the communication between caregiver and child (Cooper et al. 2005, 127–51). It describes two types of miscues: when the child appears to want support for exploration when the child really needs comfort but is uncomfortable asking for it; and the opposite, when the child appears to ask for comfort when he or she really wants to explore but is uncomfortable continuing to explore. Translating for the child in this instance is a much greater challenge for the therapist because it is likely that both partners in the dyad are uncomfortable. Directly translating in this instance could provoke even greater discomfort for one or both members of the dyad. For this reason, the therapist needs to be cautious and observe this type of miscue on more than one occasion before trying to intervene. In the case of miscues, translation works best when it directs the attention of both partners to mixed feelings rather than miscues per se. Thus, the therapist might say, "You can't decide whether you want to be next to Mommy or go look at the toy" or "Maybe you and Mommy can go over there together to see that toy." Again, the use of this type of intervention is likely to occur after the dyad has already made some gains in communicating around less disturbing issues.

There is one additional way that a therapist translates for the child to facilitate play. This relies on the therapist's knowledge of normal toddler play. By recognizing common themes in the child's play, the therapist can more easily interpret the needs expressed, anticipate an attuned response, and make suggestions that enable the caregiver to engage more comfortably in play with the child. Such comments as "I think he wants you to hold a baby, too" said to the caregiver or "Can Mommy help you protect that little lion?" said to both of them can enable the caregiver to play more responsively with the toddler.

The second specific intervention to be discussed here is modeling. Sometimes the most effective way to facilitate the caregiver-toddler play is to play with the child while the caregiver observes. This can be helpful in several ways. First, for caregivers who feel self-conscious engaging in toddler play, it can be freeing for the caregiver to see the therapist comfortably act "childlike" and perhaps foolish to elicit the silly, exuberant joy of the toddler. Second, modeling can show the caregiver play activities that the toddler likes and responds to positively. The caregiver can thus be assured that there are several good ways to play with the toddler. Finally, modeling enables the caregiver to learn how to play and which specific play activities are most enjoyable for the child.

The final two interventions are closely related: psychoeducation, or direct instruction about attachment and the needs of the toddler, and feedback to the caregiver. Both interventions should be used primarily to facilitate the use of play components by the caregiver, which in turn should facilitate the caregiver-toddler interaction. That is, they should be used only in ways that are sensitive to the needs of the dyad in treatment. There are many ways for a caregiver-toddler dyad to be attuned and playful, so all interventions must themselves be attuned to the specific dyad and what feels comfortable and playful to them. What would be playful for one dyad may be too intense and therefore uncomfortable for another dyad.

Both education and feedback can be used during the play sessions. They also can be quite effective in occasional separate sessions with just the caregiver, especially if videotapes of the play sessions are used to focus the discussion. Often, much of the formal psychoeducation is carried out during the relationship-building assessment with the caregiver at the start of treatment. It is important that the caregiver understand something about attachment and the importance of play to the attachment relationship as the caregiver makes the decision to enter caregiver-toddler play therapy.

Within play, feedback can be used at any point. Obviously, feedback needs to be both sensitive and focused on the positive. Direct feedback such as "He really likes it when you do that" or "I think he is wanting you to do that some more" overlaps with the translating interventions described earlier. Other feedback occurs in suggestions such as "He looks like he is getting very excited—maybe you could help him calm down." These work best when the activity you are suggesting is one the caregiver knows how to do but perhaps does not see the need for at the moment or is uncomfortable using in the playroom, where the therapist is perceived as being "in charge." Reminding the caregiver that you are a team working together can help alleviate the sense that the therapist is in charge. Generally, when the feedback needed emphasizes some caregiver behavior that is not helpful to the child, the feedback is best presented in a separate setting. Ideally, you would want to use a video example of the caregiver behavior where the caregiver can see that the toddler is not responding the way they expected and where they are safe to consider other ways to interact in similar occasions during future play sessions.

THE COURSE OF CAREGIVER-TODDLER PLAY THERAPY

Caregiver-toddler play therapy consists of three parts: the intake process described earlier, the middle phase when the therapist is establishing a secure base with the caregiver and supporting developmental play between the members of the dyad, and the integrative phase. In the integrative phase, the therapist is less active and the emphasis is on the emerging attached, attuned relationship between the caregiver and the toddler. At this point, the dyad need to practice regulation and achieving pleasure and joy in the relationship, while the therapist needs to serve primarily to redirect the dyad on those remaining occasions when they seem to struggle to be attuned to one another. The intake process normally will require three or four sessions. The middle phase of therapy is the longest, with the length dependent on the receptiveness of both the caregiver and toddler to the intervention. It may take as many as 15 to 20 sessions, as was the case in the therapy of Jonah and his grandmother described below. The integration phase is usually four to eight weeks, and the decision to terminate is based on the increasing automaticity of the attunement between the members of the dyad. That is, therapy ends when attuned reactions to the child by the caregiver become well-practiced to the point of becoming automatic, and the child's ability to use the caregiver for both a secure base and a safe haven is well established.

CASE STUDY[1]

Jonah, age 26 months, was brought for treatment by his maternal grandmother, who was concerned about his behavior. She described Jonah as impulsive, into everything, moody, and shy with strangers, with frequent tantrums and fights with his cousins (Benedict 2005). Jonah was placed with his maternal grandparents when he was about 21 months of age. Child Protective Services made the placement after becoming involved when his mother brought him to the emergency room injured after a fall and needing surgery and abandoned him there. According to the grand-mother, Jonah's mother was a poly-drug abuser who would bring Jonah to the grandmother's home and leave him for a week or two and then return, take him, and disappear for several weeks. Neglect was strongly suspected and possible active abuse could not be ruled out. At the time Jonah was placed with them, the grandparents were already raising another daughter's four children (ages three to seven) after that mother, who also lived in the home, was disabled in an accident. The grandmother stayed at home dur-ing the day to care for Jonah and the youngest cousin (also a boy) while the three older children attended public pre-K or elementary school.

An initial assessment was conducted, involving an intake-attachment interview with the grandmother, a joint videotaped play session with the grandmother and Jonah, and a feedback meeting with the grandmother. Although the grandfather was active in the care of the children when he was home, the grandmother was clearly the primary caregiver for all five children. Because the grandfather worked long hours, he was unable to participate in the assessment or therapy. The grandmother was clearly over-whelmed caring for five children under seven and was especially frustrated by Jonah. He seemed to be easily upset, getting angry and defiant when limits were set. He was described as running all the time, throwing constant temper tantrums, rejecting and throwing food, and generally not being af-fectionate with her, even though he resisted separations from her.

The primary problem appeared to involve Jonah's insecure attachment relationship with his "Meemaw." This could be seen in several ways. From the grandmother's point of view, he didn't seem very connected to her and she openly complained that she didn't feel the same affection and love for him she felt for her other grandchildren. She tried to play with him but didn't feel he was very responsive.

When Jonah and his grandmother played together during the assessment, their interaction was tension-filled, with the grandmother constantly giv-ing him directions he typically ignored. He would play with some of the toys while she would try to engage him in naming things, especially the animals and colors. Because she was intensely focused on instructing him, she seemed nonresponsive to him emotionally. Occasionally her play was quite intrusive, having the animals pretend to walk on Jonah or "bite him." He would respond by pushing her and the animal away. At other times, she seemed to lecture him, even commenting at length on whether the animal he was holding was an alligator or crocodile, turning to the therapist to see which it was and clearly annoyed when the therapist didn't seem to know the distinction or think it was as important as she felt it was. Jonah did not look to her for comfort or reassurance in this strange situation, did not share joint attention toward objects with her, and generally showed rather disorganized play, moving rapidly from object to object. Neither member of the dyad seemed to show any pleasure or joy in the setting, and the actual interaction between them was minimal.

In the interpretation sessions at the end of the assessment, the therapist suggested to the grandmother that Jonah was not very comfortably attached to her, perhaps because of his early history. The grandmother responded to this by agreeing and reporting that she had originally decided not to keep him and CPS had already secured a foster home for him to move to one week after he arrived. While the grandmother said she couldn't let him go at the end of the week and thus kept him, she also reported a sense that something was lacking in her relationship with Jonah. She quickly agreed to begin caregiver-toddler play therapy. She was well intentioned and genuinely wanted to be closer to her grandson, eagerly asking for help and suggestions of things she could try at home. The remainder of that feedback session and the next session were used to explain some aspects of attachment to her. She seemed to understand the concepts and did not appear to feel like a failure as a grandparent as a result of Jonah's problems.

Therapy was initiated the following week. Progress was steady but slow. This was anticipated because the amount of pleasurable and joyful interaction between Meemaw and Jonah was very limited at the beginning of therapy. It would require many brief attuned and pleasurable interactions for Jonah to begin to trust his grandmother and respond to her playful invitations. Two interventions were used at the start of therapy to provide a setting for attuned interactions to begin to take place. First, the therapist affirmed the grandmother's sense that her relationship with Jonah lacked the feelings of love and attachment she felt with her other grandchildren. In so doing, the therapist accepted the grandmother's distress about the unfulfilling relationship with Jonah as well as her frustration with his behavior.

The second intervention was done across several sessions, beginning during the intake feedback. The grandmother needed several gentle repetitions before she could begin to modify her interactions with Jonah. In this intervention, the therapist explained attunement in everyday language and encouraged the grandmother to move more toward finding ways to interact pleasurably with Jonah.

An important part of the second intervention was direct discussion of her intense focus on teaching Jonah. The grandmother reported that she felt considerable responsibility and guilt about her earlier parenting of Jonah's mother. She felt the mother's drug addiction and irresponsible behavior was the result of her (the grandmother) not trying hard enough to stimulate and teach her children when they were little. The therapist noted that teaching was a valuable thing she could offer her grandchildren, but Jonah seemed to be developmentally on schedule and showed no signs of a lack of cognitive stimulation. The therapist also indicated that many of the things the grandmother was trying so hard to teach were perhaps too advanced for even a bright two-year-old like Jonah. At the same time, the therapist noted that Jonah appeared to have been emotionally neglected during his first two years, emphasizing that he needed affection and approval more than he needed direct instruction.

While some of this work on shifting the grandmother's perception of what Jonah needed from her was started during intake with just the therapist and the grandmother present, most of the work was done in brief discussions while Jonah played. Some of the work used the "speak for the child" method. Jonah's play was largely solitary, with minimal interaction with either the grandmother or therapist. The therapist deliberately muted her affect and engagement with Jonah to avoid being more attuned and engaged than his grandmother and thus competing with her for his attention. However, the therapist would speak for Jonah, requesting the grandmother join him in his play. These requests would include simple but specific ways she could join his play. The grandmother was very responsive to these gentle instructions. Equally important was Jonah's reaction. He seemed surprised that the therapist could verbalize things he wanted and came to look to the therapist to do so several times in a session. Jonah would sometimes even nod when the therapist redirected the more intrusive of the grandmother's interactions with him. However, Jonah had little interest in playing with the therapist. If the therapist modeled a play activity with Jonah, he would immediately turn and try to play the same way with the grandmother. His obvious preference for her helped the grandmother see her importance to him, which was central to her feeling more connected to him.

Another crucial aspect of this early phase of treatment was the therapist's acceptance of the grandmother's good intentions and her constant support of the grandmother's sometimes awkward efforts. At this point in treatment, the grandmother's self-esteem was fragile and she would have found it quite difficult had she felt criticized or devalued by the therapist.

Over several sessions, the interaction between the grandmother and Jonah became increasingly playful. They seemed to enjoy each other much more, and the grandmother largely abandoned her direct teaching efforts. She was able to engage Jonah in joint attention toward objects, initiating simple games he liked and therefore repeated with her. While Jonah didn't seem to care if the grandmother came into the playroom when he began therapy, running into the room without checking to see if she were coming, he became very conscious of her presence after several sessions. He would wait to go into the room until she began to go in, and he would immediately find a toy and show it to her.

Once they were consistently enjoying playing together in sessions, a new set of challenges emerged. Jonah had shown little affect, either positive or negative, in the early sessions. He was both quiet and serious in his play with little laughter or open distress. In the second phase of therapy, Jonah began showing much more emotion. At times he was gleeful, laughing in his play with his grandmother. At other times he would get angry, either in frustration when he couldn't get the play to go the way he wanted or anger at his grandmother for talking to the therapist and not paying enough attention to him. It quickly became clear that Jonah was quite limited in his ability to regulate his emotions. When he began to show pleasure, he would get more and more excited until he lost control and began wildly throwing toys or playing with such vigor that his wild play actually became unsafe, with frequent bumps and falls in which he was hurt. Similarly, when he got angry, he almost invariably ended up pummeling his grandmother or trying to bite her. Jonah was clearly showing the lack of emotional and behavioral regulation that is typically seen with children exhibiting attachment problems.

The next goal of therapy was to empower the grandmother to regulate Jonah's emotions and behavior for him. In a healthy caregiver-infant relationship, the caregiver regulates the infant, who then has the experience of being regulated, which lays the foundation for self-regulation. Jonah's mother's neglect meant he had very limited experience of feeling regulated and safe. He had failed to develop the self-regulatory skills typical for a two-year-old. The therapist's role was to help the grandmother regulate Jonah. Modeling was not a viable option because Jonah was primarily focused on his grandmother during sessions, and the therapist's stepping in to regulate him would have likely scared Jonah and thus further dysregulated him. The therapist chose instead to translate Jonah's cues that he was getting dysregulated for the grandmother, while giving her suggestions of ways she could help him calm down and regain control. Essentially, the grandmother needed to shift her understanding of Jonah's dysregulation from her belief that he was "rebelling against everything" to the idea that he did not know how to self-regulate. Once she made that shift, she was easily able to provide the structure he needed.

Again and again in the sessions, the grandmother would engage with Jonah and increase his excitement, only to initiate calming activities before he actually lost control. She seemed to intuit that this process of regulation needed to be repeated many times. Early in this part of therapy, the dysregulation was characterized more by anger than joy. With repetition, the negative affective reactions became less frequent and were replaced by highly positive interactions. By this point, the grandmother was feeling a strong connection to Jonah. It was obvious that Jonah was very attached to her, and they came into sessions and played rather exuberantly and joyfully, largely ignoring the therapist. Therapy was terminated soon after it became clear that there was a reasonably secure attachment between them, that their interactions had become mostly joyful, that regulation and repair of dys-regulation was relatively automatic for both partners, and that the behavior problems at home had largely disappeared. The therapy, including the in-take process, took approximately eight months, with a total of 29 sessions.

CONCLUSIONS AND FUTURE DIRECTIONS

Caregiver-toddler play therapy thus has many components, all designed to facilitate attachment and an enhanced caregiver-toddler relationship. The approach begins with establishing a trusting relationship with the care-giver, moves next to creating a safe playroom environment for the toddler, and finally, uses play to modify the distressed relationship between the caregiver and toddler. Within the play, the therapist models attuned play, translates communications between the toddler and the caregiver, and oc-casionally provides direct feedback and instruction, all of these fine-tuned to the specific needs of the caregiver-child relationship. The approach is grounded in both developmental research on play and attachment and on theoretically sound clinical applications of attachment theory. While this approach has shown effectiveness in the clinical setting, much work needs to be done to establish empirical support for the effectiveness of this play therapy approach.

NOTE

1. The name and identifying information have been altered to preserve the con-fidentiality of the client and his family.

REFERENCES

Benedict, H. E. 2005a. Attachment and trauma in young children: Play therapy theory and techniques. Workshop presented at the annual meeting of the Associa-tion for Play Therapy, Nashville, Tennessee, October.
———. 2005b. Use of play themes and relationship patterns to understand young children's play. Workshop presented at the annual meeting of the Association for Play Therapy, Nashville, Tennessee, October.
Cicchetti, D., F. A. Rogosch, and S. Toth. 2006. Fostering secure attachment in in-fants in maltreating families through preventive interventions. *Development and Psychopathology* 18 (3): 623–649.

Cicchetti, D., and K. Valentino. 2006. An ecological-transactional perspective on child maltreatment: Failure of the average expectable environment and its influence on child development. In *Developmental psychopathology*, 2nd ed., vol. 3, *Risk, disorder, and adaptation*, ed. D. Cicchetti and D. J. Cohen, 146–148. New York: Wiley.

Cohen, E. 2006. Parental level of awareness: An organizing scheme of parents' belief systems as a guide in parent therapy. In *Parent-focused child therapy: Attachment, identification, and reflective functions*, ed. C. Wachs and L. Jacobs, 39–64. Lanham, MD: Rowman & Littlefield.

Cooper, G., K. Hoffman, B. Powell, and R. Marvin. 2005. The circle of security intervention: Differential diagnosis and differential treatment. In *Enhancing early attachments: Theory, research, intervention, and policy*, ed. L. J. Berlin, Y. Ziv, L. Amaya-Jackson, and M. T. Greenberg, 127–151. New York: Guilford.

Dozier, M., O. Lindbiem, and J. P. Ackerman. 2005. Attachment and biobehavioral catch-up: An intervention targeting empirically identified needs of foster infants. In *Enhancing early attachments: Theory, research, intervention, and policy*, ed. L. J. Berlin, Y. Ziv, L. Amaya-Jackson, and M. T. Greenberg, 78–94. New York: Guilford.

Kobak, R., J. Cassidy, K. Lyons-Ruth, and Y. Ziv. 2006. Attachment, stress, and psychopathology: A developmental pathways model. In *Developmental psychopathology*, 2nd ed., vol. 1, *Theory and method*, ed. D. Cicchetti and D. J. Cohen, 333–369. New York: Wiley.

Lieberman, A. 2004. Child-parent psychotherapy: A relationship-based approach to the treatment of mental health disorders in infancy and early childhood. In *Treating parent-infant relationship problems: Strategies for intervention*, ed. A. J. Sameroff, S. C. McDonough, and K. L. Rosenblum, 97–122. New York: Guilford.

Lieberman, A., and P. Van Horn. 2004. Assessment and treatment of young children exposed to traumatic events. In *Young children and trauma: Intervention and treatment*, ed. J. D. Osofsky, 111–138. New York: Guilford.

Lindaman, S. L., P. B. Booth, and C. L. Chambers. 2000. Assessing parent-child interactions with the Marschak Interaction Method (MIM). In *Play diagnosis and assessment*, 2nd ed. Ed. K. Gitlin-Weiner, A. Sandgrund, and C. Schaefer, 371–400. New York: Wiley.

Olds, D. L. 2005. The nurse-family partnership: Foundations in attachment theory and epidemiology. In *Enhancing early attachments: Theory, research, intervention, and policy*, ed. L. J. Berlin, Y. Ziv, L. Amaya-Jackson, and M. T. Greenberg, 217–249. New York: Guilford.

Siegel, D. 1999. *The developing mind: Toward a neurobiology of interpersonal experience.* New York: Guilford.

Slade, A., L. G. Sadler, and L. C. Mayes. 2005. Minding the baby: Enhancing parental reflective functioning in a nursing/mental health home visiting program. In *Enhancing early attachments: Theory, research, intervention, and policy*, ed. L. J. Berlin, Y. Ziv, L. Amaya-Jackson, and M. T. Greenberg, 152–177. New York: Guilford.

Trevarthen, C., K. J. Aitken, M. Vandekerckhove, J. Delafield-Butt, and E. Nagy. 2006. Collaborative regulations of vitality in early childhood: Stress in intimate relationships and postnatal psychopathology. In *Developmental psychopathology*, 2nd ed., vol. 2, *Developmental Neuroscience*, ed. D. Cicchetti and D. J. Cohen, 65–126. New York: Wiley.

Zeanah, C. H., J. A. Larrieu, S. S. Heller, and J. Valliere. Infant-parent relationship assessment. 1999. In *Handbook of infant mental health*, 2nd ed. Ed. C. H. Zeanah, 222–235. New York: Guilford.

Zeanah, C. H., and A. Smyke. 2005. Building attachment relationships following maltreatment and severe deprivation. In *Enhancing early attachments: Theory, research, intervention, and policy*, ed. L. J. Berlin, Y. Ziv, L. Amaya-Jackson, and M. T. Greenberg, 195–216. New York: Guilford.

Zeanah, C. H., A. Smyke, and T. Coots. 2007. Working model of the child interview training. Workshop presented at the Institute of Infant and Early Childhood Mental Health, New Orleans, June.

Zero to Three. 2005. *Diagnostic classification of mental health and developmental disorders of infancy and early childhood (DC: 0–3R)*. Rev. ed. Washington, DC: Zero to Three.

5

Ecosystemic Play Therapy with Infants and Toddlers and Their Families

Beth Limberg and Sue Ammen

INFANT MENTAL HEALTH MEETS
ECOSYSTEMIC PLAY THERAPY

Ecosystemic Play Therapy (EPT) is a dynamic, integrated therapeutic model for addressing the mental health needs of children and their families (O'Connor 1997, 2000; O'Connor and Ammen 1997). EPT is similar to other play therapy approaches in its emphasis on the warm and accepting quality of the relationship between the therapist and child and in its commitment to the importance of play as a primary treatment modality. EPT differs from nondirective play therapy approaches in that the therapist is responsible for the structure and flow of the sessions and even who participates in the sessions, depending on the child's developmental level and needs, focus of treatment, and ecosystemic variables (Ammen and Limberg 2005). EPT treatment can be designed by the therapist to range from child-led nondirective play to therapist-led developmental play with the parent-child dyad to family play therapy, as well as consultation, collaboration and/or advocacy roles with the other systems. For comparison of the different models of play therapy, including EPT, see O'Connor (2000) and O'Connor and Braverman (1997).

Infant mental health is built on a growing body of research and clinical literature that supports intervening as early as possible when a young child is experiencing emotional difficulties (Dicker and Gordon 2004). Selma Fraiberg (1980) defined *infant mental health* as the social, emotional, and cognitive well-being of a child under the age of three within the context of a caregiving relationship. The mental health treatment of infants, toddlers, and families is grounded in the belief that "the developing parent-child relationship should be placed at the center of the therapist's work from the moment a family is referred or asks for help" (Weatherston 2005, 5). The focus of treatment includes supporting the young child's social and emotional development, identifying and reducing the risk of disorder or delay, nurturing the strengths and emerging competencies of the caregiver, and strengthening family relationships (McDonough 2000, 2004; Weatherston 2005).

EPT blends well with infant mental health. EPT with young children (Ammen and Limberg 2005) is *developmentally organized* around a transactional view of development for both children and parents that starts even before birth. It is *relationship focused*, recognizing that relationships are both organizers of development and an underlying focus of all interventions with young children. It is a *strength-based* approach, which focuses on understanding adaptive functioning and identifying internal strengths and external resources when intervening with young families. Lastly, it recognizes that young children and their families are *grounded in an ecosystemic context* of multiple interacting systems that change over time, including family systems, social systems, and metasystems such as the cultural and sociopolitical contexts. It also recognizes the therapeutic ecosystem, including the systems in which our clinical work is embedded, the collaborative relations, boundaries and roles, as well as our own internal perceptions and therapeutic relationships with the infant/family. EPT with infants, toddlers, and their families is particularly useful for facilitating the development of sensory, behavioral, and emotional regulation; promoting communicative abilities including representation play skills; strengthening and healing difficulties in the parent-child relationship; and addressing issues of trauma.

DEVELOPMENTALLY ORGANIZED

A developmental frame is very important for play therapists working with infants, toddlers, and their families. Developmental change is so pronounced at this age that we must be particularly attuned to what is within the normal range and what is atypical, as well as understanding that during periods of normal stress or developmental transitions, an increase in difficult behavior and developmental regression is normal (Brazelton and Sparrow 2006). We must be attuned to the developmental levels of the parents and other family members, as well as the developmental process of the family. The play-based activities and treatment settings must be appropriate for the developmental level and capabilities of the child. For infants, the primary play object is the parent or primary caregiver. Toddlers remain highly invested in playful interactions in the context of the primary attachment relationship, and also become interested in exploration, manipulation, and beginning representational play with toys. The following discussion highlights developmental concepts and strategies particularly relevant to play therapists working with young children. It is not a substitute for a solid grounding in infant and toddler development (for excellent texts on early childhood development, see Davies 2004 and Trawick-Smith 2005).

The transactional model of development describes the developing child as "a product of the continuous dynamic interactions of the child and the experience provided by his or her family and social context. What is innovative about the transactional model is the equal emphasis placed on the effects of the child and the environment" (Sameroff and Fiese 2000, 10). In very young children, this dynamic interaction is dramatic both in terms of the rapid neurobiological maturation of the infant and in terms of the immense importance of the infant's experience of the primary caregiving relationships. Behavior is the result of both nature and nurture in interaction; through the process of coaction, nurture actually changes nature and nature changes nurture (Shonkoff and Phillips 2000). Thus, the parent-child interactions influence the neurobiological and psychosocial developmental capacities of the young child, and the child's neurobiological strengths and vulnerabilities influence the quality of the relationship. An infant with an immature sensory-regulatory system who reacts to typically soothing activities like rocking and singing by becoming more dysregulated contributes to a parent who feels inadequate and exhausted and less able to help the infant regulate. Thus, our developmental frame needs to hold the infant/toddler within this transactional relationship context.

The National Academy of Sciences monograph *From Neurons to Neighborhoods: The Science of Early Childhood Development* (Shonkoff and Phillips 2000) identifies self-regulation, communication, and relationship skills as crucial developmental tasks of early childhood that, "if mastered, appear to get children started along adaptive pathways and, if seriously delayed or problematic, can lead a child to falter" (91). These developmental tasks are often a focus of mental health treatment with young children. Regulation and communication are addressed here, relationship in the next section.

REGULATION

The young child develops self-regulation as he or she moves from needing external support to internalizing the ability to regulate emotions, behaviors, and attention. Regulatory capacity includes arousal, the infant's ability to maintain alertness and manage transitions between states; attention, the infant's ability to focus attention on a desired task or object; affective regulation, the infant's ability to recover from distress and maintain emotional stability; and action, the infant's ability to engage in adaptive, goal-directed behavior (Williamson and Anzalone 2001).

Initially, infants are regulated through the responsive actions of their caregivers. The infant who is routinely soothed when distressed learns that distress can be assuaged. Through these experiences, infants grow toward physiological homeostasis, learning to modulate physical states of sleep/waking, hunger/satiation, and learning self-calming, soothing, and settling once basic needs are met (Meléndez 2005). Infants build on this experience through sensory-motor play, learning to attend and explore the world through their senses (Drewes 2001). Self-regulation develops out of these experiences. Consistency in caregiving and daily routines "allows infants to gain a sense of security that reduces their stress when faced with new or challenging situations, helping them to self-regulate their emotions and behaviors" (Dicker and Gordon 2004, 18).

Both constitutional and environmental risk factors contribute to regulatory difficulties. Constitutional risk factors include immature neurological development, as may be seen in premature birth, and certain neurodevelopmental disorders such as autism, developmental delays, and learning disorders. Environmental risk factors include prenatal drug exposure, neglect and abuse, and exposure to violence or traumatic events. Whether the contributing factors are internal or external, regulatory difficulties become constitutionally based. The *Diagnostic Classification of Mental Health and Developmental Disorders of Infancy and Early Childhood: Revised Edition* describes *regulatory disorders of sensory processing* as "constitutionally based responses to sensory stimuli . . . [that is], a child's difficulties in regulating emotions and behaviors as well as motor abilities in response to sensory stimulation that lead to impairment in development and functioning" (Zero to Three 2005, 28). Children experience themselves and their world through their senses. A child's ability to organize these experiences in a purposeful way so as to regulate his or her affective and behavioral response is referred to as sensory integration (SI) (Williamson and Anzalone 2001). Although it is necessary for play therapists to understand sensory integration, they are not trained to treat difficulties in these areas. For proper assessment and treatment, the play therapist will consult with an occupational therapist (OT) trained in SI dysfunctions.

COMMUNICATION

Young children develop the capabilities that underlie effective communication and learning through early development of language, reasoning, and problem-solving skills. In infants our focus is on nonverbal behavioral cues and shared mutual attention; in toddlers we recognize the emergence of representational play and meta-language abilities.

Even very young children can signal their needs and wishes through behavioral cues. Kathryn Barnard, developer of the NCAST parent-child interaction scales, has identified a list of common engagement and disengagement signals that babies give to communicate in interaction (Erickson and Kurz-Riemer 1999; Sumner and Spietz 1994). Potent engagement cues include looking at the parent's face and sustained eye contact; subtle engagement cues include head raising and alerting posture with sparkle in eyes. Potent disengagement cues include crying, whining, fussing; subtle disengagement cues include a facial grimace, clinched eyes, gaze aversion, head lowering, and jerky motor movements. Sensitive caregiving involves the accurate recognition and interpretation of the baby's signals, followed by an appropriate response. (For an expanded table of infant cues, see Erickson and Kurz-Riemer 1999, 64–65.) Infants also engage in playful interactions with others, taking turns in vocal exchanges and engaging in shared attention, which allows them to communicate about a shared reality (Westby 2000).

Difficulties in infant communication may occur if the infant cues are limited or confusing, as we may see in children with developmental delays or regulatory difficulties. Difficulties in communication may also occur when parents have trouble knowing how to respond to their infant's cues, possibly because of inexperience or immaturity, as in adolescent parenthood, or because of unresolved "ghosts" (Fraiberg, Adelson, and Shapiro 1980) that cause them to misinterpret their child's cues. Parents' own mental health and cognitive, physical, or environmental problems may also keep them from being aware of the infant's cues or available to respond to them. Erickson and Kurz-Riemer (1999, 74–78) provide an excellent discussion of facilitating language development in very young children. As play therapists, we can promote both language development and attachment through guiding playful interactions around these activities between the parent and child.

Following the development of intentional nonverbal communication, we see the emergence of language, the verbal representation of internal needs and desires, and symbolic pretend play and internal mental representational abilities in toddlers.[1] Carol Westby (2000) describes the development of representational play abilities, beginning at about 18 months of age with simple symbolic play actions such as pretending to drink from a cup or feed someone else. It becomes symbolic play when the child is able to transcend the immediate reality of "I am drinking" to a created reality of "I am pretending to drink." Early representational play is based on common experiences such as eating, cooking, or gardening, and the child is dependent on realistic, life-size (for the child) props.

As children's representational play abilities develop, they are increasingly able to use smaller object-figures and even substitute objects (a block can now be a telephone or a car); their themes become more creative and less dependent upon their experience; and they begin to organize and sequence their play narratives (stories). By age two-and-a-half to three, children still use realistic props but are beginning to narrate their play with language. They are able to create complex, unplanned, but sequential play themes. Between ages three and three-and-a-half, children become less dependent on props and begin to use dolls, puppets, and small figures in their play. A significant cognitive shift occurs with the development of meta-linguistic language such as "he said," "I think," "she wants," or "they feel." The figures now began to talk and have feelings and thoughts. This indicates the child's ability to project into the thoughts and feelings of others and indicates recognition of internal mental states in themselves and others. This transition is associated with the meta-language abilities to reflect on their own behavior, to self-monitor, and to problem-solve. In play therapy, "imaginative or make-believe play is particularly important because it allows children to make the complex and frightening events in their lives manageable and comprehensible, and provides a medium for playing out different outcomes and solutions" (Ammen and Limberg 2005, 216).

Trauma has a significant impact on representation capacities, especially the meta-language abilities. Some children may reenact their trauma in repetitive play sequences that do not reduce their anxiety or give them a sense of coping; this can be seen as parallel to the intrusive, repetitive thoughts that adults with posttraumatic symptoms report. Other traumatized children may respond to the play therapy setting by being resistant or avoiding representational play or expressive play techniques (Drewes 2001).

RELATIONSHIP-FOCUSED

Effective clinical work with infants, toddlers, and their families requires a solid understanding of the development of parent-child attachment (for excellent discussions of attachment theory, see Bowlby 1988; Howe 2005; and Karen 1994). "Building a relationship between a child and primary caregiver is a basic task of the first months of life" (Dicker and Gordon 2004, 21). The child brings to this relationship his or her constitutional being—neurobiological strengths and weaknesses, sensory experience, regulatory abilities, and relational capacity—as well as experiences in the world to date. The parent similarly brings neurobiological assets— cognitive skills and deficits, regulatory and relational abilities—as well as beliefs about the world developed over time. The complex interaction between the two leads to a unique relationship, one that cannot be duplicated with another child or another parent. Bowlby (1982) identified two parental variables as strongly related to the development of a secure attachment. The first is empathic attunement and responsiveness to the infant's signals of his or her feelings and needs. The second is mutually enjoyable interactions between a parent and infant. In infancy the primary play object is the mother or primary caregiver. Play interactions occur frequently, making up about a third of the ongoing interactions that occur daily between mothers and infants. "When mothers and infants enjoy their early play interactions, they are likely to continue to express enjoyment in their later interactions" (Roggman, Boyce, and Newland 2000, 303).

Ideally, this infant-caregiver dance is interactively coordinated with respect to the child's needs and affective experience. When the dance is not coordinated, the infant may experience a breakdown in mutual regulation leading to sleeping and eating problems and disruptive behaviors due to an inability to self-regulate. Alternatively, the infant may become emotionally constricted and depressed in an effort to self-regulate. Both infant and parent are active participants in this attachment relationship; problems with the infant or parent, or even just a mismatch between them, may contribute to a lack of coordination in their attachment dance (O'Connor and Ammen 1997).

Weston, Ivins, Heffron, and Sweet (1997) proposed that the "centrality of relationships" should be an organizing construct for the field of infant mental health because relationships are both organizers of development and the basis of all interventions with young children. EPT also evaluates and implements treatment within the context of the child's primary relationships—both as a focus of the treatment and as a way to facilitate the treatment.

> The younger the child, the more vital are the roles of the parents and the family. In therapy situations with young children, the therapist must keep the parents-caregivers in a more prominent role than that of the therapist. For this reason, the therapist's relationship with the parent-figure is at least as important as his or her relationship with the young child. Often the therapeutic effect results from play-based interactions that help parents [and children] experience the relationship differently, combined with verbal reflections and interpretations that help them understand the child's experience and behaviors differently. (Ammen and Limberg 2005, 212)

Parent-child attachment is so crucial to the well-being of young children that addressing relationship problems should be a priority in infant mental health treatment. Even when relationship problems are not a focus of treatment, parent-child relationship strengths should be used to facilitate the treatment of other problem areas. The consistent involvement of parents in the young child's treatment is developmentally necessary (Heffron 2000; Lieberman and Knorr 2007; Pawl and St. John 1998).

STRENGTH-BASED

A strength-based approach focuses on the perspectives of child and family—their motivations and intentions—rather than on psychopathology.

> Every family we serve has *vulnerabilities*. Their vulnerabilities are what bring them to our attention. While it is important to understand the babies' and families' vulnerabilities and risk factors, these are *deficits*, things that they *lack*. *You can't build on what isn't there.* A deficit model ultimately prevents us from identifying what the baby and family can build on, what their strengths are [emphasis in original]. (Maury and Monzon-Kong 2002.)

Shifting from a deficit- to a strength-based model is challenging. Sometimes focusing on what the family has (strengths and resources) makes them feel like we are not hearing their concerns and struggles. Madsen (2007) eloquently notes that a strength-based approach needs to "shift from 'pointing out strengths' to eliciting richer stories and supporting previously obscured experiences." It follows that we need "to address, not just presenting problems, but also the organizing life stories within which they are embedded," with an emphasis on "inviting the enactment of empowering life stories" through our therapeutic interactions. He recommends a relational stance with families through which we continually "search for elements of competence, connection, and hope" (Madsen 2007, 7–9).

CONTEXTUALLY GROUNDED IN
THE CHILD'S ECOSYSTEM

When doing EPT with young children, the play therapist recognizes that children exist within the context of multiple interacting systems (Ammen and Limberg 2005). The play therapist must consider the larger family system, including understanding how the family defines its membership (parents, partners of parents, siblings, grandparents, elders, neighbors, etc.), how authority and responsibility are assigned/granted within the family (based on age, based on gender, etc.), and even what the family expects from therapy.

Multidisciplinary assessment and collaboration is critical to successful work with infant/toddler families. A young child is often brought for mental health services without a thorough evaluation. Play therapists need to know that something that looks like a behavioral or emotional problem may actually be rooted in a medical concern or a sensory integration problem. Even at such a young age, infants and toddlers may already be or may need to be involved with multiple community systems, including medical systems, child welfare, legal systems, child care, schools, churches, and community centers. A family's experience with community systems as either helpful or intrusive must be considered when attempting to engage additional services for families.

The play therapist must be aware of the cultural context of the family. Childcare practices, for example, are organized within cultural frameworks for caregiving practices, based in the values placed on children and the images of who these children will grow to be (Meléndez 2005). Some cultures value independence, and so their childrearing practices include opportunities for children to explore on their own, take risks, and succeed or fail, all toward the goal of autonomy. Other cultures value interdependence, and so provide opportunities for children to learn within relationships and accept help, all toward the goal of inter-reliance. Working within the cultural context of the family becomes particularly challenging when that context differs significantly from our own. Real or perceived differences in beliefs and expectations must be addressed respectfully (Barrera and Corso 2003). Matters of privilege (socioeconomic status and class, gender, ethnicity and race, religious beliefs and practices, sexual orientation, immigration or migration status, etc.) can also significantly affect how a family participates in treatment.

All of these systems influence the child and family both directly through interactional experiences and indirectly through the meanings that they place on these experiences. The participants in these systems (e.g., parents, teacher, physician) each have their own perspective about why the infant/ toddler is behaving in a particular way, and these beliefs influence how they respond to the child's behavior. It is not unusual for the perceptions of the child and those of the other participants in the child's ecosystem to be at odds. As EPT therapists, we must try to understand the perceptions of all of the relevant participants and work to increase the understanding between them (Ammen and Limberg 2005).

As therapists, we too approach our client-families from our own perspective, which is determined in part by our own history of experiences and by our training. Wright (1992) notes that countertransference issues are particularly significant when working with very young children, because the preverbal and vulnerable state of the child taps our own preverbal and primary emotional processes. We may be drawn to rescue the infant or may overidentify with the affective state of the infant, feeling emotional hunger, rage toward the parent, or detached hopelessness. Home-based interventions mean limited control of the therapeutic environment, which can contribute to the therapist feeling overwhelmed or ineffective. Therapists need to identify the sources of their affective reactions, including what is really happening in the present between the parent and infant, what is being triggered in the therapist because of one's own experiences, and what is being triggered in the therapist-parent relationship. When working with young children and families, ongoing reflective supervision is critical, regardless of one's level of experience (Heffron 2005; Parlakian 2001).

PLAY THERAPY INTERVENTIONS WITH
INFANT/TODDLER FAMILIES

Choosing activities that are developmentally based is common ground for play therapists and infant mental health specialists alike (Drewes 2001; James 1989; Lieberman and Knorr 2007; O'Connor and Ammen 1997; Shelby 2000). Play serves as a way for children to organize their understanding of the world, and play interactions promote the young child's development in both social and cognitive domains. Early sensory-motor play teaches the child about his or her world. Shared communicative gestures like the coordination of joint attention between a parent and young child toward an object or toy promotes both language and regulatory functioning. Later pretend play contributes to the child's development of symbolic representation abilities, further strengthened by the parent's involvement, which facilitates higher levels and longer episodes of symbolic play among toddlers (Roggman, Boyce, and Newland 2000).

Because the parent-child relationship is central to treatment, all activities are designed to support attachment and the child's development within relationship. Play therapists support these goals by introducing and modeling activities that address the unique clinical needs of the infant or the infant-parent dyad and by guiding the parent's understanding of the interaction. The EPT is in a unique role when working with infant/toddler families: though fully engaged in guiding the therapeutic process, the EPT keeps the focus on the interaction between the parent and child.

STRENGTHENING DEVELOPMENT
THROUGH RELATIONSHIP

Mother-infant play in the early months of infancy has been described by Stern (1977) as "episodes of social interaction that are initiated by mutual gaze, maintained by variations in the intensity and tempo of interactive behaviors, and ended by a breaking of attention" (Roggman, Boyce, and Newland 2000, 308). Mimicking these early interactions, play therapy activities that include mutual gaze and touch can be used to teach the parent to read the baby's engagement and disengagement cues. "Peek-a-boo" is one such game that draws on these early experiences—the parent and infant repeatedly and playfully engage and disengage with each other behind hands or a small blanket. The play therapist further enhances the parent's abilities to recognize and respond to his or her baby's cues by reflecting directly on the interaction or by using videotape to help the parent reflect (for more on the use of videotaping in infant mental health, see McDonough 2000, 2004; Erickson and Kurz-Riemer 1999). The play therapist might reflect positively on the parent's sensitivity in this game or on the infant's responsiveness. The play therapist might take on the "voice" of the baby, delighting in this new game, or reflect on the parent's emotional response to the game, especially if the interaction seems to trigger a "ghost" that has been interfering with the parent's ability to fully engage with the infant.

Recognizing that relationship and development are inextricably intertwined, the play therapist may introduce more "baby games" to the play therapy session. In typical development, these games are aimed at creating or strengthening the engagement of early attachment, predictably involving considerable eye contact and touch. In play therapy, these games are used to recreate, repair, or restore these early experiences. Contests that promote eye contact (breath holding contests, staring contests) and activities that promote touch (holding hands, cuddling while reading a book together) can be made up by the creative play therapist to suit any parent-child dyad. Security, another significant component of early attachment, can also be facilitated through play by modifying daily routines to include playful, nurturing opportunities, such as adding book time to the bedtime ritual or playing with shaving cream together in the bath.

In toddlers, a developing sense of self and differentiation becomes important. Games that promote exploration and experimentation, such as "hide and seek" and "find the missing object" stimulate curiosity and contribute to the toddler's growing sense that he or she is special and capable. Mastery activities, discussed in the next section, further promote this developing sense of self. Janine Shelby (2000) and Athena Drewes (2001) suggest several more developmental play therapy activities in their writings.

Play therapists are also sensitive to the parents' developmental needs, recognizing that their life experiences will affect how they parent their own children (Fraiberg, Adelson, and Shapiro 1980; Lieberman, Padrón, Van Horn, and Harris 2005). Play provides a nonthreatening way for parents to engage with their infants and toddlers, and in some cases, the play therapist is the first person to introduce the parent to this avenue of engagement. Some parents may have good skills, but do not know how to apply them with their challenging child. In these situations, the play therapist may assist the parent in adapting typical activities for the unique needs of their child. For a child with sensory integration difficulties, for example, the parent and child relationship can become strained when the child repeatedly rejects the parent's bids to play. By teaming up with an OT, the play therapist can identify activities that do not trigger the child's sensory sensitivities but do support parent-child interaction—for example, introducing shaving cream art into the bath can return bath time to a nurturing and engaging ritual.

ADDRESSING TRAUMA

As with play therapy treatment for other concerns, the ultimate goal of trauma treatment is to restore the infant/toddler's developmental trajectory within the parent-child relationship (Drewes 2001; Lieberman and Knorr 2007; O'Connor and Ammen 1997). Helping parents prepare for treatment is often the first step. The play therapist may need to help parents understand their child's symptoms within the context of the child's distress (Lieberman and Knorr 2007; Shelby 2000), respond empathically while managing their child's behaviors (Gaensbauer 2004), and understand their own feelings of guilt or remorse for failing to protect their child from the traumatic event (Shelby 2000).

The next step is to restore the infant/toddler's sense of security. Environmental changes that remove reminders of the trauma and explicit statements of safety and protection can repair the child's sense of trust in the adult to protect him or her (Lieberman and Van Horn 2004; Shelby 2000). For example, one mother took her young child from room to room in their apartment following a burglary, pointing out the new locks on the windows and stating how the room was now safe because the burglar could not open the window. Stimulating curiosity by exploring novel situations can also contribute to a renewed sense of security in a toddler (Drewes 2001). Child-led play therapy that utilizes concrete retrieval cues (physical props) to direct the play (Shelby 2000) is also effective, especially when the therapist narrates the play for the child, explicitly commenting on themes of protection and security. This narration can also correct the child's misunderstandings of the event. Egocentricity, mixed with a still immature understanding of cause and effect, often leads toddlers to misunderstand the cause of a traumatic event, sometimes believing that their thoughts and feelings and actions caused the event (Lieberman and Knorr 2007).

Finally, we work to restore the infant/toddler's sense of competence. Toddler fears are sometimes amorphous, manifesting themselves as fear of "monsters." Several play therapy techniques take advantage of this developmental phase to help young children gain mastery over adversity. Remembering that toddlers gain mastery by doing things over and over again (Shelby 2000), the play therapist may have the toddler draw the "monster" and then tear it up, or make the monster out of play dough and then smash it. These techniques make the fear/monster concrete for the child and then allow the toddler to use his or her whole body to destroy it, gaining mastery over it. Knowledge of typical developmental idiosyncrasies also allows the play therapist to take advantage of the toddler's capacity for magical thinking, as monster spray, "No Monsters" signs, and flashlights to drive away monsters become common tools in the toddler's arsenal to banish monsters. For one boy, reminded of several traumas by the sounds of sirens, "magic" lotion applied carefully to his ears protected his ears from the harsh sounds, making the sounds less scary. Janine Shelby reminds us that "treatment designed to induce a sense of mastery over the feared event is more efficacious than techniques designed to help children merely express their feelings" (Shelby 2000, 75).

CASE ILLUSTRATION

The authors work with young children and their families in both community mental health and private practice settings. We have great respect for the families who have shared their stories with us and wish to carefully safeguard their privacy. Therefore, this case illustration is not about any one family. Instead, "Jessie" and her family represent a composite of several children and families. The clinical issues presented, however, represent very real issues that families face and bring to treatment. In the case presented, all services, from intake to discharge, are provided in the family's home or in their community.

Jessie and Her Grandparents

Jessie is a 21-month-old girl of European descent, brought to treatment because of excessive tantruming. Jessie's grandparents report that Jessie tantrums (screams and drops to the floor) frequently throughout the day, with tantrums sometimes lasting longer than an hour. Some of Jessie's tantrums are predictable; for example, she will consistently tantrum and scream when she is strapped into her car seat. Most of her tantrums, however, seem to occur without provocation, and what upsets her some days does not appear to upset her on other days. Her grandparents report that Jessie appears anxious to them. She will insist on having everything where she left it, frequently moving objects on the table back to their original spots if they have been moved in her absence. She also insists that the cupboards be closed and will tantrum if they are left open. Finally, her grandparents report that Jessie seems "less lively" than she was as an infant. As an infant, they report, Jessie was quite engaging and social. Now, she does not seem particularly excited to play new games with them, to go to new places, or to explore new toys.

Jessie has lived with her paternal grandparents since her birth. Her parents' persistent drug use has made them inconsistent participants in Jessie's life. Despite Jessie's premature birth and likely in utero drug exposure, she met her early developmental milestones on time. Over the past year, Jessie's development seems to have slowed some, but she is still within the normal range in all areas except expressive language, which appears slightly delayed. Jessie does not sleep well and is a picky eater. She has not gained weight as expected over the past year.

When Jessie was 10 months old, her house caught fire (faulty wiring) and burned to the ground in the middle of the night. Her grandfather was able to rescue Jessie but unable to rescue her older sister, who had been asleep in a loft above Jessie's crib. Jessie's sister died in the fire. Jessie was "bright red" when she was removed from the fire, but was otherwise unharmed. Almost a year has passed since the fire.

Getting Started

The initial assessment with Jessie and her grandparents included both an evaluation of Jessie's symptoms and an appraisal of her functioning within her primary relationships (Zero to Three 2005). The play therapist turned to Jessie's grandparents for more information about the behaviors that have brought Jessie to treatment. They were most concerned with Jessie's tantrums, and secondarily concerned with her anxiety and lack of interest in people and things that once interested her. Although neither grandparent identified the fire as the cause of Jessie's behaviors, the play therapist was especially attuned to the effects of trauma on young children, and wondered if some of Jessie's anxious and withdrawing behaviors might be related to this. But first, the therapist attended to the grandparents' primary concerns. She asked Jessie's grandmother to track Jessie's tantrums more carefully. This tracking, as it turned out, opened the door to understanding Jessie's story.

In the first week of tracking, Jessie's grandmother noticed that her tantrums were not as random as previously thought. Grandma noted that, in addition to tantruming when she did not get her way (a typical tantrum trigger for toddlers), Jessie also tantrumed when her routine was changed and when Grandma was running water for dishes or running the bath. After discussing the significance of routines for children who are anxious, the play therapist and Grandma hypothesized about why running water might upset Jessie. When nothing came to Grandma's mind immediately, the therapist asked Grandma to talk more about the fire and the sights and sounds of that night. As Grandma talked about the firefighters, she wondered if the sound of running water might remind Jessie of the fire hoses from the fire. The next week, Grandma identified another tantrum trigger—the sound of fire sirens from the station a few blocks away, a sound that the adults had "tuned out" over the years. Grandma and the play therapist hypothesized that Jessie's tantrums were, at least in part, her response to sounds that reminded her of the fire hoses and sirens she heard on the night of the fire 11 months ago. Jessie appeared to be reacting to reminders of the trauma she experienced in the fire.

In addition to tracking symptoms, the play therapist was careful to assess these symptoms within a multi-disciplinary context. The therapist encouraged Jessie's grandparents to take her to a pediatrician to evaluate and track her weight. Once they have confirmed that Jessie's lack of weight gain is not caused by medical issues, they can work with the pediatrician to ensure that Jessie is getting proper nutrition. Next, Jessie's premature birth and exposure to toxins in utero puts her at risk for sensory integration difficulties, which can mimic anxiety symptoms. An evaluation with a trained OT indicated that Jessie's sensory processing is remarkably on target. Her symptoms do not appear to represent additional sensory concerns.

While seeking to understand Jessie's symptoms, the play therapist also sought to understand her functioning within her primary caregiving relationships. Observation suggested that Jessie feels safe in the presence of her grandparents. She references them when the play therapist arrives, and she seeks them out for help with new activities and for comfort. Both grandparents clearly enjoy Jessie, smiling at her frequently and responding with ease to her requests for help. They appear comfortable setting limits with her. Even so, the play therapist questioned if these relationships have been strained by Jessie's experience of the traumatic fire. Trauma can cause development to stall or regress, and Jessie's "less lively" behavior over the past year may be an indicator of this kind of a stall. Even though Jessie turns to her grandparents for safety and support (as an infant would), she is not utilizing them as a secure base from which to explore her environment (as would be expected of a toddler). Reestablishing this sense of security, then, is where the play therapist decided to start, knowing that further trauma treatment can only progress when this security is restored.

TREATING TRAUMA WITHIN RELATIONSHIP

Grandparents as a Secure Base

The relationship between the infant/toddler and the caregiver is central to EPT with young children. If the relationship is struggling, it becomes the focus of treatment; if the relationship is strong, it is used to facilitate treatment. In Jessie's case, it appeared that trauma had interrupted the progression of Jessie's development in relationship. In early sessions, play was used to pull Jessie back into engagement with her grandparents. Infant games, such as "this little piggy" and "itsy bitsy spider," created playful opportunities for touch and eye contact, typical nurturing experiences for infants. As Jessie was reminded of the joys she experienced in relationship, exploratory games such as "peek-a-boo" and "hide-and-seek" were introduced. These games pulled her back into exploring the world while tolerating separations, typical developmental tasks of the toddler. Reestablishing these capacities allowed Jessie to move into what happens next, to use play to make sense of her early trauma experience.

Grandparents as Cotherapists/Collaborators

The ongoing involvement of Jessie's grandparents in her therapy was grounded in several developmental needs. First, when addressing trauma in play therapy, the young child must feel safe within the context of a sensitive caregiving relationship. Whenever possible, the play therapist utilizes the caregiving relationship to bolster the child's sense of security in therapy. The involvement of the grandparents also provided a sense of continuity for Jessie. By observing how the therapist responded to behaviors and questions surrounding the trauma, the grandparents could respond similarly when questions or behaviors arise outside of the play therapy sessions. Developmentally, this is crucial. Jessie had not yet developed the ability to "hold in mind" the therapist. She would not store up her thoughts and her questions, to be asked conveniently during a weekly session. Recognizing the need for an "in-home" expert, the play therapist regularly discussed with the grandparents the effects of trauma on children Jessie's age and the role of play therapy in healing trauma. The grandparents wanted to help Jessie heal from such an ordeal, and this healing will in turn help them to heal.

Preparing Grandparents to Support Jessie

Before any of the above could take place, the grandparents needed to be ready to support Jessie in her therapeutic endeavors. A caregiver's psychological availability to an infant is a significant factor in assessing the severity of a trauma as experienced by the infant. The degree to which the caregiver can act as a buffer, help the infant understand the events, and help the infant cope notably mediates the infant's experience of the event (Zero to Three 2005). Understandably, Jessie's grandparents were also traumatized by the fire in their home that killed their other granddaughter and could have killed Jessie.

Early in treatment, the clinician made time to meet independently with the grandparents to assess their needs and the supports they had received thus far. She found that recognizing that the tantrum triggers were related to trauma helped Jessie's grandmother see the importance of addressing the trauma. Jessie's grandfather, however, initially resisted the idea that a child as young as Jessie could have any memories of the fire. The therapist also explored the grandparents' spiritual and cultural beliefs about death in general, about the death of a child, and about a parent's responsibility to care for and protect children. All of these beliefs will affect their understanding of the fire, and the understanding that they want Jessie to have. The goal of these discussions is not necessarily to change their belief, simply to make them explicit as having a role in how the grandparents interpret the events of their lives. In this discussion, Jessie's grandfather disclosed that he was struggling with his guilt and grief over not rescuing Jessie's sister. He was experiencing less joy and interest in his life, and this was clouding his interactions with Jessie. With this understanding, therapy focused on helping the grandfather grieve, as well as positively re-engage with his granddaughter.

Using Play to Make Sense of Trauma

When Jessie's relationship with her grandparents was back on its developmental trajectory, the play therapist turned to the trauma. After considering interventions that were developmentally in sync with Jessie's abilities, the therapist introduced toys that would encourage play about the fire: a dollhouse with people, a fire truck, and an ambulance. The introduction of these concrete cues into child-led play focused Jessie's attention on the issue at hand, without constraining her exploration of the materials or the event that was causing her continued distress (Shelby 2000). Ideally, the therapist would introduce life-size props for Jessie, but in this case, the therapist did not have such props and gambled on Jessie's developing representational abilities to make use of smaller props. The therapist initially used the props as though they were life-size, using the hose on the fire truck to "spray" Jessie and her grandparents with water, and encouraging Jessie to do the same. Jessie played along and eventually turned the hose on the house, where she reenacted the fire over and over again: the fire, the fire trucks arriving (sirens blaring), the firefighters turning the hoses on the house, and the ambulance leaving. Jessie played out the fire over and over again, each time taking a bit more control of the situation, gaining mastery. The therapist and grandparents narrated Jessie's play for her, adding a language component to an experience that occurred when Jessie was still preverbal. Drawing on earlier discussions with Jessie's grandparents about their beliefs surrounding the fire, the therapist narrated a story of fire and being afraid, then of protection and care and being safe together. The play therapist, also trained in using EMDR (Eye Movement Desensitization Reprocessing) with young children, utilized this intervention to help Jessie stay present in the play (for more information on the use of EMDR with very young children, see Lovett 1999; McGuinness 2001; Tinker and Wilson 1999). As Jessie started incorporating a dollhouse baby into her play, the therapist focused the narration on the baby.

Over time, Jessie's play became less emotionally charged, and her grand-parents reported fewer tantrums during the week. The therapist now shifted focus to the community. Grandma started desensitizing Jessie to the fire sirens, going on walks with Jessie down the block, closer and closer to the source of the sirens, the fire station. At the same time, the therapist contacted the fire station to ask for their help. With the grandparents' permission, the play therapist told the fire chief about Jessie, her early trauma, and her current fears. She asked for an opportunity to bring Jessie to the fire station to explore the fire trucks, and ultimately, to allow herself to be seat-belted into the fire truck. The fire chief and his crew were eager to support Jessie in this endeavor, and scheduled a morning "off" for the firehouse. Barring a multi-alarm fire, no calls would come into the firehouse during Jessie's visit.

On the morning of Jessie's visit, the fire station was quiet. Jessie brought her fire truck and the dollhouse baby, and she held them tightly as she and the therapist explored the station and the fire trucks, guided by the fire chief. The therapist was attuned to Jessie's anxiety and allowed Jessie to set the pace. When Jessie started to withdraw, the therapist supported her with soothing words and with EMDR. After a time, Jessie climbed into the cab of the fire truck. To the therapist's surprise, Jessie not only allowed herself to be seat-belted in, but also insisted on hitting the siren—repeatedly. Having mastered the siren, Jessie climbed down, and the therapist thought that they were ready to leave. As the therapist was thanking the fire chief, Jessie approached the back of the ambulance. She indicated that the back should be opened, and when this was done, she placed the dollhouse baby in the back. She then indicated that the doors should be closed. She played this scene several times: open the doors, put the baby in the back, close the doors, open the doors, take the baby out, put the baby back in, close the doors. Not sure what was happening, the play therapist narrated the events. Finally, Jessie had the doors closed and started to walk away. When the therapist reminded Jessie that the baby was still in the back of the ambulance, Jessie merely replied, "Baby stays."

Intended as a desensitization technique to address Jessie's fear of sirens and difficulties being belted in, the trip to the fire station appears to have provided Jessie with an opportunity for representational play more consistent with 21-month-old capacities—that is, the opportunity to play through the trauma using life-size "toys." With the life-size ambulance, Jessie was able to show clearly the final piece of her trauma experiences, the loss of her sister who ultimately went into the ambulance and "stayed."

Wrapping It Up

Following the trip to the fire station, the frequency and intensity of Jessie's tantrums decreased still further. Jessie's grandparents felt as though their granddaughter was back to her playful, engaging self. They also felt more confident in their ability to care for Jessie. They have joined a grandparents group, and are finding this to be a tremendous source of support both in raising Jessie and in grieving the loss of their other granddaughter. The therapist concluded with one last piece of information for the grandparents. Having already explained how trauma can affect young children, the therapist forecast for the grandparents that Jessie will likely bring up the trauma in the future, reexamining her understanding of the fire and the loss of her sister as she grows and is able to comprehend the event in different ways.

CONCLUSIONS

EPT provides mental health clinicians with a strong theoretical basis for mental health practice with infants, toddlers, and their families because of its emphasis on relationships, development, and the ecosystem. This chapter has provided an overview of key concepts and theories used in EPT, along with a case example of EPT used with a toddler and her family.

NOTE

1. Most of the content in the following paragraphs about representational play development is adapted from Ammen and Limberg (2005, 216–217).

REFERENCES

Ammen, S., and B. Limberg. 2005. Play therapy with preschoolers using the ecosystemic model. In *The handbook of training and practice in infant and preschool mental health*, ed. K. M. Finello, 207–232. San Francisco: Jossey Bass.

Barrera, I., and R. M. Corso. 2003. *Skilled dialogue: Strategies for responding to cultural diversity in early childhood*. Baltimore: Brookes.

Bowlby, J. 1982. *Attachment*. 2nd ed. New York: Basic.

———. 1988. *A secure base: Clinical applications of attachment theory*. London: Routledge.

Brazelton, T. B., and J. D. Sparrow. 2006. *Touchpoints: 0–3*. Rev. ed. New York: DaCapo/Perseus.

Davies, D. 2004. *Child development: A practitioner's guide*. 2nd ed. New York: Guilford.

Dicker, S., and E. Gordon. 2004. *Ensuring the healthy development of infants in foster care: A guide for judges, advocates, and child welfare professionals*. Washington, DC: Zero to Three.

Drewes, A. A. 2001. Developmental considerations in play and play therapy with traumatized children. In *School-based play therapy*, ed. A. A. Drewes, L. J. Carey, and C. E. Schaefer, 297–314. New York: Wiley.

Erickson, M. F., and K. Kurz-Riemer. 1999. *Infants, toddlers, and families: A framework for support and intervention.* New York: Guilford.

Fraiberg, S., ed. 1980. *Clinical studies in infant mental health: The first year of life.* New York: Basic.

Fraiberg, S., E. Adelson, and V. Shapiro. 1980. Ghosts in the nursery. In *Clinical studies in infant mental health: The first year of life,* ed. S. Fraiberg, 164–197. New York: Basic.

Gaensbauer, T. J. 2004. Traumatized young children: Assessment and treatment process. In *Young children and trauma: Intervention and treatment,* ed. J. D. Osofsky, 194–216. New York: Guilford.

Heffron, M. C. 2000. Clarifying concepts of infant mental health: Promotion, relationship-based preventive intervention, and treatment. *Infants and Young Children* 12 (4): 14–21.

———. 2005. Reflective supervision in infant, toddler, and preschool work. In *The handbook of training and practice in infant and preschool mental health,* ed. K. M. Finello, 114–136. San Francisco: Jossey Bass.

Howe, D. 2005. *Child abuse and neglect: Attachment, development, and intervention.* New York: Palgrave Macmillan.

James, B. 1989. *Treating traumatized children: New insights and creative interventions.* Lexington, MA: Lexington.

Karen, R. 1994. *First relationships and how they shape our capacity to love.* New York: Oxford University Press.

Lieberman, A. F., and K. Knorr. 2007. The impact of trauma: A developmental framework for infancy and early childhood. *Psychiatric Annals* 37 (6): 416–422.

Lieberman, A. F., E. Padrón, P. Van Horn, and W. W. Harris. 2005. Angels in the nursery: The intergenerational transmission of benevolent parental influences. *Infant Mental Health Journal* 26 (6): 504–520.

Lieberman, A. F., and P. Van Horn. 2004. Assessment and treatment of young children exposed to traumatic events. In *Young children and trauma: Intervention and treatment,* ed. J. D. Osofsky, 111–138. New York: Guilford.

Lovett, J. 1999. *Small wonders: Healing childhood trauma with EMDR.* New York: Free Press.

Madsen, W. C. 2007. *Collaborative therapy with multi-stressed families.* 2nd ed. New York: Guilford.

Maury, E. H., and M. Monzon-Kong. 2002. Topic 1: Strength-based interventions. In *Learning Lab B Curriculum for Infant-Preschool Providers.* Sacramento, CA: WestEd.

McDonough, S. C. 2000. Interaction guidance: An approach for difficult-to-engage families. In *Handbook of infant mental health.* 2nd ed. Ed. C. H. Zeanah Jr., 485–493. New York: Guilford.

———. 2004. Interaction guidance: Promoting and nurturing the caregiving relationship. In *Treating parent-infant relationship problems: Strategies for intervention,* ed. A. J. Sameroff, S. C. McDonough, and K. L. Rosenblum, 79–96. New York: Guilford.

McGuinness, V. 2001. *Integrating play therapy and EMDR with children.* Colorado Springs, CO: First Books Library.

Meléndez, L. 2005. Parental beliefs and practices around early self-regulation: The impact of culture and immigration. *Infants and Young Children* 8 (2): 136–146.

O'Connor, K. J. 1997. Ecosystemic Play Therapy. In *Play therapy theory and practice: A comparative presentation,* ed. K. J. O'Connor and L. M. Braverman, 234–284. New York: Wiley.

———. 2000. *Play therapy primer.* 2nd ed. New York: Wiley.

O'Connor, K. J., and S. Ammen. 1997. *Play therapy treatment planning and interventions: The ecosystemic model and workbook.* San Diego: Academic.

O'Connor, K. J., and L. M. Braverman, eds. 1997. *Play therapy theory and practice: A comparative presentation.* New York: Wiley.

Parlakian, R. 2001. *Look, listen, and learn: Reflective supervision and relationship-based work.* Washington, DC: Zero to Three.

Pawl, J. R., and M. St. John. 1998. *How you are is as important as what you do in making a difference for infants, toddlers, and families.* Washington, DC: Zero to Three.

Roggman, L. A., L. Boyce, and L. Newland. 2000. Assessing mother-infant interaction in play. In *Play diagnosis and assessment.* 2nd ed. Ed. K. Gitlin-Weiner, A. Sandgrund, and C. Schaefer, 303–339. New York: Wiley.

Sameroff, A. J., and B. H. Fiese. 2000. Models of development and developmental risk. In *Handbook of infant mental health.* 2nd ed. Ed. C. H. Zeenah Jr. , 3–19. New York: Guilford.

Shelby, J. S. 2000. Brief therapy with traumatized children: A developmental perspective. In *Short-term play therapy for children,* ed. H. G. Kaduson and C. E. Schaefer, 69–104. New York: Guilford.

Shonkoff, J. P., and D. A. Phillips, eds. 2000. *From neurons to neighborhoods: The science of early childhood development.* Washington, DC: National Academy of Sciences.

Stern, D. 1977. *The first relationship.* Cambridge, MA: Harvard University Press.

Sumner, G., and A. Spietz, eds. 1994. *NCAST caregiver/parent–child interaction feeding manual.* Seattle: NCAST Publications.

Tinker, R. H., and S. A. Wilson. 1999. *Through the eyes of a child: EMDR with children.* New York: Norton.

Trawick-Smith, J. 2005. *Early childhood development: A multicultural perspective.* Rev. ed. Upper Saddle River, NJ: Prentice Hall.

Weatherston, D. J. 2005. Returning the treasure to babies: An introduction to infant mental health services and training. In *The handbook of training and practice in infant and preschool mental health,* ed. K. M. Finello, 3–30. San Francisco: Jossey-Bass.

Westby, C. 2000. A scale for assessing development of children's play. In *Play diagnosis and assessment.* 2nd ed. Ed. K. Gitlin-Weiner, A. Sandgrund, and C. Schaefer, 15–57. New York: Wiley.

Weston, D. R., B. Ivins, M. C. Heffron, and N. Sweet. 1997. Formulating the centrality of relationships in early intervention: An organizational perspective. *Infants and Young Children* 9 (3): 1–12.

Williamson, G. G., and M. E. Anzalone. 2001. *Sensory integration and self-regulation in infants and toddlers: Helping very young children interact with their environment.* Washington, DC: Zero to Three.

Wright, B. 1992. Treatment of infants and their families. In *Countertransference in psychotherapy with children and adolescents*, ed. J. R. Brandell, 127–139. Northvale, NJ: Jason Aronson.

Zero to Three. 2005. *Diagnostic classification of mental health and developmental disorders of infancy and early childhood (DC: 0–3R).* Rev. ed. Washington, DC: Zero to Three.

6

Parent-Child Attunement Therapy for Toddlers: A Behaviorally Oriented, Play-Based Parent Training Model

Stefan C. Dombrowski, Susan G. Timmer, and Nancy Zebell

BASIC RATIONALE AND THEORY

Basic Rationale

Toddlerhood is a critical period that lays the foundation for later development. It is important for fostering attachment security, solidifying the relationship between caregivers and children, and developing cognitive and language skills (Cicchetti and Toth 1995). Toddlerhood also requires a new set of developmental tasks that focus on self-development (Cole 1990), emotion regulation (Smetana et al. 1999) and social representational models (Toth et al. 1997).

Certain types of dysfunctional caregiver-toddler relationship patterns can contribute to less than optimal social-emotional development and a variety of pathological symptoms that might elicit need for prevention or intervention. Examples include coercive interactional styles, abusive caregiving, exposure to domestic violence, and neglectful parenting. Such dysfunctional relationship patterns have the potential to alter optimal social-emotional development and contribute to symptoms such as extreme temper tantrums, reduced frustration tolerance, and somatic complaints (Lieberman 2004; Osofsky 2005). If the caregiver-toddler attachment relationship is jeopardized, then this inability or difficulty to establish or maintain a sense of attachment security with caregivers might manifest in internalizing behaviors (e.g., separation anxiety, stranger anxiety, social withdrawal, and a restricted range of affect; Cicchetti 1989; Osofsky 1995; Pynoos 1990; Scheeringa and Gaensbauer 2000). Or, such difficulties could manifest in externalizing behaviors including aggression, noncompliance, and controlling behavior

(Cicchetti 1989; Osofsky 1995; Pynoos 1990; Scheeringa and Gaensbauer 2000).

Accordingly, there is significant need for empirically supported therapeutic approaches that address these difficult behaviors. Parent-Child Attunement Therapy (PCAT) is a promising behaviorally based, play therapeutic modality that is suitable for this purpose (Dombrowski, Timmer, Blacker, and Urquiza 2005). PCAT is based upon the rich clinical and empirical tradition of Parent-Child Interaction Therapy (PCIT), which has been documented in preschool and early elementary school children to improve behavioral adjustment and establish a stronger bond between caregivers and children (Herschell and Mc-Neil 2005). PCAT has a sound theoretical basis, predicated to a large degree upon the theoretical perspective of PCIT. As a result, PCAT promises to be a viable intervention for toddlers (age 12 to 36 months) with externalizing problems and attachment difficulties. There also is recognition of the need for additional research on the effectiveness of PCAT.

PCAT represents an adaptation of Parent-Child Interaction Therapy (PCIT) and is guided by a similar theoretical approach and clinical tradition, appropriately modified for the toddler stage of development (Dombrowski et al. 2005; Eyberg 1988; Hembree-Kigin and McNeil 1995). Like PCIT, PCAT focuses on enhancing the caregiver-child relationship and improving the toddler's behavior through in vivo parent-coaching sessions. This is accomplished by increasing caregivers' attention to children's positive and appropriate behavior, decreasing attention to inappropriate behavior, and instructing parents on how to follow their children's lead in play in a nondirective fashion (Dombrowski and Timmer 2001; Paravicini 2000; Paravicini, Urquiza, and Blacker 2000). Because the goals of PCAT involve consistent attention to children's appropriate behavior, caregivers become more accessible and the behavior of both the caregivers and the toddlers becomes more predictable. Since inconsistent responsiveness and a lack of positive interactions characterize family contexts that promote externalizing behaviors in children (Cerezo and D'Ocon 1999; Wolfe 1987), we argue that PCAT is well suited for toddlers who display externalizing behaviors and who might possibly suffer attachment difficulties.

Basic Theory

Because PCAT represents an adaptation of PCIT, much of the theory underlying PCIT also is applicable for PCAT. Like PCIT, PCAT is influenced by an amalgam of different theories, including developmental, social learning, behavioral, and traditional play therapy (Eyberg 1988). The progenitor of PCIT, Sheila Eyberg, was influenced in large measure by the tenets of Dr. Constance Hanf (1968, 1969), who developed a two-stage operant model for modifying the oppositional behavior of youngsters. The first stage entailed teaching the technique of differential reinforcement, whereby caregivers were taught to attend to their children's positive behaviors and to ignore all undesirable behaviors. The second stage entailed teaching parents to proffer clear directions, consistently praise compliance with parental requests, and use time-out procedures for noncompliance.

PCAT is different from PCIT in that less emphasis is placed upon the use of the time-out procedure, which was thought to be developmentally inappropriate at certain stages. Instead, parents are taught to use redirection and ignoring of behavior, which were thought to be sufficient to manage most difficult behaviors and were more developmentally appropriate for younger toddlers. Consistent with Hanf's approach, PCAT uses in vivo therapy, coaching parents and children together directly in a live session. When creating PCIT, Eyberg also infused traditional play approaches within an operant model and understood the importance of predicating both upon a solid developmental framework. In so doing, PCAT, like PCIT, places emphasis on teaching parents the nondirective play (e.g., Axline 1947) therapy skills of following the toddler's lead, describing the toddler's play activities, praising, imitating and reflecting verbal and nonverbal behavior, and displaying high levels of enthusiasm. In addition, PCAT is predicated upon the developmental psychology literature, particularly that of Mary Ainsworth (1969) and Diana Baumrind (1968), and attempts to foster the establishment of a nurturing environment via behavioral mechanisms. It also recognizes that a developmental perspective is an important component of effective treatment and that many of the caregiver-child problems arise out of a developmental need on the part of the child to assert independence and free himself or herself from inappropriate developmental expectations held by the parent (Hembree-Kigin and McNeil 1995).

Though not expressly discussed in Hembree-Kigin and McNeil's (1995) widely referenced book on PCIT, PCAT, like PCIT, draws upon social learning theory, and specifically the work of Patterson's (1982) coercive interaction theory. Patterson's theory posits that children's behavior problems can be fostered and subsequently maintained by problematic parent-child interactions via a coercive interactional cycle. This cycle tends to involve habitual, aversive, and escalating negative interactions that are maintained via negative reinforcement and are representative of a power struggle in the relationship between caregiver and child.

Developmental Considerations Regarding
Use of Behavior Management

When deciding which behavior management strategies to use with younger children, it is important to consider their developmental phase and cognitive capabilities. Table 6.1 describes different strategies taught in

Table 6.1. Developmental Considerations in the Use of Behavior Management with Young Children

Behavior Management Strategy	Cognitive Prerequisites	Developmental Considerations
Childproofing	—	Removing dangerous or treasured objects from the reach or vision of the child protects the child, removes a source of worry and/or annoyance from the relationship, and facilitates positive child behavior.
Redirecting (3 months +)	• Child must be able to adjust behavior in response to external events and stimuli. • As child becomes able to recall the memory of the disallowed pleasurable activity, parent will need to accompany redirecting with heightened enthusiasm, and possibly a reasoned explanation for the change in activities.	Allows the parent to effectively maintain a stable and positive level of emotional arousal, forestalling the need for more coercive management strategies.
Direct Commands (9–12 months +)	• Child must be able to respond to warning signals ("Hot! Don't touch!"), showing the ability to comply with simple commands. • Child must understand the words and syntax the caregiver uses when giving the command (e.g., if the child does not know "red" from "blue," he or she will not be able to identify a red bag and take it to the caregiver).	Children will self-initiate inhibitive behavior (i.e., parents' "Don't" commands like "No") before they self-initiate "Do" commands. Most situations requiring children to comply are situational (e.g., "Please wash your hands"), depend on the demands of the moment, and do not assume the child will know what to do without parental guidance. To maximize compliance, commands should be stated simply and positively. The more complex the command, the greater the load on memory capacity, and the greater the chance of noncompliance.

Behavior Management Strategy	Cognitive Prerequisites	Developmental Considerations
Establishing Rules (9–12 months +)	• Some memory capacity is essential for remembering prohibited and allowed behaviors. • Child must show at least rudimentary self-control or impulse control.	Complying with "Don't" rules concerning safety emerges early, and children are generally compliant with these rules. Establishing rules helps to organize both parents' and children's beliefs and expectations for appropriate social behavior.
Active Ignore/ Selective Attention (12–18 months +)	• Child must show at least rudimentary self-control or impulse control. • Child must value attention from an adult more than the pleasure of performing a disallowed task. • Child must recognize the association between losing the adult's attention and the inhibition of the prohibited act.	This strategy is effective if the reinforcing value of caregiver attention is greater than the value of the immediate pleasure of doing the disallowed activity. Selective attention should not be used if the activity is dangerous or highly stimulating.
Two Choices Time-Out Removal of Privileges (30 months +)	• Child must be able to symbolically represent two competing activities and outcomes, and recognize that he or she must choose one option. • If child cannot self-soothe, time-outs should not be used. • To effectively use the strategy of removing privileges, child must be able to symbolically represent the choices and the effect of losing a privilege. Child also must associate the inhibition of the undesirable behavior with retaining the privilege.	Parents may use the two-choice strategy with children who are not cognitively mature enough, and it may appear as though they are making a choice when they are simply complying with the first request. Time-outs are most effective as a way of removing a child from a highly arousing but undesirable activity, giving the child time to calm down. At the same time, this strategy is a punishment (removal of the privilege of playing at that moment) and should not be relied upon as a behavior management strategy.

PCAT, the ages at which they can be considered for use, and their cognitive prerequisites. We briefly review these strategies below.

The first two strategies listed in table 6.1, childproofing and redirecting, do not have any cognitive prerequisites but have fundamental neurological requirements. Infants' neurophysiology must be organized to a level that allows the child to perceive and respond to environmental input. Their behavior must reflect responses to changing events and stimuli in the environment. It is possible to control the child's environment (i.e., childproof) at any age, although this is most important when children begin to grab objects (depth perception and prehensile strength have matured) and have some mobility. At this point, removing dangerous or precious objects from the infant's reach can help minimize both parents' and children's anger and frustration. Similarly, when infants can adjust their behavior to respond to external events and stimuli (e.g., show interest in toys dangling in front of them), they can be distracted or "redirected" from a less desirable to a more desirable activity. Infants have the cognitive capacity to be redirected beginning at approximately three months of age (Kopp 1982). This strategy of substituting a positive stimulus with an equally attractive positive stimulus is an effective way of maintaining a steady level of positive arousal.

Between approximately 9 and 12 months of age, infants begin to be able to respond to warnings and prohibitions as they occur in the moment (Kopp 1982). When children are able to respond appropriately to warnings (e.g., "Hot!" "Don't touch!"), this demonstrates the development of internal self-control. When parents observe their children's ability to comply with simple rules and commands, they can use direct commands to manage their infants' and toddlers' behavior, but should be aware that memory capability and receptive language ability constrain the degree to which these are useful tools for the parent. For example, an infant asked to bring a red book might bring a blue book (not distinguishing between red and blue) or any object that happened to be within reach (not understanding what a "book" is). Additionally, simple and understandable commands must also be able to be performed by the very young child. For example, infants 9 to 12 months generally are not able to control their negative affect without help from caregivers. Hence, the direct command "Don't cry" could not be expected to yield compliance.

Research has shown that infants begin to initiate self-inhibitive behavior between 12 and 18 months (e.g., Kochanska, Coy, and Murray 2001), controlling their behavior and impulses in accordance with caregivers' rules and wishes. The motivation to accede to caregivers' wishes is a complex phenomenon, believed to be related to the quality of the parent-child relationship (Kochanska and Aksan 1995). Cognitively, infants who are able to control impulses to touch or play with forbidden objects show a memory capacity sufficient to remember the prohibitions, an awareness of what behavior is acceptable (or not) to the caregiver, and an ability to evaluate the consequences of compliance with caregivers' expectations. With these cognitive abilities in place, parents may effectively use the "Active Ignore" (i.e., selective attention) to eliminate undesirable behavior. The "Active Ignore" is most effectively used when children understand that this is a strategy parents use when they are trying to get their children to engage in more positive behavior, although this is not essential. The parent uses a cue (e.g., "When Sammy plays gently with the toys, then I can play with him") and plays alone, not interacting with the child while he or she is behaving negatively. When the child begins to play appropriately, the parent draws attention to the fact that the child is now playing appropriately, so they can play together again. The parent is encouraged to use a high level of enthusiasm at this point, in order to magnify the difference between the parent's ignore and engagement. This behavior management strategy makes few demands on infants' cognitive systems. The infant must have a sense of social awareness and a recognition of "ignoring" (this emerges as early as three months, according to research using Tronick's "Still-Face" paradigm (e.g., Gusella, Muir, and Tronick 1988). They must also have an understanding of the effects of their behavior on their environment, what behavior should be stopped, how to perform the desirable behavior, and the ability to control the impulse to do the undesirable behavior. While it is possible to use the "Active Ignore" with infants of about 12 months of age, the effectiveness of this strategy depends on the caregivers' ability to support the infant's positive behavior and help regulate her or his physical arousal.

The behavior management strategy used in PCAT requiring the most cognitive maturity is the Two Choices/Time-Out/Removal of Privileges sequence. In this sequence, parents initially respond to undesirable behavior by giving the child two choices: perform a desirable behavior or suffer a consequence (a time-out or a removal of some privilege). In order to solve the two-choice problem, children must be able to recall an image of themselves engaged in each of these options and evaluate their desirability. Recall memory and representational thinking are generally thought to emerge at about 18 months of age. The evaluation of the desirability of the two options requires slightly more cognitive capacity. Between the ages of 18 and 24 months, children begin to understand social rules (Gralinski and Kopp 1993), remember the associated positive and negative emotions of different situations (Wellman and Woolley 1990), and make the connection between the associated affect of behaviors (e.g., time-outs) and decisions to engage in those behaviors (Repacholi and Gopnik 1997). These cognitive skills underlie the ability to understand the two-choice sequence. However, understanding the elements of the two-choice sequence and actually negotiating it successfully (e.g., deciding to stop throwing Legos and play with them on the table) are very different. Children's self-control at this age has been noted as limited, and their compliance closely tied to the immediate pleasure of the action more than the need to follow rules (Kopp 1989). For example, when given a choice to play gently with a toy or have it taken away, a child may be able to play gently for a few minutes but be unable to sustain this less stimulating activity. At young ages, when a toddler chooses the desired activity (e.g., playing gently), the caregiver may also need to provide attention and enthusiasm in order to compensate for giving up the undesirable activity.

The usefulness for the toddler of taking a time-out is proportional to the limitations of his or her memory, self-control, and emotional regulation. In a perfect world, the time-out removes the child from a source of negative emotional arousal or great temptation and allows the child to become calm. It also makes it difficult for the child to obtain attention from caregivers or other children. In reality, young children often scream in protest at being removed from a highly arousing (but forbidden) activity, and the process of enforcing time-out is as much a source of negative physical arousal as the original prohibited activity. As a general rule, caregivers should not be encouraged to use time-out as a behavior strategy if other strategies will work (e.g., redirection, active ignore, removal of privilege). Also, if children cannot negotiate the two-choice sequence, they should not be put in time-out. Children from 30 to 36 months should be able to successfully negotiate time-outs: they should understand that they have broken a rule or done something that has a consequence of a time-out (e.g., been defiant, hit someone), show effortful control—that is, the ability to control a dominant (prohibited) response on their own and perform a subdominant one (e.g., Putnam, Gartstein, and Rothbart 2006) by discontinuing the prohibited behavior, sustaining an unstimulating activity (e.g., sitting in a time-out chair) for a specified time period (Kochanska, Coy, and Murray 2001), and again show effortful control by complying or otherwise behaving appropriately upon release from a time-out. Younger children or cognitively delayed children who are placed in time-out may be able to perform the time-out sequence with their caregivers' support, but they are not likely to internalize the lessons that are meant to be learned.

PLAY INTERVENTION PROCEDURES

PCAT has been discussed as effective in increasing positive caregiver-toddler interactions, enhancing the parent-toddler relationship, reducing parenting stress, and decreasing dysfunctional parent-child relationship patterns (Dombrowski et al. 2005). PCAT alters particular PCIT techniques to be more developmentally appropriate for children younger than 30 months of age. (A summary of the similarities and differences from PCIT is provided

Table 6.2.   Comparison of PCAT and PCIT

Similarities	Unique to PCAT
1. Initial coaching/training sessions	1. Simpler, more developmentally appropriate language
2. Similar technology (e.g., remote hearing device, two-way mirror)	2. Reduced session length (30 to 45 minutes)
3. Collection of data	3. Greater emphasis on parent enthusiasm, including nonverbal indicators of approval (e.g., clapping)
4. Avoidance of criticism, commands, and threats	4. Using behavior management strategies appropriate for the level of the child's cognitive abilities
5. Increased praise, reflections, and descriptions	5. Flexibility to deal with diaper soiling
6. Limiting of questions	6. Fatigue of toddler and caregiver
7. Daily homework assignment (i.e., practice of PCAT skills)	7. Greater emphasis on increasing positive touching (e.g., hugs)
8. Emphasis on nondirective play	8. Developmentally younger toys

in table 6.2.) To attain this goal, PCAT offers a structured, individualized, behavioral, yet manualized approach.

Like PCIT, PCAT has a strong assessment component, requiring the collection of observational data on the quality of caregiver-toddler interactions and information about the nature and severity of the toddler's behavior problems and caregiver's stress pre (i.e., baseline) and post intervention. Baseline data are collected during the initial clinical interview. At this time the caregiver completes standardized assessments (e.g., child behavior problems, parenting stress, parental psychological symptoms) and participates in a 15-minute, semistructured play with the child. The caregiver-child play is observed by the therapist and videotaped for later review. After the initial assessment, the caregiver is introduced to the mechanics and rationale of PCAT in a didactic training session. During this session, the caregiver and toddler are instructed in the mechanics of PCAT and the caregiver is provided with a rationale for practicing concepts. The rationale is tailored to the specific needs the caregiver described, and to the strengths and concerns the therapist observed in the semistructured play.

Following this didactic session, the caregiver is taught Child Directed Interaction (CDI) skills (e.g., how to praise the toddler for engaging in appropriate behavior; how to follow the toddler's lead in play). These are similar to those taught in PCIT, but adjusted slightly to be more developmentally appropriate for toddlers. For example, PCAT uses nondirective types of verbalizations and communication (e.g., appropriately praising, describing, and reflecting the toddler's behavior using simple words, short sentences, and a high degree of enthusiasm), but makes less use of "reflecting" the child's speech as a tool for enhancing the caregiver-child relationship, since toddlers have little speech.

In PCAT, the therapist coaches parents as they play with their children, using the parent as the primary agent of therapeutic change. The therapist stands in an observation room on the other side of a two-way mirror from the dyad, communicating with the caregiver via a remote hearing device. The therapist instructs and models for caregivers such skills as how to differentially reinforce toddlers for appropriate behaviors (e.g., enthusiastic praise after putting pegs in a hole; ignoring when the toddler displays temper outbursts), and how to move from trying to control their toddler's play to describing the play in a way that conveys interest in the toddler's activity. During initial sessions, the therapist asks the caregiver to repeat almost verbatim. The therapist models both the verbal (e.g., "Good job playing gently with the truck") and nonverbal (e.g., giving the toddler a hug after putting the toys away) aspects of communication. As treatment progresses, the therapist gradually encourages the caregiver to become more independent by furnishing more general instructions (e.g., "Go ahead and describe what Henry is doing") or prompting the caregiver ("Henry is really playing gently with the truck"). This practice is designed to increase the amount of initiative the parent takes in interactions with the toddler and to reduce the parent's dependence on the therapist. In addition to providing coaching on styles of interaction, the therapist also provides information about children's general psychological and behavioral development, and the specific caregiver behaviors that seem to have the greatest impact on the child's development.

In each PCAT session, the therapist coaches and models verbalization patterns and behavioral techniques designed to improve caregiver-toddler relationships and decrease the toddler's behavior problems. The therapist tries to show caregivers that praise and positive attention increase their children's appropriate behaviors. Similarly, caregivers learn that their attention is sufficiently powerful that ignoring inappropriate behavior and redirecting the toddler toward a more appropriate behavior is often enough to forestall tantrums. Caregivers are also taught to minimize the use of questions and commands. When commands are necessary, caregivers are taught to keep them simple, direct, and positively stated. Criticism and threats are strongly discouraged, since these verbalizations almost always lead to a downward-spiraling cycle of negative interactions.

Caregivers are taught and coached to implement strategies that increase the power of their positive attention to shape behavior. This is an important goal of PCAT. Caregivers are taught to describe the toddler's play in a way that conveys interest in, rather than control of, the toddler's activity. For example, caregivers are taught to describe what the toddler is doing and how to imitate, reflect, and elaborate the toddler's own *appropriate* verbalizations or actions. Additionally, the caregiver is taught to use simple, developmentally appropriate language, a high level of enthusiasm, and nonverbal methods of conveying approval (e.g., "Great job!" stated enthusiastically, followed by hand clapping).

Caregivers are also taught to minimize the use of verbalizations that require a behavioral or verbal response from the child, such as questions and commands. When parents use these kinds of verbalizations, they expect the child to respond, and if the child does not respond they are more likely to escalate the strength of their demands to obtain recognition of their bid for attention. Bousha and Twentyman (1984) indicate that excessive parental control during playtime is a characteristic of abusive mother-child dyads. This coercive style of interaction may evoke in the child resistance to complying with caregiver commands (Kochanska and Aksan 1995). This is the beginning of a cycle that Patterson (1982) labels a coercive process, in which the child's opposition and defiance subsequently elicits a more coercive response from the parent in an attempt to obtain compliance. This parental response is typically met by an angrier, more defiant response from the child. Thus the interaction continues to escalate on both sides until either the parent or the child gives in. Once this pattern is established in a dyad's behavioral repertoire, it may be difficult for either parent or child to enter into any interaction without thinking that it may decay into a coercive exchange, thus impeding the development of a healthy, secure parent-child relationship.

Instead of using coercive control to manage the toddler's behavior, caregivers are taught to ignore mildly inappropriate behavior or redirect inappropriate behavior toward more appropriate and praiseworthy activity. For instance, the caregiver might remove a dangerous toy (e.g., a sharp pencil) from the toddler's hands and provide the child with a functionally similar toy (e.g., a crayon). Or, for example, the caregiver might physically redirect a child if the toddler attempts to climb on top of the table. In this example, the caregiver would be instructed to return the toddler to the play location, use enthusiasm to draw the toddler's attention to a different (less dangerous) activity, and possibly move the chair in a way that makes the table less accessible.

Therapists give caregivers many reasons for changing their well-established patterns of interaction with their toddlers. They teach caregivers about normal toddler behavior and show how positive PCAT strategies support healthy cognitive development. They teach caregivers about their children's cues and signals, and how PCAT strategies help to keep them calm (i.e., emotionally regulated) and happy. And they show caregivers how PCAT strategies will help reduce their toddlers' problem behaviors and help them manage future problems.

Structure of PCAT Sessions

Because younger toddlers tire easily (and caregivers of younger toddlers tire easily), PCAT sessions are often 15 to 30 minutes shorter than PCIT sessions, lasting only 30 to 45 minutes. Children sit at a table with their parents in PCIT sessions. Because younger toddlers have difficulty sitting at a table for extended periods of time, PCAT therapists give parents the choice to conduct sessions either on the floor, allowing the toddler to move around the room, or at a table. Some therapists move the table and chairs out of the room, and lay down a blanket to encourage (but not require) the play to take place in a specific area of the therapy room. This strategy allows the toddler to explore the environment, and removes the inevitable and unprofitable struggle between a caregiver and toddler.

The following is an excerpt of a PCAT coaching session:

[Caregiver and toddler are sitting on the floor while the toddler plays with a red fire truck.]

Toddler: Mee, mee, mee, mee [as he rolls the red fire truck].

Therapist: Tell Maxwell, "Maxwell, you're making the sound of the fire truck."

Caregiver: Maxwell, you're making the sound of the fire truck [reflecting toddler's verbalizations].

Therapist: Great—By reflecting Maxwell's verbalization you are showing him that you are interested in how he is playing.

Toddler: Uck . . . uck [attempting to say "truck"].

Therapist: Say, "Yes. You're playing with a red fire truck" [therapist uses a lot of enthusiasm].

Caregiver: Yes! You're playing with a red fire truck! [reflecting and elaborating on Maxwell's verbalizations and describing his behavior].

Therapist: Great enthusiasm and reflecting. Again, your reflections show interest in what he is doing by restating what he says, and you also help to support his language development.

Toddler: [Pushes truck away and goes over to bookshelf and tries to climb up on shelf.] Up!! Up!!!

Therapist: Ignore this and redirect him. Get the race car and have a lot of fun rolling it on the floor. Maybe make some noise as you roll it.

Caregiver: Vroom, vroom, vroom! [rolling the race car on the floor]. Errrrkkkk . . . [turning the car around to come back].

[Maxwell focuses his interest on the race car and forgets about climbing.]

Therapist: Notice how Maxwell forgot about climbing and came over to you to play with the race car when you made that fun. Ignoring and redirecting is a great way to get him to stop doing something without getting into a struggle with him.

Therapist: Tell Maxwell that you really like playing with him and give him a pat on his back.

Caregiver: Max, this is *so* fun playing with you! [pats Maxwell on his back].

Therapist: Excellent praise. Maxwell smiled when you patted him on the back. Your attention is so important to him, and will help to make him want to please you.

This example of PCAT coaching tried to convey a sense of the range of information the therapist can give the caregiver, although normally the therapist would not talk quite so much after every parent verbalization. In this example, the therapist labeled and praised the caregiver's appropriate verbalizations (e.g., "Excellent praise"), gave rationales for the therapist's directions in terms of their positive effect on the relationship with the child, their connection with cognitive development, and their use in behavior management.

EMPIRICAL SUPPORT

Evidence Supporting PCIT

Since PCAT is a relatively new, yet very promising, therapeutic modality for improving the behavior of toddlers, there is presently a dearth of available peer-reviewed empirical literature attesting to its effectiveness. Accordingly, our review is broader in scope and examines the effectiveness of PCIT, from which PCAT was derived. Since PCAT uses some of the same approaches as PCIT, the empirical literature regarding PCIT may have some parallels for PCAT.

There have been numerous studies demonstrating the efficacy and effectiveness of PCIT for reducing child behavior problems. Schuhmann and her colleagues (1998) published the first results of a study of the efficacy of PCIT, randomly assigning 64 clinic-referred 3- to 7-year-old children either to PCIT or a wait list. Results showed significant increases in positive parent verbalizations (e.g., praise), decreases in negative verbalizations (e.g., critical statements), and clinically significant improvements in parents' assessments of their children's behavior problems and their own role-related stress. This study also demonstrated that these treatment effects were stable four months after completing PCIT (Schuhmann et al. 1998). A study of long-term treatment maintenance was performed subsequently, examining the maintenance of treatment effects three to six years after completing treatment (Hood and Eyberg 2003). This study included 23 of the families from the original study and found stable treatment effects on children's behavior. Chaffin and colleagues (2004) examined the efficacy of PCIT for a population of 110 physically abusive parents and their 4- to 12-year-old children randomly assigned to PCIT, PCIT plus individualized services targeting parent problems (e.g., depression, marital problems, substance abuse), or a standard community group. They found that participation in PCIT, compared to the community treatment group, reduced the likelihood that a parent had an allegation of physical abuse within 850 days of beginning treatment. They found no added benefit of extra, individualized services to the efficacy of PCIT. In 2004, Nixon, Sweeney, Erickson, and Touyz reported the results of their comparison of one- to two-year post-treatment outcomes for 54 preschoolers, randomly assigned to standard PCIT, an abbreviated form of PCIT, or a wait list control group. Nixon et al. (2004) found clinically significant decreases in child behavior problems and parent role-related stress, increases in parent positive verbalizations and child compliance, and decreases in parent commands. While these studies provide evidence for the efficacy and robustness of PCIT, none included children younger than three years in their samples.

Studies using performance outcome information from PCIT participants in a community-based mental health setting have shown the effectiveness of PCIT for children in the two- to eight-year age range. One study explored the effectiveness of PCIT for maltreated children, using a sample of 136 two- to eight-year-old children with and without a history of maltreatment (Timmer et al. 2005). A second study explored the effectiveness of PCIT for children when participating with non-relative foster parents compared with non-maltreating biological parents, using 173 two- to eight-year-old children (Timmer, Urquiza, and Zebell 2006). In both of these studies, parents reported significant reductions in their own psychological distress and role-related stress, and in child behavior problems.

A study investigating the generalization of PCIT outcomes to the school setting (McNeil et al. 1991) included 30 two- to seven-year-olds in their sample, assigning them to one of three groups: treatment group (with behavior problems), control group with no behavior problems, and a behavior-problem control group. An examination of their findings revealed improvements in observed classroom comportment (e.g., appropriate, compliant, and on-task behaviors) of children in the treatment group from pre- to posttreatment, and decreases in teachers' reports of behavior problems. These results suggest that the positive effects of participating in PCIT with parents in the clinic also extend to school settings.

A study examining the stability of the McNeil et al. (1991) findings collected observational and teacher reports 12 to 18 months after the treatment group (N=10) completed PCIT (Funderburk et al. 1998). This study showed some decay in behavior problems in the classroom, with ratings reverting to pretreatment levels. However, children's improved compliance with teachers' directives was stable from posttreatment to the follow-up assessment. While the effectiveness studies have included two-year-olds, they have not discussed the degree to which the process of treatment might vary by the age of the child, nor have they addressed the consistency of effectiveness across age groups. Thus, additional empirical research on the use of PCAT with toddlers is desirable to augment that which has been conducted already by Dombrowski et al. (2005).

CASE ILLUSTRATION

Method

Subject

The subject of this study is L., a 23-month-old male toddler, and his 25-year-old biological mother. The referral for treatment stated that the toddler had been removed at birth from his parents' care due to his mother's drug use and his father's unwillingness and inability to care for L. and his three siblings (all under four years of age). L. was born to his mother when she was in jail. It is suspected that L. had been prenatally exposed to drugs, since his mother was reported to have used drugs before going to jail, though this was not documented. L. lived with the same foster family from birth until the time he was reunified with his biological parents and siblings at 22 months of age. Shortly after reunification, the toddler was referred to the University of California, Davis Children's Hospital for mandated PCAT because of concerns about temper tantrums (including throwing objects), aggression toward his younger sister, and head banging when his parents set limits on his behavior. A detailed session-by-session description is furnished in table 6.3.

Measures

Five measures were used to evaluate the effectiveness of PCAT in this case study: the Dyadic Parent-Child Interaction Coding System (DPICS), the Achenbach Child Behavior Checklist (CBCL), the Eyberg Child Behavior Inventory (ECBI), the Parenting Stress Index—Short Form (PSI-SF), and the Emotional Availability Scales (EA).

Table 6.3. Session-by-Session Detail of Case

Pretreatment	*Assessment to determine client's suitability for PCAT*

- Inclusion criteria are as follows:
  - o Child is between 12 and 36 months of age.
  - o Child has a significant caregiver who is willing to participate in treatment with the child.
  - o Child has externalizing behavior problems (e.g., temper tantrums, aggressiveness, biting, head butting).
- Parent completes standardized measures and observational assessment.

Session 1   *Didactic session*

- Therapist describes behavioral approach to treatment and behavior management.
- Therapist describes how the skills learned in PCAT will improve the child's behavior. Therapist explains how they will handle each problem area. In L.'s case, tantrums were noted as a big problem for the parent. The therapist describes how the following PCAT skills could help with temper tantrums, and that the therapist would help her master these skills:
  1. Help parent to recognize signs of distress in L.
  2. Teach parent to describe and praise L.'s positive behaviors (e.g., quiet, calm behavior).
  3. Teach parent to use strategies for avoiding tantrums if possible (e.g., redirecting and distracting).
  4. If tantrums are unavoidable, teach parent how to minimize the attention she gives L. when he is having a tantrum.
  5. Teach parent how to assist the child to regulate his emotions. Parent will learn calming strategies and verbal prompts to help L. reenter play with positive behaviors and attitudes (e.g., "when-then" statements such as, "When L. is quiet, then he can come play with me").
  6. Show parent that continued use of the PRIDE skills after a temper tantrum will help repair any lingering emotional distress between parent and child.

Sessions 2–3   *Coaching sessions: Setting rules, positive communications, modeling*

- Therapist teaches parent about rules for special playtime and helps parent set up rules for the child's behavior at home.
- Therapist focuses on helping the parent to recognize how she interacts with L., labeling and reinforcing her use of praises, descriptions, and reflections. Therapist teaches how to convert commands and questions into descriptive statements, points out to parent effects on child of using positive communications with child.
- Therapist finds an opportunity to show parent how she can "teach" the child positive behavior by modeling that behavior. For example, when L. put play food in his mouth, the therapist told the parent to show L. how to pretend to eat the food by saying, "I'm *pretending* to eat the food" while putting the food near her mouth.

- Therapist should communicate with parent that part of the effectiveness of the behavior management skills depends on making sure they contrast dramatically with the "fun times." The purpose of these early sessions is to hone the parent's ability to be positive and fun with the child.
- **Goals**: Parent should recognize child's positive behavior. Child should attempt to draw parent into play, enjoying playing with parent in a relaxed and easy manner.

Session 4–6   *Coaching sessions: redirection, active ignore*
- Therapist continues to work with parent to help her establish and enforce rules, and then use positive communication strategies and modeling to forestall behavior problems.
- Therapist introduces some stress into the play by changing activities during the session. Therapist teaches the importance of preparing the child for a transition, then coaches the parent through the transition using redirection, enthusiasm, and active ignore (including "when-then" statements). Therapist talks about the importance of helping the child to "recover" (i.e., calm down and be able to play with parent). Therapist repeats this process at cleanup, working the parent through transition to cleanup, and cleaning up toys.
- Child is rewarded with juice and crackers for effective cleanup.
- **Goals**: As in early sessions, parent should recognize child's positive behavior. Parent should recognize signs of distress in child. Parent should be able to state expectations for child's behavior in different settings (i.e., rules). Child should attempt to draw parent into play, enjoying playing with parent in a relaxed and easy manner. Child should prefer playing with parent to being ignored. Child should respond to redirection. Parent should report some improvement in frequency of problem behaviors. If these goals have not been achieved, therapist should inquire about the parent's use of these skills at home, parent's mental health, and about life stressors that may interfere with treatment effectiveness. If barriers are identified, therapist will work with parent to overcome them.

Session 7–9   *Coaching sessions: incentives, logical consequences, review*
- Therapist continues to work with parent to help her establish and enforce rules, and then use positive communication strategies and modeling to forestall behavior problems. Additionally, therapist continues to help parent use redirection and active ignore, noting whether the parent is able to use these tools without coaching.
- Therapist introduces concept of logical consequences and incentives, if child is cognitively mature enough to understand them. A logical consequence of L. throwing a car across the room would be putting the car away so that L. could not play with it. L.'s mother offered stickers, juice, and crackers as incentives for L. to clean up (e.g., "When you help Mommy clean up, then you will get a sticker!").

(*continued*)

Table 6.3. (*continued*)

- Therapist reviews with the parent the skills they have acquired and how they are being used. Additionally, therapist inquires about challenges the parent may be experiencing. If necessary, the therapist will design strategies for the parent, enabling her to manage these challenges.
- **Goals**: As in early sessions, parent should recognize child's positive behavior. Parent should recognize signs of distress in child. Parent should be able to state expectations for child's behavior in different settings (i.e., rules). Child should attempt to draw parent into play, enjoying playing with parent in a relaxed and easy manner. Child should prefer playing with parent to being ignored. Child should respond to redirection and incentives for good and compliant behavior. Parent should report improved child behavior. If these goals have not been met and the barriers have been identified but are still interfering with treatment progress, the therapist may consider referrals for other services.

Session 10   *Review and termination assessment*

- Therapist reviews with the parent the child's strengths and challenges, also discusses which PCAT strategies seem to work best for the parent and why, the skills she has acquired, and the improvements she has witnessed. The therapist further inquires about continuing challenges the parent may be experiencing and works with the parent to establish effective strategies for the parent's use.
- Therapist does 15-minute observation of parent and child play and administers standardized measures, as at pretreatment.

Dyadic Parent-Child Interaction Coding System. The DPICS is a behavioral coding system designed to assess the quality of parent-child social interactions through observation of parent-child dyads (Eyberg and Robinson 1982). The DPICS consists of behavioral categories for both children and caregivers. Although the DPICS was designed to measure 20 different nonverbal and verbal parent-child behaviors and verbalizations (e.g., whining; laughing), parental verbal behavior was given primary consideration during PCAT coding sessions. The therapist coded the mother's use of praise, descriptions, reflections, questions, commands, and critical statements in the first five minutes of each treatment session. Half of these sessions were recoded in order to ensure the reliability of the therapist's codes. Intraclass correlation coefficients (a measure of intercoder reliability) for the coding categories were the following: descriptions/reflections = 0.76; praises = 0.94; questions/commands = 0.97.

Consistent with the PCIT coding approach, PCAT coding notes the frequency of verbalizations thought to be important in enhancing the caregiver-child relationship and reducing dysfunctional relationship patterns. Specific "mastery" criteria are established at PCIT levels with respect to the number of parent descriptions and reflective statements, praises, questions, and commands uttered in five minutes of free play. Parents are taught to make at least 25 descriptive and reflective statements, 15 praises (at least 8 of which are specific, labeled praises), and no more than 3 questions or commands. Questions and commands are discouraged during playtime as they serve to remove control from the child. The following is a more precise operational definition of descriptions, reflections, praises, questions, and commands:

Descriptions: Statements or sentences that describe the child, the objects with which the child is playing, and the activity in which the child is engaging (e.g., "You're playing with the red truck" or "You're sitting in your seat").

Reflections: Statements that repeat or rephrase a preceding toddler verbalization (e.g., toddler states, "Want car"; caregiver states, "You want the car").

Praises: Positive evaluation of products, attributes, or behavior of the child. There are generally two types of praise that are coded: labeled and unlabeled. Labeled praises are very precise, describing the reason the praise was offered (e.g., "Good job rolling the truck!"). Unlabeled praises are vague and nonspecific (e.g., "Great job!").

Questions: Verbal statements that invite or call for a reply (e.g., "Do you want to play with the dolls?").

Commands: Directions from caregivers to toddler indicating that a verbal or motor activity should be performed (e.g., "Pick up the car from the floor").

Child Behavior Checklist. The CBCL (Achenbach, 1991) is a standardized instrument that lists 112 problem child behaviors. This version is completed by a parent or regular caregiver, and describes the behavior of children between the ages of 4 through 16 years. Separate norms are provided for both boys and girls in three age groups. Normative data is derived from a large, sociologically diverse population of both nonreferred and clinically referred children and their parents. The CBCL is comprised of a Total Problem score, two broad-band scales (internalizing, externalizing), eight narrow-band scales for each age group and sex (e.g., withdrawn, somatic complaints, delinquent behavior, aggressive behavior). The clinical cut-off scores for the broad-band scales is a T-score greater than or equal to 65.

Eyberg Child Behavior Inventory. The ECBI is a 36-item scale that measures specific behavior problems exhibited by children age 2 to16 years. Parents indicate the frequency of certain behaviors (Intensity score) and whether they are considered to be problems (Problem score) (Eyberg and Robinson

1982; Eyberg and Ross 1978). The ECBI has been standardized on a number of populations (Eyberg and Robinson 1982; Eyberg and Ross 1978). Test-retest reliability scores across a three-week time span on the ECBI Intensity and Problem scales were .86 and .88 respectively (Robinson, Eyberg, and Ross 1980). The published clinical cut-off scores are an Intensity score of greater than 131 or a Problem score of greater than 16.

Parenting Stress Index—Short Form. The PSI-SF (Abidin, 1995) is a 36-item inventory designed to identify parent-child dyads that are experiencing stress and are at risk for developing dysfunctional parenting and child behavior problems. The PSI-SF consists of three subscales: Difficult Child, Parent Distress, and Dysfunctional Parent-Child Relationship. The PSI-SF also contains a measure of defensive responding. Low scores (< 15th percentile) on this scale have been shown to indicate either that parents are minimizing problems associated with the parent role, that they do not have a close relationship with the children and are therefore unaffected by their behavior, or that they are simply not stressed by situations that stress normal parents. The test-retest and internal consistency reliability of the PSI on various scales range from .68 to .84 (Abidin, 1995).

Emotional Availability Scales. The EA Scales (Biringen, Robinson, and Emde 1998) consist of four global parent scales and two child scales that measure specific dimensions of the caregiver-child relationship. Parent scales measure their sensitivity to the child, their nonhostility, nonintrusiveness, and ability to structure the interaction. Child scales measure their responsiveness to the parent and the degree to which they involve the parent in their activities. Parent sensitivity scores reflect the degree to which the parent perceives and responds to the child's cues, the parent's engagement and interest in the child's activity, and the affective quality and conflict management. Parental structuring scores measure the parent's ability to give structure to an interaction (i.e., scaffold) so that the child responds positively. Parent nonintrusiveness refers to the parent's ability to give structure to the interaction without over-controlling and diminishing the child's autonomy. Parental nonhostility scores reflect the degree to which the parent's actions and tone of voice convey anger, impatience, or boredom. Child responsiveness refers to the degree to which the child responds to the parent in a positive, emotionally available manner, and the degree to which the child balances autonomous pursuits and interest in the parent's activities. Child involvement measures the degree to which the child involves the parent in his or her play, taking into account the balance of child-initiated and parent-initiated interactions. Higher scores reflect more optimal emotional availability. According to Biringen (1998, cited in Easterbrooks, Biesecker, and Lyons-Ruth, 2000), parent sensitivity scores above 4 are in the optimal range. Additionally, nonhostility scores above 4 and nonintrusiveness and structuring scores above 3, and child responsiveness and involvement scores above 4 are in the optimal range.

Procedure

While learning PCAT, caregivers are taught to follow their child's lead in play, to praise the child for behaving appropriately, and to limit the number of questions and commands elicited during play. Caregivers are also taught to ignore inappropriate behavior and to redirect the child's behavior when appropriate. Mastery of these skills is believed to result in decreased numbers of problem behaviors and improvements in the parent-child relationship.

Prior to the initial didactic session, before each weekly coaching session, and at the end of treatment, the mother and toddler were coded for five minutes using the DPICS. (The caregiver was instructed to follow the toddler's lead in play, during which time the trained therapist coded the parent-child interactions.) Following the five-minute DPICS coding, the therapist coached the parent on appropriate parent-child interaction through the use of a one-way mirror and a bug-in-the-ear device. In this case study, the mother and the toddler participated in an initial pretreatment DPICS coding session followed by a teaching session to familiarize the parent with the terminology, nine coaching sessions, and a posttreatment assessment. During the posttreatment session, the caregiver and child were observed and videotaped as they played together in 15 minutes of semistructured play. This was coded using the DPICS and the EA scales. Additionally, the caregiver was asked to complete a battery of standardized measures (e.g., ECBI, PSI, CBCL) during the initial intake interview and after the last PCAT session.

Results

Figures 6.1 and 6.2 present the results of DPICS coding. As shown, the mother's use of praise, descriptions, and reflections significantly increased from pretreatment to posttreatment. In the first five minutes of the observational assessment (a child-directed activity; CDI task) at pretreatment, the mother praised her son five times. In contrast, during the first five minutes of the posttreatment observational assessment (CDI task), the mother used 46 praises, well beyond the 15-praise mastery threshold. A similar increase was reflected in the number of descriptions and reflections provided by the mother. At pretreatment, the mother had 12 descriptions/reflections, below the mastery threshold of 25. This increased to 59 descriptions/reflections by posttreatment, representing another significant gain. The number of questions the mother asked her child decreased from a pretreatment level of 50

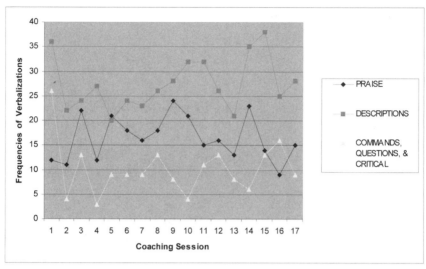

Figure 6.1. Number of Verbalizations by Caregiver

to a posttreatment level of 2. Overall, the mother attained mastery on all criteria coded within PCAT.

Table 6.4 shows the mother's ratings of her child's behavior at pretreatment and posttreatment, as well as ratings of her own functioning. In contrast to scores on observational measures, the mother rated the child's problem behaviors as having increased slightly from pre- to posttreatment

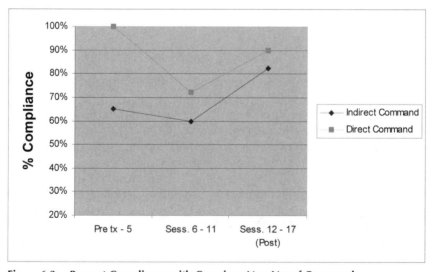

Figure 6.2. Percent Compliance with Caregiver *Non-Use* of Commands

Table 6.4. Measures of Child and Parent Functioning: Pretreatment, Posttreatment, and at Five-Month Follow-Up (after In-Home Support)

Measures	Pretreatment	Posttreatment	Five-Month Follow-Up
ECBI (T-scores)			
Intensity score	55	65*	42
Problem score	59	65*	52
CBCL (T-scores)			
Anxious/depressed	52	61	58
Withdrawn	59	54	50
Sleep problems	50	50	50
Somatic problems	50	61	50
Aggression	67+	61	51
Destructive behavior	51	50	50
Internalizing	56	58	55
Externalizing	62+	56	49
Total problem score	58	57	49
PSI-SF (Percentile scores)			
Parent distress	7.5	5	7.5
Dysfunctional relationship	50	45	75
Difficult child	90*	85*	35
Defensive responding	5*	5*	15+

+ Borderline range; * Clinical range

on both the ECBI and the CBCL. In the case of the ECBI intensity score, a measure of more everyday problem behaviors, the score moved from below the clinical cut-off into the clinical range. In contrast, scores on the PSI-SF decreased very slightly. It is interesting to note that the mother showed elevated levels of defensive responding (lower percentile scores indicate higher defensive responding), perhaps indicating a desire to present herself and her relationship with her son in a positive light.

Table 6.5 shows the results of the EA rating of this dyad. Pretreatment scores on parent emotional availability scales are mixed: some are optimal (nonhostility), some are in the low-optimal range (sensitivity), and some are non-optimal (structuring, nonintrusiveness). The child's emotional availability scores were all nonoptimal. The mother's sensitivity scores were in the low-optimal range throughout the observational assessment. Throughout pretreatment CDI and Cleanup tasks (first and last five minutes), her affect was positive and consistent, and she was engaged in her interaction with the child, although the child did not respond to her overtures with a similar level of enthusiasm. In CDI, the mother played with the child for a short time, but the child's interest in the play waned, and the mother questioned him about what he wanted to do. The child got down from his chair and walked around the therapy room, while the mother directed his

Table 6.5. Mean Parent and Child EA Scores and Percent of Total Score Averaged across CDI, PDI, and Cleanup Tasks

	Pretreatment	% Score	Posttreatment	% Score
Parent Scales				
Sensitivity (9-pt. scale)	5.33	59%	6.67	74%
Non-hostility (5-pt. scale)	4.67*	93%	5.0	100%
Non-intrusiveness (5-pt. scale)	2.33***	47%	4.0	80%
Structuring (5-pt. scale)	3.0***	60%	4.33 *	87%
Child Scales				
Responsiveness (7-pt. scale)	3.0***	43%	4.67 *	67%
Involvement (7-pt. scale)	3.0***	43%	4.67 *	67%

* One out of three at risk/nonoptimal score (e.g., CDI, PDI, or Cleanup)
** Two out of three at risk/nonoptimal scores
*** Three out of three at risk/nonoptimal scores

attention to the toys on the table, asking him to help her clean them up. She continued to direct his cleaning up until the therapist switched the activity to Parent Directed Play. During the cleanup, L. ignored his mother's requests to pick up the toys and tantrumed. Her lower structuring and non-intrusiveness scores reflect the raters' observation of her inability to support his play activities and the degree to which she directed the play. The child's low responsiveness and involvement scores reflect the raters' note of his continual need to be prompted by his mother in order to sustain his engagement with her and his tantrum during the cleanup segment.

At posttreatment, most of the mother's and child's emotional availability scores improved, shifting to the optimal range. The dyad showed one nonoptimal score in parent structuring and child responsiveness and involvement. During the posttreatment DPICS, mother and son sat together on the floor playing with play dough forms. The mother followed the child's lead and elaborated his play. The child was highly engaged in play with his mother, handing her the play dough forms and saying, "Here, Mommy!" At one point he tried to take a sticker off a toy, but his mother successfully redirected his attention elsewhere.

The child's and his mother's emotional availability scores showed great improvement from pre- to posttreatment. Overall, the mother tried to verbally engage the child pre- and posttreatment. However, the mother was less directive, more positive, and more creative in her play with the child at posttreatment than pretreatment. She also seemed more comfortable playing with her son at posttreatment and involved herself in his play more easily. The mother did not seem as disturbed by his noncompliance by posttreatment, handling the "active ignore" with ease, although she did need some assistance from the therapist. The child, for his part, appeared more cheerful and talkative. He spent more time interacting positively with his mother, and was able to control his negative emotions quickly (once given the "active ignore" framework).

Discussion

The results of this single case study suggest that PCAT was successful, increasing the number of positive caregiver-toddler interactions and improving the emotional availability of this dyad. The mother learned how to play with L., responding appropriately to his cues. In turn, L. responded positively to his mother's praise and was involved with her in his play. However, the scores on the standardized measures suggest that PCAT might not have been completely successful in shifting the mother's perception of her son's behaviors. Additionally, this mother showed a tendency to minimize her own stress in parenting (reflected by her elevated defensive responding score on the PSI-SF), which suggests that she also may have minimized her child's behavior problems pre-treatment. The mother reported behavior problems on ECBI and CBCL in the normal range although she reported concerns about temper tantrums (including throwing objects), aggression toward his younger sister, head banging, and noncompliance. It is difficult to use standardized measures as indicators of treatment-related reductions in behavior problems when parents minimize the child's problems at the start of treatment.

Post-PCAT In-Home Services

Over the last several weeks of treatment, the mother reported that she and her husband were fighting a lot, and that L.'s behaviors were becoming more difficult to manage. While the mother was able to forestall many tantrums and control the ones that occurred, L.'s tantrums were lasting longer, and he was having a harder time calming. Furthermore, the family was experiencing severe financial distress, had no transportation, and reported no social support. Just as treatment was scheduled to end, the father was incarcerated for problems unrelated to their domestic difficulties and the mother was distressed. Given these multiple risks and their lack of transportation, the family was referred for further in-home mental health services. The plan was to reduce the occurrence and length of L.'s temper tantrums, coaching the mother to use a time-out procedure in conjunction with the other behavior management skills she had learned in PCAT (e.g., redirecting, active ignore, when-then statements, PRIDE skills). Table 6.4 shows the mother's ratings of the child's behavior at a follow-up assessment approximately five months after the end of PCAT services and after receiving in-home PCIT-based support services. The mother's ratings of the child's behavior problems at this time are well within normal limits. These further reductions in behavior problems may result from the family's adjustment to their father's absence, an absence of marital conflict, the mother being able to effectively use the time-out procedure, or some combination of all of these reasons. The progress of this case suggested that life events and family contexts often serve as barriers to observable treatment effectiveness.

Barriers to Treatment Effectiveness

An obstacle to measurable treatment success in this PCAT case was the quality of the marital relationship and family stressors. When the mother began reporting that she and her husband were fighting, causing her to leave the home several times, she reported increased numbers and duration of temper tantrums (including screaming, hitting, and throwing toys) at home and in the clinic. Children in families characterized by interparental violence have been found to exhibit more externalizing behaviors (Jouriles, Murphy, and O'Leary 1989). Furthermore, marital conflict has been shown to be a source of emotional insecurity in children, which mediated the relationship between the conflict and externalizing behaviors (Davies et al. 2002). PCAT effectiveness depends on the parents' developing consistent and contingent parenting infused with warmth, creating a predictable and safe (i.e., more secure) environment for the child. By disrupting the predictability, warmth, and safety of the home environment, interparental violence could also disrupt the child's emotional security. Subsequently, the child may exhibit behavior problems, even when one parent is participating in PCAT and making notable progress. In L.'s case, the parents were told of the consequences on L.'s behavior of their marital discord. They were referred to marriage counseling in order to provide more stability for L.

A second potential obstacle to treatment effectiveness in this case was L.'s prenatal exposure to drugs and subsequent removal from his mother's care. Unfortunately, the therapist did not specify which drugs L.'s mother had been using or whether she also abused alcohol, so it is difficult to know whether to expect any effects on L.'s behavior or cognition. Studies of the effects of prenatal exposure to alcohol (i.e., fetal alcohol spectrum disorders) on children have consistently described severe cognitive effects (e.g., Mattson et al. 1999; Streissguth, Barr, and Sampson 1990). Studies of cocaine and polydrug drug use on children have found consistent effects on attention and systems of inhibitory control. L. was too young to test either cognitive effects or inhibitory control when he participated in PCAT, and his emotional dysregulation could be attributed to environmental stressors rather than neurological deficits. However, the possibility existed that negative sequelae of prenatal exposure to alcohol and other drugs could have interfered with the treatment process such that we would observe improvements in the mother's parenting skills without decreases in the frequency of L.'s problem behaviors.

As an added stressor, L.'s biological father was incarcerated near the end of treatment. While this effectively ended the turmoil of interparental violence, L.'s mother reported that she was quite depressed by this event. Apart from losing her primary social support when her husband was jailed, the family's income was severely diminished and they had to depend on public transportation. She also reported that L. was throwing more temper tantrums. Empirical studies have found effects of environmental stressors and the experience of poverty on psychopathologies such as depression and anxiety in both children (Wadsworth and Achenbach 2005) and adults (Johnson et al. 1999). While L. and his family were living in poverty throughout treatment, the sudden loss of transportation and income from the father may have caused increased anxiety and depression in L. and his mother. Research suggests that we would expect that the mother's depression and anxiety would impair her ability to accurately interpret L.'s needs (Zahn-Waxler et al. 1990), and would lead her to perceive his behaviors as more negative (Youngstrom, Izard, and Ackerman, 1999). Depression and anxiety in young children could be expected to manifest in angry outbursts, tantrums, aggression, and anxiety (NICHD Early Child Care Research Network, 1999). In L.'s case, although the mother reported improvements in her relationship with L. and greater confidence in her ability to manage his difficult behaviors, the mother's and child's responses to these negative life circumstances seemed to have mutually and increasingly negative effect. The mother's depression seemed to make it more difficult for her to tolerate his temper tantrums, which in turn seemed to increase L.'s anxiety and the severity of his temper tantrums. Without additional support and intervention, this negative cycle of interactions threatened to erase the previous gains the dyad had made. Fortunately, the mother elected to receive home-based support services posttreatment, which helped her continue to use the skills she acquired in PCAT during this difficult period in the family's life.

CONCLUSIONS AND FUTURE DIRECTIONS

The ultimate goal of PCAT is to assist caregivers in forming and maintaining a secure, nurturing, and positive relationship with their child while instructing the caregivers in appropriate limit setting via the use of redirection and ignoring of inappropriate behavior. Some of the goals for children include the development or increase of prosocial behaviors such as sharing and taking turns. Another goal is to decrease inappropriate behavior such as temper tantrums, noncompliance with parental requests, and defiance. These goals are monitored and measured at each session to determine progress. While this treatment modality cannot hope to alleviate all the mental health problems in toddlers, we believe that making the caregiver-child relationship a more predictable, positive, and safe environment will go a long way in facilitating normal, healthy developmental trajectories.

NOTE

Correspondence regarding this chapter should be directed to Susan Goff Timmer, PhD, CAARE Diagnostic and Treatment Center, Department of Pediatrics, UC Davis Children's Hospital, 3300 Stockton Blvd., Sacramento, CA 95820. Voice: 916-734-6630. E-mail: susan.timmer@ucdmc.ucdavis.edu.

REFERENCES

Abidin, R. R. 1995. *Parenting stress index.* 3rd ed. Charlottesville, VA: Pediatric Psychology Press.

Achenbach, T. M. 1991. *Manual for the Child Behavior Checklist/4-18 and 1991 Profile.* Burlington: University of Vermont, Department of Psychiatry.

Ainsworth, M. D. 1969. Object relations, dependency, and attachment: A theoretical review of the infant-mother relationship. *Child Development* 40 (4): 969–1025.

Axline, V. M. 1947. *Play therapy: The inner dynamics of childhood.* Oxford: Houghton Mifflin.

Baumrind, D. 1968. Authoritarian vs. authoritative parental control. *Adolescence* 3:255–272.

Biringen, Z., J. Robinson, and R. Emde. 1998. Emotional Availability Scales. 3rd ed. Unpublished manual, Colorado State University.

Bousha, D. M., and C. T. Twentyman. 1984. Mother-child interactional style in abuse, neglect, and control groups: Naturalistic observations in the home. *Child Development* 49:1163–1173.

Cerezo, M. A., and A. D. D'Ocon. 1999. Sequential analyses in coercive mother-child interaction: The predictability hypothesis in abusive versus nonabusive dyads. *Child Abuse and Neglect* 23:99–113.

Chaffin, M., J. Silovsky, B. Funderburk, et al. 2004. Parent-child interaction therapy with physically abusive parents: Efficacy for reducing future abuse reports. *Journal of Consulting and Clinical Psychology* 72:491–499.

Cicchetti, D. 1989. How research on child maltreatment has informed the study of child development: Perspectives from development psychopathology. In *Child maltreatment: Theory and research on the causes and consequences of child abuse and neglect,* ed. D. Cicchetti and V. Carlson, 377–431. New York: Cambridge University Press.

Cicchetti, D., and S. L. Toth. 1995. A developmental psychopathology perspective on child abuse and neglect. *Journal of the American Academy of Child and Adolescent Psychiatry* 34:541–565.

Cole, D. A. 1990. Relation of social and academic competence to depressive symptoms in childhood. *Journal of Abnormal Psychology* 99:422–429.

Davies, P. T., G. T. Harold, M. C. Goeke-Morey, and E. M. Cummings. 2002. Child emotional security and interparental conflict. *Monographs of the Society for Research in Child Development* 67 (3): vii–viii.

Dombrowski, S. C., and S. G. Timmer. 2001. Parent-Child Attunement Therapy with a 23-month-old maltreated toddler. Paper presented at the second annual PCIT conference, Sacramento, California.

Dombrowski, S. C., S. G. Timmer, D. Blacker, and A. J. Urquiza. 2005. A positive behavioral intervention model for toddlers: Parent-Child Attunement Therapy (PCAT). *Child Abuse Review* 14:132–151.

Easterbrooks, M. A., G. Biesecker, and K. Lyons-Ruth. 2000. Infancy predictors of emotional availability in middle childhood: The roles of attachment security and maternal depressive symptomatology. In Mapping the terrain of emotional availability and attachment, special issue, *Attachment & Human Development* 2 (2): 170–187.

Eyberg, S. M. 1988. PCIT: Integration of traditional and behavioral concerns. *Child and Family Behavior Therapy* 10:33–46.

Eyberg, S. M., and E. A. Robinson. 1982. Parent-child interaction training: Effects on family functioning. *Journal of Clinical Child Psychology* 11:130–137.

Eyberg, S. M., and A. W. Ross. 1978. Assessment of child behavior problems: the validation of a new inventory. *Journal of Clinical Child Psychology* 7:113–116.

Funderburk, B. W., A. M. Eyberg, K. Newcomb, C. B. McNeil, T. Hembree-Kigin, and L. Capage. 1998. Parent-child interaction therapy with behavior problem children: Maintenance of treatment effects in the school setting. *Child and Family Behavior Therapy* 20:17–38.

Gralinski, J. H., and C. B. Kopp. 1993. Everyday rules for behavior: Mothers' requests to young children. *Developmental Psychology* 29 (3): 573–584.

Gusella, J. L., D. Muir, and E. A. Tronick. 1988. The effect of manipulating maternal behavior during an interaction on three- and six-month-olds' affect and attention. *Child Development* 59 (4): 1111–1124.

Hanf, C. 1968. Modifying problem behaviors in mother-child interaction: Standardized laboratory situations. Paper presented at the meeting of the Association of Behavior Therapies, Olympia, Washington, April.

———. 1969. A two-stage program for modifying maternal controlling during the mother-child interaction. Paper presented at the meeting of the Western Psychological Association, Vancouver, British Columbia, Canada, April.

Hembree-Kigin, T. L., and C. B. McNeil. 1995. *Parent-child interaction therapy.* New York: Plenum.

Hershell, A. D., and C. B. McNeil. 2005. Parent-child interaction therapy for children experiencing externalizing behavior problems. In *Empirically based play interventions for children,* ed. L. A. Reddy, T. M. Files-Hall, and C. E. Schaefer, 169–190. Washington, DC: American Psychological Association.

Hood, K. K., and S. M. Eyberg. 2003. Outcomes of parent-child interaction therapy: Mothers' report of maintenance three to six years after treatment. *Journal of Clinical Child and Adolescent Psychology* 32:419–429.

Johnson, J. G., P. Cohen, B. P. Dohrenwend, B. G. Link, and J. S. Brook. 1999. A longitudinal investigation of social causation and social selection processes involved in the association between socioeconomic status and psychiatric disorders. *Journal of Abnormal Psychology* 108:490–499.

Jouriles, E. N., C. M. Murphy, and K. D. O'Leary. 1989. Interspousal aggression, marital discord, and child problems. *Journal of Consulting and Clinical Psychology* 57 (3): 453–455.

Kochanska, G., and N. Aksan. 1995. Mother-child mutually positive affect, the quality of child compliance to requests and prohibitions, and maternal control as correlates of early internalization. *Child Development* 66:236–254.

Kochanska, G., K. C. Coy, and K. T. Murray. 2001. The development of self-regulation in the first four years of life. *Child Development* 72:1091–1111.

Kopp, C. B. 1982. Antecedents of self-regulation: A developmental perspective. *Developmental Psychology* 18 (2): 199–214.

———. 1989. Regulation of distress and negative emotions: A developmental view. *Developmental Psychology* 25 (3): 343–354.

Lieberman, A. F. 2004. Traumatic stress and quality of attachment: Reality and internalization in disorders of infant mental health. *Infant Mental Health Journal* 25 (4): 336–351.

Mattson, S. N., A. M. Goodman, C. Caine, et al. 1999. Executive functioning in children with heavy prenatal alcohol exposure. *Alcoholism: Clinical and Experimental Research* 23:1808–1815.

McNeil, C. B., S. M. Eyberg, T. H. Eiserstadt, K. Newcomb, and B. W. Funderburk. 1991. Parent-child interaction therapy with behavior problem children: Generalization of treatment effects to the school setting. *Journal of Clinical Child Psychology* 20:140–151.

NICHD Early Child Care Research Network. 1999. Chronicity of maternal depressive symptoms, maternal sensitivity, and child functioning at 36 months. *Developmental Psychology* 35:1297–1310.

Nixon, R. D. V., L. Sweeney, D. B. Erickson, and S. W. Touyz. 2004. Parent-child interaction therapy: One- and two-year follow-up of standard and abbreviated treatments for oppositional preschoolers. *Journal of Abnormal Child Psychology* 32 (3): 263–271.

Osofsky, J. D. 1995. Perspectives on attachment and psychoanalysis. *Psychoanalytic Psychology* 12 (3): 347–362.

———. 2005. Professional training in infant mental health. *Infants and Young Children* 18 (4): 266–268.

Paravicini, S. F. 2000. Parent-child attunement therapy: Development of a program for children one to three years old. *Dissertation Abstracts International* 60 (9-B). (UMI No. AAI9945876).

Paravicini, S. F., A. J. Urquiza, and D. M. Blacker. 2000. Parent-Child Attunement Therapy: Development of a program for children one to three years old. Paper presented at the first annual PCIT conference, Sacramento, California.

Patterson, G. R. 1982. *Coercive family process.* Eugene, OR: Castalia.

Putnam, S. P., M. A. Gartstein, and M. K. Rothbart. 2006. Measurement of fine-grained aspects of toddler temperament: The early childhood behavior questionnaire. *Infant Behavior and Development* 29 (3): 386–401.

Pynoos, R. S. 1990. Post-traumatic stress disorder in children and adolescents. In *Psychiatric disorders in children and adolescents*, ed. B. Garfinkel, G. Carlson, and E. Weller, 48–63. Philadelphia: Saunders.

Repacholi, B. M., and A. Gopnik. 1997. Early reasoning about desires: Evidence from 14- and 18-month-olds. *Developmental Psychology* 33 (1): 12–21.

Robinson, E. A., S. M. Eyberg, and W. A. Ross. 1980. The standardization of an inventory of child conduct problem behaviors. *Journal of Clinical Child Psychology* 9:22–29.

Scheeringa, M. S., and T. J. Gaensbauer. 2000. Post-traumatic stress disorder. In *Handbook of infant mental health*, ed. C. H. Zeanah, 369–381. New York: Basic Books.

Schuhmann, E., R. Foote, S. M. Eyberg, S. Boggs, and J. Algina. 1998. Parent-child interaction therapy: Interim report of a randomized trial with short-term maintenance. *Journal of Clinical Child Psychology* 27:34–45.

Smetana, J., C. Daddis, S. L. Toth, D. Cicchetti, J. Bruce, and P. Kane. 1999. Effects of provocation on maltreated and non-maltreated preschoolers' understanding of moral transgressions. *Social Development* 8:335–348.

Streissguth, A. P., H. M. Barr, and P. D. Sampson. 1990. Moderate prenatal alcohol exposure: Effects on child IQ and learning problems at age 7.5 years. *Alcoholism: Clinical and Experimental Research* 14:662–669.

Timmer, S. G., A. J. Urquiza, and N. Zebell. 2006. Challenging foster caregiver–maltreated child relationships: The effectiveness of Parent Child Interaction Therapy, *Child and Youth Services Review* 28:1–19.

Timmer, S. G., A. J. Urquiza, N. Zebell, and J. McGrath. 2005. Parent-Child Interaction Therapy: Application to physically abusive and high-risk dyads. *Child Abuse and Neglect* 29:825–842.

Toth, S. L., D. Cicchetti, J. Macfie, and R. N. Emde. 1997. Representations of self and other in the narratives of neglected, physically abused, and sexually abused preschoolers. *Development and Psychopathology* 9:781–796.

Wadsworth, M., and T. Achenbach. 2005. Explaining the link between low socioeconomic status and psychopathology: Testing two mechanisms of the social causation hypothesis. *Journal of Consulting and Clinical Psychology* 73:1146–1153.

Wellman, H. M., and J. D. Woolley. 1990. From simple desires to ordinary beliefs: The early development of everyday psychology. *Cognition* 35 (3): 245–275.

Wolfe, D. A. 1987. Child-abusive parents: An empirical review and analysis. *Psychological Bulletin* 97: 462–482.

Youngstrom E., C. Izard, and B. Ackerman. 1999. Dysphoria-related bias in maternal ratings of children. *Journal of Consulting and Clinical Psychology* 67:905–916.

Zahn-Waxler, C., R. J. Iannotti, E. M. Cummings, and S. Denham. 1990. Antecedents of problem behaviors in children of depressed mothers. *Development and Psychopathology* 2:271–291.

7

Theraplay with Zero- to Three-Year-Olds

Evangeline Munns

BASIC RATIONALE

Theraplay is a treatment method that is ideally suited for the zero- to three-year-old population for a number of reasons. First, it tries to replicate what normal parents do with their young children. Theraplay goes back to the roots of connectedness, which normally begins in the first years of a child's life. One of its main goals is to enhance the attachment between parent and child, which is one of the most important developments in childhood. Research from around the world has shown that if a child does not have a secure attachment with a chief caregiver, then there is a strong likelihood that the child will develop emotional, social, or behavioral problems later on in life, unless remediating factors intervene (Rutter 1994; Schore 1998; Spratt and Doob 1998; van IJzendoorn, Juffer, and Duyvesteyn 1995; Webber-Stratton and Taylor 2001).

Second, Theraplay places an emphasis on physical contact with the child, which is exactly the kind of sensory stimulation a baby needs. The tactile sensory system is the most advanced sensory system when a child is born (Eliot 2000). (Touch includes four sensory abilities: cutaneous touch, temperature, pain, and proprioception.) The infant can perceive and process tactile stimuli especially in the oral region, and that is one of the reasons that the baby often mouths objects in its attempts to explore its world. The majority of Theraplay activities, especially with a young child, involve touch.

Third, Theraplay has many activities incorporating the vestibular system—a sense that allows us to perceive our body movements and balance and is the second most highly developed sensory system at birth (Eliot 2000).

Babies take delight in motions such as rocking, bouncing, being carried, and gentle jiggling, and can be comforted by these repetitive movements. Theraplay activities with very young children will often include nursery rhymes that encompass simple repetitive rhythms such as bouncing or rocking.

Fourth, Theraplay is not a verbal therapy. Words are not as meaningful to young children as they are to adults. Theraplay is an action-oriented, physical, fun type of play therapy that children usually love.

Fifth, one of the main tenets of Theraplay is to build the self-esteem of the child, emphasizing the child's positive attributes. This, along with the sensitive, nurturing caretaking of the child, contributes to the child's positive "internal working model" (Bowlby 1988), that he or she is a valued, important little person.

Overall, Theraplay helps parents to be attuned to their child's needs and to be contingently responsive along with taking pleasure in each other. If this indeed takes place, the parent helps the child to become self-regulated and in this process, attachment is strengthened (Booth 2000; Gerhardt 2004).

Theraplay for the zero to three age group needs to be modified because of the rapid growth in all aspects of the young child, especially in the development of the brain. Particularly in the first year, there is a spurt of growth in synaptic connections between neurons. This is followed by a "pruning" of connections that are not used, which results in a deterioration or fading away of such synapses (Gerhardt 2004). By the end of the third year, nine-tenths of the brain is developed. The Theraplay modifications will be discussed after first giving a background to Theraplay and describing its classic approach.

HISTORY AND BACKGROUND

Theraplay was founded by Dr. Ann Jernberg, a psychoanalytical psychologist, in 1967 when she was given a federal grant to enhance the bonding between mothers and their children in a Head Start program in Chicago (Jernberg and Booth 1999; Munns, 2000). Because it was found to be clinically effective in a short period of time, it became more widely known. Today it is practiced around the world, with its international headquarters located at the Theraplay Institute in Chicago.

Theraplay has been used individually, with families (most often), and in a group format, whether it is peer groups or parent-child groups. Parent-child groups with young and older children have been found to be very helpful not only for parent-child relationships, but also as a format for children to learn social skills and for parents to be supportive with each other (Martin 2000; Munns and Ahmad 2006; Sherman 2000).

THEORY

The theory underlying Theraplay rests on attachment theory. The main purpose of Theraplay is to enhance the attachment between child and parent. The most important relationship a child has is its first one with its major caregiver. If that is not a strong, healthy, secure attachment, then the child will likely have difficulties in his or her life later on, growing up and as an adult, unless there are remediating factors such as having another nurturing figure who cares for the child in a responsive, consistent way (Fonagay 2003). Theraplay goes back to the stage where the attachment process was derailed and tries to replicate what a normal parent would do with a child at that age. At times this may mean incorporating some regressive activities (such as feeding, rocking the child in a blanket, caring for hurts, etc.). Theraplay goes back to that early stage with the goal of forming a secure attachment. In this process the parent is guided to be attuned to the child's cues and to regulate the child's emotions, which in turn helps the child to achieve self-regulation (Booth 2005).

RESEARCH

Attachment theory is well supported by research worldwide, but Theraplay needs further research, although a good start has been made in this direction. There are many case studies supporting Theraplay (Jernberg and Booth 1999; Munns 2000), a number of studies using pre and post scores (Makela and Vierikko 2004; Munns, Jensen and Berger 2000), and an increasing number using control groups. The research studies using control groups do point to the effectiveness of Theraplay (Ammen 2000, showing a significant increase in empathy scores of high-risk teenage mothers with their infants; Meyer and Wardrop 2006, indicating a significant drop in behavior problems; Ritterfield 1990, significant increases in expressive language and positive social-emotional scores; Sui 2006, a significant increase in self-esteem scores and a significant decrease in internalizing symptoms; Wettig, Franke, and Fjordback 2006, showing a significant decrease of symptoms in children with attention/hyperactivity and social/emotional disorders; Yoon 2007, finding a significant improvement in social/emotional behavior and a reduction in parental stress scores). More research is in progress (Lassenius-Panula and Makela 2007; Weir 2007). In addition, there is growing evidence of the importance of touch (Field, 1995; Thayer, 1998), which is a strong factor in Theraplay.

WHAT IS THERAPLAY?

Theraplay is a structured form of play therapy that is short-term (12 to 16 half-hour sessions weekly over a period of approximately 4 months, but sometimes longer with severe problems). Theraplay has been used successfully for a wide age range (infants to adults) and a wide spectrum of social, emotional, and behavioral difficulties (Munns 2003, 2005). It is nonverbal (no interpretations are made, although some reflections are sometimes given), with an emphasis on focusing on the positive strengths of the child (problems are not discussed with the child, and bizarre behavior is ignored). No toys are used and minimal supplies are needed, so it is cost-effective. It is based on interactions between therapist and child, while parents first observe for about four sessions and then participate directly with their child under the guidance and support of the therapist. The Theraplay session is ideally followed by a half-hour parent counseling session where a debriefing of the Theraplay session takes place, along with a discussion of home and school behavior. Parents are encouraged to try Theraplay activities at home every week. Toward the end of the treatment period, parents are increasingly given a leadership role in the sessions.

The agenda for each session is preplanned by the therapist, integrating information from a detailed family history including each parent's history, as well as information from a parent-child assessment using the Marschak Interaction Method (MIM). The MIM is a family assessment tool based on simple activities requiring parent-child interactions that give a picture of how parents structure, challenge, engage, and nurture their children and how their children respond (DiPasquale 2000).

Each Theraplay session is based on goals for the four underlying dimensions of Theraplay—structure, challenge, engagement, and nurture.

DIMENSIONS

Structure

Every child needs structure in her or his life. Children need consistent routines such as times for feeding, bathing, playing, and sleeping, so they can establish a rhythm and predictability in their daily lives. This helps to regulate them. They need rules to govern their behavior and to establish a safe environment for them. Structure gives them a sense of security. Often, in treatment, children are referred because they are impulsive, lacking in control of their feelings, aggressive, defiant, restless, and dysregulated. Theraplay would emphasize structure in these children's lives. Activities and games with clear rules and signals to start or end—such as "Red light" or "Simon says" or balloon races—might be used.

One of the intentions of structuring activities is to have the child cooperate with simple directions, first with the therapist and then with the parents.

Challenge

Challenge helps the child take appropriate risks and expand his or her world. The child learns that he or she can take some chances, and this can bring rewards. In mastering new skills, the child gains a sense of competence and self-confidence. It is important to offer challenges that are in the scope of the child's abilities to master. Success brings a sense of pride and accomplishment. Failure can bring a loss of self-esteem, shame, and fear.

The parent at home will present challenges even for the very young child, such as learning to sit up alone, to walk, to throw and catch objects, and so on. Children love challenges when they feel they can succeed. Praise and encouragement are important to support the child's attempts. This is especially important for children who are withdrawn, timid, frightened, or overprotected. In Theraplay such children are supported in trying simple activities such as keeping a balloon up in the air; bursting a soap bubble with both hands, then with one finger, and the like; blowing ping-pong balls while on their tummy; imitating a clap pattern (e.g., patty-cake and later, other more complicated sequences). Challenging activities are also given to children that have a lot of inner tension and need a safe outlet for their aggression. An activity such as a cotton-ball fight or paper punch (punching through a tautly held newspaper sheet) might be included in the session.

Engagement

Engagement is a way of directly interacting with the child. It may include playfully intruding into the child's space. Care is taken to be aware of the child's acceptance or rejection of this playful intrusion, particularly with very young children or with those who have been previously abused. If signs of aversion are displayed in a preverbal child such as head turning away, facial frown, downcast eyes, and so forth, then the therapist stops and tries to find another way that is more appealing to the child. Activities are not forced on the child.

Usually children love to be engaged, and there are hundreds of ways of interacting that children find delightful. Young children usually enjoy singing and nursery rhymes such as "This is the way a horsy rides" while being bounced on the adult's ankle. Another favorite is "This little piggy went to market," where the adult wiggles each of the child's fingers or toes and ends up with a gentle tickle under the child's chin. Mirroring is another popular activity (parent mirrors the child's movements and sounds). Engaging activities often involve a face-to-face position with good eye contact. This kind of stimulation has a direct effect on the hard wiring of the brain (Gerhardt 2004; Schore 1998). Mirror neurons are excited in the child's brain in the same area of the brain that excitation takes place in the adult's brain resulting in "brain to brain" connection (Siegel 1999). Young children need this kind of stimulation so their brains can develop in an optimal way and so they develop a sense of empathy with others (Gerhardt 2004).

In Theraplay, engaging activities are emphasized for children who are withdrawn, who resist intimacy (autistic children), or who are lethargic or depressed.

Nurture

This is one of the most important dimensions of Theraplay. All children need nurturing, especially the very young and those who have been ne-glected, deprived, or abused. Ordinarily, a young child at home receives much nurturing such as cuddling, rocking, caressing, patting, kissing, feed-ing, bathing, powdering, grooming, singing songs such as "I love you," et cetera. All of these activities make the child feel valued, important, accepted, cared for, and loved. Theraplay tries to replicate this, and some form of nur-turing takes place in every session, regardless of the child's age. Nurturing activities are activities such as lotioning or powdering of "hurts" on the child's hands or feet; feeding the child a snack; making powder handprints; combing the child's hair; face painting; rocking the child in a blanket while singing a special song about the child while the child sucks on a lollipop, a bottle, or from a juice box. If a child resists nurturing (often a child with a poor self-image will resist), then another way is found that the child can accept. For example, a child might resist lotioning of "hurts," so the thera-pist may do an outline of the child's hands and then wash and powder or lotion the hands. Once the child experiences lotioning in this way, then he or she usually accepts caring of "hurts" in the next session.

If a child is tactile defensive, it is important to get an accurate assessment, because this may be a result of sensory motor processing difficulties or pos-sibly poor attachment or abuse. If this is a sensory motor difficulty, then further treatment with an occupational therapist might be recommended (Chaloner 2006).[1]

The discussion that follows has been garnered partly from my own ex-perience, but also from seasoned Theraplay therapists working with zero to three-year-olds (Ammen 2000; Booth 2000; Chaloner 2006; Rubin and Mroz 2006). Note that not all of the points below have been discussed with all of these authors. However, it is predicted that there would have been general agreement if this had been done.

MODIFICATIONS

It was previously mentioned that Theraplay needs to be modified for children zero to three years of age. Modifications need to be appropriate to the child's developmental stage. For infants and toddlers, although the therapist tries to follow his or her agenda and direct the child, there may be many times when the child's lead should be followed until the therapist can reengage the child. The therapist has to be very attuned to the child, being especially sensitive to nonverbal communication. This does not mean that the therapist only follows the lead of the child. The therapist can attempt to follow her or his agenda, but if the child shows aversion, resistance, fear, or a lot of anxiety, then the therapist needs to stop and find another way to reach her or his goals. The therapist must always be aware of the child's maturity level and what the child can or can't do. The following are important considerations:

- Young children's attention spans are relatively short. Activities need to be appropriate in length, and the whole session may be shortened to say 20 minutes rather than a half hour, depending on the child.
- They need varied stimuli, otherwise they may lose interest.
- They need more than words, because often they can't understand words (although they do react to tone of voice). So visual stimuli along with movement can often catch their attention.
- Babies tire easily.
- Remember the importance of appropriate amounts of sensory stimulation in all sensory modalities, but not to the extent of overwhelming the sensory systems. The therapist needs to know when to soothe the child and when to stimulate him or her. This helps the child toward self-regulation. Note that it is often difficult to tell if a child has a true regulatory problem before six to eight months, because this can sometimes be resolved through maturation of the child (Chaloner 2006).
- Use a gentle voice. Avoid loud sounds that can be alarming to the child.
- Children love rhythm in song and action.
- Take small steps—don't make sudden, abrupt changes.
- Give lots of warm physical affection as modeling for the parent, but also focus on the parent interacting with their child in this way.
- Allow for some freedom of movement. Don't try to have the child sit for too long.
- Get down on the floor with the child (note that Theraplay therapists do this with all ages).
- If the child is under age two, then have the parents nearby during the observation period. Don't try to separate the parents from the child, until the child is comfortable with the therapist. This may mean that the parents are directly involved from the beginning without the observation sessions first.

CASE EXAMPLE

Some of the Theraplay principles and activities might be best illustrated with a case example of a two-and-a-half-year-old boy with severe aggressive behavior. We shall call him Jason (not his real name). Jason was referred to our mental health children's center for biting (to the point of drawing blood), hitting, spitting, and swearing and being defiant. He had been dismissed from several day care centers, and his parents had consulted with several mental health agencies to no avail. The aggressive behavior was also seen at home to the point that a pet cat would hide under furniture when Jason entered the room. Neighborhood children had ceased to play with him because of his fighting. Even older children were frightened of him (a note of pride was heard as the father said this).

After taking an in-depth family history, including the family history of each parent, it was revealed that both mother and father had come from backgrounds of physical abuse and addictions. The maternal grandmother had used drugs and the paternal grandfather was a binge alcoholic who beat his wife and son repeatedly. The biological parents had also used drugs and alcohol in the past. Jason's father had been jailed a number of times for the use of drugs, assault, and robbery. The father had just been released from jail at the beginning of therapy. When asked about his occupation, he replied, "I'm a bum."

The mother had been placed in an abusive foster home as an infant, but later returned to the care of her addicted teenage mother and maternal grandmother. The mother ran away from home at the age of 13 years and was a street child for a number of years. She had stopped using cocaine and was trying hard to establish a stable home for Jason. The mother had been quite aggressive growing up and as an adult. Her ambition for her son was high—she expected him to go to university and had already taught him the alphabet. Both parents wanted a better life for their son and were highly motivated to put effort into this.

The Marschak Interaction Method (MIM), an assessment of family relationships, revealed that the parents gave a lot of attention and praise to their son and could take delight in his behavior. However, they also gave a lot of power to their son. He often made the decision to start or stop activities. Parents tended to accede to his demands or would coax him. They were nurturing to him, but tended to be rough in touching him. Goals from this assessment were:

1. To enhance the attachment between parents and child, especially between mother and child
2. For parents to be more gentle in their physical contact with him

3. For Jason to be more cooperative and to support the parents in taking charge of his behavior
4. To reduce Jason's aggressive behavior

The parents observed Jason with the therapist behind a one-way mirror for the first four sessions as an interpreting therapist explained the purpose of each activity, as well as guiding the parents to be more attuned to Jason's needs. Jason did not have difficulty separating from his parents, except for the beginning of the fifth session when he was not feeling well. He was easily engaged by the therapist and took delight in many of the activities. However, at the beginning, he attacked her a few times by hitting, scratching, and spitting. Each time she immediately stopped him, said firmly "No hurts," and diverted his attention to another activity. Jason needed frequent reminders to be gentle in his touch.

Parents came into the therapy room halfway through the fifth session, when they directly interacted with their son under the guidance of the therapists. Whenever Jason was aggressive to his parents, he was immediately stopped with a "No hurts" and a more appropriate action was modeled for him by the therapist. The therapists stressed structure and nurturing activities with Jason. He soon became more obedient, stopped his aggression, and was spontaneously affectionate with the therapist. After a half hour of Theraplay activities, parent counseling took place, as well as a debriefing of the Theraplay session. Home and day care progress was discussed, and the parents were encouraged to do Theraplay activities at home. The parents were advised to stop any aggression immediately in a consistent fashion and to do nurturing activities with him. Below is the agenda used in the fifth session (note that the parents observed for the first 5 to 10 minutes of this session and then came into the Theraplay room).

Agenda

Entrance (note that this entrance was modified, because Jason did not want to separate from his parents at the beginning of this session): Follow the leader

Hello song (for structure and a clear beginning to the session): "Hello, Jason, hello, Jason, hello, Jason, I'm glad you came to play."

Inventory (for self-esteem building) noting positive attributes of the child: "Jason, I see you have brought your sparkling eyes, shiny brown hair, rosy cheeks, and strong arms. Look at these hands!"

Lotioning of hurts (for nurturing): "Oh, oh, I see a boo-boo here. That needs looking after." The therapist proceeded to lotion all of the hurts on his hands.

Song (for engagement and body image): "Head and shoulders."

Activity (for engagement and body image): "Squeaky body parts." The therapist makes a funny noise as she presses different parts of his body—nose ("honk-honk"), chest ("erk!"), shoulders ("ohoo!"). The therapist makes up noises for different body parts and repeats them in sequence. (Jason laughs a lot during this activity).

Activity (for structure): Hopping from one side of the room to the other side.

Activity (preparing to engage parents): Rolling up in blanket pretending to be a hot-dog.

[The parents enter the room.]

Activity (for connecting to Jason and nurturing): Parents pretend to find Jason and then unroll the blanket with many delighted exclamations on having found him. (Jason wants this activity repeated, but the therapist moves on to the next activity.)

Activity (for nurturing): Jason is rocked in the blanket while adults sing "Rock-a-bye, Jason," and then is lifted up into a parent's arms. This is repeated with the other parent.

Activity (for nurturing): "Cotton-ball soothe." Therapist models gentle touch by moving a cotton ball on Jason's face, shoulders, arms, and hands. Parents imitate this with Jason and with each other.

Activity (for challenge): "Cotton-ball guess." Jason closes his eyes and guesses where his parents are touching him with the cotton ball.

Activity (for nurturing, structuring, and body image): "Body outline." Adults make an outline of Jason's body as he lies on a piece of paper. Everyone joins in, filling in the different body parts with colored crayons, with many positive comments.

Activity (for nurturing): Feeding of potato chips directly into the mouth of Jason by therapists and later by the parents. The therapists feed the parents as well. (Both parents needed nurturing, as well as the child.)

Activity (for definite ending and structure): "Good-bye song": "Good-bye, Jason, good-bye, Mommy, good-bye, Daddy, good-bye, Sue and Linda. We're glad you came today."

Big circle hug.

At this point one of the therapists took Jason into another room to play or do crafts while the parents remained with the other therapist for a counseling session and to focus on what had just happened in the Theraplay session.

Progress

Remarkably, Jason stopped biting children in his day care by the third Theraplay session. By the fifth session he had stopped being aggressive with his father, the chief caregiver (a stay-at-home dad), but was still swearing and spitting at his mother (who worked long hours during the night and did not come home until morning, when she went to sleep). By the seventh session, the neighborhood children were playing again with Jason and the cat did not hide from him. Theraplay was ended after the ninth session because most of the goals had been reached. The parents (especially the father) were relating to Jason in a positive, relaxed, but firm way. The mother still needed to be more directive with him, but he was much more obedient with her than previously. Four checkups were planned for the year, and the parents were advised to seek marital counseling.

Jason progressed well at home, at day care, and in the neighborhood for almost a year. Then the father started to use drugs again and accidently smashed his wife's car. She ordered him out of the house and hired a nanny. She also found a new boyfriend. The disruption in Jason's home life was a setback for him, and he started to be aggressive again. The mother asked for Theraplay again.

Theraplay was resumed, but this time it took place in the home with the hope that there would be better generalization of treatment effects, especially with the mother's interactions with her son. Again, Jason's behavior significantly improved. However, after treatment during checkup contact, it was noted that whenever the mother discontinued a relationship with a partner or hired a new nanny, Jason's behavior deteriorated. The treatment ended with a discussion on the importance of stability in Jason's home life. The mother agreed to strive for this. Individual psychotherapy was needed for the mother, but she was unable to afford this financially.

The prognosis was guarded for this family because of the frequent change of caregivers for Jason. However, at the end of both series of treatment, Theraplay had reduced Jason's aggression and had helped him to be a more cooperative, happier child, who was able to relate more positively to his parents, other adults, and peers.

CONCLUSIONS AND FUTURE DIRECTIONS

On a clinical level, Theraplay has a good reputation for being a highly effective treatment method, in a short period of time, that is cost-effective and particularly suited for infants and toddlers with its concrete, nonverbal, playfully engaging approach. Since Theraplay tries to replicate normal parent-child interactions, it is easily understood by parents and clinicians alike. It is often highly enjoyable for both parents and child as they find new ways of taking delight in each other. Parents become more attuned and responsive to their child's needs, while children usually become more accepting of their parents' overtures. Attachments between parent and child are usually strengthened.

What is crucial for the acceptance of Theraplay is more evidence-based studies using randomly assigned control and treatment groups, as well as studies comparing Theraplay to well-validated treatment methods. For now and the future, this is a direction that Theraplay clinicians are well aware of and must continue to pursue. With cutting-edge research from psycho-biologists indicating that we need to pay more attention to non-verbal therapies and the importance of touch for children, it may be that treatment methods like Theraplay will soon be at the forefront of therapies widely used for helping children and their families form healthy relationships and/or attachments.

NOTE

1. More information about this area can be obtained directly from Barry Chaloner by e-mail: pals@frontier.net, or at www.pals4schools.com.

REFERENCES

Ammen, S. 2000. A play-based teen parenting program to facilitate parent/child attachment. In *Short-term play therapy for children*, ed. H. Knudson and C. Schaefer, 345–369. New York: Guilford.

Booth, P. 2000. Forming an attachment with an adopted toddler using the Theraplay approach. *Signal: Newsletter of the World Association for Infant Mental Health* (July–September).

———. 2005. Current Theraplay best practices: Focusing on attunement and regulation in play. *Theraplay Newsletter* (Summer): 5–8.

Bowlby, J. 1998. *A secure base*. New York: Basic.

Chaloner, B. 2006. One therapist's journey as a Head Start mental health consultant integrating child-centered with sensory/Theraplay-based approaches to play therapy with at-risk children. *Theraplay Newsletter* (Winter): 8–10.

DiPasquale, L. 2000. Marschak Interaction Method. In *Theraplay: Innovations in attachment-enhancing play therapy*, ed. E. Munns, 27–54. Northvale, NJ: Jason Aronson.

Eliot, L. 2000. *What's going on in there? How the brain and mind develop in the first five years of life*. New York: Bantam.

Field, T. 1995. *Touch in early development*. Hillsdale, NJ: Erlbaum.

———. 2000. *Touch therapy*. New York: Churchill Livingstone.

Fonagay, P. 2003. The development of psychopathology from infancy to adulthood: The mysterious unfolding of disturbance in time. *Infant Mental Journal* 24 (3): 212–239.

Gerhardt, S. 2004. *Why love matters: How affection shapes a baby's brain.* New York: Brunner-Routledge.

Jernberg, A., and P. Booth. 1999. *Theraplay: Helping parents and children build better relationships through attachment-based play.* San Francisco: Jossey-Bass.

Lassinius-Panula, L., and J. Makela. 2007. Effectiveness of Theraplay with symptomatic children ages 1 to 6: Changes in symptoms, parent-child relationships and stress hormone levels of children referred to psychiatric care in three university hospital districts in Finland. Paper presented at the International Theraplay Conference in Chicago, July 2007.

Makela, J., and I. Vierikko. 2004. From heart to heart: Theraplay research at SOS Children's Villages, Finland. Paper presented at the International Theraplay Conference in Chicago, July 2007.

Martin, D. 2000. Teacher-led Theraplay in early childhood classrooms. In *Theraplay: Innovations in attachment-enhancing play therapy*, ed. E. Munns, 321–338. Northvale, NJ: Jason Aronson.

Meyer, L., and J. Wardrop. 2006. Research on Theraplay. *Theraplay Institute Newsletter* (Summer): 8–11.

Munns, E., ed. 2000. *Theraplay: Innovations in attachment-enhancing play therapy.* Northvale, NJ: Jason Aronson.

———. 2003. Theraplay: Attachment-enhancing play therapy. In *Foundations of play therapy*, ed. C. E. Schaefer, 156–174. Hoboken, NJ: Wiley.

———. 2005. Theraplay with adolescents. In *Play therapy with adolescents*, ed. L. Gallo-Lopez and C. E. Schaefer, 30–47. Northvale, NJ: Jason Aronson.

Munns, E., and C. Ahmad. 2006. Theraplay groups with parents and their preschool children. *Theraplay Institute Newsletter* (Winter): 10–11.

Munns, E., D. Jensen, and L. Berger. 2000. Theraplay and the reduction of aggression. In *Theraplay: Innovations in attachment-enhancing play therapy*, ed. E. Munns, 14. Northvale, NJ: Jason Aronson.

Ritterfeld, U. 1990. Theraplay auf dem Prufstand: Bewerting des Therapieereflgs an Beisp Sorachhaufulliger Vorschulkinder. [Putting Theraplay to the test: Evaluation of therapeutic outcome with language-delayed preschool children.] *Theraplay Journal* 2:22–25.

Rubin, P., and J. Mroz. 2006. Infant/toddler attachment therapy: A place for Theraplay. Paper presented at the 18th annual ATTACh Conference on Attachment and Bonding, St. Louis, October 2006.

Rutter, M. 1994. Clinical implications of attachment concepts: Retrospect and prospect. Paper presented at the International Conference on Attachment and Psychopathology, Toronto, October.

Schore, A. 1998. Early trauma and the development of the right side of the brain. Paper presented at the conference "The Long Shadows of Trauma," Toronto, November.

Sherman, J. 2000. Multiple-family Theraplay. In *Theraplay: Innovations in attachment-enhancing play therapy*, ed. E. Munns, 195–210. Northvale, NJ: Jason Aronson.

Siegel, D. 1999. *The developing mind.* New York: Guilford Press.

Spratt, J., and A. Doob. 1998. *Can problem behavior in childhood be an introduction to future delinquency?* Workshop paper W-98-29ES. Ottowa: Human Resources Development, Canada.

Sui, A. Forthcoming. Theraplay in the Chinese world: An intervention program for Hong Kong children with internalizing problems. Doctoral dissertation.

Thayer, S. 1998. Encounters. *Psychology Today* (March): 31–36.

van IJzendoorn, M., F. Juffer, and M. G. C. Duyvesteyn. 1995. Breaking the intergenerational cycle of insecure attachment: A review of the effects of attachment-based interventions on maternal sensitivity and infant security. *Journal of Child Psychology and Psychiatry* 36 (2): 225–248.

Webber-Stratton, C., and T. Taylor. 2001. Nipping early risk factors in the bud: Preventing substance abuse, delinquency, and violence in adolescence through interventions targeted at young children (0 to 8 years). *Prevention Science* 2:165–192.

Weir, K. 2007. A research project on adopted children will begin in August 2007 at California State University at Fresno. Announcement at the International Theraplay Conference in Chicago, July 2007.

Wettig, H., U. Franke, and B. Fjordback. 2006. Evaluating the effectiveness of Theraplay. In *Contemporary play therapy*, ed. C. Schaefer and H. Knudson, 103–135. New York: Guilford.

Yoon, J.-H. 2007. Effects of family group Theraplay to enhance interactions between child and mother in low-income families. Poster presentation at the International Theraplay Conference in Chicago, July 2007.

II

APPLICATIONS TO SPECIFIC POPULATIONS

8

Situational and Story-Stem Scaffolding in Psychodynamic Play Therapy with Very Young Children

Theodore J. Gaensbauer and Kim Kelsay

With the recognition that children's play provides a unique and privileged window into the child's mind, the facilitation of expressive play has historically been a cornerstone of psychodynamically based psychotherapeutic work with children (Erikson 1950; Freud 1946; Waelder 1933; Winnicott 1968). In keeping with this important tradition, our focus in this chapter is on the question of how best to promote therapeutically meaningful expressive play in very young children. In addressing this issue we will take as our point of departure one of the most important and enduring debates within the psychodynamic play therapy movement (Newell 1941), namely to what extent should the child be encouraged to play freely and spontaneously without the intervention of the therapist versus to what extent should the therapist actively intervene in the play process? For reasons that we will outline below we believe that, given the unique challenges associated with involving very young children in expressive play therapy, significant activity on the part of the therapist is called for. By providing a scaffolding framework for helping young children make use of play as a communicative vehicle, the active, flexible, and dynamically attuned therapeutic structuring of play situations can be an especially effective vehicle for accessing the very young child's inner world and for facilitating therapeutic processing of both internally and externally derived emotional conflicts, including psychological trauma.

In recent years there has been a striking convergence of interest among clinicians and developmental researchers in the use of structured paradigms to identify early mental processing. A recent product of this convergence, the MacArthur Story Stems Battery (Bretherton et al. 1990), a series of standardized structured play situations designed to assess a full range of developmental themes in young children, has provided solid support for the clinical use of structured play. This battery has proved to be remarkably effective in eliciting thematic differences in children's responses to the various stimulus situations depending on their developmental experiences. Structured play approaches have also enjoyed a long history in child psychotherapy (Conn 1939; Levy 1939; Solomon 1938). In what follows, we will discuss developmental factors that need to be taken into account in doing play therapy with very young children and provide background history on the use of structured play situations in developmental research and in clinical settings. We will then present our own perspective on these issues and describe a number of case examples illustrating how therapeutic scaffolding can be utilized for both diagnosis and treatment. We will conclude with a discussion of how such approaches might lend themselves to systematic psychotherapy research with young children.

THE RATIONALE FOR THERAPEUTIC SCAFFOLDING

The cornerstone of psychodynamic play therapy has been to help children communicate their inner thoughts and feelings for the following purposes: gaining insight into the sources of their emotional distress and behavioral symptoms; facilitating psychological processing of conflict situations; identifying maladaptive defenses; strengthening adaptive coping mechanisms; and promoting psychological integration of internal and external stressors. To these ends, psychodynamic play therapists have generally advocated nonintrusive therapeutic approaches that allow children to play in unstructured and spontaneous ways in order that they may freely and without outside influence communicate what is on their minds. Interestingly though, in the many discussions that have taken place over the years about the advantages of nonintrusive approaches as opposed to more active and structured approaches in gaining access to the child's inner world, the age of the child has been given relatively little consideration.

It is our contention that given their level of development, very young children are much less likely to reveal their inner thoughts and feelings spontaneously than they are when the therapist actively provides opportunities for these thoughts and feelings to be expressed. There are a number of reasons why we believe this to be the case. The most straightforward is that young children are still in the process of learning how to play. Although in the past decades we have learned that infants' capacities for memory and internal processing are much more complex than was long appreciated, infants' play activities are nevertheless primarily sensorimotor in nature.

Around age two, a number of developmental transitions occur that open up new worlds for the child. These advances include the development of

language fluency, symbolic play, emotional regulation and the appreciation of differing emotional states, a sense of an autobiographical self, and
increased understanding of narrative structure (Bloom and Tinker 2001).
Although these developmental attainments are crucial prerequisites for the
development of expressive play, at age two they are all still in emergent
stages. Even as children's play moves beyond the concrete and imitative
and becomes more symbolic in nature, the cognitive-affective schemata
upon which this early play is based are likely to be highly egocentric,
closely tied to immediate experience, relatively segmented, and expressed
primarily through behavioral enactments. It is only over the next two years
or so that children become increasingly able to use play props to represent
their physical and social worlds in miniature and to creatively manipulate
these props independently of the immediate stimulus situation. Over time,
the growing capacity to manipulate different scenarios through play will
help children make meaningful associative links between the disparate
mental schemata that they accumulate through experience and will facilitate an increasingly coherent understanding of their relationship to the
world around them.

How is it that young children learn to use these various developmental
attainments in the service of creative play? The answer is clear. It is through
the developmental guidance and scaffolding that is provided by adults. By
their sensitive caregiving and attentiveness, parents convey to children that
their communications, including play, are valued and evoke meaningful
responses. But caregivers do much more than simply encourage the child's
expressiveness. They provide sensitive scaffolding that is crucial to the
child's advancement in all of the areas mentioned above. Without parents'
recognition of where the child is in his or her developmental understanding
and their provision of the contingent structuring that allows the child to
take the next step forward, the child will have great difficulty making these
developmental advances. For example, as children move from preverbal to
verbal levels of development they depend heavily on caregivers' abilities to
identify and empathically communicate their understanding of the child's
wishes, to provide verbal frameworks and emotional labels for their experiences, and to teach and model adaptive ways of expressing these emotions
and wishes. By sensing what a child is trying to convey and facilitating that
communication by adding important words or concepts that the child has
not quite grasped, they gradually expand the child's understanding and
communicative skills. Over time, they help the child put his or her experiences into increasingly sophisticated narrative contexts, not only through
direct explanations, but through more general scaffolding such as that
provided by storytelling and reading books (Nelson 1990). Documenting the crucial role of caregivers in helping children communicate their
experiences, research on early memory has unequivocally demonstrated

that young children are much more able to convey what they know when appropriate cues are provided (Fivush 1993).

Translating these developmental considerations into the treatment situation, we must recognize that young children will not consistently, or even frequently, play out their internal representations spontaneously. Since they are not purposefully participating in therapy and because the therapy situation will be unfamiliar and potentially anxiety provoking, in an unstructured situation young children are likely to gravitate toward play materials and activities that are familiar and pleasurable, as opposed to activities that are associated with psychic conflict. Very young children will also have limited abilities to search out the expressive play materials available in a playroom on their own. Since the likelihood of a young child enacting any particular cognitive-affective schema is highly dependent on the types of stimulus cues available, minimal structuring of the playroom that makes expressive toys such as dolls and dollhouses, puppets, toy animals, and drawing materials readily accessible will be necessary at the very least. Many children, particularly those with developmental delays or those who have been maltreated, may have difficulty playing creatively or using play materials in a symbolic way. But even in optimal caregiving situations, children between the ages of three and four will have difficulty creating sustained story lines on their own. Symbolic play narratives are likely to be short, easily disrupted, and highly dependent on caregiver support.

An additional consideration is that, of any age group the communicative ability of very young children will be most vulnerable to outside influences. Maltreated children are likely to have considerable fear about communicating their experiences because of explicit or implicit threats. However, even very expressive children with well-meaning parents may be hesitant to talk about difficult subjects unless they receive explicit parental permission (Hirshberg 1993). It is not uncommon for parents to report that their young children have not talked about even the most compelling of emotional experiences, including traumas or the death of a parent, despite the fact that numerous indicators of emotional preoccupation were evident. A simple recommendation that caregivers take the initiative in encouraging their children to talk about their experience can result in a rush of thoughts and feelings from the child. As described below, the opportunity for parents to observe the child's reenactments in play situations that pertain to real life experiences can help them to appreciate how much the child has been affected by these experiences.

For all of these reasons, in facilitating a psychodynamic therapeutic process with young children we believe that, just as parents have the responsibility of providing the necessary structure within which children can grow, therapists have a responsibility to actively help young children communicate what they have experienced. In a therapeutic context, this involves the provision of cues or play settings that can serve as evocative stimuli for the child but that do not lead the child in any particular direction. Historically, this kind of therapeutic activity has been referred to as "structured," "directed," "controlled," or "guided" play. Since these terms can imply a particular agenda on the part of the therapist, we prefer the term "scaffolding" to describe what we are proposing. Developmentally, "scaffolding" refers to the process whereby an adult, without directly intervening or controlling, provides crucial framing that allows the child to make advances along a particular developmental trajectory. The trajectory originates with the child, but the child would have difficulty making the advances on his or her own. Our view of therapeutic scaffolding is very similar. The goal is to provide situational or play settings that can foster the expression of thoughts and feelings that children carry within but that they are unlikely to express without assistance. The scaffolding is done in ways that fully respect the child's autonomy, do not impose the therapist's values on the child, respond empathically and contingently to the child's handling of the play setting, and lead to increasingly self-directed and spontaneous play expression.

HISTORICAL BACKGROUND AND OVERVIEW

Developmental psychologists have used structured experimental situations to explore the perceptions, memory capacities, and cognitive functioning of young children for over a century. Based on children's responses to an initial stimulus, inferences are drawn as to the internal representations and mental processing that explain these responses. Based on the understanding gained from the initial responses, subsequent experimental stimuli can be presented in order to gain further insight into the children's thought processes. This kind of sequential exploration of children's mental processing can be carried out using different groups of children or can involve a series of experiments with the same child. Perhaps the foremost representative of this latter method of study, utilizing close observation of young children's spontaneous play combined with the timely introduction of structured stimuli that promoted further elaborations of the child's internal schemata, was Jean Piaget (1952, 1954).

In infancy, inferences about children's inner world will be based almost entirely on their nonverbal behavioral and emotional responses to concrete situations involving stimuli they have experienced in their everyday life. Designed for use with this age group, perhaps the most productive structured situation in the history of child development has been the "Strange Situation" paradigm developed by Ainsworth and her colleagues (1978). Assessing infants' responses to a series of separations from their caregivers, developmental psychologists have been able to make valid judgments about the quality of the infant's attachment to (or "internal working model" of) that caregiver, judgments that have strong predictive implications for the infant's current and future social-emotional functioning (Carlson and Sroufe 1995). Building on the work of Spitz (1965), Ainsworth, and many others, I [Gaensbauer] and my colleagues used a series of structured situations including free play, comparison of approaches by an unfamiliar adult and by the child's caregiver, interactive play tasks, mild frustrations, and a brief separation from the caregiver to assess emotional regulation and caregiver-child interaction in both normal and maltreated infants ranging in age from 3 to 24 months (Gaensbauer 1982a; Gaensbauer and Harmon 1981; Gaensbauer and Mrazek 1981; Gaensbauer, Mrazek, and Emde 1979). Infants' behavioral and emotional responses to the stimuli presented to them in this kind of structured playroom setting were quite productive in delineating not only emotional vulnerabilities and attachment patterning but also cognitive-affective schemata that pointed to specific caregiving experiences (Gaensbauer 1982b; Gaensbauer and Harmon 1982).

Beyond infancy, developmental psychologists and clinicians have utilized an immense array of stimulus situations to assess the increasingly complex social-emotional and cognitive functioning seen in the period between two and five years. Among the most productive has been the story stem technique, in which through doll play and a brief verbal description the child is presented with the beginning of a story and is then asked to "show and tell what happens next." In recent years, with the support of the MacArthur Foundation, a consortium of developmental researchers and clinicians brought together a number of evocative story stems tapping into a range of emotionally compelling developmental themes, including attachment security, responses to authority, peer rivalry, moral dilemmas, family conflict, oedipal relationships, and emotional regulation (Bretherton and Oppenheim 2003). This group of story beginnings, termed the MacArthur Story Stem Battery (MSSB; Bretherton et al. 1990), has been used in a number of studies in both clinical and nonclinical settings and has proved to be remarkably productive as a vehicle for eliciting narratives that capture the young child's inner world (Emde, Wolf, and Oppenheim 2003). A listing of the stories and a representative example (the lost keys) of how the story stems are presented to the child are provided at the end of this chapter.

That the MacArthur story stem approach is particularly applicable for the two- to five-year-old age group is exemplified by the finding that in a nonclinical sample, at age three almost half of the children could acknowledge a moral dilemma in the stories, at age four over 75 percent, and at age five over 90 percent (Oppenheim et al. 1997). Studies in nonclinical samples have shown significant correlations between the children's parental representations as reflected in their story stem responses and independent measures of that relationship, including attachment security (Bretherton et al. 1990; Solomon, George, and DeJong 1996). Story stem responses have also been shown to correlate with parent and teacher behavior ratings of internalizing and externalizing behaviors, both concurrently and prospectively (Von Klitzing et al. 2000; Warren, Oppenheim, and Emde 1996). In the clinical setting, the story stems of abused and/or neglected children have been found to differ significantly from those of nonclinical children (Macfie et al. 1999; Toth et al. 1997) as have narratives of children from battered women's shelters (Grych et al. 2002). Individual responses of abused children have shown remarkably clear evidence of very specific experiences in the parent-child relationship (Buchsbaum et al. 1992). Narratives of maltreated children have also been found to show positive changes over time following adoption (Hodges et al. 2003).

The MSSB and similarly structured diagnostic batteries such as the Children's Apperception Test (Bellak and Bellak 1987), the Berkeley Puppet Interview (Measelle et al. 1998), or the Children's Play Therapy Instrument (Kernberg, Chazan, and Normandin 1998) fit naturally into a systematic evaluation of the young child. More difficult to describe systematically is the use of play scaffolding in individual treatment, where the therapeutic focus will be on the specific problems that have brought the child to treatment rather than on a broad spectrum of developmental issues.

From a clinical standpoint, perhaps the most notable practitioner of the "structured" approach was David Levy. Based initially on a research interest in children's normative responses to developmental situations postulated by psychoanalytic theory to be potential sources of psychic conflict, in what constituted perhaps the earliest form of a story stem battery, Levy (1933) developed a series of specific play situations to examine children's attitudes and emotional reactions. These included standardized play dramatizations involving sibling rivalry, conflicts with peers, reactions to the discovery of genital differences, fantasies about childbirth, separations from parents, and responses to parental punishments. Over time, as he recognized the revealing nature of the children's responses, he began using the standardized situations in the context of therapy, introducing them at moments in the therapeutic process when the relevant issue had come to the surface. Most relevant to current clinical practice, by the late 1930s he had begun to combine structured and spontaneous play in the form of what he termed "Release Therapy" or "Abreaction Therapy" (Levy 1938, 1939). In this therapy, children who had been frightened by a specific event were presented with play situations that either recapitulated that event or promoted the unfettered expression of aggressive behavior, such as bursting water balloons. Children were encouraged to respond to the dramatization in any way they wished, with the goal of allowing them to abreact feelings associated with the frightening event and/or to release inhibited feelings. The therapist generally did not intervene once the stage was set. Hambidge (1955), a later collaborator of Levy's, used the term "structured play therapy" to describe this approach and, much as we are proposing here, outlined how such situational play structuring would be naturally interwoven with spontaneous play.

Play scaffolding in individual therapy places great responsibility on the knowledge and skills of the therapist. A major concern about the use of structured situations in therapy has been that therapists will either directly impose their own formulations and values on the child or by intruding on children's spontaneous play will indirectly disrupt children's ability to fully express their own ideas. Another potential concern has been the potential for bypassing or overriding the child's defenses and thus confronting the child with therapeutic issues and emotions that the child is not ready to handle. Psychoanalytically oriented therapists have also expressed concerns about contamination of the therapist-patient relationship, thereby interfering with the use of transference as a therapeutic tool (Newell 1941).

With these concerns in mind, we would like to elaborate on our approach to therapeutic scaffolding. Rather than viewing such structuring as controlling or disruptive of the child's autonomy, we see it as a way of establishing a dialogue with patients whose language skills are limited and whose primary communicative currency is play action. In the course of psychodynamic psychotherapy with an adult, the therapist not only attends to the spontaneous material the patient presents, but is likely to ask the patient to elaborate on certain experiences or feelings that the therapist believes are important to the patient's problems. Not infrequently, patients will avoid difficult subjects and it will be necessary for the therapist to actively address this avoidance through interpretation or tactful redirection. In our view, the introduction of a structured play situation with a young child is the equivalent of asking questions of an adult. For example, if there has been a recent stressful event, by recreating a concrete or symbolic play scene that replicates the event's context in sufficient detail for the child to recognize the references and then either implicitly or explicitly asking the child what happens next, we are essentially asking the child, "How did you feel when this happened?"

In the preverbal child, the "structured recreation" of a stressful event is likely to involve concrete behavioral or interactional exposure to stimulus situations that are similar to the situation that caused the original stress. This is likely to be done in the form of graduated doses in a supportive and affectively positive way for purposes of desensitizing the infant to the stressor, with a close monitoring of the infant's affective and behavioral responses in order to determine the infant's readiness to handle the exposure (Gaensbauer and Siegel 1995). An example would be an 18-month-old child who experienced a facial burn with painful medical treatments and who subsequently resisted any caregiving intrusions, including baths and diaper changes. In stepwise fashion over time, his parents used the playful, loving application of a soothing lotion to his body and eventually his face as a "structured" vehicle for helping him overcome his traumatically derived resistance to being touched.

As children become more capable of symbolic play, they will be increasingly able to engage in structured play scenes using toys. We have had the not uncommon experience that once children "get it," that is, recognize that the scene corresponds to something within their own experience, they immediately become engaged, as if internalized memories and feelings have just been waiting for the means to get out (Gaensbauer 1995). Either through their direct participation in the play scene or through other behavioral manifestations, the child will convey his or her memories, affective reactions, defensive operations, and personalized understanding of the situation. An example would be a 21-month-old dog bite victim, whose initial response to a scene of a boy doll and a toy dog clearly reflected his fear and anger. He defensively moved away from the scene but immediately began to hit the playroom wall with a baton he was holding (Gaensbauer and Siegel 1995). Similar to the adult patient, the child's initial response will lead to further questions or observations on the part of the therapist that will often be best conveyed through additional slight modifications in the play scene. For example, in the case of the child who was bitten by a dog, an additional character such as a mother doll could be introduced (i.e., "How did you feel when your mother came to help you?"), an affective reaction could be labeled (i.e., "The boy doll is scared or angry"), a new character and a subsequent action could be demonstrated through medical toys (i.e., "How did you feel when the doctor treated your bite?"), or a reassuring reminder such as removing the dog could be carried out (i.e., "The boy is now safe").

Although there is a long history of using guided play for specific stress situations, such as in the aftermath of a discrete trauma (Gaensbauer 1994, 1997, 2000; Levy 1939; Maclean 1977) or in anticipatory preparation for a stressful event such as a hospitalization or medical procedure (Cassel 1965; Rae et al. 1989), we believe that such scaffolding is applicable to the full range of the environmental factors influencing the young child's development (Russ 1995). By taking a detailed developmental and interactional history, the therapist will likely have a very good idea of the factors contributing to the child's symptoms (e.g., family tension, separation experiences, disciplinary battles, past stressful events, etc.) and the settings where these symptoms are being manifested (e.g., bedtime, visitation or day care transitions, mealtime, etc.). In addition, given their immaturity and dependence on caregivers, most of the very young child's key life experiences can be readily captured in a play setting.

If and when guided play is introduced, it is fluid in nature, taking the form of a vehicle for dialogue rather than a rigid formula, and it is not utilized if the child is spontaneously elaborating on his or her experiences in a productive way. Following Piaget, except when a complete change of scene is called for, the therapist's active interventions are likely to involve very small additions or modifications to the scene, with the goal of helping the child take one small step further in the elaboration of her or his experience. Since young children tend not to carry out sustained spontaneous play, even when their attention is clearly captured, their participation in a play scene can be very transient. The therapeutic process thus often takes place in "rounds" or brief bouts of engagement alternating with other activities. The therapist's introduction of a new variation often provides the incentive for the child to return to the scene. Between "rounds," if the parents are present the therapist has the opportunity to talk to them about therapeutic issues that have come up both in the sessions and at home. Structuring or scaffolding thus does not occur throughout a therapeutic session but only at opportune times as judged by the therapist. There is plenty of time for spontaneous play, both in response to the play stimulus and in general.

In keeping with the goals of psychodynamic work, the opportunity to reenact or communicate about stressful experiences in the young child's life can serve a variety of therapeutic purposes. It allows children to fully express their memories and understanding of the experiences or situations that have caused them stress and to abreact difficult feelings. Over time, the repeated reworking of a compelling therapeutic theme through play can help children to identify and increasingly regulate their emotional responses to the stresses they have encountered. Even in preverbal infants such as the child described above with the facial burn, situational exposures that trigger responses associated with a stressful event but in a nonstressful environment are promoting psychological reprocessing and integration of that event. In other words, new internal schemata are being formed. With children over the age of two, the playing out of difficult experiences can help the child develop a more complete narrative understanding of what has occurred and help to correct the inevitable fragmentation, distortion, and overpersonalization that typically characterizes young children's perceptions. The opportunity for children to creatively write their own script as to "what happens next" also can serve the purpose of mastery by allowing for the carrying out of reparative fantasies and alternative outcomes that help alleviate the child's feelings of helplessness.

Within the framework of such therapeutic re-creations, the therapist has a variety of traditional play therapy techniques through which he or she can provide support, guidance, and interpretation. These include direct participation in the play through action or through verbal observations, identification of important affects and motives, provision of narrative commentary regarding sequences and meanings, corrections of distortions in the child's understanding of the situation, promotion of mastery through compensatory play scenarios, facilitation of the expression of inhibited affects such as anger, and the teaching of alternative adaptive modes of responding to the situation. The reader is referred to the excellent chapter on play therapy with preschool children by Benham and Slotnick (2006) for a detailed review of the therapist's options once meaningful play has been mobilized.

We are in strong agreement with Benham and Slotnick (2006) that individual psychotherapy with the very young child is not indicated without significant parental involvement. If it is appropriate and they can handle it, we believe that having parents participate in sessions is ideal and can be enormously helpful. Seeing the child respond in a meaningful way to a particular story stem can provide parents with a clearer understanding about how the child is being affected by the situation. This in turn can become the basis for more informed understanding about what the parents can do to help the child with that situation. In sessions, as the child is reliving events that have been stressful, parents can provide feedback and comfort to the child in ways that they had not been able to previously for lack of understanding of the child's inner feelings (Gaensbauer and Siegel 1995). Finally, the parents' presence facilitates the development of "co-constructed narratives," in which a dialogue about the situations of stress is established between parent and child that can serve to promote ongoing communication and problem solving in the home environment (Fivush and Fromhoff 1988).

CLINICAL EXAMPLES

Therapeutic scaffolding in order to facilitate children's expression of their internal representations can be helpful in a wide range of clinical situations. In the following vignettes we will provide examples that illustrate this broad degree of applicability.

Providing an Opportunity for Children to Express Memories of a Past Experience

The following case illustrates the usefulness of having expressive toys readily available and of providing verbal and play action guidance in order to facilitate children's communication of their memories of important past events. In this case a four-year-old child referenced experiences that occurred prior to 28 months of age. In previous publications, Gaensbauer (1995, 2002, 2004b) has reported on a series of children between the ages of two and five years who in response to appropriate stimulus cues reenacted salient aspects of traumatic experiences that had occurred in the preverbal period.

Four-year-old Joseph was being seen because of aggressive behavior toward his grandmother and especially toward his stepmother, with whom he had been living the previous three months. In an initial parent session, his father reported that Joseph had been living with his father and his father's parents until his father's recent marriage and that he had not seen his mother since she had been arrested for a white-collar crime when he was 28 months of age. The father also reported that prior to her arrest, his mother had been very overprotective and paranoid, including taking Joseph into an unlighted closet with her for long periods. At the current time it was very hard for Joseph to be alone or in the dark. After his mother was taken away Joseph asked for her several times over the first few days but then had not asked about her again. His father reported that Joseph had not shown any symptoms related to his mother's leaving and that "he doesn't even remember her now."

Joseph's grandmother brought him to the first session. Upon entering the playroom, in an action that took his grandmother aback, he almost immediately went over to the dollhouse and put a baby doll that was lying about into a toy standup cupboard. Making the association to being held in the dark by his mother, the therapist asked if it was dark in the "closet." Joseph didn't say anything but instead put a toy lamp in the cupboard with the baby doll. At other points in the session he put the baby doll in a toy wardrobe and placed several other doll figures in tight places, including the oven of a toy stove. Since from the history it appeared that the recent back-and-forth visitation between grandparents' home, father's home, and preschool was part of his stress, the therapist brought out a second dollhouse, cars, and a play "school," and then spent time identifying dolls that would represent a mother, father, grandparents, and child. Joseph showed relatively little interest in this play, other than putting the baby to bed and knocking over the various dolls and furniture. When not presented with a specific play situation, his play was relatively disorganized and unfocused.

Joseph's father brought him to the second session and told the therapist that when Joseph's grandmother had told him about the closet play he (the father) had cried. To acquaint his father with the playroom setting, the therapist pointed to the dollhouse and encouraged Joseph to help identify the dolls used in the previous session. Soon after, Joseph put the mother doll in a small box that was part of the dollhouse furniture. When the therapist asked why the mother doll was in the box, Joseph again put a toy lamp in the box, saying "It's not so dark." When the therapist commented that Joseph didn't like the dark and asked why, Joseph said he was scared of monsters. His father, who was quite stunned by this play, asked him, "Did anyone ever put you in the dark?" Joseph in a confused way first said yes, then no. He then turned to his father and asked, "Did anyone ever put me in a closet?" His father responded, "I don't know," whereupon Joseph said, in a more declarative than interrogative tone, "When I was a baby."

Obtaining the father's approval, the therapist explained to Joseph that when he was a baby, his mother had put him in the dark. He then asked Joseph if he remembered that and Joseph said no. The references to his mother soon led into a discussion of his stepmother, as the therapist and his father helped him to distinguish between the mother who had taken care of him when he was a baby and his current mother figure. At one point, when the therapist asked him if he knew where his mother was, he said he didn't and then said, "Let's not talk about this anymore."

By pure coincidence, later in the session Joseph began playing with a Fisher Price "town" with a miniature police station and jail. Noting this, Joseph spontaneously said, "Someone has to go to jail . . . someone has been bad." When his father asked who had to go to jail, of the large number of dolls lying on a table Joseph specifically picked up the mother doll! He put the doll in the jail cell, and said, "You have to stay there." Soon after he turned to his father and said, "Remember when you called the police?" As his father wasn't sure what he was referring to, Joseph added, "When Caitlin . . . " Still confused, his father said, "Your cousin?" and then, having an insight, asked, "Kennedy?" Joseph immediately responded, "Yes." His father, rather shaken, then turned to the therapist and explained that "Kennedy" referred to his mother. The father explained that he had not called the police when Joseph's mother was arrested but that a policeman had come to the door and asked that his father leave the house with Joseph. Joseph and his father were thus outside and watched the police take his mother away. That was the last time that Joseph saw her.

These initial two sessions highlighted for his father and grandmother the degree to which Joseph had remembered and been affected by the loss of his mother and by the anxiety-provoking experiences he had experienced in her care. They also helped to explain the fear that he was continuing to show in the dark and when left alone. Placing a lamp in the cupboard with the dolls was clearly an adaptive step toward mastering this fear. While Joseph clearly retained internal representations of his mother, they were vague, fragmented, and confused. He clearly needed the scaffolding of his father and the therapist to make sense of them and to obtain a more accurate narrative about what had occurred. The recent significant loss of time with his grandmother and the confusion of his stepmother with his biological mother had triggered feelings of anger both about his mother's early caregiving and her abandonment, which were being taken out on both of his current female caregivers. His difficulty in responding in any coherent way to the play setting involving the two dollhouses and the "school" pointed to his confusion about his current schedule and the need for much more explanation on the part of his caregivers.

Identifying Aspects of a Trauma Needing Therapeutic Attention

It is often difficult to predict what aspects of a trauma have been most salient for the child or the most stressful. For this reason, exposure of the child to every aspect of a traumatic experience through guided play situations can be helpful in identifying those experiences that most need to be addressed in treatment.

When he was 18 months of age, a dog bumped John to the ground and appeared to be licking his face, with no growling or other indicators of aggression. Only as his mother pulled the dog away did she see that John had been severely bitten and a large segment of his upper lip torn away with profuse bleeding. John began crying as she picked him up. He was immediately taken to the emergency room, where he received stitches while being held down screaming and struggling. His injuries subsequently interfered with his eating and required several follow-up medical procedures.

At age three he was referred for an evaluation. Over the course of three sessions and in the midst of spontaneous play that was quite informative in itself, the therapist introduced two specific play settings. The first was the situation in which he had been bitten. The second involved a hospital scene. In response to the dog bite scene, he expressed generalized feelings of anger at the dog, such as knocking the dog figure off the table. However, he seemed at a loss as far as playing out what happened. While not avoiding the scene, he didn't carry out any play actions that had specific relevance to what had happened to him, nor did he show much emotional reaction to the scene.

In contrast, when the therapist presented the hospital scene he became immediately engaged and played out a number of aspects of his medical treatments. He pressed a toy knife on a boy doll's face, took a toy medicine bottle and put it to the boy doll's mouth (reminiscent of how he had been fed during his healing process), and took a parrot toy and bit all of the doctor dolls and then threw them and the hospital furniture across the room. He then pressed the parrot toy forcefully against the therapist's upper lip and pretended to be a giant marching around the room with a scary, gruff voice.

The structured play helped confirm (there was other clinical information that suggested this would be the case, including the fact that he showed little fear of dogs) that the child's traumatic affects were much more tied to his medical treatments than they were to the dog bite itself and that these medical experiences would need to be the primary focus of treatment. Indeed, after the session in which the hospital play was carried out, he told his mother that he thought it was the doctors who had injured his lip.

Exploring Psychodynamics When a Complete Development History Is Lacking

In contrast to clinical situations where the therapist has knowledge of the child's developmental history, with maltreated children or children in foster care it is often the case that the therapist will have little information about the child's past. Structured play such as the MacArthur story stems can be a means of exploring not only major themes troubling to children, but also important prognostic variables such as children's ability to regulate their emotions and the nature of their representations of parental figures and adults. With story stems the therapist is able to gain rapid and efficient access to the child's internal world, while familiarizing the child with a vehicle for communication that can be used for the subsequent scaffolding of important themes in treatment.

Stephen was a five-year-old living with a new foster family and attending a therapeutic preschool for abused children. Although it was known that he had been removed from his biological family due to abuse, the foster family and clinical team had little other information regarding Stephen's past. As the MacArthur story stems were administered, Stephen was clearly captivated and engaged, with a bright affect throughout. His stories were detailed and centered on themes of chaotic aggression and uncertainty about his location. For example, when presented with the exclusion story stem "The kiss," (in which two parents sitting together on a couch ask the boy doll "David" to go upstairs and play quietly in his room; they then kiss), Stephen told the following story: "The brother is upstairs and they kick the ball and it hits Mom in the head. Dad comes upstairs and asks in an angry voice, 'Who did it?' The brother says, 'He did it.' The other brother says, 'No, he did it.' They got sent to bed. Mom and Dad were in bed. Dad slept on the couch. He sleeps there every day. The boy tiptoes out the door to the other house. He gets all his clothes and he lives there. He wakes up in the morning and no one wakes up. He goes to school but he doesn't know what school. He walks to the other school. All the schools in the world are gone." In other stories, the boy "David" also ended up going between houses and often all the characters died. The story stems indicated that Stephen had surprisingly good affect regulation despite the atmosphere of angry conflict that characterized his home environment, but that he was having great difficulty making sense of his moves from one house to another and feeling secure with the adults in these homes.

Assessing the Child's Understanding of Parental Divorce and Visitation

Structuring of play is not only helpful in situations where there have been discrete stressful events, but also in assessing children's understanding of a variety of common situations that can produce emotional distress. A common one is parental divorce, with its attendant complicated visitation arrangements.

Sandra was two years old when her mother brought her for evaluation because of the considerable anger she was showing toward her mother following visitations with the father. Following her parents' separation when she was four months old, her mother had been the primary caregiver of her and her older brother, with two daytime visits and one overnight visit each week with her father. The divorce had been very acrimonious, including arguments during visitation exchanges. A fifty-fifty custody-sharing arrangement on a five-two-two-five schedule had been instituted two months prior to the evaluation.

In the first session, Sandra was very hyper and moved from toy to toy in a very unfocused way. She also showed an indiscriminate pattern of relating. Showing no shyness with the therapist, she immediately ran into the office from the waiting room ahead of her mother. On leaving the first session, she darted into the open door of a colleague's office and climbed on his couch. Since her verbal skills were not sufficient to gain a sense of her feelings about the visitation schedule, in the second session the therapist brought out two dollhouses and a mother, father, brother, and baby doll. He then set up separation situations in which the child dolls were saying goodbye to one or the other of the parents. Sandra had trouble sustaining any consistent identification of the dolls, particularly the mother and father dolls. She showed particular resistance to identifying a mother doll, exemplified by the fact that on several occasions as the therapist was holding a clearly female doll with a dress, she identified it as "da-da." She seemed unable to relate to the separation scenes. She tended to grab all the dolls and put them together someplace—on a bed or in the garage of one of the houses.

The overall impression was of confusion, inability to engage the situation, avoidance of the mother dolls, and a sense of inner chaos that was reflected not just in her response to the play setting but in her overall functioning. The confusion was understandable in light of the intense parental conflict and the recent dramatic change in the visitation schedule, and, similar to Joseph's case described above, pointed to the need to help her develop a cognitive map about what was happening. The responses to the play also suggested difficulties in the relationship with her mother, over and above the problems with reunions. Her mother, while committed to her child, was often distracted, busy, and emotionally unavailable, whereas her father was much more emotionally attentive. The anger toward her mother following reunions and her doll play expressed not only her difficulty with transitions but also her emotional preference for her father. Over time the play platform established in these initial sessions provided the vehicle for Sandra to express the anger and upset that she was experiencing that was being channeled into hyperactivity, behavioral acting out, and emotional detachment. It also allowed her parents and the therapist to play out the visitation patterns with toys in ways that she could increasingly comprehend. Finally, it alerted her mother to problems in her interactions with Sandra that needed to be addressed.

Helping Children Deal with Everyday Stressors

Sandra's and Joseph's struggles to make sense of their visitation schedules point up another way in which guided play can be extremely useful. Young children experience a variety of stressful situations for which parents try to prepare them, including not only divorce and visitation scheduling, but a variety of everyday events such as parental absences for work or illness, deaths of pets, day care arrangements, family travel, medical procedures, and so forth. Often this preparation comes in the form of a verbal explanation, such as "Your mother will be back from her trip on Tuesday" or "You'll see your father next Friday" or "The doctor is going to have to give you a shot today." Unfortunately these verbal explanations often have little meaning to young children who are not able to create an internal map based on words alone. We thus recommend that parents accompany their verbal explanations with play action demonstrations, so that children not only hear the words but are able to see in concrete terms what is happening. One might, for example, explain that a parent is going on a long trip by putting a parent doll in a toy airplane and flying it to a far side of the room. The young child is provided not only with a tangible visual image of the parent going far away, but also with concrete evidence that the parent still exists and will be returning. A four-year-old child facing an MRI procedure was helped to anticipate what she would experience when the therapist created a "cave-like space" by taping a rounded sheet of typing paper to a table in the form of an open-ended, horizontal half cylinder. The therapist then placed a baby doll on a bed and pushed the bed into the open space underneath the paper, giving the child a sense of how she would be enclosed. As he was doing this, the therapist also demonstrated the kinds of noises the child was likely to hear.

Other structuring techniques, such as drawing, can also supply children with tangible references that they can turn to in dealing with everyday stresses. The Draw-A-Book technique utilized by Benham (personal communication) can be particularly effective in this regard. The technique involves drawing a series of pictures in the form of a book or Sunday cartoon in order to provide a complete story about something the child is experiencing. The "book" concludes with an ending that achieves some sort of resolution or closure. Children's participation in the storybook construction can be quite revealing. In helping a four-year-old child deal with the frequent business travels of his mother, in the first frame of the story the therapist drew a picture of his mother saying goodbye to him at school. The therapist then asked the child what he should draw in the next frame to capture what the child was doing at school. The child told him he should draw the child with a sad face looking out the window of the school and watching his mother leave, poignantly conveying his feelings of missing her. His mother and the therapist were able at this point to empathize with his sad feelings, while proceeding to complete the story book by drawing his father picking him up after school (the parents were divorced), playing with him and putting him to bed, and so on. The story ended with a happy reunion upon the mother's return. The child kept the book with him and would review it with both his parents. It was quite helpful in reducing the child's distress during his mother's absences.

Assessing Play Content and Process for Diagnostic Purposes

The use of a story stem battery can be helpful in differentiating among possible causes of a child's behavioral difficulties. Terence was a five-year-old attending a therapeutic preschool. Although he had a history of abuse, the behavioral problems he was showing in class were not typical of what might be expected given this history. More than their emotional content, what was most striking about Terence's responses to the MacArthur story stems was his preoccupation with sensation. As the examiner got out the toys and dolls he nicely told her to be quiet. Although very interested in the stories he refused to manipulate the dolls himself, even when encouraged. There were frequent references to story characters being too loud, of dogs scratching him and barking loudly, and vivid descriptions of various sensations such as the color, feel, or sound of things. The stories were unusual in this regard and pointed to the rich and potentially overwhelming world of sensations that this boy lived in. Subsequent therapy focused on helping him deal with his sensory integration issues, including work with an occupational therapist.

Use of Elicited Play as a Mechanism for Mastery

Among the most productive uses of scaffolded play is as a vehicle for helping the child to work through and master difficult feelings associated with a trauma. Such scaffolding can take a variety of forms, including storytelling, drawings, or play reenactment. The following vignette illustrates how these various methods were combined to help a child overcome difficult feelings associated with an auto accident that were seriously impairing her relationship with her mother. This case has been previously reported in detail (Gaensbauer 2004a).

Three-year-old Katie was seen one month after she and her mother were involved in an auto accident. Katie was unhurt but her mother was knocked unconscious for several minutes and bled from a scalp laceration. She and her mother were taken to the hospital in separate ambulances. At the hospital, in contrast to her older sister who had not been in the accident, Katie refused to get up on the bed to give her mother a kiss. Following the accident, Katie showed a number of posttraumatic symptoms, but most troubling was her anger toward and withdrawal from her mother, whom she refused to let hold her. Among other things, she blamed her mother for "driving on the grass" and for not hearing her calls for help. Initially, through storytelling by her mother at home and through drawings done both in sessions and at home, her mother and the therapist were able to portray the various situations and help her to understand what had happened and that her mother was not at fault. There was a significant reduction in her anxiety symptoms and her anger at her mother as a result.

As Katie became increasingly comfortable talking about the auto accident, her mother observed that she continued to have a very hard time talking about the hospital. That this was a difficult moment was evidenced by the fact that the first time the therapist drew a picture on a blackboard of a child with a sad facial expression standing by the mother in bed, Katie immediately wanted to erase the picture. Eventually, she was able to deal with the scene, including participating with the therapist in drawing the "red spots" that her mom had on her face as a way of helping to desensitize her to the frightening images of her bleeding mother. The degree to which Katie had been preoccupied with her failure to get up on her mother's bed and give her mother a kiss only became clear when, during one of our discussions, Katie said that "Amy [her sister] got up on the bed and I didn't." This comment allowed her mother and the therapist to empathize with how scared she had been because her mother looked different.

At this point, the therapist suggested playing out the accident with toys. With Katie's participation, the entire sequence of accident, ambulance ride, and hospital treatment was played out, with two notable moments. The first occurred when, as she and the therapist were putting the mother doll in the ambulance, Katie put the doll representing herself in the ambulance with the mother. The second occurred when, as the scene of the mother at the hospital was being played out, Katie immediately put her doll in the bed next to the mother. Her mother and the therapist were then able to talk about how much she wanted to be with her mother in the ambulance and how much she wanted to give her mother a hug at the hospital but was scared. Katie proceeded to enthusiastically participate in getting out medicine bottles and bandages that she and the therapist used to help the mother doll feel better.

Her mother described this as a breakthrough session, as Katie became much more relaxed at home and much more comfortable and affectionate with her mother. Her distress about being separated in the ambulance and her fear, guilt, and sense of alienation for having reacted differently from the rest of her family had played major roles in her anger and withdrawal from her mother. Her ability to articulate these feelings in discussions that occurred at home and in the office, combined with the opportunity through the structured situation to play out reparative fantasies of what she wished had happened, were crucial to therapeutic resolution of her internal conflict.

RESEARCH IMPLICATIONS AND FUTURE DIRECTIONS

Research using the MacArthur Story Stem Battery and similarly constructed paradigms has provided strong evidence that structured story stems can provide unique access into the young child's inner world. Combined with long-standing clinical practice, we believe that the field has reached a point of great promise for systematic research on the value of structured situations in psychodynamic play therapy with individual children. Most straightforward would be studies comparing the kind of scaffolding play approaches we are describing here with other forms of play therapy with young children, such as client-centered and/or unstructured psychodynamic approaches. The format of such studies might be similar to the studies of Cohen, Mannarino, and their colleagues (Cohen and Mannarino 1996, 1997), which demonstrated the superiority of a structured, 12-session cognitive-behavior protocol compared with an unstructured client-centered approach in the treatment of sexually abused preschool children. In support of the kind of therapeutic structuring described here, it is relevant to note that although the treatment utilized in these studies was termed cognitive-behavioral therapy, the structured protocols made strong use of expressive elements such as drawing, writing, and parent-child communication to promote abreaction, narrative construction, and reparative intrapsychic meaning. Indeed, the importance of these expressive components was highlighted in a subsequent intervention study using a very similar protocol with a group of older sexually abused children. A significant proportion of the children reported that the aspect of treatment that they found most helpful was the opportunity to talk about their traumatic experience (Deblinger et al. 2006). Similar comparative studies could also be done in the diagnostic arena, contrasting the efficiency and diagnostic value of information obtained through structured approaches such as the MSSB as compared with the information gained by more traditional play methods.

The use of relatively standardized play vehicles with young children also has the potential for developing important information about psychotherapeutic process, including increasing specificity in the delineation of the kinds of interventions that contribute to psychodynamically meaningful therapeutic processing in young children (Russ 1998). Since it is occurring in a relatively fixed location, scaffolded play therapy with

---

MacArthur Story Stem Battery Story Stems

1. Warm-up: Birthday
   Theme: Introduction, modeling of narration with family figures
2. Spilled juice
   Theme: Parental responses to accident
3. The lost dog/reunion with the lost dog
   Theme: Loss and reunion
4. Mom's headache
   Theme: Dilemma about empathy with mother versus loyalty to friend
5. Gift to mom and dad
   Theme: Pride/preference for one parent (Oedipal theme)
6. Three's a crowd
   Theme: Dilemma of loyalty to friend versus empathy toward sibling
7. Hot gravy
   Theme: Disobedience/parental empathy versus authority
8. The lost keys
   Theme: Parental conflict
9. Stealing candy
   Theme: Transgression/getting caught/shame
10. Departure story
    Theme: Separation from parents
11. Reunion
    Theme: Attachment
12. The bathroom shelf
    Theme: Dilemma of obedience to mother versus empathy to sibling
13. Outing to the park
    Theme: Mastery/pride
14. The exclusion story/the kiss
    Theme: Exclusion from the parental relationship (Oedipal theme)
15. The cookie jar
    Theme: Conflict between loyalty to parent and loyalty to sibling
16. Family fun
    Theme: Family fun

---

very young children lends itself to systematic data gathering, including video recording. Also available are the extensive collection of social-emotional and cognitive rating scales that have been developed for the MSSB, including measures of theme content, affective quality and coherence, attachment relatedness, narrative complexity and style, and representations of self and others, to list just a few (Emde, Wolf, and Oppenheim 2003). These rating scales offer great promise as mechanisms for assessing ongoing treatment processes and in identifying therapeutic interventions that lead to higher levels of functioning and psychological integration on the children's part.

The MSSB or other story stems designed to pull for particular emotional themes have also been useful in measuring the treatment outcome. For example, in their work with children who have witnessed domestic violence, Lieberman and her colleagues have used the parental conflict story stem "Lost Keys" as an outcome measure to document the effectiveness of child-parent psychotherapy (Lieberman, pers. comm.; Lieberman and Van Horn 2004).

In summary, it is our experience that providing scaffolding to very young children in the context of play therapy makes it possible for children to express and make sense of their inner world in ways that they would not be able to do on their own. It is consistent with the current state of knowledge regarding cognitive and emotional development—that is, that early development is largely influenced by the support provided within relationships (Shonkoff and Phillips 2000). We believe that it is also consistent with the principles of respect for the child's autonomy and facilitation of self-healing through play that have constituted essential elements of psychodynamic play therapy from its beginnings.

The Lost Keys

Story theme: Parental conflict
Props: None
Characters: Mother, father, child
Setting: Mom and Dad facing each other, child observing
Examiner: Susan/George comes into the room and sees Mom and Dad looking at each other like this. Look at my face (show angry expression).
M (angrily): You lost my keys!
F (angrily): I did *not*!
M: Yes, you did, you always lose my keys!
F: I did not lose them this time.
E: Show me and tell me what happens now.
Issue prompt (if child does not enact end or resolution of conflict):
E: What's going to happen about Mom and Dad's argument?

REFERENCES

Ainsworth, M. D. S., M. D. Blehar, E. Waters, and S. Wall. 1978. *Patterns of attachment: A psychological study of the Strange Situation.* Hillsdale, NJ: Erlbaum.

Bellak, L., and S. S. Bellak. 1987. *Children's Apperception Test.* Larchmont, NY: CPS.

Benham, A. L., and C. F. Slotnick. 2006. Play therapy: Integrating clinical and developmental perspectives. In *Handbook of preschool mental health: Development, disorders, and treatment,* ed. J. Luby, 331–371. New York: Guilford.

Bloom, L., and E. Tinker. 2001. The intentionality model and language acquisition: Engagement, effort, and the essential tension in development. *Monographs of the Society for Research in Child Development* 66 (45): i–viii, 1–91.

Bretherton, I., and D. Oppenheim. 2003. The MacArthur Story Stem Battery: Development, administration, reliability, validity, and reflections about meaning. In *Revealing the inner worlds of young children: The MacArthur Story Stem Battery and parent-child narratives,* ed. R. N. Emde, D. P. Wolf, and D. Oppenheim, 55–80. New York: Oxford University Press.

Bretherton, I., D. Oppenheim, H. Buchsbaum, R. N. Emde, and the MacArthur Narrative Group. 1990. The MacArthur Story Stem Battery (MSSB). Unpublished manual, University of Wisconsin, Madison.

Bretherton, I., D. Ridgeway, and J. Cassidy. 1990. Assessing internal working models of the attachment relationship: An attachment story completion task for three-year-olds. In *Attachment in the preschool years,* ed. M. T. Greenberg, D. Cicchetti, and E. M. Cummings, 273–310. Chicago: University of Chicago Press.

Buchsbaum, H. K., S. L. Toth, R. B. Clyman, D. Cicchetti, and R. N. Emde. 1992. The use of a narrative story stem technique with maltreated children: Implications for theory and practice. *Development and Psychopathology* 4:603–625.

Carlson, E. A., and L. A. Sroufe. 1995. Contribution of attachment theory to developmental psychopathology. In *Developmental psychopathology,* vol. 1, *Theory and methods,* ed. D. Cichetti and D. J. Cohen, 581–617. New York: Wiley.

Cassell, S. 1965. Effect of brief puppet therapy upon the emotional response of children undergoing cardiac catheterization. *Journal of Consulting Psychology* 29:1–8.

Cohen, J., and A. P. Mannarino. 1996. A treatment outcome study for sexually abused preschool children: Initial findings. *Journal of the American Academy of Child and Adolescent Psychiatry* 35 (1): 42–50.

———. 1997. A treatment outcome study for sexually abused preschool children: Outcome during a one-year follow-up. *Journal of the American Academy of Child and Adolescent Psychiatry* 35 (9): 1228–1235.

Conn, J. H. 1939. The child reveals himself through play: The method of the play interview. *Mental Hygiene* 23:49–69.

Deblinger, E., A. P. Mannarino, J. A. Cohen, and R. A. Steer. 2006. A followup study of a multisite, randomized, controlled trial for children with sexual abuse–related PTSD symptoms. *Journal of the American Academy of Child and Adolescent Psychiatry* 45 (12): 1474–1484.

Emde, R. N., D. P. Wolf, and D. Oppenheim, eds. 2003. *Revealing the inner worlds of young children: The MacArthur Story Stem Battery and parent-child narratives.* New York: Oxford University Press.

Erikson, E. H. 1950. *Childhood and society.* New York: Norton.

Fivush, R. 1993. Developmental perspectives on autobiographical recall. In *Child victims, child witnesses: Understanding and improving testimony*, ed. G. S. Goodman and B. L. Bottoms. New York: Guilford.

Fivush, R., and F. Fromhoff. 1988. Style and structure in mother-child conversations about the past. *Discourse Processes* 11: 337–355.

Freud, A. 1946. *The psycho-analytical treatment of children*. London: Imago.

Gaensbauer, T. J. 1982a. Regulation of emotional expression in infants from two contrasting caretaking environments. *Journal of the American Academy of Child Psychiatry* 21 (2): 163–171.

———. 1982b. The differentiation of discrete affects: A case report. *Psychoanalytic Study of the Child* 37:29–66.

———. 1994. Therapeutic work with a traumatized toddler. *Psychoanalytic Study of the Child* 49:412–433.

———. 1995. Trauma in the preverbal period: Symptoms, memories, and developmental impact. *Psychoanalytic Study of the Child* 50:122–149.

———. 1997. Traumatic stress disorder. In *DC: 0–3 Casebook*, ed. A. Lieberman, S. Wieder, and E. Fenichel, 31–46. Arlington, VA: Zero to Three.

———. 2000. Psychotherapeutic treatment of traumatized infants and toddlers: A case report. *Clinical Child Psychology and Psychiatry* 5:373–385.

———. 2002. Representations of trauma in infancy: Clinical and theoretical implications for the understanding of early memory. *Infant Mental Health Journal* 23:259–277.

———. 2004a. Traumatized young children: Assessment and treatment processes. In *Young children and trauma*, ed. J. Osofsky, 194–216. New York: Guilford.

———. 2004b. Telling their stories: Representation and reenactment of traumatic experiences occurring in the first year of life. *Journal of Zero to Three* 25 (5): 25–31.

Gaensbauer, T. J., and R. J. Harmon. 1981. Clinical assessment in infancy utilizing structured playroom situations. *Journal of the American Academy of Child and Adolescent Psychiatry* 20:673–691.

———. 1982. Attachment behavior in abused/neglected infants: Implications for the concept of attachment. In *The development of attachment and affiliative systems*, ed. R. N. Emde and R. J. Harmon, 263–279. New York: Plenum.

Gaensbauer, T. J., and D. Mrazek. 1981. Differences in the patterning of affective expression in infants. *Journal of the American Academy of Child and Adolescent Psychiatry* 20:673–691.

Gaensbauer, T. J., D. Mrazek, and R. N. Emde. 1979. Patterning of emotional response in a playroom laboratory situation. *Infant Behavior and Development* 2:163–178.

Gaensbauer, T. J., and C. H. Siegel. 1995. Therapeutic approaches to posttraumatic stress disorder in infants and toddlers. *Infant Mental Health Journal* 16:292–305.

Grych, J. H., T. Wachsmuth-Schlaefer, and L. L. Klockow. 2002. Interparental aggression and young children's representations of family relationships. *Journal of Family Psychology* 16 (3): 259–272.

Hambidge, G. 1955. Structured play therapy. *American Journal of Orthopsychiatry* 25:601–617.

Hirshberg, L. M. 1993. Clinical interviews with infants and their families. In *Handbook of infant mental health*, ed. C. H. Zeanah, 173–190. New York: Guilford.

Hodges, J., S. Hillman, K. Henderson, and J. Kaniuk. 2003. Changes in attachment representations over the first year of adoptive placement: Narratives of maltreated children. *Clinical Child Psychology and Psychiatry* 8 (3): 351–367.

Kernberg, P. F., S. E. Chazan, and L. Normandin. 1998. The Children's Play Therapy Instrument (CPTI): Description, development and reliability studies. *Journal of Psychotherapy Practice and Research* 7 (3): 196–207.

Levy, D. M. 1933. The use of play technique as experimental procedure. *American Journal of Orthopsychiatry* 3:266–275.

———. 1938. Release therapy in young children. *Psychiatry* 1:387–390.

———. 1939. Release Therapy. *American Journal of Orthopsychiatry* 9:713–736.

Lieberman, A. F., and P. Van Horn. 2004. *"Don't hit my mommy!" A manual for child-parent psychotherapy with young witnesses of family violence*. Washington, DC: Zero to Three.

Macfie, J., S. L. Toth, F. A. Rogosch, J. Robinson, R. N. Emde, and D. Cicchetti. 1999. Effect of maltreatment on preschoolers' narrative representation of responses to relieve distress and of role reversal. *Developmental Psychology* 35:460–465.

Maclean, G. 1977. Psychic trauma and traumatic neurosis: Play therapy with a four-year-old boy. *Canadian Psychiatric Association Journal* 22:71–76.

Measelle, J. R., J. C. Ablow, P. A. Cowan, and C. P. Cowan. 1998. Assessing young children's views of their academic, social, and emotional lives: An evaluation of the self-perception scales of the Berkeley Puppet Interview. *Child Development* 69 (6): 1556–1576.

Nelson, K. 1990. Remembering, forgetting, and childhood amnesia. In *Knowing and remembering in young children*, ed. R. Fivush and J. A. Hudson. Cambridge, UK: Cambridge University Press.

Newell, H. W. 1941. Play techniques in child psychiatry. *American Journal of Orthopsychiatry* 11:245–251.

Oppenheim, D., R. N. Emde, M. Hasson, and S. Warren. 1997. Preschoolers face moral dilemmas: A longitudinal study of acknowledging and resolving internal conflict. *International Journal of Psychoanalysis* 78 (5): 943–957.

Piaget, J. 1952. *The origins of intelligence in children*. New York: International Universities Press.

———. 1954. *The construction of reality in the child*. New York: Basic.

Rae, W., F. Worchel, J. Upchurch, J. Sanner, and C. Daniel. 1989. The psychosocial impact of play on hospitalized children. *Journal of Pediatric Psychology* 14:617–627.

Russ, S. W. 1995. Play psychotherapy research: State of the science. In *Advances in clinical child psychology*, ed. T. Ollendick and R. Prinz, 17:365–391. New York: Plenum.

———. 1998. Play therapy. In *Comprehensive clinical psychology*, ed. A. Bellack and M. Hersen, 5:221–243. Oxford: Elsevier Science.

Shonkoff, J., and D. Phillips, eds. 2000. *From neurons to neighborhoods: The science of early childhood development*. Washington, DC: National Academy Press.

Solomon, J. C. 1938. Active play therapy. *American Journal of Orthopsychiatry* 8:479–498.

Solomon, J., C. George, and A. DeJong. 1996. Children classified as controlling at age six: Evidence of disorganized representational strategies and aggression at home and at school. *Development and Psychopathology* 7:447–463.

Spitz, R. 1965. *The first year of life: A psychoanalytic study of normal and deviant development of object relations.* New York: International Universities Press.

Toth, S. L., D. Cicchetti, J. Macfie, and R. N. Emde. 1997. Representations of self and other in the narratives of neglected, physically abused, and sexually abused preschoolers. *Development and Psychopathology* 9 (4): 781–796.

Von Klitzing, K., K. Kelsay, R. N. Emde, J. Robinson, and S. Schmitz. 2000. Gender specific characteristics of five-year-olds' narratives and associations with behavior ratings. *Journal of the American Academy of Child and Adolescent Psychiatry* 39:1017–1023.

Waelder, R. 1933. The psychoanalytic theory of play. *Psychoanalytic Quarterly* 2:208–224.

Warren, S., D. Oppenheim, and R. Emde. 1996. Can emotions and themes in children's play predict behavior problems? *Journal of the American Academy of Child and Adolescent Psychiatry* 35:1331–1337.

Winnicott, D. W. 1968. Playing: Its theoretical status in the clinical situation. *International Journal of Psychoanalysis* 49:591–598.

9

Play Therapy Techniques with Very Young At-Risk Children in Child Care Settings

Jane Robinson and Roxanne Grobbel

At-risk children under the age of five are a large population, often forgotten, whose mental health needs are seldom met. Early intervention and prevention that focuses on attachment, resiliency, and play would help to strengthen their growth and development into functioning adults.

Devonte, a two-year-old African American boy, bites and kicks others in the classroom. He seems angry and aggressive. His father is in and out of his life and is a drug dealer on the streets. Devonte was nearly expelled. He will follow his father's angry path if there is not early intervention for him and his mother.

Jeremy, a three-year-old Haitian boy, born prematurely, kicks, bites, and hits children and teachers in the preschool classroom. He is disruptive, throwing and breaking toys. When he was hospitalized for the first 10 months of his life, his mother was unable to visit him regularly. Influenced by cultural values, she feels a sense of shame about having a disabled child. Jeremy is at risk because of his insecure attachment to his mother.

Brittney is a two-and-a-half-year-old asthmatic Hispanic preemie, a victim of neglect. Children's Protective Services removed her from the home of her single, drug-addicted mother. First placed in a foster home, she was later transferred to her paternal grandparents and then to her father's care. Her attachments are extremely unstable. Like other seriously deprived children, she hugs and kisses others indiscriminately.

These children are examples of a large number of high-risk children who spend the majority of their waking hours in child care centers in the care of low-paid, undereducated teachers. The children and their caregivers urgently need mental health services.

At-risk children under five years of age are a large, yet often forgotten, population with many risks and needs. In the United States approximately 21 percent of children under five years of age live in poverty. They experience a number of life conditions that put them at risk for emotional, social, and behavioral disturbance (Annie E. Casey Foundation 2006). It is estimated that three out of five of these children spend the majority of their waking hours in child care settings five days a week (Simpson et al. 2001). Almost two million of these were enrolled (in 2004) in publicly funded early childhood programs (National Child Care Information Center 2006). These are the children of working parents, many of them single and of ethnic minorities, who often must place their children in poor-quality child care because of economic necessity and lack of choice. These child care centers are often staffed with teachers who are underpaid, undereducated, and face many of the same risk factors as the children (Helburn and Bergmann 2002). They are poorly equipped to promote the social and emotional well-being of the children in their care.

Many of these young at-risk children show symptoms of developmental and speech delays, poor social skills, inability to self-regulate, and inability to learn (Aber, Jones, and Cohen 2000; Osofsky 2004; Siegel 1999), in addition to signs of insecure/disruptive attachment, poor relationships with adults, depression, and out-of-control aggressive behavior. Yet 75–80 percent of children and youth in need of mental health services do not receive them (Kataoka, Zhang, and Wells 2002), and a study by Ringel (2001) found that 88 percent of minority children have unmet mental health needs. The necessity for early childhood mental health services is further indicated by a study of more than 3,800 preschool-aged children, which reported that 21 percent of the sample met the criteria for a psychiatric disorder and 9.1 percent of this at-risk group met the criteria for a severe disorder (Lavigne et al. 1996).

Children who are at risk for social and emotional problems are also at risk for expulsion from preschool. A recent Yale Child Study Center (Gilliam 2005) found expulsion rates for pre-kindergarten students were three times higher than the rate for K–12 students. African American preschoolers were 3 to 5 times more likely to be expelled than their Caucasian, Latino, or Asian American peers, and boys were 4.5 times more apt to be expelled than girls.

The most important finding of this study was that expulsion rates significantly decrease with access to on-site or regular mental health consultation. The Yale study further indicated that teachers and parents require assistance to cope with the social and emotional problems of these children, thus emphasizing the need for on-site mental health programs. Several presenters at Head Start's recent National Research Conference also indicated an urgent need to integrate early childhood mental health services into child development centers throughout the United States.

This chapter will provide an overview of our All 'Bout Children Inc. (ABC) multi-faceted intervention program, which focuses on at-risk young children, their families, and child care center staff. We will begin with a portrayal of a population of at-risk children, then move to a discussion of attachment, resiliency, and infant mental health and social emotional well-being. We will describe the program interventions, highlight child-centered play therapy and the rationale for its use, and conclude with discussion of program evaluation and research.[1]

RISK FACTORS

There are multiple layers of risk factors: individual, family, and community. The first layer that inhibits the healthy development of children includes poverty, violence, lack of stimulation, poor nutrition, abuse, and neglect, as well as physiological/ biological factors such as cerebral palsy, Down syndrome, autism, birth defects, and sensory integration disorders (Osfosky and Thompson 2000).

Children are further impacted by familial risk factors such as single-parent families, poor parenting skills, domestic violence, substance abuse, mental illness or parental depression, young or immature parents, under-educated parents, family disruption (moves, loss of job, illness, death, divorce, incarceration), isolation, lack of insurance, parents not active on child's behalf, and absence of family support.

The third layer includes community risk factors such as violent neighborhoods, racism, lack of supportive social service agencies, lack of community activism, and substandard housing and educational systems.

Perhaps the most important community factor is the lack of quality child care. Most child care center teachers are undereducated, poorly paid, rarely respected, and teaching in schools that do not meet minimum standards (Greenspan 2000).

The above risk factors impact the growth of the very young child in all areas at a crucial time when development is extremely rapid. Risk factors increase stress. Stress or prolonged exposure to severe or unpredictable stress during the early years can alter the brain's development and adversely impact the child's physical, emotional, cognitive, and social growth (Perl-mutter 2006; Shonkoff and Phillips 2000; Siegel 1999). Changes occur in these areas:

1. *Physical growth.* Infants begin as totally dependent beings and ideally grow to become increasingly independent, physically active, and curious as they explore their world. Risk factors can delay children from reaching their physical developmental milestones.

2. *Brain development.* Ninety percent of brain growth takes place in the first three years of life. The experiences of very young children are crucial in organizing the way the basic structures of the brain develop (Siegel 1999; Perlmutter 2006). "The genes and experiences shape how the neurons connect to one another, in this way forming the specialized circuits that give rise to mental processes" (Zigler, Finn-Stevenson, and Hall 2002, 32).

3. *Emotional growth.* When young children's needs are not met or they are not nurtured, talked to, or made to feel safe, they do not learn to self-regulate or self-control (Siegel 1999).

4. *Cognitive growth.* As infants, children can only cry to get their needs met. During the early childhood years they learn language and are able to express themselves and be understood. Children evolve from not understanding the world around them, seeing only black and white, to being able to complete a puzzle, understand how things work, problem solve, identify letters and words, and create their own ideas. Again, risk factors may impede cognitive development (Siegel 1999).

5. *Social growth.* Children progress from being concerned with only getting their immediate needs satisfied, toward learning to work independently and cooperatively with others as a part of a family, classroom, and society. The impact of risk factors often manifests in attachment issues and poor relationships with adults. The importance of the relationship with a primary caregiver (parent or teacher) is immense (Bowlby 1988). It is through healthy attachments that children learn about themselves and the world. If risk factors create attachment issues, there is no social road map for the children to follow for future relationships. Without the opportunity for positive relationships with adults, they often become aggressive or withdrawn and have limited ability to develop self-control or to interact positively with others (Siegel 1999).

Chronic fear or stress can raise the cortisol hormone levels in the brain, which means that regions of the brain involved in complex thought often do not function (Siegel 1999). One of the most significant risk factors for young children today is time spent in child care settings. The National Institute of Child and Human Development reports a correlation between time spent by preschoolers in child care and both elevated stress levels (reflected in cortisol hormone tests) and a higher incidence of problem behavior (cited in Langlois and Liben 2003).

Siegel (1999) further points out that early relationship experiences have a dominant influence on the brain because the same neural pathways that are responsible for social perception also direct the creation of meaning, organization of memory, capacity for interpersonal communication, and regulation of bodily states and emotion.

ATTACHMENT

Bowlby described attachment as the "lasting psychological connectedness between human beings" (1969, 194). The definition of attachment has been further expanded as a reciprocal, enduring emotional and physical affiliation between a child and a caregiver. It's the base from which children explore their physical and social environments and form their concepts of self, others, and the world (James 1994). It is attachment that allows for infants' survival; it is through the relationship with the caregiver that they seek to get their most basic needs met.

In relationships that are secure, the caregiver is able to perceive and respond appropriately to the emotional signals of the infant or child. The infant uses the caregiver's behavior to organize his or her own mental and emotional processes; thereby the child learns how to calm himself or herself during frightening or anxious times and gains a sense of safety when distressed. This appropriate attunement response in turn increases the child's positive emotional states and helps regulate negative states. When this occurs, the sense of being soothed is encoded in implicit memory and then becomes a mental model of attachment, which helps the child to have a secure base and the ability to self-soothe (Siegel 1999).

Thus, the ability to attach or bond with another person is vital to a child's mental health. The basis for wellness and resilience, especially for the young child, is found in warm relationships, as indicated in the rapidly expanding body of attachment theory literature (Ainsworth et al. 1978; Bowlby 1977, 1980, 1988; Brauner 2004; Crowell and Feldman 1991; Greenberg 1999; Howes and Ritchie 1998; Siegel 1999).

Bowlby's work is considered seminal, and his thesis is best expressed in his own words:

> Intimate attachments to other human beings are the hub around which a person's life revolves, not only when he is an infant or a toddler or a school child, but throughout his adolescence and his years of maturity as well, and on into old age. From these intimate attachments, a person draws his strength and enjoyment of life and, through what he contributes, he gives strength and enjoyment to others. (1980, 442)

Since secure attachment is created through relationships, it is necessary to have consistency in child care so these relationships can be formed (Ainsworth et al. 1978; Siegel 1999). From the formation of a secure base the child is able to explore the world, develop relationships, and grow and separate in a healthy way (Ainsworth et al. 1978).

The quality of a child's attachment has been divided into four categories:

1. *Secure.* The parent is available and responsive to the child and the child is able to explore the world freely and feel safe (Bowlby 1980). At approximately six months old, the child has the capacity to picture and process the activity of the relationship between self and others. This relationship is then remembered and becomes the basis for secure attachment (Siegel 1999).
2. *Insecure.* The caregiver is not consistent in creating a safe environment for the child. The parents will often fail to notice or misinterpret the child's cues. The child may either be:
   a. Anxious/resistant. The child is uncertain that the parent is available and responsive. A parent will enter a room and the child will cry and the parent will be unable to soothe the child (Ainsworth et al. 1978).
   b. Anxious/avoidant. The child has no confidence that the parent is available. When a parent enters the room, the child will avoid the parent by not paying attention to the parent, turning away from the parent or continuing to play (Ainsworth et al. 1978).
3. *Disorganized.* The child feels both comforted and frightened by the parent, which results in confusion. Inconsistent parental behavior, which becomes a source of both fear and reassurance, appears to contribute to a disorganized attachment style (Main and Solomon 1986). A caregiver will enter a room and the child will freeze with a trance-like expression; fall, huddle, and cry; or cling while crying hard and leaning away from the caregiver (Siegel 1999).
4. *Disrupted.* This is a new classification (Osofsky 2004) in which the child has no consistent primary caregiver with whom to form a healthy attachment. As a result the child is unsure whether anyone will respond to her or his needs. These children are often in foster care or moved from family member to family member and then perhaps moved back with the parent.

Unlike securely attached children, children with an insecure disorganized attachment pattern are more prone to learning difficulties and aggressive behavior (Lyons-Ruth, Alpern, and Repacholi 1993); they are more likely to associate with peer groups where delinquency, substance abuse, and other risky or deviant behaviors are common (Coie et al. 1992).

Longitudinal studies by the Minnesota Parent-Child Project consistently indicate that children in high-social-risk environments, who showed early insecure attachment relationships, were significantly more likely to have poor peer relations and exhibit symptoms of depression and aggression (Urban et al. 1991).

Thus attachment research concludes that *all future relationships are influenced by the first relationships in a child's life.* It is the gentle touch, kind and soft connection, the tone of voice that makes the child feel safe to explore his or her world, learn cognitive skills, affiliate with others, and learn social skills (Bowlby 1988).

RESILIENCY

Attachment is generally viewed as a major factor in promoting *resiliency*, which is fundamental to social and emotional wellness in children. Resiliency refers to children's above-average ability to cope with and master adverse life situations—as Cowen has suggested, "swimming well when all known precursors say they should sink" (1991, 406–407). Hoyt-Meyers et al. (1995) attribute the fact that resilient children beat heavy odds to a fortuitous combination of *protective* child attributes: a warm, caring family environment; the child's temperament; and support sources—collectively called the "triad of protective factors" (cited by Werner and Smith 1992, 326; also referred to by Garmezy 1985). Also relevant is current research concerning genetic factors influencing resilience (Brazelton 2006; Siegel 1999).

Researchers typically view resilience phenomena in the context of risk and protective factors (Coie et al. 1993; Fraser 1997). *Risk* refers to "variables associated with a high probability of onset, greater severity, and longer duration of major mental health problems, or the maintenance of a problem condition" (Coie et al. 1993, 1013). *Protective* factors, on the other hand, are "those internal and external factors that help children resist or ameliorate risk" (Fraser 1997, 3–4). Studies conducted at different times and places, with diverse subjects, have found a common core of protective factors. Environmental factors that facilitate the development of resiliency consist of caring and support, positive expectations, and opportunities for children to participate (Benard 1993). Factors that focus on the child's attributes include social competency (flexibility, empathy), problem-solving skills, autonomy (internal locus of control, self-efficacy, initiative, self-control), and sense of purpose (Anthony and Cohler 1987; Benard 1993; Hunter 1998; Devereux 2001). These are the qualities All 'Bout Children looks to foster in children in our preventive intervention program.

Preschool can be changed from a possible risk factor (Langlois and Liben 2003), inducing stress and impeding the positive growth of vulnerable children, to a protective environment that promotes the factors that encourage resiliency. The well-known Perry Preschool Project, using an experimental design, has reported the positive lifetime effects of a high-quality preschool program, emphasizing resiliency and secure attachments, on 123 African Americans born in poverty-ridden neighborhoods. The experimental and control subjects were followed from age 3 and 4 to age 40. The experimental group subjects were more likely to graduate from high school, had more stable job histories, enjoyed higher earnings, and committed fewer crimes than the control subjects who did not attend a similar program (High/ Scope Educational Research Foundation 2005).

EARLY CHILDHOOD SOCIAL AND EMOTIONAL WELL-BEING

Mental health for the young child is relationship based. The child's physical and mental growth and survival is dependent, as earlier indicated, upon her or his relationship with an adult, which determines the child's social, emotional, and cognitive well-being.

Healthy young children with good mental health generally experience themselves and the world in a positive way and have enough confidence in themselves and others to believe that problems can be solved. When young children are upset or display challenging behaviors, they are dependent upon their caregivers to determine the causes and ascertain a way to help. Unfortunately, most parents and child care workers have no training in mental health, and lack the knowledge and skills they need to respond to a troubled child (Zigler, Gilliam, and Jones 2006).

Therefore, any therapeutic work with very young children ideally includes the caregiver—mother, teacher, father, or foster parent (Raver and Knitzer 2002). The mental health of the caregiver is also important, as it can significantly impact the child's mental health. Children of depressed parents often have adjustment problems and are vulnerable to clinical depression, academic difficulties, social withdrawal, and aggressive behaviors (Downy and Coyne 1990).

When unstable mental health or other risk factors create a stressful, insecurely attached situation for a young child, relationships formed in child care can provide the positive protective environment that is needed. When a young child is in day care from a very early age, attachment with caregivers on-site is crucial.

PROGRAM OVERVIEW

All 'Bout Children Inc. (ABC) is a 501(c)3 nonprofit grassroots community agency providing consultation, training, play therapy, and counseling for young children 18 months to 5 years of age, their teachers, and families. Most of the children come from low-income, mainly single-parent, poorly educated minority (Haitian, African American, and Central and South American) families living in neighborhoods that are prone to violence. These at-risk children frequently show signs of insecure/disruptive attachment, lack of school readiness, speech delays, poor social skills, inability to self-regulate, and learning difficulties. The interventions recommended in this chapter focus on enhancing children's resiliency factors—attachment, initiative, and self-control—which in turn improve children's ability to cope and relate to both other children and adults (Devereaux 2001). Our ABC program focuses on caring and support, positive expectations, building interpersonal and cognitive competence skills, and providing opportunities to participate constructively—all of which fosters a resilient outcome.

This is an integrated approach utilizing universal, selective, and indicated preventive interventions to ensure that "no child is left behind" (Coie 1993; see figure 9.1). It emphasizes primary attention to *universal* preventive interventions (environmental change), such as education for teachers, staff, and parents through workshops, modeling therapeutic responses in the classroom, and reflective supervision. These universal interventions are designed to affect *all* teachers and children. *Selective* intervention is provided through small group play therapy for children detected to be at an increased risk for emotional and behavioral disorders. *Indicated* preventive interventions target high-risk individuals with specific identifiable symptoms, for whom the risks and challenges are the greatest (Weissberg, Kumpfer, and Seligman

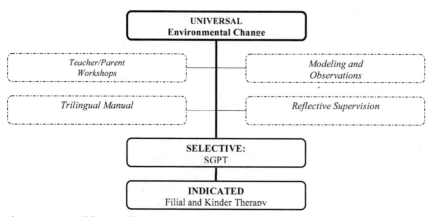

Figure 9.1. Building Wellness and Resilience: Approaches to Prevention

2003). They include filial therapy for children and their caregivers (parents, foster parents, teachers, or any adult-child relationship in need of improvement) and individual play therapy. Thus, all children benefit from universal psycho-educational interventions, many (about 20–40 percent) need selective small group play therapy interventions, and a few (perhaps 5–15 percent) require indicated filial therapy interventions.[2] Assignment to the selective and indicated interventions are based on DECA scores and teacher, parent, and counselor observations.

The recommended interventions focus on both the caregiver and the child. Problematic early relationships are linked to subsequent problems relating to social and emotional health, brain development, adult relationships, and learning and problem-solving issues (Siegel 1999). The crux of this multi-intervention approach is teaching staff and parents basic child-centered play therapy techniques to aid them in managing feelings and behavior, thereby becoming "therapeutic agents" while improving or repairing their own relationships with the child.

Using these interventions, preschool can change from a possible risk factor to a protective environment that increases the factors which foster resiliency (Reynolds and Temple 2006). Findings show that especially for economically disadvantaged children, significant gains in cognition, social-emotional development, and educational performance take place when children are enrolled in a child development center that includes well-trained and well-paid staff and where comprehensive on-site services provided for children and their families are delivered in a consistent and concentrated manner (Helburn and Bergman 2002).

According to Fonagy (1998), the preschool environment affords an opportunity for the enhancement of self-concept through healthy relationships with teachers and other parent surrogates, thus reducing the chances of potential difficulty in later years. Through these relationships, children are able to achieve social and emotional wellness. The child development center's programs emphasizing social and emotional development are as important as those focusing on linguistic and cognitive development (Shonkoff and Phillips 2000).

As very young children spend more hours in school, many preschoolers spend more awake time with their teacher than with their parent; as the school becomes an extension of the family, often the teacher becomes the second parent. Therefore we need to assist the teachers and child care center staff in creating healthy relationships and attachments as well as in understanding their responsibility to the children.

Building a positive warm relationship between teacher and child is a major dynamic of this program and of creating a therapeutic environment in the preschool classroom. Teachers are taught the knowledge, skills, and positive attitudes necessary for secure attachment to take place. Studies indicate that mental health nonprofessionals can be trained to provide this therapeutic relationship as effectively as mental health professionals (Cowen, Dorr, and Pokracki 1972; Truax and Carkhuff 1967). As the teacher develops a nonjudgmental and accepting relationship with the child, a safe space is provided for the child to learn and grow emotionally.

Haim Ginott stated the power of the teacher:

> I have come to a frightening conclusion. I am the decisive element in the classroom. It is my personal approach that creates the climate. It is my daily mood that makes the weather. As a teacher, I possess tremendous power to make a child's life miserable or joyous. I can be a tool of torture or an instrument of inspiration. I can humiliate or humor, hurt or heal. In all situations it is my response that decides whether a crisis will be escalated or de-escalated and a child humanized or dehumanized.
>
> How parents and teachers talk tells a child how they feel about him. Their statements affect his self-esteem and self-worth. To a large extent, their language determines his destiny. (Ginott 1972, 15–16)

PREVENTIVE INTERVENTION IN ACTION

The importance of educating the child development center teachers and staff is evident from the moment the children and their families walk through the front door of a child care center. Often the first person they meet is the receptionist. She or he is the hub of the school, knows all the children and families, and interacts with them daily. Therefore it is important for the receptionist to become a therapeutic agent as well.

For example, when a child is crying and does not want to leave his mother or even be in school, the receptionist can say, "Stop that, you are a big boy. Quit crying."

Or the receptionist can say, "It's hard to leave Mom. You wish you could go home. Mom has to go to work. She can take you to your class. She will be back at the end of the day."

In the second response the receptionist is acknowledging the child's feelings, using reflective listening, and setting limits in a caring way.

The second person the family encounters when coming to school is the teacher. As the young child enters the classroom, the teacher has an opportunity to observe the parent-child relationship. The teacher also has an opportunity to model a secure relationship for the parent by the way in which he or she greets the child who is having a difficult time separating. The teacher must understand that the child may be insecurely attached, frightened, hungry, or tired from not having slept the night before. For at-risk children there may be many reasons for the child to be upset; there may be violence in the house or neighborhood, or Mom is overwhelmed because she does not know if she can pay the bills for this week. The teacher has an opportunity to "humanize or dehumanize," to be in a comforting or threatening relationship with the child by the choice of response.

If the teacher responds, "Stop crying. Grow up. What is the matter with you?" the teacher has harmed the child and taught the parent it is okay to denigrate the child. However, if the teacher has been taught to be a "therapeutic agent," he or she will be ready to acknowledge the child's feelings, assist the child to make a positive start for the day, and model for the parent how to be effective. The teacher can say, "Hi, Johnny, I am so glad to see you today. It is hard to leave Mommy. You wish you could go home right now. We have lots of toys on the table for you and your friends. Mommy can walk you over there and say good-bye. She will be back at the end of the day to get you."

UNIVERSAL INTERVENTIONS

Let us now be specific about the preventive intervention approach we utilize. Our first interventions are *universal* interventions, educating the teachers and parents to be therapeutic agents. This process includes workshops for teachers, directors, and support staff; modeling in the classroom by professionals; and reflective supervision.

Teacher Workshops

The teachers in child care centers are underpaid, undereducated, and asked to perform tasks that require skills and knowledge they do not have. Often these teachers have only a high school education; live in the same neighborhoods as the children; and cope with the same poverty, violence, and lack of social support (Helburn and Bergmann 2002). Yet they are responsible for caring for children at the critical time when the children's brains are developing and attachments are being formed (Siegel 1999). Therefore, it is essential to give these teachers appropriate tools and techniques with which to relate to these children, to help them to develop social and emotional health, and to be effective teachers in the classroom (Raver and Knitzer 2002). Of course, this cannot happen overnight.

Prior to the teacher workshop, our All 'Bout Children counselors develop a relationship with the teachers to use as a foundation upon which workshops are based. Teachers are observed in the classroom, as to their interactions with children, their strengths, and those areas in which they could use help. The ASK checklist (appendix 9-A), an instrument developed by ABC to measure classroom atmosphere and the teacher's attitude, skill, and knowledge regarding managing feelings and behaviors, is used as a baseline measure. With this understanding of the staff, counselors present a six-hour workshop on child-centered play therapy; filial therapy (adult-child relationship); protective factors (attachment, initiative, and self-control); and the attitude, skill, and knowledge needed to provide a therapeutic environment.

Workshops are based on a 52-page manual, *A Way of Being with Children: Managing Feelings and Behavior in the Classroom*, which is available in English, Spanish, and Creole (see list of contents in appendix 9-B). The six-hour workshops build upon the areas of attitude, knowledge, and skill.

1. *Attitude* describes how the teacher relates with children and the importance of the teacher and the school as an extension of the family. Attitude reflects how the teacher perceives her job: is it just a paycheck, a career, or a calling? In addition, the attitude section concerns acceptance of children and understanding that they are doing the best they can at this moment, but with patience and guidance children can reach their potential.
2. *Knowledge* is learning what is developmentally appropriate; how words and actions impact the child's brain; how children grow; and the impact of attachment, sensory integration, resiliency, and emotional intelligence (Goleman 1995). The workshop also explains the importance of such subjects as active/reflective listening, encouragement, consistency with setting limits, and natural consequences of action and choices. Attention is focused on setting limits using Landreth's ACT model (2002b): Acknowledge a feeling, Communicate a limit, and Target an alternative behavior. Videos and role-playing are used to help teachers understand the feelings and intentions that drive children's behavior.
3. *Skill* is the application of knowledge gained to actual classroom experience. Role-playing is used in workshops to practice knowledge gained. Also, the counselor models therapeutic responses and limit setting in the classroom after the workshop. The teacher can then practice—again through role-playing—therapeutic responses and take part in reflective supervision, which encourages a nonjudgmental relationship between the teacher and the counselor or director.

Modeling

Attitude, skill, and knowledge become the backbone of helping the teacher to become a therapeutic agent. After teacher workshops—to the extent that staff resources permit—counselors participate in the classroom, modeling the newly learned attitude, skill, and knowledge. Modeling means the counselor demonstrates, hands on, what was learned and discussed in the workshop. The concepts become concrete actions that facilitate learning. The counselor maintains a nonjudgmental, reflective manner that allows the teacher to witness and learn lessons in a nonthreatening environment. This enables the teacher to be comfortable with new techniques. The counselor creates the same environment for the teacher that the workshops encourage the teacher to create for the children. The modeling takes place naturally as events unfold in the classroom.

Consider the example of a child having a difficult time sitting at circle time. A teacher who had attended a workshop but was unable to apply the new attitude, skill, and knowledge might say to the child, "You can never sit still. You never do what you are supposed to. You are never going to make it in this world. I knew you would act this way." This abrasive attitude and response can be harmful to the child. The counselor can teach through example in the classroom, demonstrating a more therapeutic response by stating to the child, "It's hard to sit still. Right now everyone is listening to the story. You can jump around when you go outside." The counselor can allow the teacher to try the alternative response the next time and help her find the correct words. Afterward, in reflective supervision, the counselor can discuss the incident with the teacher and refer to the workshop or manual as a reminder. The counselor suspends judgment, acknowledges feelings, and teaches in a proactive, encouraging manner that builds the same positive relationship between teacher and counselor that we want the teacher to have with the child.

Reflective Supervision

As previously stated, an important part of promoting the mental health of a child care center is the implementation of reflective supervision for staff (Fenichel 1992; Harden and Lythcott 2006; Shahmoon-Shanok 2006). As with child-centered play therapy and filial therapy, the relationship is also the foundation for reflective supervision. Reflective supervision promotes learning in the context of the relationships and interactions in which it occurs. The supervisee learns from the modeling of the supervisor (Bertacchi and Norman-Murch 1999). In 1992 a multidisciplinary group assembled by Zero to Three and the National Center for Clinical Infant Programs studied supervision from the perspective of practice with infants, toddlers, and their families. They agreed on the effectiveness of reflective supervision in this setting and defined the essential features of effective supervision: (1) reflections, (2) collaboration, and (3) regularity (Fenichel 1992).

In order to practice reflective supervision there must be a secure, safe, nonjudgmental relationship that is open to change. Often the areas that most need supervision are those that make one feel vulnerable and incompetent; therefore there must be a trusting, respectful relationship. Reflective supervision is used to consider one's own behavior, beliefs, conflicts, and values as well as those of the system or program. The process should center on the supervisee's strengths, and any problems should be jointly assessed and solved. Advice or opinions are not given by the supervisor; rather it is a session that encourages self-examination and problem-solving (Fenichel 1992; Gilkerson and Shahmoon-Shanok 2000; Pflieger 2002).

Collaboration in reflective supervision requires shared power, clear mutual expectations, open communication, and lack of judgment or criticism from either the supervisor or supervisee. Each person must feel comfortable to raise differences of opinion and perceptions, explore conflicts, and share goals. Supervision must occur regularly to protect against burnout or negative attitudes (Fenichel 1992).

Reflective supervision includes four key concepts: trust, respect, modeling, and cultural acceptance. In an atmosphere of trust and respect the teacher, or supervisee, becomes open to change. The supervisor allows the teacher to lead and listens to the teacher's point of view, using the art of reflective listening. Reflective supervision is an effective way of providing ongoing support to teachers, parents, and other trainees in order to maintain and deepen the above-mentioned attitude, skill, and knowledge components imparted in the workshops. Reflective supervision involves a dialogue between teachers and the supervisor/counselor, which enables the teachers to problem-solve, individually and as a team, and to develop more positive relationships with the children in their classrooms.

Supervision opens a dialogue to discover common ground and creates a bridge to different cultures. It allows for diverse people to feel safe together and to work together as a team (Gilkerson and Shahmoon-Shanok 2000). In child care settings there are many professionals and nonprofessionals with differing backgrounds, education levels, and cultural beliefs. However, they all must work together in an environment that is emotionally charged. These complex emotional situations evoke strong feelings and complex responses that are often difficult to sort out in order to respond in a supportive manner. Reflective supervision allows the teacher to step back from these intense emotional experiences and sort through thoughts, feelings, and reactions (Fenichel 1992; Gilkerson and Shahmoon-Shanok 2000).

In our literature search, we were able to find only one example of an experimentally designed study of the effects of reflective supervision on teachers' performance. In their study of a sample focused on factors influencing the morale and turnover rate of 80 preschool teachers (39 percent Latino, 39 percent African American), Howes, James, and Ritchie (2003) reported that teachers' "responsive involvement" with children—similar to ABC's child-centered approach emphasizing teacher-child attunement—was significantly greater for those teachers (N=27) who had the opportunity to benefit from regularly scheduled "reflective supervision."

Reflective supervision may be implemented in many ways in the preschool setting, including in staff, administrative, and clinical meetings; group and peer supervision (Gilkerson and Shahmoon-Shanok 2000); formal weekly individual and monthly group conferences; and informal contexts such as creating celebrations, developing school rituals, and impromptu discussions. The teacher becomes the client as much as the child. When the counselor reflects and joins with the teacher there is opportunity for change (Gilkerson and Shahmoon-Shanok 2000).

The following is an example of reflective supervision. A preschool teacher had a four-year-old student who ran out of the room constantly, screaming, "I can't do this. I don't know where my mother is." Teachers felt helpless, chasing after him down the hall and telling him, "You know better than to leave the class. You know your mom is at work and she will be here at 5:00. Be a big boy and stop running." The teachers used the counselor as a sounding board to understand what feelings the child was experiencing, how to reflect those feelings, and how to set limits.

The counselor listened to and reflected the teachers' concerns, feelings, and frustrations. This enabled them to create appropriate and feasible solutions to the situation. The counselor emphasized to the teachers the necessity for choices. The classroom team worked together to decide what choices they could use to help the child remain in the classroom. The counselor worked with the child in the classroom, modeling play therapy techniques that would assist the teachers in coping with an out-of-control child. The counselor modeled reflective statements such as, "You really miss your mom. It's hard to stay in class when you are sad, even if you know your mom is coming at 5:00." Limit setting was also modeled: "You really miss your mom and you want to run in the hallway. Now is the time for being in class. You can play in the class while you wait for her."

Often, during the four weeks before the child was able to stay in the classroom, the counselor and teacher would have informal reflective supervision in the hall, in the restroom, or in the classroom. Teachers used the supervision time to express their frustration, analyze what might be going on for the child, and explore possible solutions and alternatives. The teachers in the class watched the counselor model reflective statements and limit setting and learned to use these methods to help the child remain in the classroom. Through reflective supervision, the teachers discovered a way to help the child develop self-control so he would be able to utilize an inner locus of control in order to remain in the classroom. With the support of the counselor teaching quietly through reflective supervision, teachers figured out how to view the child, think through his problem, and work as a team.

Reflective supervision also provides parallel care for the teachers, who should be nurtured by their supervisors and school administrators. Reflective supervision can change the internal working of the child care center so that it promotes the mental health of the staff as well as the children and families (Harden and Lythcott 2006).

Parent Workshops

The workshops for the parents include the same attitude, skill, and knowledge components as for the teachers, except the emphasis shifts to the family and home relationships. Educating parents through workshops that focus on child-directed play therapy skills, consistent discipline strategies, and strengthening child's social skills has been effective with parents of at-risk young children (Reid, Webster-Stratton, and Baydar 2004). Our workshops are usually presented for four evenings, each session one-and-a-half hours long. It is very difficult to get a large group of parents who work all day to commit to this time. The most successful incentives are to offer some food, prizes, and babysitting. Parents of at-risk children cannot afford babysitters and often do not have anyone to take care of the children. The ABC interns and facilitators often take care of the children; at times teachers have been paid to stay with the children.

The most opportune time to reach the parents in the child care setting is in the morning when they drop their children off and in the evening when they pick them up. The playroom can have an open door policy. Parents often hesitate to trust anyone. They are frequently frightened. As with the children and teachers, it is necessary to build a trusting relationship. Therefore, the counselor approaches the parent with a nonjudgmental, client-centered approach. With time, the parents become curious about what is going on in the playroom and why their children are doing better, thus affording the counselor the opportunity to extend an invitation to join actively in filial therapy. Change takes time. When the well-trained mental health counselor is on the premises for at least 20 hours a week, the parents begin to accept her or him and join in playroom activities. Our services are available on-site and are less threatening since they involve play. The caregiver does not have to go to an agency, where therapy may be unavailable or unaffordable. This is an opportunity to get all of the adults in the child's life on the same page, so change can then happen.

SELECTIVE INTERVENTIONS

Small Group Play Therapy

The second of the multiple interventions is *selective*. Children who need extra help or are detected to be at risk for emotional and behavioral disorders are placed in small group play therapy (SGPT).

According to many child development specialists (Russ 2004), psycho-therapists (Hunter 1998), and pediatricians (Ginsburg 2006), play is the child's most powerful tool for learning and growing. It is the "language" with which children first communicate to others. Play is to the child what verbal communication is to the adult; hence it is the most effective vehicle through which adults can understand and guide children (Axline 1969; Kottman 1995; Landreth 2002a). Through play children learn about their world; understand how things work; express feelings and thoughts; and develop new physical, cognitive, and social skills and bonds (Landreth 2002a; Axline 1969). Toys and games are used instead of words to express the same feelings that adults have, such as fear, happiness, anger, and so on, but which children usually cannot express verbally (Landreth 2002a). Children may have a difficult time trying to explain how they feel or how they are affected by what they have experienced. Through play, children attempt to work out their problems and conflicts (Frank 1982). Play therapy can increase children's feelings of self-worth and self-acceptance, through a relationship with a caring adult who stimulates play and who models the core conditions for healthy relationships (i.e., congruence, acceptance, and understanding). Secondly, play therapy encourages children to understand their use of play as a way to express, explore, and work through their interpersonal conflicts and issues. And third, play therapy helps children to understand the purpose of their play, in its relationship to associating with past childhood events and its connection to feelings and behavior exhibited outside of the playroom (White and Allers 1994).

Preschools make ideal settings for play therapy intervention in that play is still accepted as the child's primary learning mode; emotional and social learning, rather than purely academic concerns, still have a primary place in the curriculum. The model of play therapy used in our program is a child-centered approach that creates an atmosphere of freedom and safety.

The therapist follows the child's lead, striving to listen and understand. Self-direction opportunities are maximized and the accepting nonjudgmental relationship allows the child to explore new ways of feeling and behaving (Sweeney and Homeyer 1999). The therapist actively reflects the child's thoughts and feelings so that the child can accept and learn to deal with them (Landreth 2002a). The intent of child-centered play therapy is to allow the child the freedom to be who she or he is. The use of empathetic understanding, acceptance, warmth, and behavioral limits provides an environment in which the child can grow and develop new behaviors. If the therapist is not directing the session, the child is allowed to explore the issues that are most significant to her or him (Sweeney and Homeyer 1999; Landreth, 2002a).

The following attitudes and techniques are emphasized:

1. *Acceptance*: being nonjudgmental, warm and caring, recognizing potential for growth in each child (Axline 1969; Zigler, Finn-Stevenson, and Hall 2002).
2. *Reflective/empathic listening*: acknowledging feelings, assisting the child in understanding and expressing his or her own feelings and others' feelings (Axline 1969; Ginott 1969; Landreth 2002a). For example, a child's comment "I hate you" is often reflected back as "You seem really angry."
3. *Encouragement*: instead of praise, encouragement builds self-esteem and fosters the child's ability to internalize appropriate behavior. Encouragement means valuing and accepting the child as he or she is, pointing out positive behavior, showing faith in the child so that the child can come to believe in himself or herself, recognizing effort and improvement rather than requiring achievement, and showing appreciation for contributions. For example, the adult might say "You were able to put the puzzle together by yourself" instead of "Good boy!" (Dinkmeyer and McKay 1982; Landreth 2002a).
4. *Building self-responsibility* and inner locus of control through the use of reflection, limit setting, and choices: "That's up to you to decide" (Axline 1969; Kottman 1995; Landreth 2002a).
5. *Enlarging the meaning*: for example, "It's scary when you don't know what is going to happen." The response to a child taking a toy from another child might be, "You would like to play with Scott but are not sure how to say, 'Can I play with you?'"
6. *Consistency*: the adult demonstrating to the child that she or he will be present and truly hear the child (Norton and Norton, 1997).
7. *Entering the child's world*. Play provides the vehicle to communicate with the child. The child leads as the director, the adult is the actor. By staying present with the child, the therapist can see the world as the child perceives it and understand the feelings driving the child's behavior. Playing together creates a bond and a relationship of respect for the child and his or her inner world. Imagination creates possibilities for change (Landreth 2002a; Snyder, Snyder and Snyder, 1985).
8. *Setting limits when limits have to be set*. Limits should not be set unless a child is hurting himself, the toys, or someone else. These are not stated at the beginning of the session. Children are told upon entering the playroom, "In here, you can do almost anything. We will let you know the things you may not do." As stated earlier, limits are set according to Landreth's ACT (2002b). The counselor Acknowledges a feeling ("You're mad"), Communicates a limit ("Bobby is not for hitting"); and Targets an alternative ("You can say 'Don't take my toys'" or "You can hit the stuffed animal or the pounding block").

9. *Natural consequences of action.* Choices allow the child to feel the consequences of her or his actions (Landreth 2002a). For example, "If you choose to throw the cars, you choose not to play with the cars. If you choose to slide the cars on the floor, you choose to play. You can decide."

Play therapy as an intervention may be conducted in a small group format. Small group play therapy allows the group members to learn more about themselves through interaction with other group members (Landreth 2002a). The discovery that one's own experience has been shared with others is an important therapeutic factor. Group play therapy allows for countering the elements of secrecy, isolation, and being different and allows for vicarious learning. As pointed out by many authors, the group therapy playroom is a microcosm of the larger society in which children live their everyday lives (Ginott 1969; Slavson 1948; Sweeney and Homeyer 1999; Yalom 1995). Group play therapy involves the application of individual play therapy principles in an interactive group context while maintaining active contact with each individual child.

Summarizing the rationale for group play therapy, Sweeney and Homeyer mention the following interrelated advantages for children (1999): promotion of spontaneity; vicarious learning; opportunities for self-growth and exploration; learning about limit setting and reality testing; improving social skills; and observing positive attachments among other children and between other children and the group therapist.

Applying the intervention guidelines detailed above, the play therapy group is for children identified at-risk through our early detection pretests, who need extra attention to assist them in managing their feelings and behavior. The child-centered play therapy group provides a laboratory in which children can experiment with learning how to interact with their peers, express their emotions and feelings in an appropriate manner, and create an internal locus of control.

While ABC uses a small group play therapy format, because of its therapy team approach, children are able to receive benefits of both group and individual therapy. ABC's small group sessions are conducted by a team consisting of a therapist and graduate intern and/or undergraduate intern and/or lay facilitator. In most cases there is a one-to-one ratio of adults to children. All interns and facilitators are trained in child-centered play therapy techniques and work only with a qualified counselor. Children receive the social benefits of the group while benefiting from the individual attention of one adult listening, watching, and reflecting with each child individually.

Our groups are made up of three to four children. While most of the children in SGPT are age three to four, some are as young as 20 months. The toys are adapted for the age of each group. The group sessions are 30 minutes long. In child care centers the groups need to be conducted in the morning, because children eat lunch around 11:30 and are down for naps by 12:00–12:15. Many of the children begin their days at the centers by 7:30 a.m. For each child ABC has a permission slip signed by the parents, with an explanation of the research and permission to videotape for teaching and research purposes.

Limit Setting and Choices

The playroom becomes a laboratory for the children to figure out how to participate at their developmental level. As explained above, the at-risk child is often developmentally, socially, and speech delayed. The children often act out their needs in an impulsive manner. Patience is needed to teach children other ways to express their feelings, from standing up to a bully to hitting a stuffed animal instead of a person.

Limit setting in a kind but firm manner is very important. The child learns what it feels like to know what is expected without judgment. In the playroom there is opportunity to teach children what to say. Often adults will tell a very young child, "Use your words." An 18-month-, 2-, 3-, or 4-year-old child often does not know what words to use. This is an opportunity to walk children through the process of relating to others in a compassionate way.

Imagine two children fighting over a toy, yelling, "Mine!" "No, mine!" What does an adult do? She or he yells, "Give that back. You have to share in this room." Using child-centered play therapy, the facilitator can empathize with the victim: "It doesn't feel very good when Johnny takes that toy from you." At the same time, the counselor can reflect with the perpetrator: "It is hard to wait for a toy. Toys are not for grabbing. You can ask, 'Can I play? or Can I have a turn?'" In this way, children begin to understand what it feels like when something is taken away from them and at the same time learn how to play with another child. This is an example of the ACT method of limit setting. The T (target an alternate behavior) becomes the words the child can learn to communicate with his or her peers.

Another example: Jane is crying because someone has hit her. She is sobbing; the counselor reflects, "Sam hurt you." Jane says yes (still crying). Jane will work through the crying if the counselor continues to talk. To tell a child that he or she must stop crying is to deny the child's feelings. The counselor can give the child words. "Jane, you can say, 'Sam, you hurt me. Stop it.'" If Sam replies, "Jane took my toy," the counselor may respond, "Maybe, Jane, you could ask to use the toy. Sam, maybe you could tell Jane you will give it to her when you are through."

Choices become very valuable for these young children. The choice should not be that the child cannot come into the playroom, but the choice is not to play with a toy. The key components of choices (Landreth 2002a) are (a) understanding that the child makes the choice; (b) the locus of control is with the child; (c) there is no judgment in the choice giving and there is no "good" or "bad" choice. Only *two* choices are given. And when the child balks at the choices, the choices are repeated. This will work only if the adult is consistent and follows through with the choice. Most important is "Big choices for big kids. Small choices for little kids" (Landreth 1990). This is not a time-out. The child knows why he is not participating or is not getting to use a toy. Choices are not a threat. A threat is when you state: "If you do that one more time, I am going to take that away from you." By using choices, the adult is giving the child opportunity to learn to problem solve and think about the consequences of actions rather than reacting impulsively.

Often children who struggle with safety and attachment issues become persistently aggressive with swords, snakes, or other toys and hurt others in the group. Limit setting becomes an important way for these children to learn to be aware of others.

For example: Danny loves to play swords with other children. He is careless in the way he plays, and he hurts others. The counselor can set a limit by stating, "You really love to play with the sword. The sword is not for hitting people. You can pretend or hit the stuffed animal (bop bag)." Danny refuses. The counselor can offer choices after setting limits, "You really like to play swords. If you choose to hit the stuffed animal or pretend, you choose to use the sword. If you choose to hit others in the group, you choose not to play with it. You can decide." Danny continues to play recklessly and hits another child. The counselor then states, "You like playing swords. I see you have chosen not to play with the sword." Danny cries, "I won't do it again." The counselor states, "The minute you hit someone is the minute you chose not to play." The counselor takes the sword away from Danny. He hangs onto the sword begging to use it. "I won't hit anyone again." The counselor remains calm and continues to reflect with Danny, "You are really upset with the choice you made. Maybe next time you will choose differently." In the meantime, the other children in the group are listening, watching, and learning. The counselor can comment to them, "You are noticing that Danny decided not to play with the sword. He seems to not like the choice he made. Maybe next time he will make a different choice."

In this example Danny is working on his own issues, and the other children are learning from his actions. This is a key concept of small group play therapy. In our model, there is more than one adult in the room. Therefore the counselor can remain focused on and reflecting with the child who is upset. The other adults can be reflecting the concerns of the other children in the group.

INDICATED INTERVENTIONS

The third area of our multiple interventions includes filial and kinder therapy. Teacher- or parent-child therapy is a powerful tool. The counselor helps the teacher and the parent change their perception of the child and gives them tools for managing the child's feelings and behavior; then the possibility for the child to change is dramatic. As both the parent and the teacher begin to perceive the child differently, the child begins to perceive himself differently. When the same techniques are used at school and at home, an environment is created that allows for the child's growth and development. Stress is reduced for everyone, and the atmosphere changes.

Filial Therapy

Filial therapy involves training caregivers (teachers and parents) in the attitudes, knowledge, and skills of play therapy. It is an intervention adaptation of child-centered play therapy, selectively used to improve parents' and teachers' ways of perceiving, communicating with, and relating to the child. Developed by Guerney (1964), this model has been used for more than 40 years. An entire issue of the *International Journal of Play Therapy* (2002), devoted to filial therapy, underscored the broad applicability of this modality. Meta-analysis of 93 studies has indicated an improvement in children's emotional and behavioral problems, with the largest effects being with treatments that included the parents (Bratton et al. 2005). Moreover, Landreth (2002a) has cited a number of outcome studies concerning the effectiveness of a 10-week filial therapy model with ethnically diverse clients.

It is easier to engage reluctant and untrusting parents in filial therapy when the services are on-site at the child care center. The counselor has the opportunity to meet and talk with the parents in the morning when the parents bring the child to school or in the afternoon when the child is picked up, thus building rapport with them. Another opportunity for informal contact is by leaving the door open to the playroom. Parents or teachers can stop by for a chat, or the counselor can invite them in to see the playroom. In this way, the counselor can build a relationship, affording a more positive response when the counselor invites the caregiver into the playroom to play with her or his child.

Kinder Therapy

Kinder therapy (filial therapy with teachers and children) has been shown to be effective in making teachers therapeutic agents with children.

Teachers who received the play therapy training were more skillful in their preschool classrooms when compared with control group teachers who had not participated in the special training (Post et al. 2004). However, a follow-up study found that the use of these skills in the classroom was not maintained one year later. Even so, teachers continued to have a more positive view of their skills and the children. Researchers noted the need for in-vivo training (modeling) in order for teachers to maintain their skills (Hess, Post, and Flowers 2005).

If a teacher is having difficulty relating to a certain child in her classroom, she might say "Oh, no, I was hoping Johnny would be absent today. I wonder what trouble he is going to cause today? He makes my life impossible. My day is ruined." Her relationship with this child needs improvement. This is an opportunity to get the teacher into the playroom with the child. If we can change the adult's attitude toward the child, then chances are we can change the child's behavior. The teacher has been taught the basics of filial therapy in the workshop. Those skills are refreshed in the playroom as she is invited to play with the child, letting the child take the lead. We then have the ability to model—to demonstrate in vivo and help the teacher see the child's strengths. At the same time, the child gets the attention he or she needs and comes to perceive the teacher in a different light.

PROGRAM EVALUATION AND RESEARCH

Professionals providing services to clients are of course very interested in learning whether their services are actually helping the clients. Today's emphasis is on evidence-based practice; professional accountability is legislatively mandated, incentives are given by managed health care systems for practice-effective research studies, and most funding strategies are outcome-based. Professionals should use empirical methods to evaluate programs and treatment outcomes.

Therapists must consider the many reasons for conducting program evaluation. It can help determine whether the program interventions are effective and in fact are helping the children, parents, and teachers. It can also help in deciding which services to provide and in verifying whether the needs and goals of children, parents, and staff are met. Program evaluation and research can be used to determine the strengths and weakness of the program so modifications can be made. Information gained from program evaluation can be used to justify program expenses. It also offers validation of the program for grant writing, as it provides the accountability and evaluation that foundations and grantors require.

After developing an early childhood mental health program in a child development center, you will begin to notice changes in children's behavior in the playroom and changes in families. You may begin to wonder about changes teachers are seeing in the classroom and may feel the environment calming. You will probably notice that positive changes are occurring and want more than anecdotal stories. You will want, in short, to have empirically based research.

Program evaluation is a work in progress; it will constantly grow and modify to meet your needs as your work continues. It need not be a daunting task. You can begin simply. First, find an instrument that measures the desired outcomes of your intervention. There are numerous standardized tests to measure school readiness (such as the National Reporting System, used by Head Start), resiliency factors, or behavioral concerns (such as DECA).

If there is not a standardized or normed instrument available, you may consider designing your own simple measure. Our ASK and PVRs (appendixes 9-A and 9-C) are measures we developed for use with our workshops, which we hope to get normed through future research. We also designed the Teacher's List of Concerns (TLC; appendix 9-D) to ensure that no child will fall through the cracks.

Pre and post tests on the children can be completed at the beginning and end of the school year or of a prearranged intervention period. Consider who you would like to complete these measures: teachers? parents? therapists? or some combination thereof?

Develop and administer pre and post tests for teacher and parent workshops. Select or develop an instrument to measure whether workshop participants have learned the information you proposed to teach. Consider creating and using an instrument to measure the teachers' ability to apply the knowledge and skill in the classroom.

There can be impediments to conducting effective evaluation or research. It requires participation on the part of teachers, staff, and parents. This is made easier if a relationship exists between counseling professionals and Child Development Center (CDC) staff and parents. One benefit of using person-centered therapy is that relationships are constantly being built and strengthened, thereby making it easier to get the cooperation of the staff because they already feel heard and a part of the program. Modest incentives (we offered $1 per completed test) for teachers and parents to complete measures on the children can also be effective. Perhaps with the help of a research consultant you can decide whether to use a simple "before and after" or an experimental design, if a comparable control group is available.

The ABC research team continues to conduct research and program evaluation. Valuable experience was gained during our initial exploration project. Our ongoing study has allowed us to develop a methodology for implementation and follow-up with a small group of children from three classrooms and their preschool teachers. The original modest sample, 45 children from three classrooms, decreased to a final number of 26 due to children changing schools, which indicated the need for a larger sample size to account for attrition. All teachers completed pre and post tests on each child using the above-mentioned Devereux Early Child Assessment (DECA), assessing within the child protective factors (resiliency) of initiative, self-control, and attachment, as well as behavioral concerns. ABC also used Child's Future (developed by Dr. Dirk Hightower),[3] which is a subjective view of the child's future based on theory of self-fulfilling prophecy. After a brief orientation and use of incentives (breakfast or lunch), we were able to obtain a 100 percent response rate from the preschool teachers.

In this pilot study, teachers attended two three-hour workshops in the fall and winter. They also received modeling in the classroom for an average of 20–30 minutes weekly, as well as approximately 30 minutes of reflective supervision per week. Due to lack of funding and staff, we were unable to provide modeling in the classroom for more time and in a consistent manner. Twenty-two of the twenty-six children received 30–60 minutes of SGPT per week. Three of the families received filial therapy aimed at improving relationships and communication between caregivers and children.

Teachers were rated in their classrooms by counselors using ASK (appendix 9-A), an instrument we devised to measure classroom atmosphere and teachers' attitude, skill, and knowledge regarding managing feelings and behaviors, at the beginning and the end of the school year. Before and after the workshops, teachers' and parents' attitude, skill, and knowledge were measured using Play Vignette Responses (PVRs) (see appendix 9-C), a tool designed to give us insight into their perception of managing feelings and behavior and to note what was learned in the workshop and what areas of the workshop needed improvement or emphasis. Sample questions from the play vignettes follow:

1. Two children are fighting over one toy. You say:
   a. Stop that!
   b. You have to share in school.
   c. You both want the same toy.
   d. Why are you two fighting?
2. A child at cleanup time is pretending to be a turkey instead of cleaning up. You say:
   a. I told you, it is cleanup time!
   b. Stop acting silly!
   c. If you don't clean up right now you are going in time-out.
   d. You're having fun pretending, but it is time to clean up now. You can play again when we go outside.

3. A child cries and says, "I want my mommy." You say:
   a. You miss your mommy.
   b. She'll be back. You don't have to cry.
   c. No, you don't.
   d. Don't worry. We are going to have fun.
4. A child shows you her picture and says, "Look what I did." You say:
   a. Wow, that's beautiful.
   b. I like your picture.
   c. What is it?
   d. You want me to see what you did.

Paired sampled t-tests were used to compare Time 1 and Time 2 scores on the three measures: initiative, attachment, and self-control. The overall DECA scores showed a significant increase in Overall Resiliency ($t = -3.36$, $p = .003$). Among the subscales, significant increases were found among Initiative ($t = -2.83$, $p = .009$) and Attachment scores ($t = -2.47$, $p = .021$). Interestingly, Self-Control did not increase significantly ($t = -1.47$, $p = .155$) and Behavioral Concerns did not decrease significantly ($t = -2.02$, $p = .054$). This warrants further investigation to explore the possibility that children's increase in self-expression was viewed as lack of control or a behavioral concern. There was also a significant increase in the Child's Future scores ($t = -4.34$, $p = 000$) indicating the teachers' improved positive view of the child.

We believe that the children's improvement in Attachment and Initiative are probably spontaneously generalized from SGPT sessions to the classroom, thus contributing to teachers' perceptions of increased "Behavioral Concerns" as measured by DECA.

We are now exploring a way that might help manage this discrepancy: We now solicit in an open-ended questionnaire the Teacher's List of Concerns (TLC), consisting of classroom teachers' list of three behavioral concerns (rank-ordered) about specific children recommended for SGPT. With additional funding, the same questionnaire would be administered to the parents. These lists of concerns are obtained at six-week intervals. To ensure program accountability, lists of the three concerns would be monitored by play therapists on a weekly basis, so no child's needs would be ignored if funding were available for additional staff.

After each SGPT session, the supervising play therapist, as well as graduate and volunteer assistants, completes a structured checklist measuring the children's social-emotional behavior during the session (SGPT Checklist, appendix 9-E). A detailed assessment of progress in relation to teacher and parent concerns is included. We then have multiple data sources. It may well be that the discrepancy between play therapists' and teachers' and parents' perceptions is more apparent than real.

This reconnaissance experience has confirmed that the tests are feasible for use by ABC in preschools. Moreover, we find that DECA resilience-related scores will be especially helpful as one early detection device (among others) for identifying children at risk for emotional or behavioral problems. We were able to refine the measurements used after determining what we wanted to measure and which scales would do so most accurately.

While our staff has also become familiar with the utilization of ECERS-R for studying preschool classroom environments, we have found the ASK to be a more useful measurement of the classroom milieu.

We have also learned from experience over the past four years that many children who test as at-risk may not need therapy but can be helped by being continued in the regular preschool classroom, *provided that the teachers have the opportunity for ongoing support from the mental health professional's training sessions, modeling, and reflective supervision.*

In sum, the results of this small pilot study suggest the intervention methods of the program are effective in increasing the resilience of children, particularly in the key areas of attachment and initiative. The strength of the results is particularly striking when considering the modest scope of our intervention repertoire. The results indicate that additional implementation and extension of the program are warranted. We continue to search for funding for the resources needed to support the staff required for program expansion and replication.

To evaluate further the effectiveness of our program, we are now studying not only resiliency factors and behavioral concerns using DECA, but also school readiness utilizing the National Reporting System (U.S. Department of Health and Human Services, 2007). In accordance with our experimental design, one school will serve as the experimental group receiving teacher workshops, classroom modeling, and small group play therapy. Another similar school will serve as the control group; it will receive services the following year. We are administering pre and post NRS and DECA tests to all classes in both schools. Having completed observations, we are forming groups for small group play therapy and are planning a refresher workshop for teachers and staff.

We have found that as the relationship and trust builds between teachers/staff and therapist, the program grows; of course, the program must be flexible in order to improve it. As with the children, change relies heavily on the relationship, as well as consistently helping teachers and therapists to recognize the "just noticeable differences" in the children's behavior. We noticed that the shift in the CDC staff is gradual and that a program can always use more staff. Workshops for CDC staff are necessary on a consistent basis to continue to reinforce the model, and they must be scheduled around the needs of the CDC. It is important that the therapist be available to model in the classroom and for consultation with teachers. Involving parents increases effectiveness.

CASE STUDIES

Justin

Teachers' Attitude

In preschool, Justin, a three-year-old child, was out of control. He destroyed the classroom every morning, knocking all the toys off the shelves and dumping blocks and Legos. The school wanted to expel him. All the school staff saw a very defiant, misbehaving, out-of-control child who was disrupting the classroom and the entire school. The teachers could not cope with him. He spent many hours in the director's office alone. We had just begun to provide small group play therapy at this school. The teachers were doubtful that anything would help this child or any other child through play. The teachers felt he was impossible and nothing would work. According to the teachers, what he needed was some really strict, harsh discipline. One of the teachers who had been at the school for many years said that this idea of play therapy was ridiculous. She was out to show us it would not work.

History of Disruptive Attachment

The maternal grandparents and the paternal grandfather shared temporary custody of Justin. The grandparents were in a custody battle in the courts to gain sole custody of him. Justin's mother was an alcoholic, had been on drugs, and had just had her second child. She did not have time for Justin. She left her parents' house when she had the second baby and lived with the father, leaving Justin to stay with his grandmother. The paternal grandfather had adopted Justin's father at a very young age. Justin's father served time in jail. He spent some time living with Justin's paternal grandfather. The maternal grandmother and the mother fought and argued constantly. The paternal grandfather was determined: "This child is not going to be like my son. I'm going to be really tough on him." The custody battle between the grandparents continued for two years. Justin was caught in the web of these adults. He had little consistency in his relationships and no secure attachment. Justin never knew when he was going to be with his dad, his grandfather, or his grandmother. At times he was told he would be with one person and then end up with another. This is an example of disrupted attachment. Justin needed to be able to play out his concerns in a way appropriate for his developmental level. He also needed to find a safe place to be. The only consistent factors in his life were his school and his teacher.

Importance of Toys to Express a Feeling

We began with SGPT for Justin. He enjoyed coming to group and was in a group with a few older boys. The boys would often play with swords, vying for possession of them. During an early session, Justin quickly found the sword and hid it, covering it with his shirt. He excitedly said to the counselor, "Look what I've got," and started to giggle. This play let us know that he had a sense of humor, resiliency, and charm. During other sessions, he would lock up both the counselor and the male facilitator with the handcuffs. We would not be allowed to move. Justin's most telling play was the use of a large yellow rubber snake as a lasso and fishing pole. Limits were set: "It is fun to swing the lasso (snake). The lasso can hurt others. You can swing the lasso in the corner away from others." We set the limits several times. Finally, Justin had a choice to make: "If you choose to swing the lasso around the group, you choose not to play lasso. If you choose to swing it away from others, you choose to swing the lasso." Justin chose not to play with the snake.

The counselor had the snake in her hand and Justin hung onto the snake for 20 minutes. He cried and cried. This choice was not about getting to hold onto the snake and play with it. It was about the larger meaning of needing to hold onto his family. He stated, "I hate my life." The idea that the snake was a lasso also seemed to represent the idea of roping in his family—to hang on to his family any way he could. The next session he made the same choice, but with more acceptance of his choice. He begged for only 10 minutes. By the fifth time, Justin made a choice to swing the snake away from others. His need to use the snake changed into another metaphor. The snake turned into a fishing pole. It was as though he was going to catch his family. By the time Justin left preschool to go to kindergarten, he was explaining to others about limits and choices. Justin would tell the other children in the group that they could swing the snake in the corner away from everyone else. He became empathic and caring of other people's feelings.

The Adults' Change in Attitude

Over a period of time Justin learned to express his feelings in an appropriate manner. It was a gradual process. There were times when the counselor had to take him out to the playground by himself, just to scream, hide, and throw things. The teachers were all upset with this kind of behavior. During the early process, they were very skeptical of the outcome. His teacher would question Justin's going to SGPT sessions. She wanted to say that if he behaved he could go to the group. We stayed reflective and showed empathy with the teacher: "It is very difficult to deal with a child who is out of control and destroys the room the very first thing in every morning. It is very disconcerting to have to pick up Legos day after day." The counselor spent many hours with the teachers after the first six-hour workshop. She or a facilitator would model in the classroom how to use encouragement and reflection with Justin. Reflective supervision was a part of this process, providing empathic listening with the teachers.

Attitudes gradually changed over the year. Teachers became more willing to try new and different ideas and became more comfortable as they built their skills by experiencing the new techniques in the classroom setting. Justin's paternal grandfather was willing to come to parenting workshops. Justin's maternal grandparents were not willing to come at any time. The mother came for a few filial sessions. His father also came to a few sessions. Justin's paternal grandfather was willing to try new ideas using choices and consequences, and learned to play with Justin in parent-child therapy sessions. In the playroom, Justin used the sword with his grandfather. Justin would stab his grandfather and his grandfather would let Justin be powerful. Justin also used the handcuffs and the snake as a lasso and fishing pole. The teachers were using encouragement and some limit setting.

ABC counselors continued to offer additional on-site workshops and modeled for the teachers ways to handle Justin's fear, hurt, and frustration. By the time Justin graduated from preschool, his teachers loved him and his behavior was socially acceptable. His grandfather had created a safe and positive environment at home. Adopted by his grandfather, Justin is now in fourth grade, and while he has recently developed some school problems, he is at the top of his class at a parochial school. His grandfather has also adopted Justin's two younger siblings. The lead teacher now tells all of the teachers at the workshops, "Listen, these ideas may seem strange, but I saw them work."

Discussion

Without the on-site services, Justin would have been expelled from school, fought with his grandfather, and gone down a very different path. Often children like Justin have so much pain and so much expected of them, that the only way they can express their feelings is through acting out. There is always a reason for a child's behavior. Very young children have difficulty verbalizing what they are feeling. We have to listen with our eyes and facilitate increased awareness in the adults that work with them. The attitude, knowledge, and skills of Justin's teacher helped not only Justin but all of the children in his class. As each teacher improves her attitude, knowledge, and skills there is a positive influence on many of the children in the classroom. Children in future classrooms will also benefit from the reflection, encouragement, and nonjudgmental limit setting that teachers learned in workshops and reflective supervision, thus illustrating the psycho-educational benefits of the universal component of preventive intervention and the philosophy of "teach one, reach many."

Mikey and Jack

Mikey (four years old) and Jack (two years old) now attend one of our schools. These brothers come from a family in chaos. The mother now lives with her mother and the boys. The father left home when Mikey was two and Jack was two days old. The mother seems depressed and has poor parenting skills. The father has been ordered by the court to take anger management classes. He is living with his girlfriend, who apparently has an alcohol problem. The paternal grandparents seem caring, but appear to have a poor relationship with their son. The paternal grandmother stated that her son needs help in disciplining his children. The father was over-heard threatening Mikey that if he did not stop crying he was going to take him into the bathroom. To which Mikey cried, "Daddy, don't hurt me."

Neither Mikey nor Jack is able to separate from their parents. They both cry and have temper tantrums at their classroom doors every morning. Mikey seems hypervigilant and frightened. He exhibits extreme separation anxiety. His speech is delayed. Mikey could not stay in the classroom. He would run out of the classroom at least four or five times a day. Sometimes he would run out of the school, climb the fence, and run around the school, crying, "I can't do this. I can't do this. I can't find my mommy. Where is my mommy?" This behavior, obviously not safe for the child, the teachers, or the remainder of the class, put the whole school on edge and demoralized and frustrated the teachers. How exhausting it was for everyone to have to be constantly alert, wondering when Mikey was going to run out again. (This type of behavior causes children to be expelled from preschools.)

Jack, Mikey's two-year-old brother, also appeared sad. His speech was better, but he too could not separate from his parent. Jack stayed in his room, rarely smiled, and always had a worried expression on his face.

The brothers were assigned to SGPT at least twice a week. Mikey also received speech therapy. It took six weeks to get Mikey to stay in the class-room. The teamwork of the counselors, teachers, and supervisory staff made this possible.

The counselor would come into the classroom to model limit setting with Mikey for the teachers. She would stand at the door. Mikey would pull on the door, push the counselor away, and climb on and under the coun-selor to try to open the door. On one occasion, after 20 minutes, Mikey finally said he was hungry and wanted his snack. He sat down at the table and remained in the room. The counselor and the classroom team started to put together reflections, limit setting, and choices for Mikey. Through brainstorming, they figured a way to keep the class going and still have someone with Mikey when he felt he had to run.

The teachers began to understand Mikey's fear through role-play situa-tions in reflective supervision and supplementary workshops. The coun-selor, seeing his teacher in the hall, would ask, "How is it going today?"

Some days the teacher would say, "Better." Other days she would say that Mikey was having a rough day. The counselor was able to use encouragement and reflection with the teacher and create a support system for coping with a very difficult classroom situation.

The parents each came into the playroom for filial therapy sessions with the children. The teachers participated in kinder therapy sessions. We are now making some progress. Mikey is able to stay in the classroom, and Jack seems happier. Each boy still has difficulty in leaving the mother. We hope their separation anxiety will be resolved by the end of the school year.

Dante and Demitri

Dante, now five years old, was aggressive and destructive in the playroom and the classroom. Counselors had worked in SGPT extensively with him while he was in preschool. Gradually he worked through many of his problems, learned social skills, and developed self-control. His brother, Demitri, two years younger and also aggressive, was in SGPT. While in kindergarten, Dante returned to the preschool for a day. He came to the counselor to hand her a large toy lion. He said, "My brother stole this lion from the playroom." Whenever he comes with his mother to pick up his brother, he peeks his head into the playroom and says. "Hi, Ms. Play Therapy." This is a child who used to tear up the playroom and used every four-letter word. He often refused to return to class after SGPT. The mother attended a parenting workshop and filial sessions. His younger brother has played with the lion for the past two years. His 6-foot-5-inch father has a tattoo of a lion on the back of his right hand.

Damian and Robert

A teacher at the school was having difficulty with her oldest son, Damian. His previous preschool had stated that they could no longer have Damian in the classroom. He was destructive, "bad," and difficult. Once at our child care center, he was selected for SGPT. Damian attempted to destroy the playroom every week. He would pounce on a large stuffed monkey while making everyone in the playroom stay away. He would try to knock down all the toys. Finally, one day, as he left the mess in the playroom, he stated, "Now I can have a good day."

His mother was fearful that he would never be able to handle kindergarten. She came into the playroom and had filial sessions with Damian and her younger son, Robert. Counselors worked with the mother reflecting and modeling therapeutic responses, including setting limits, offering choices, and acknowledging his feelings. When Damian went to kindergarten, he had a few incidents. His mother talked with counselors about choices and consequences. Within two months of kindergarten, he was doing well. He is now in first grade, doing well academically and socially. In a follow-up interview, his mother reported that the head aftercare teacher said, "Damian is able to follow the rules, take turns and be kind to others, better than any of the other children, even the older children."

Jim

Jim, a two-year-old boy, normally a joy to his teachers, began to act out. He was having temper tantrums, hitting others. His mother was going to have a baby. The teachers were all talking to him about how wonderful it was going to be to have a new baby. He was going to be a big brother now. The teachers were all excited the day his brother was born. They were all standing around him saying, "How exciting, you have a new baby brother. You are a big brother now." They did not let up. Jim was crying all day long. One teacher stated, "Don't worry about him. He will never remember this." No one considered that Jim's routine was disrupted; Mom didn't bring him to school but Grandma and Grandpa brought him. They never brought him to school before. Daddy wasn't around and Mommy had to go to a hospital. Nobody was hearing him.

This scenario was brought up and discussed at a teacher workshop. The counselor had the teachers role-play the situation. One teacher played Jim and was sitting on the floor. The other teachers could not think of what they could have said to Jim to make him feel safe and heard. The other teachers stood around the teacher playing Jim, talking excitedly about the new baby over his head. One teacher said, "I got it. We were not acknowledging this child. He felt ignored and uncared for." The role-play was processed by asking the person playing Jim (sitting on the floor at the feet of all these women) how she felt. She said, "Frustrated, ignored, mad, hurt, and confused." The teachers learned about the power of their words, acknowledging feelings, and being sensitive to a young child's point of view.

CONCLUSION

Our goal is to have an on-site early childhood social and emotional wellness program in every child care center/preschool. An early intervention and prevention program creates an opportunity for positive change to occur in the lives of children, their teachers, and their parents. The use of preventive play groups for children, involvement and education of teachers and parents, and the support of reflective supervision allows the counselor to focus on children's resiliency factors rather than pathology. An on-site program promotes play therapy and social and emotional mental health and wellness for all children and their caregivers.

Consider the impact of just one teacher in a school with a mental health program. She has 20 children each year in her classroom. If she teaches for 10 years, she will impact 200 children. Her therapeutic attitude and skills will affect her relationships with children in her personal life, friends, and coworkers. Teaching the child-centered play therapy techniques helps the teacher to reduce her stress as well as become a therapeutic agent. The analogy of a single pebble dropped into a pond creating a ripple effect across the water illustrates the training of one teacher whose therapeutic expertise will affect not only one child but will ripple through her entire community.

The importance of play as essential to the social, emotional, cognitive, and physical well-being of children has been emphasized by the American Academy of Pediatrics (Ginsberg 2006). The need to attend to children's social and emotional well-being was reiterated at the Head Start National Conference in June 2006 by numerous presenters who stressed the need for early childhood mental health services in Head Start programs.

This chapter has presented an overview of such a program, sponsored by All 'Bout Children (ABC), a grassroots South Florida community agency providing a comprehensive program for at-risk young children, age 18 months to 5 years, typically from low-income minority ethnic groups.[4] We have detailed our multifaceted preventive intervention services, including workshops for parents and teachers; early detection of children at risk for emotional and behavioral problems through DECA and other instruments; small group play and filial therapy; and modeling and reflective supervision for caregivers. To ensure accountability, our services are evidence-based; we have built into our program systematic evaluation and experimentally designed research. While still a work in progress, our ABC program to date shows a promising increase in children's overall resilience in coping with personal, family, and neighborhood risk factors. We are studying the effectiveness of the program on learning readiness, and if future funding is available we plan to do a longitudinal follow-up study of learning readiness for both experimental and control groups.

We strongly believe that by incorporating early childhood mental health services on-site in child development centers, the slogan "No child left behind" will increasingly become a reality.

APPENDIX 9-A. ASK SCALE

Date_____ Teacher _____

School _____

	Never				Often
Demonstrates acceptance of the child	1	2	3	4	5
Refrains from using judgmental language	1	2	3	4	5
Listens empathically	1	2	3	4	5
Encourages creativity	1	2	3	4	5
Focuses on present issues	1	2	3	4	5
Demonstrates high expectations of child	1	2	3	4	5
Uses encouragement instead of praise	1	2	3	4	5
Fosters the child's ability/desire/will to learn	1	2	3	4	5
Encourages child to fulfill potential	1	2	3	4	5
Focuses on child's strengths	1	2	3	4	5
Allows/encourages child to express feelings	1	2	3	4	5
Acknowledges/reflects the child's feelings	1	2	3	4	5
Helps child to identify/understand his/her feelings	1	2	3	4	5
Helps child to act constructively on his/her feelings	1	2	3	4	5
Follows the child's lead	1	2	3	4	5
Encourages the child to solve his/her own problems	1	2	3	4	5
Allows child to choose/direct activity/discussion	1	2	3	4	5
Acknowledges gradual/incremental changes in child's behavior	1	2	3	4	5
Announces plans regarding activities	1	2	3	4	5
Gives a timed warning for transition to new activities	1	2	3	4	5
Uses limit-setting as an opportunity to teach	1	2	3	4	5
Limits and consequences are reasonable	1	2	3	4	5
Limits and consequences are consistent	1	2	3	4	5
Remains calm and neutral when setting limits	1	2	3	4	5
Creates a warm and friendly atmosphere	1	2	3	4	5

APPENDIX 9-B. A WAY OF BEING WITH CHILDREN: MANAGING FEELINGS AND BEHAVIOR IN THE CLASSROOM

Contents

Please note: (1) Supplementary information concerning the dynamics of depression will be included in our updated trilingual (English, Spanish, and Creole) manual. (2) Similar parent-focused content is contained in the parents' manual, *Managing Feelings and Behavior at Home.*

APPENDIX 9-C. PLAY VIGNETTE RESPONSES

School_____

Date_____   A_____ B_____

1. Two children are fighting over one toy. You say:
   a. Stop that!
   b. You have to share in school.
   c. You both want the same toy.
   d. Why are you two fighting?
2. A child at cleanup time is pretending to be a turkey instead of cleaning up. You say:
   a. I told you, it is cleanup time!
   b. Stop acting silly!
   c. If you don't clean up right now you are going in time-out.
   d. You're having fun pretending, but it is time to clean up now. You can play again when we go outside.
3. A child cries and says, "I want my mommy." You say:
   a. You miss your mommy.
   b. She'll be back. You don't have to cry.
   c. No, you don't.
   d. Don't worry. We are going to have fun.
4. A child shows you her picture and says, "Look what I did." You say:
   a. Wow, that's beautiful.
   b. I like your picture.
   c. What is it?
   d. You want me to see what you did.
5. A child is going down a slide in a dangerous way. You say:
   a. Stop that! I have told you not to go down headfirst.
   b. Why did you do that? You know better.
   c. If you choose to go down head first, you choose not to use the slide. If you choose to go down feet first, you choose to use the slide. Which do you choose?
   d. That's dangerous, and I can't have you do that in school, because if something were to happen to you that would be terrible. You could hurt yourself and you could hurt someone else. So I don't want to see you do that again.
6. For the first time, Johnny was able to stay in line without touching someone. You say:
   a. Why don't you do that all the time?
   b. Not say anything to Johnny.
   c. You are able to stay in line today.
   d. What a good boy.

7. When it is almost time to move from center time to playing outside. You . . .
   a. Turn off the lights and say "Clean up now."
   b. Give a five-minute warning.
   c. Threaten the class that they'd better clean up or you won't let them go out to play.
   d. Expect the children to clean up right away when you say to.
8. Sarah cries about everything during the day. You feel . . .
   a. Sarah is impossible and just wants everything her way.
   b. Sarah is having difficulty adjusting to school.
   c. Sarah is spoiled and needs Mom to discipline her.
   d. You wish Sarah was not in your class.
9. The class is really noisy and running around too much. You feel . . .
   a. There goes Johnny creating havoc in the class.
   b. I wish I could get another job.
   c. They are still excited over the game they were playing outside.
   d. Why do they always act that way when we have to get ready for lunch?
10. A child comes and says, "Johnny pushed me again." You feel . . .
    a. Johnny pushes people for no reason.
    b. It is mostly Johnny's fault.
    c. You need to find out what happened before assigning blame.
    d. Johnny is struggling with how to express himself appropriately.
11. You find that you have a child that is developmentally delayed in your class. You think . . .
    a. She will be a real problem.
    b. Poor child, she won't be able to do much.
    c. This could be an opportunity for all of us to learn.
    d. Why do I always get these children in my class?
12. The classroom looks great and the children are excited about the new theme for the week. You think . . .
    a. That was a lot of work, but it really helps the children to learn.
    b. I really have the ability to set the stage.
    c. I have created a special feeling for the children.
    d. All of the above.
13 A child has just been reunited with his mother and is in day care for the first time. He has a very bad day and is trying to hit and kick you. You . . .
    a. Want him out of your class.
    b. Are sure he should be in another school.
    c. Feel he is doing this to you on purpose.
    d. Feel he is struggling and needs a lot of understanding from you.

14. A child invites you to play. You . . .
    a. Direct the play.
    b. Allow the child to be the director.
    c. Give ideas of other ways to play.
    d. Try to fix the child's struggles.
15. The brain of a three-year-old is
    a. 50 percent developed.
    b. 90 percent developed.
    c. 30 percent developed.
    d. None of the above.
16. The way a teacher talks to a child
    a. Can affect the child's self-esteem, self-worth.
    b. Has no effect at all.
    c. Doesn't bother the child for long.
    d. None of the above.
17. Encouragement is
    a. The same as praise.
    b. Helping the child to say "I can."
    c. Not necessary—praise is all that is needed.
    d. Of little value.
18. Which sentence is not encouraging?
    a. You were able to do that.
    b. You worked hard on that.
    c. What a beautiful picture!
    d. That is up to you to decide.
19. Which sentence is an example of reflective listening?
    a. Why did you do that?
    b. Why are you so sad?
    c. I know just how you feel—when I was a little boy . . .
    d. You seem upset.
20. Setting limits should be
    a. Firm.
    b. Kind.
    c. Neutral.
    d. All of the above.
21. Natural consequences of actions
    a. Place the responsibility on the child.
    b. Place the responsibility on the teacher to teach.
    c. Are judgmental.
    d. None of the above.
22. A child won't participate in anything and roams the room. You say:
    a. Come on, everyone has something to do.
    b. You have to do this.

c. Why aren't you playing?

d. It's hard to figure out what to do.

23. A child is playing building blocks. You say:

    a. What are you doing?

    b Why are you doing that?

    c. Why don't you build the blocks this way—it would be better.

    d. You are building them high.

24. Sally is trying to put a difficult puzzle together. You say:

    a. Here, let me help you.

    b. You put this piece in first.

    c. You are working hard on that puzzle.

    d. Why did you pick that piece?

25. A child says, "I don't want to do this. It's too hard." You say:

    a. You can do it.

    b. It's easy. Don't make it so hard.

    c. You're not so sure you can do it.

    d. Why can't you just try.

26. A child says, "Ms. Patty, I had a bad dream last night." You say:

    a. It was only a dream. There is nothing to be scared about.

    b. You had a scary dream.

    c. What was the dream about?

    d. I can't talk right now. I have to put the mats out.

27. Bobby takes a car and tries to take it apart. You say:

    a. Bobby, toys are not for breaking.

    b. You can't do that [you grab the toy].

    c. What are you doing?

    d. [quickly raising your voice] Stop that!

28. A child is building a castle. He is very serious about the project. You say:

    a. If you don't make it stronger, it will fall down.

    b. Let me show you how to make it stronger.

    c. It is important to make a strong castle.

    d. None of the above.

29. What do you anticipate when you come into the classroom in the morning?

30. How do you feel about the children at the end of the day?

APPENDIX 9-D. TEACHER'S LIST OF CONCERNS (TLC)

Child's Name_____Teacher_____
Date_____ ID_____ School_____

During the past week, how often did the child . . .

	N/A	Never	Rarely	Occasionally	Frequently	Very Frequently
_____	0	1	2	3	4	5
_____	0	1	2	3	4	5
_____	0	1	2	3	4	5
_____	0	1	2	3	4	5
_____	0	1	2	3	4	5
_____	0	1	2	3	4	5

Comments:_____
_____
_____
_____

APPENDIX 9-E. SMALL GROUP PLAY THERAPY (SGPT) CHECKLIST

Child's Name_____ Date_____ Group___
Individual___ Filial___

During the session, how often did the child . . .

	N/A	Never	Rarely	Occasionally	Frequently	Very Frequently
Play	0	1	2	3	4	5
Interact/play with peers	0	1	2	3	4	5
Accept 2nd choice when 1st unavailable	0	1	2	3	4	5
Verbalize needs/wishes	0	1	2	3	4	5
Accept limit setting	0	1	2	3	4	5
Share with others	0	1	2	3	4	5
Handle frustration appropriately	0	1	2	3	4	5
Do things for himself/herself	0	1	2	3	4	5
Interact positively with adults	0	1	2	3	4	5
Throw or destroy property	0	1	2	3	4	5
Hit/fight with other children	0	1	2	3	4	5
Show empathy	0	1	2	3	4	5

Comments_____
_____
_____
_____

Signature_____

NOTES

1. Our heartfelt thanks go to Dr. Howard J. Parad and Dr. Linda Hunter for their insight, support, and constant encouragement, which motivates the continued growth of our work.

2. Of course, the actual percentages of at-risk children receiving selective and/or indicated preventive interventions will vary with your assessment of the number and degree of risk and protective factors. The at-risk determination based on Devereux Early Childhood Assessment (DECA) Protective Factor Scale T-score is a child's scoring a "less than or equal to 40 or a Behavioral Concerns Scale greater than or equal to 60" (Le Buffe and Naglieri 1999, 18).

3. Used with permission of Dr. Dirk Hightower, Children's Institute, Rochester, N.Y.

4. We gratefully acknowledge support from Allegany Franciscan Ministries Inc. for funding ABC's program "Building Wellness, Resilience, and School Readiness: A Preschool Preventive Intervention Project," now in progress in preschools in Palm Beach, Florida.

REFERENCES

Aber, J. L., S. Jones, and J. Cohen. 2000. The impact of poverty on the mental health and development of very young children. In *Handbook of infant mental health*, 2nd ed., ed. C. H. Zeanah Jr., 113–128. New York: Guilford.

Ainsworth, M. D. S., M. C. Blehar, E. Waters, and S. Wall. 1978. *Patterns of attachment: A psychological study of the Strange Situation.* Hillsdale, NJ: Erlbaum.

Annie E. Casey Foundation. 2006. Kids Count state level data online. October. http://www.aecf.org/kidscount/sld/compare_results.jsp?i=190 (accessed December 3, 2006).

Anthony, E., and B. Cohler. 1987. *The invulnerable child.* New York: Guilford.

Axline, V. 1969. *Play therapy.* New York: Ballantine.

Benard, B. 1993. Fostering resiliency in kids. *Educational Leadership* 51 (3): 44–49.

Bertachhi, J., and T. Norman-Murch. 1999. Implementing reflective supervision in non-clinical settings: Challenges to practice. *Zero to Three* 20 (1): 18–23.

Bowlby, J. 1969. *Attachment and loss*, vol. 1, *Attachment.* New York: Basic Books.

———. 1977. The making and breaking of affectional bonds. *British Journal of Psychiatry* 130:201–210.

———. 1980. *Attachment and loss*, vol. 3, *Loss: Sadness and depression.* New York: Basic.

———. 1988. *A secure base: Parent-child attachment and healthy human development.* New York: Basic.

Bratton, S. C., D. Ray, T. Rhine, and L. Jones. 2005. The efficacy of play therapy with children: A meta-analytic review of treatment outcomes. *Professional Psychology: Research and Practice* 36 (4): 376–390.

Brauner, T. 2004. Efficacy of attachment-oriented family therapy interventions for children with developmental disabilities: An exploratory-descriptive study of process and outcome in a therapeutic preschool. PhD diss., Smith College.

Brazelton, E. 2006. A question of resilience. *New York Times Magazine*. April. http://www.nytimes.com/2006/04/30/magazine/30abuse.html?pagewanted=1&ei=5090&en=556898e2c03cc09d&ex=1304049600&partner=rssuserland&emc=rss (accessed December 8, 2006).

Burns, B., S. Philips, H. Wagner, R. Barth, D. Kolko, Y. Campbell, and J. Landsverk. 2004. Mental health need and access to mental health services by youths involved with child welfare: A national survey. *Journal of the American Academy of Child and Adolescent Psychiatry* 43 (8): 960–970.

Campbell, F. A., C. T. Ramey, E. P. Pungello, J. Sparling, and S. Miller-Johnson. 2002. Early childhood education: Young adult outcomes from the Abecedarian Project. *Applied Developmental Science* 6:42–57.

Coie, J. D., J. E. Lochman, R. Terry, and C. Hyman. 1992. Predicting early adolescent disorder. *Journal of Consulting and Clinical Psychology* 60 (5): 783–792.

Coie, J. D., N. F. Watt, S. G. West, J. D. Hawkins, J. R. Asarnow, H. J. Markman, S. L. Ramey, M. B. Shure, and B. Long. 1993. The science of prevention: A conceptual framework and some directions for a national research program. *American Psychologist* 48:1013–1022.

Cowen, E. L. 1991. In pursuit of wellness. *American Psychologist* 46:404–408.

Cowen, E. L., D. A. Dorr, and F. Pokracki. 1972. Selection of nonprofessional child aides for a school mental health project. *Community Mental Health Journal* 8:220–226.

Crowell, J. A., and S. S. Feldman. 1991. Mothers' working models of attachment relationships and mother and child behavior during separation and reunion. *Developmental Psychology* 27 (4): 597–605.

Devereux. 2001. DECA program/classroom strategies guide: Using the environment to promote resilience. *Enhancing social and emotional development*, 17–31. Villanova, PA: Devereux Foundation.

Dinkmeyer, D., and G. D. McKay. 1982. *How to talk so kids can learn at home and at school*. New York: Simon & Schuster.

Donohue, P., B. Falk, and A. G. Provet. 2000. *Mental health consultation in early childhood*. Baltimore: Brookes.

Downy, G., and J. C. Coyne. 1990. Children of depressed parents: An integrative review. *Psychological Bulletin* 108:50–76.

Fenichel, E. S., with NCCIP Work Group on Supervision and Mentorship. 1992. Learning through supervision and mentorship to support the development of infants, toddlers and their families. In *Learning through supervision and mentorship to support the development of infants, toddlers and their families*, ed. E. Fenchel, 9–17. Arlington, VA: National Center for Clinical Infant Programs. http://eric.ed.gov/ERICDocs/data/ericdocs2/content_storage_01/0000000b/80/23/eb/eb.pdf (accessed November 14, 2006).

Fonagy, P. 1998. Prevention: The appropriate target of infant psychotherapy. *Infant Mental Health Journal* 19 (2): 124–150.

Frank, L. 1982. Play in personality development. In *Play therapy: The dynamics of the process of counseling with children*, ed. G. Landreth, 19–32. Springfield, IL: Charles C. Thomas.

Fraser, M. W., ed. 1997. *Risk and resilience in childhood*. Washington, DC: NASW Press.

Garmezy, N. 1985. Stress-resistant children: The search for protective factors. In *Recent research in developmental psychopathology*, book supplement, *Journal of Child Psychology and Psychiatry*, 213–233. Oxford: Pergamon.

Gilkerson, L., and R. Shahmoon-Shanok. 2000. Relationships for growth: Cultivating reflective practice in infant, toddler, and preschool programs. In *WAIMH handbook of infant mental health*, vol. 2, *Early intervention, evaluation, and assessment*, ed. J. D. Ososky and H. E. Fitzgerald, 34–79. New York: Wiley.

Gilliam, W. S. 2005. *Prekindergarteners left behind: Expulsion rates in state prekindergarten program*. FCD Policy Brief Series no. 3. New York: Foundation for Child Development.

Ginott, H. 1969. *Between parent and child*. New York: Avon.

———. 1972. *Between teacher and child*. New York: Macmillan.

Ginsburg, K. 2006. The importance of play in promoting healthy child development and maintaining strong parent-child bonds. American Academy of Pediatrics. http://www.aap.org/pressroom/playFINAL.pdf (accessed November 2, 2006).

Goleman, D. 1995. *Emotional intelligence: Why it can matter more than IQ*. New York: Bantam.

Green, B. L., J. Simpson, M. C. Everhart, and E. Vale. 2003. The benefits of integrated mental health consultation in Head Start: A qualitative inquiry. http://www.npcresearch.com/Files/MHC%20article_final.pdf (accessed October 9, 2006).

Greenberg, M. T. 1999. Attachment and psychopathology in childhood. In *Handbook of attachment*, ed. J. Cassidy and P. R. Shaver, 469–496. New York: Guilford.

Greenspan, S. I. 2000. *The four thirds solution: Solving the child-care crisis in America today*. Cambridge, MA: Perseus.

Greenspan, S., and S. Wielder. 1998. *The child with special needs: Encouraging intellectual and emotional growth*. Cambridge, MA: Perseus.

Guerney, B. G. 1964. Filial therapy: Description and rationale. *Journal of Consulting Psychology* 28:303–310.

Harden, B. J., and M. K. Lythcott. 2006. Therapy and beyond: Mental health services for young children in alternative settings. In *Mental health in early intervention: Achieving unity in principles and practice*, ed. G. M. Foley and J. D. Hochman, 343–381. Baltimore: Brookes.

Helburn, S. W., and B. R. Bergmann. 2002. *America's child care problem: The way out*. New York: Palgrave Macmillan.

Hess, B. A., P. Post, and C. Flowers. 2005. A follow-up study of kinder training for preschool teachers of children deemed at-risk. *International Journal of Play Therapy* 14 (1): 103–115.

High/Scope Educational Research Foundation. 2005. Lifetime effects: The High/Scope Perry Preschool Project. http://www.highscope.org/Research/PerryProject/perrymain.htm.

Howes, C., J. James, and S. Ritchie. 2003. Pathways to effective teaching. *Early Childhood Research Quarterly* 18 (1): 104–120.

Howes, C., and S. Ritchie. 1998. Changes in child-teacher relationships in a therapeutic preschool program. *Early Education and Development* 9 (4): 411–422.

Hoyt-Meyers, L., E. L. Cowen, W. C. Work, P. A. Wyman, K. B. Magnus, D. B. Fagen, and B. S. Lotyczewski. 1995. Test correlates of resilient outcomes among highly stressed second- and third-grade urban children. *Journal of Community Psychology* 23: 326–338.

Hunter, L. B. 1998. *Images of resiliency: Troubled children create healing stories in the language of sand play.* Palm Beach, FL: Behavioral Communications Institute.

James, B. 1994. *Handbook for treatment of attachment-trauma problems in children.* New York: Free Press.

Kataoka, S., L. Zhang, and K. Wells. 2002. Unmet need for mental health care among U.S. children: Variation by ethnicity and insurance status. *American Journal of Psychiatry* 159 (9): 1548–1555.

Kottman, T. 1995. *Partners in play: An Adlerian approach to play therapy.* Alexandria, VA: American Counseling Association.

Lamb, M. E., M. H. Borenstein, and D. M. Teti. 2002. *Development in infancy: An introduction.* 4th ed., 205–244. Mahwah, NJ: Erlbaum.

Landreth, G. 1990. *Cookies, kids, and choices.* VHS. Denton: University of North Texas.

———. 2002a. *Play therapy: The art of the relationship.* 2nd ed. New York: Brunner-Routledge.

———. 2002b. Therapeutic limit setting in the play therapy relationship. *Professional Psychology: Research and Practice* 33 (6): 529–535.

Langlois, J. H., and L. S. Liben. 2003. Child-care research: An editorial perspective. *Child Development* 74 (4): 969–975.

Lavigne, J. V., R. D. Gibbons, K. K. Christoffel, R. Arend, D. Rosenbaum, H. Binns, N. Dawson, H. Sobel, and C. Isaacs. 1996. Prevalence rates and correlates of psychiatric disorders among preschool children. *Journal of the American Academy of Child and Adolescent Psychiatry* 35 (2): 204–214.

Le Buffe, P. A., and J. A. Naglieri. 1999. *Devereux early assessment user's guide.* Lewisville, NC: Kaplan Press.

Lyons-Ruth, K., L. Alpern, and B. Repacholi. 1993. Disorganized infant attachment classification and maternal psychosocial problems as predictors of hostile-aggressive behavior in the preschool classroom. *Child Development* 64:572–585.

Main, M., and J. Solomon. 1986. Discovery of an insecure-disorganized/disoriented attachment pattern: Procedures, findings and implications for the classification of behavior. In *Affective development in infancy*, ed. T. B. Brazelton and M. Yogman, 95–124. Norwood, NJ: Ablex.

McKenna, J. J. 1986. An anthropological perspective on the Sudden Infant Death Syndrome (SIDS): The role of parental breathing cues and speech breathing adaptations. *Medical Anthropology* 10:8–92.

National Child Care Information Center. 2006. Number of children in early care and education programs. http://nccic.org/poptopics/number-kidsece.pdf (accessed November 21, 2006).

Norton, C. C., and B. E. Norton. 1997. *Reaching children through play therapy: An experiential approach.* Denver: Publishing Cooperative.

Osofsky, J. D. 2004. Statement of Dr. Joy Osofsky before the Subcommittee on Substance Abuse and Mental Health Services Committee on Health, Education, Labor and Pension Hearing on "Mental Health in Children and Youth: Issues throughout the Development Process." www.zerotothree.org/policy (accessed October 2, 2006).

———. 2004. *Trauma and the young child.* New York: Guilford.

Osofsky, J. D., and M. D. Thompson. 2000. Adaptive and maladaptive parenting: Perspective on risk and protective factors. In *Handbook for early intervention,* ed. J. P. Shonkoff and S. J. Miesels, 54–75. Cambridge: Cambridge University Press.

Peisner-Feinberg, E. S., M. R. Burchinal, R. M. Clifford, M. Culkin, C. Howes, S. L. Kagan, et al. 1999. *The children of the cost, quality, and outcomes study go to school: Technical report.* Chapel Hill: Frank Porter Graham Child Development Center, University of North Carolina.

Perlmutter, D. 2006. *Raise a smarter child by kindergarten.* New York: Morgan Road.

Pflieger, J. 2002. Reflective supervision. *Head Start Bulletin,* no. 73. http://www .headstartinfo.org/publications/hsbulletin73/hsb73_32.htm (accessed November 12, 2006).

Post, P., M. McAllister, A. Sheely, B. Hess, and C. Flowers. 2004. Child-centered kinder training for teachers of preschool children deemed at-risk. *International Journal of Play Therapy* 13 (2): 53–74.

Powell, D., G. Dunlap, and L. Fox, L. 2006. Prevention and intervention for the challenging behaviors of toddlers and preschoolers. *Infants and Young Children* 19 (1): 25–35.

Raver, C. C., and J. Knitzer. 2002. *Ready to enter: What research tells policy-makers about strategies to promote social and emotional school readiness among three- and four-year-old children.* Policy Paper no. 3. New York: National Center for Children in Poverty.

Reid, M. J., C. Webster-Stratton, and N. Baydar. 2004. Halting the development of conduct problems in Head Start children: The effects of parent training. *Journal of Clinical Child and Adolescent Psychology* 33: 279–291.

Reynolds, A. J., and J. A. Temple. 2006. Economic returns of investments in preschool. In *A vision for universal prekindergarten,* ed. E. Zigler, W. Gilliam, and S. Jones. New York: Cambridge University Press.

Ringel, J. S., and R. Sturm. 2001. National estimates of mental health utilization for children in 1998. *Journal of Behavioral Health Services and Research* 28 (3): 319–333.

Russ, S. W. 2004. *Play in child development and psychotherapy: Toward empirically supported practice.* Mahwah, NJ: Erlbaum.

Shahmoon-Shanok, R. 2006. Reflective supervision for an integrated model: What, why, and how? In *Mental health in early intervention: Achieving unity in principles and practice* ed. G. M. Foley and J. D. Hochman, 343–381. Baltimore: Brookes.

Shonkoff, J. P., and D. A. Phillips, eds. 2000. *Neurons to neighborhoods: The science of early childhood development.* Washington, DC: National Academy Press.

Siegel, D. J. 1999. *The developing mind: How relationships and the brain interact or shape who we are.* New York: Guilford.

Simpson, J. S., P. Jivanjee, N. Koroloff, A. Doerfler, and M. Garcia. 2001. Promising practices in early childhood mental health. In *Systems of care: Promising practices in children's mental health,* 2001 series, 3. Washington, DC: Substance Abuse and Mental Health Services Administration.

Slavson, S. R. 1948. Play group therapy for young children. *Nervous Child* 7:318–327.

Snyder, M., R. Snyder, and R. Snyder Jr. 1985. *The young child as person: Toward the development of healthy conscience.* New York: Human Services Press.

Sweeney, D., and L. Homeyer. 1999. *The handbook of group play therapy.* San Francisco: Jossey-Bass.

Truax, C. B., and R. P. Carkhuff. 1967. *Toward effective counseling: Training and practice.* Chicago: Aldine.

Urban, J., E. Carlson, B. Egeland, and L. A. Sroufe. 1991. Patterns of individual adaptation across childhood. *Development and Psychopathology* 3:445–460.

U.S. Department of Health and Human Services. 2007. Head Start National Reporting System Direct Child Baseline Assessment (2006–2007).

Weissberg, R. P., K. L. Kumpfer, and M. E. P. Seligman. 2003. Prevention that works for children and youth. *American Psychologist* 58 (6/7): 425–496.

Werner, E., and R. Smith. 1992. *Overcoming the odds: High risk children from birth to adulthood.* Ithaca, NY: Cornell Press.

White, J., and C. Allers. 1994. Play therapy with abused children: A review of the literature. *Journal of Counseling and Development* 72 (4): 390–394.

Willoughby, M., J. Kupersmidt, and D. Bryant. 2001. Overt and covert dimensions of antisocial behavior in early childhood. *Journal of Abnormal Child Psychology* 29 (3): 177–187.

Yalom, I. 1995. *The theory and practice of group psychotherapy.* 4th ed. New York: HarperCollins.

Zeanah Jr., C. H. 2000. *Handbook of infant mental health,* 2nd ed., 110–135. New York: Guilford.

Zigler, E., M. Finn-Stevenson, and N. W. Hall. 2002. *The first three years and beyond: Brain development and social policy.* New Haven, CT: Yale University Press.

Zigler, E., W. Gilliam, and S. Jones. 2006. *A vision for universal preschool education.* New York: Cambridge University Press.

10

Issue-Specific Guided Play to Support Infants, Toddlers, and Their Families in Health Care Settings: Rationale and Interventions

Joy Goldberger and Anne Luebering Mohl

Children age six months to three years have been documented as being the most vulnerable to persistent emotional sequelae of hospitalization. However, these children are inconsistently provided with age-appropriate emotional and developmental support in health care settings. This article discusses planned, systematic play as one necessary facet of emotional and developmental support to hospitalized infants and toddlers and their families and suggests categories and methods of issue-specific play interventions.[1]

Numerous studies have clinically documented how profoundly deleterious institutional care can be for very young children (Bowlby, Robertson, and Rosenbluth 1952; Freud 1952; Freud and Burlingham 1944; Maki et al. 2003; Provence and Lipton 1962; Robertson 1958; Rutter et al. 2007; Spitz 1945). Classic longitudinal research has also documented the vulnerability of children from six months to six years of age, particularly to extended or repeated hospital stays. Some of the detrimental effects of hospitalization in infancy persist into the school years (Meijer 1985) and, indeed, often through adolescence (Douglas 1975; Quinton and Rutter 1976). An important converse, noted by Green and Solnit (1964), is that a single illness from which the mother believed the infant might not recover was associated with subsequent emotional problems based on the mother's belief that the child remains vulnerable ("vulnerable child syndrome"). Current research about early brain development and the impact of early trauma in shaping brain structures and pathways (Anand and Scalzo 2000; Porter, Grunau, and Anand 1999; Tupler and DeBellis 2006) supports these important classic studies and makes finding ways to help mediate the pain and trauma young children often experience in association with their medical care even more imperative.

Although much has been done to improve the experience of hospitalized children, the quality and sophistication of emotional and developmental care may not always match the quality and sophistication of technological care. Minde (2000) provides a comprehensive overview of the complexity of the environment, noting dramatic alterations for number of caregivers (minimum of 40 different contacts daily for hospitalized infants, compared to 6.6 per day and 8.4 per week for healthy 36-month-olds) and unpredictable routines, at an age when children particularly need sensitive and predictable caretaking experiences to develop patterns of trust. The American Academy of Pediatrics Committee on Hospital Care (2006) has recognized the importance of meeting the psychosocial needs of children as they relate to medical care and has recommended that hospitals incorporate child life into pediatric settings. Although the implementation of this recommendation will be beneficial, the 15:1 patient to child life specialist[2] ratio will not always prove adequate to address the psychosocial needs of all children that result from their medical care. In particular, the needs of infants and toddlers are often overlooked because their needs are not verbalized and/or are not readily observable to the untrained eye. Financial constraints to providing child life care within hospitals, combined with the misconception that infants and toddlers are the least likely patients to be impacted by the stress of health care experiences, may lead to inadequate child life staff dedicated to these youngest patients.

Many acute medical and surgical interventions are now provided either on an outpatient basis or with only a brief hospital stay. The increase in survival rates of infants with complex and fragile medical conditions and the implementation of diagnosis-related groups are changing the nature of inpatient populations; they are more complex and are receiving more intense levels of care (American Academy of Pediatrics Committee on Hospital Care 2006). In addition, many infants and toddlers are likely to experience the extended and repeated hospital admissions that have been found to increase the likelihood of persisting emotional consequences to hospitalization (Douglas 1975; Meijer 1985; Quinton and Rutter 1976). Even a single overwhelming outpatient experience can cause immediate and enduring changes for toddlers (Stashinko and Goldberger 1998). Inpatients with lengthy or repeated admissions may have reduced contact with primary caregivers due to socioeconomic pressures for mothers to remain at or return to work, the increasing numbers of adolescent mothers, and the noteworthy numbers of single-parent families. Job responsibilities, cultural differences, financial constraints, parental inexperience, needs of siblings, discomfort in medical settings, and distance are some of the many variables that inhibit parents' physical availability. Even when parents may be physically available, they may be rendered emotionally unavailable to their infants due to fear, guilt, grief, and other stressors. Thus, although hospital policy may now actively encourage family involvement, infants' emotional experience during hospitalization still remains a significant concern. Estimates suggest that over 65 percent of pediatric hospital beds are filled by children under four years of age (American Academy of Pediatrics Committee on Hospital Care 2006); yet this inpatient group at greatest risk for psychosocial sequelae often does not receive adequate emotional care or age-appropriate environmental adaptations (Wagner and McCue 1987). Although longitudinal studies describe resilient children who recover well from emotionally difficult situations when positive characteristics and factors are cultivated (Rouse 1998; Rutter 1999), infants and toddlers not experiencing individualized, loving care and in-depth relationships may not have enough support to overcome repeated traumatizing inpatient or outpatient experiences.

The experience of hospitalization is a known stress experience in early childhood (Rutter 1987), although it is not always recognized and addressed as traumatic. It is often assumed that infants and young children will not remember painful or frightening medical experiences, but recent research has demonstrated that infants remember experiences for increasing durations as they get older. Even before three months of age, infants demonstrate that they recognize situations and actions that they have previously experienced (Rovee-Collier 1990, 1993, 1999). Even when children do not explicitly remember past experiences, they have been shown to display a physiological reaction to stimuli from their past (Newcombe and Fox 1994). Evidence that infants remember medical events was first described by Engel and Reichsman (1956) in their observations of an infant who was fed through a gastrostomy tube for the first two years of her life, and, as an adult, held her own baby in the position that she experienced during her own feedings as an infant, although she would not have seen this position in the care of other infants nor have been expected to remember it (Engel et al. 1974). More recent research indicates that infants remember traumatic experiences (Fivush 1998; Gaensbauer 1995, 2000, 2002, 2004), specifically traumatic medical experiences (Peterson and Parsons 2005; Peterson and Rideout 1998), even in the first months of life. Although verbal recall of difficult medical experiences becomes more fluent and accurate over the second and third year (Peterson and Parsons 2005; Peterson and Rideout 1998), Gaensbauer (1995, 2000, 2002, 2004; Gaensbauer et al. 1995) presents case studies of children who had traumatic medical and nonmedical experiences before they were verbal and who spontaneously acted them out with play materials even years later. Clearly, experiences that very young children find to be overwhelming have the potential to remain with them for some time.

In 1987, Rutter suggested directed and specific play as one of the facets of care that could prevent or remediate some of the most frequent emotional and developmental challenges for hospitalized infants and toddlers. Brazelton and Sparrow (2006) describe the benefits of demonstrating and encouraging imitation during routine exams and office visits, and believes that by age 15 months a child shows "that by using a new cognitive acquisition—symbolic play—he can transfer his anxiety about the doctor to a doll and can receive reassurance from watching procedures with the doll" (150). Brazelton and Sparrow further recommend that parents seek out and use play specialists if their young child is hospitalized, with the goal of helping him or her master the potentially overwhelming situation. Gaensbauer (1995, 2000, 2002; Terr et al. 2006) describes how his treatment of children who were traumatized as infants and toddlers included directly providing the materials that enabled the children to "play out" the details of their experiences. However, it is likely that the vast majority of very young children are not offered the opportunity to engage in therapeutic play experiences in which individualized materials for expressive and descriptive play are provided and thematic material is recognized and addressed. Thus, one recommendation is that hospital staff—child life specialists, pediatric nurses, and pediatricians—be trained to guide families upon discharge to anticipate and support young children's need to play through their medical experiences once at home.

THE CHALLENGE OF PLAY IN THE CONTEXT OF HEALTH CARE

Numerous authors have emphasized the interplay between the appropriateness of the infant's environment and each infant's unique sensitivities, needs, and abilities to respond (e.g., Brazelton 1976; Brazelton and Nugent 1995; Erikson 1963; Greenspan 1995; Greenspan and Porges 1984; Jones 1979; Nugent et al. 2007). A. E. Gottfried (1985) describes consistent findings replicated across researchers and populations, indicating that the availability of play materials and parental involvement correlates positively with subsequent developmental outcomes. Wachs (1985) found seven play and environmental factors in infancy to affect cognitive development at five years of age: availability of stimulation materials, variety of stimulation materials, responsivity of physical environment, and regularity of scheduling positively affected cognitive development; ambient background noise, overcrowding, and physical restraint were negatively related to cognitive outcome.

Measuring the health care environment in comparison to the "ideal" supportive environment for infant and child development reveals the shortcomings of the typical hospital or outpatient center (see, for example, Greenspan and Porges 1984). Core concerns regarding parental involvement, the appropriateness of the environment, and the availability of play materials merge in the care of infants and toddlers in hospitals.

Opportunities to nurture the infant's emotional health with relaxed, enjoyable, expressive playful interactions may be all too rare in hospitals or even home care for medically complex children. Parents may feel the pressures of competing emotional and social "burdens," and the interactional synchrony that is the basis of adult-infant communication may be compromised by both the child's condition and the parent's state of mind. This is especially true for infants and toddlers with permanent disabilities who may be poorer "senders of cues" and may have more difficulty engaging in social contact that rewards the caregiver (Greenspan 1988; Williamson 1988: Zeitlin and Williamson 1994). Babies with temporary disabilities created by their medical condition or care may also be especially affected. Infants and toddlers who are limited by health care equipment or by their condition (e.g., those tethered to an IV pole, oxygen, or ventilator; those with weakness and/or awkwardness imposed by disability or paraphernalia of illness such as IV armboards or casts; those with an inability to produce sounds because of tracheostomy or need for a ventilator) may have difficulties producing expressive language, as well as with normal types of communication such as pointing, using rudimentary words along with gestures, or engaging in and sustaining reciprocal exchanges (Goldberger 1990; Goldberger and Wolfer 1991; Greenspan 1988; Greenspan, DeGangi, and Wieder 2001). Lack of emotional rewards combined with the infant's weakness may make it difficult for parents to sustain playful interaction (Greenspan 1988; Grenspan, DeGangi, and Wieder 2001), and social interactions may not be felt by the baby or parents to be gratifying or meaningful. Even if parents are present and are able to be sensitive to their child's needs, there are times when neither parents nor staff can be responsive to a child's overt cues (cries that say "Pick me up and help me escape this painful procedure" or "Please feed me").

The hospital environment can be chaotic, overstimulating, or understimulating. Ambient background noise, physical restraints, and a seemingly endless stream of unpredictable strangers contribute to the stressfulness of the environment. Human and mechanical sounds, movements, and sights may be perceived by the infant as disjointed and hard to interpret (e.g., hearing people without seeing them; feeling the stomach filling during tube feedings without the social-emotional-kinesthetic-auditory-visual events that normally accompany eating). Staff may "round" on children talking among themselves about the child without any sustained interaction with the child. Feeding, so important in infancy, may be stopped and started out of synchrony with a baby's hunger, pending medical consideration and upcoming procedures. For infants who have been hospitalized more often than not, and who are fed through tubes, regularity of scheduling and diurnal rhythms may be weakly experienced. Disciplines that provide services by consult may arrive ready for interaction just when an exhausted or uncomfortable baby has finally fallen asleep. All of these challenges are compounded for children with developmental challenges or sensory deficits, as well as for their parents.

Toys may be unavailable, inappropriate, out of sight of restrained or confined infants, or in sight but out of reach. Additionally, individual play programs, such as those provided by services such as Child Life (American Academy of Pediatrics Committee on Hospital Care, 2006) may not have staffing in quantities realistic to provide for all who need it.

Play is recognized as essential in children's ability to make sense of and cope with the world, whether at home or in a stressful environment such as the hospital (Bolig 1984; Brazelton and Greenspan 2000; Thompson and Stanford 1981). In varying degrees, play in hospitals may be facilitated by adults. Ideally, it should include a range of free play and more structured play opportunities that are supervised by a skilled adult (such as a child life specialist) who is aware of individual patient and family needs and is able to use play as a means of assisting very young children to play through and master past experiences (Bolig 1984). For those who provide support and intervention outside of the medical setting, it may be important to ask about, learn the components of care, and be prepared to work through a child's past health care experiences, using appropriate play materials. This chapter will focus on play that is adult-designed and adult-initiated in order to respond to the unique and specific concerns of infants and toddlers in health care settings. Guided issue-specific play, together with regular opportunities for free play, should continue and optimize development and enrich the family's involvement with the child by normalizing the environment and counterbalancing the stressful and confining hospital setting. In this context, play will be considered "issue-specific" when it is individualized for each patient and structured to achieve goals specific to the experiences and needs of an individual child and his or her family. Issue-specific play may be primarily *preventive* (e.g., opportunities for free and expressive play to continue development and adjustment; preparation for medical events) or primarily *remedial* (e.g., play that addresses stranger or separation anxiety exacerbated by hospitalization; play that follows a stressful medical experience). Play that is preventive is aimed at preventing negative socio-emotional outcomes; remedial play is planned to decrease the traumatic effects of hospitalization and other health care–related experiences.

PLAY THAT IS PRIMARILY PREVENTIVE

When play for infants and toddlers in health care settings is initiated with regard to a specific concern, its goal is to support universal developmental needs and progression. In the first years of life, play that is provided preventively should include rich opportunities for unstructured play for the purpose of expression, for a sense of control and mastery, and for the caregiver's ongoing assessment of the child's status (Bolig, Fernie, and Klein 1986). In addition, structured, issue-specific play can help provide family support, age-appropriate opportunities, and a forum for addressing feelings related to separation from home and family.

Family Support

Stressed, fearful, grieving, overwhelmed parents may be so focused on "what is wrong" with their child that they have little reserve available to appreciate their infant's areas of health. Parents may be so cautious of medical equipment that they avoid handling their infant, and staff should be alert for parents' fears and encourage them to interact physically with the infant as much as is possible given their medical state. Hospital staff who are familiar with a variety of medical conditions and paraphernalia and who also know child development can help parents recognize safe ways to interact and play and can reinforce parents' positive perception of their infant.

Marney was a newborn, the first child in a young family. At birth she was rushed to a major medical center for surgery within 24 hours. Despite the fact that the birth defect was significant, it was in no way life-threatening. When Marney's father arrived at her bedside, he sat at a distance and made little eye contact or attempts to hold or touch her. He focused on questions that related to the surgery that she would face and what her life would be like. The child life specialist offered to show the father photographs of Marney's birth defect as a bridge to seeing what he feared, and afterward the father tentatively glanced at the baby's actual body, which had been well camouflaged by her diaper and gown. Soon after, the father was shown some of her very healthy and intact capacities, such as her attentiveness, responsiveness, and synchronous movements to her father's voice; her ability, if held "en face," to imitate her father's tongue thrusts; and her willingness to visually track a red ball. From then on, Marney's father gingerly held and fed his baby, and began tentatively establishing his role as "Daddy."

It seems likely that, when parents have already cared for and become attached to their infant at home, materials that encourage the continuity of patterns of nurturing and pleasure are of importance in the hospital. The familiarity of play with family can provide a sense of normalcy to a hospitalized child. Seeing their baby play may optimize parents' hopes and perceptions of their baby's recovery. Even in the most dismal of medical situations, a young child's spark of interest may help fuel and comfort parents. For many parents whose self-image as parents has been diminished by the expertise of medical staff in so many areas of their child's life, play can become the one area where they remain the experts about their child.

When physical care must be performed by others, play can become crucial as the vehicle through which parents and siblings remain irreplaceable for the child. Similarly, when parents may be somewhat detached from their infant as a result of emotional, social, or financial constraints, play is an ideal means to comfortably maintain their sense of connection. Indeed, Rutter (1981) states that it is actually play rather than physical care that is the most significant facilitator of infant-parent attachment. For child life staff who have contact with families over time, observation of patterns of play between parents and infants, informed by knowledge of qualitative evaluation tools such as the Functional Emotional Assessment Scale (Greenspan, DeGangi, and Wieder 2001), the Brazelton Neonatal Behavioral Assessment Scale (Brazelton and Nugent 1995), or the Newborn Behavioral Observations system (Nugent et al. 2007), should provide insight into areas where a family might need psychosocial support and help staff in forming goals on behalf of children and families.

Developmentally Appropriate Opportunities

An appropriate play environment for a young infant should include visual, auditory, tactile, and kinesthetic input from both people and toys (A. E. Gottfried 1985) and ample opportunities for self-determined, intrinsically motivated play (A. W. Gottfried 1985). However, for some infants, simultaneous sensory input from more than one or two systems may be overwhelming (Greenspan and Porges 1984; Greenspan and Wieder 1998). Health care staff can join parents in recognizing signs of infants' pleasure, sensory tolerance, and cues to disengage. While they are sick, babies' tolerances for stimulation may be higher or lower than their typical levels, and a child with disabilities may also need special accommodations such as positioning, increased physical contact, or brighter lighting to be able to play with success and satisfaction. An infant's ability to focus on an interesting play environment rather than the medical environment surrounding him has been anecdotally observed to decrease the worried, hypervigilant appearance of sick young infants. Close attention by parents and staff is required to ensure that play materials remain within reach when an infant's position is changed so that the child is not frustrated by seeing playthings that are out of reach.

Whether a baby is developing typically or with differences, it is important to consider the developmental tasks that the child would be working on in a nonhospital environment and try to mirror those in the hospital setting. For example, after the infant attains a developmental age of four months, it becomes increasingly important that appropriately sized and weighted materials be available for reaching, bringing to mouth, banging, turning, prodding, and otherwise "making work" and that adults facilitate the necessary positioning if infants are too weak to master this on their own (Williamson 1988). This can be particularly challenging for babies who are small as well as weak, as staff and parents are likely to naturally offer play opportunities befitting a baby of that size, while the baby has the cognitive and physical desires of others her developmental age. It is the challenge of those who provide hospital care as well as early intervention in the home to find materials that meet the criteria of requisite novelty, cognitive challenge, and increased opportunities for satisfying sound production and movement, while not taxing weak infants with little reserve. As at home, toys offered for play in the hospital must continue to provide increasing complexity, opportunities for social involvement and initiative, and symbolic play (Piaget 1962). When the infant or toddler is immobilized for any reason, providing channels for exploration, interest through novelty and variety, and release for energy and frustration resulting from excessive confinement are necessary in continuing age-appropriate development.

Katie, an active 18-month-old, sustained a simple fracture when her leg became tangled in a climbing structure. In the emergency room, her leg was placed in a spica cast; she was immobilized from above her waist down to the foot of the injured leg and to the knee of the other leg. Her movement was severely restricted, and Katie's parents were in a state of high anxiety about how to manage this sudden challenge to their skills as parents of an active toddler. When the child life specialist in the emergency department asked what they thought would be the biggest problem areas for Katie and the hardest times of day, they responded that decreased time with other children would be difficult, since she was highly social in day care but would be cared for in the home while in the cast, and that she would be unable to engage in the "wild running and rowdy play" that she seemed to use to calm herself at the end of the day. The child life specialist offered several ideas to her parents and suggested that they form a plan that worked for them:

- *Offer Katie small toys that she could throw into a metal basin, making noise and dispelling some energy.*
- *Provide toys that require pounding and physical force such as clay, toys with balls and hammers, and playing catch.*
- *Find surprising novelty toys (such as a Nerf ball ice cream cone, in which pressing a button propels the ice cream from the cone), accenting the following features during play: being "one up" in the sense of having power over surprised adults; and commanding the space through which the ice cream travels.*
- *Create a routine based on Katie's typical past daily rhythms but adapted to current circumstances, including both active and quieter times, and incorporating both predictability and the requisite novelty to be stimulating.*
- *Acquire a bean bag chair for positioning, to use alone or in conjunction with a toy wagon, so that Katie can be fairly upright at times and reclining at others, but remaining in the midst of activity.*

- *Form simple events such as "parades" in which Katie is an equal participant, joining cousins, neighborhood children, and interested parents, with musical instruments or household objects to create a band that marches through the neighborhood.*
- *Engage in journaling and photographing the events of Katie's recuperation to form them into a story organized with a beginning, middle, and end, along with anecdotes that will help Katie remember this time with a sense of mastery and closeness, and with positive family memories. The more difficult events and feelings should be included, as they too were real, but with recognition of how well Katie overcame these situations.*

Katie's parents later responded that they made use of many of these ideas, and Katie's recuperation was much more manageable than they had anticipated.

Babies who are not able to have food by mouth must be given particularly close consideration, since feeding is a foundation for reciprocal positive engagement with the external world and the alert attention needed for playful interactions. Feeding, like no other experience, can provide rich input simultaneously to each and every sensory system: the sight of the caregiver and sound of her voice, the kinesthetic sense of being moved through space to a comfortable and familiar position, the warm sensation of being held and touched, and obviously taste and aroma. There is the equally rich framework for infants to have early successful experience with "language," as their cries result ideally in a contingent response, and their gestures evoke a response and communication with the caregiver. These combine into early cognitive schemata about the infant's evolving sense of being a causal agent in a social interaction, and about what works and what doesn't work while being fed. When babies are unable to eat in the usual fashion, special care must be taken to simulate for them the experiences that feeding normally provides.

Cassie was born with several congenital anomalies. Most relevant to our discussion, and likely to her experience, was a severe defect of her trachea and esophagus, so that any liquids in her mouth posed a significant risk for aspiration. To protect her airway while more serious medical issues were being addressed, she was required to stay in a fixed upright position in her crib. She could not be taken out and held. The goal for Cassie focused on being as attentive as possible to her natural awake-alert timing, and to make the most of a structure for diurnal rhythms. Each day, Cassie's parents were encouraged to climb onto a stool at the right height to be able to surround her in as close an embrace and replication of feeding as possible and to provide a pacifier, shaped as closely like the one she would eventually be fed with, for her to suck. The cloth holding the pacifier was dipped in formula so that she could experience the aroma and retain positive associations with it. Three or four times daily, family members cuddled, "rocked," and sang to Cassie. As she got older, in addition to the pacifier, Cassie was provided with small teething toys and other safe materials to maintain a sense of pleasure in oral experience. This routine was reserved solely for the family. Cassie's transition to beginning oral feedings was still challenging, as she was more prone to gagging and to fatiguing than the typical infant her age. However, the transition was not met with the refusal or struggle that is common under similar circumstances with little or no issue-specific plan and intervention.

Medical Play and Preparation for Medical Experiences

When able to be mobile, healthy infants and toddlers at home would be actively exploring and manipulating their immediate environment; supervised opportunities to touch and play with hospital equipment used in their care is important for a hospitalized child of any age (Petrillo and Sanger 1980) and may also parallel the expected developmental norm of imitating household activities. For example, an infant with an IV would see many caregivers paying attention to bags of IV solution and associated equipment. A parent or staff member might hold the baby so she can touch and explore the bags and examine the pump, and later give her some tubing similar to her own to explore. Opportunities to handle IV tubing, oxygen cannulas, nasogastric tubes, syringes, anesthesia masks, and stethoscopes satisfy curiosity, and children subsequently are less likely to disturb their own equipment. This exploration can serve to maximize infants' self-perception of being actively involved in the environment in which they are immersed. For children with more complex medical needs, a developmental progression of interest can be expected. A child who is developmentally 10 to 12 months might simply want to play repeatedly with a syringe and plunger like the one used to put medicines into his IV, but soon after, he may be likely to imitate adult use of the syringe on a doll. In general medical play, as long as the child's play is not harmful to him or to others, the role of the adult facilitator is to enable the child to lead, without teaching or prodding. Observations made of the child's affect and actions during this play can be used to guide future play specific to an observed issue.

There is also a more formalized conceptualization of preparation called "psychological preparation." The core tenets of psychological preparation for medical experiences—(a) anticipating stress points and (b) planning and rehearsing coping strategies—were developed initially by John Wolfer and Madelon Visintainer (1975, 1979) based on existing theories of stress and coping combined with child development theory. Their methods were refined as part of a more comprehensive play program during the ACCH Child Life Research Project (Gaynard et al. 1990; Wolfer et al. 1988), which incorporated more recent coping theory (Lazarus and Folkman 1984) and evaluated the reactions of children from three to twelve years of age, with strongly positive results (Gaynard et al. 1990; Wolfer et al. 1988). Although no data exist at this point to evaluate the effectiveness of psychological preparation with younger children, these tenets can be adapted and incorporated into our care of infants and toddlers.

In preparing infants and toddlers for upcoming medical procedures, knowledge of development allows us to predict what aspects of the experience babies are likely to find challenging and to prepare for them in ways that are meaningful at their developmental level. For example, even very young infants demonstrate awareness of strange situations and strangers in unusual clothing. We can predict that seeing hospital staff dressed in surgical garb, hats, and masks is likely to be upsetting. Babies can be prepared for surgery by "practicing" peek-a-boo with surgical caps, masks, and gowns so that when the infant sees people wearing these items, their familiarity may decrease distress. With guidance from professionals, parents are the ideal facilitators of this play (Wolfer and Visintainer 1979). As infants mature to the age when separation from familiar caregivers becomes stressful, games of peek-a-boo and other forms of play involving going away and coming back again (pop-up toys, bubbles, toy cars) may help them cope with separation.

At the beginning of their second year, when toddlers become interested in imitating adults' actions, child life or other hospital staff can help toddlers and their parents use medical materials and dolls to play through the sequence of events that the child will experience. It is important that the equipment that is used in this play be as close to realistic as the child can tolerate, and sized appropriately for dolls. The toddler may not initially understand that the content of the play is specific to her or him and may show little interest, but during the actual procedure, the process will be familiar, and the child will know that she or he has been told. If the child experiences repeated new procedures, such preparation play will take on more meaning.

As development progresses into the third year, the child will begin to include expressions of affect into medical play. At this age, some practicing of coping strategies can be incorporated into preparatory play. Young children can rehearse such strategies as staying still for procedures (first showing wiggling to the doll then showing the doll how to stay very still) or blowing the feelings away. These can be practiced by having the child "teach" the doll what to do during the easier and harder parts of the procedure. It is also important at this age that hospital staff prepare a toddler in advance for any postsurgical alterations in the child's perception of his body (e.g., place a cast like the one the child will receive on a stuffed toy; place a doll in traction; insert a tracheostomy tube in a doll and practice suctioning; place an ostomy bag on a stuffed animal's abdomen; place Band-Aids or gauze and tape over the site of an anticipated surgical incision).

David and his father met with a pediatric nurse in preparation for David's surgery the next day. Because David was only 14 months old and had little expressive language, his father was skeptical but indulged the nurse, who wanted to replicate the impending events on a doll. Just as David would experience, they gave the doll "sleep medicine so the doll won't feel his operation" and placed bandages, doll-sized drainage tubes, and facsimile traction equipment on the doll, just like David would have. David seemed minimally attentive as the nurse described that for weeks the doll would eat and sleep and play in bed, and showed him how the tubes would be cleaned. He came and went to the medical play setting, gathering other toys without actually playing with them.

Postoperatively, David was in his room and agitated, although his pain seemed well managed. He repeatedly pointed to the window, and eventually his father realized that he wanted that doll, which was resting on the windowsill. David pointed to the doll's arm: David had an IV; his doll didn't. When the nurse placed a small imitation IV on the doll's arm, David settled down and no longer was interested in the doll.

Several days later, David's two older brothers came in for their first visit with him. Again, David pointed for the doll and then pointed to each of the tubes on the doll. Although he didn't have words, his actions spoke volumes about his sense that he had been told what his experience would be.

Although preparatory play is typically initiated in advance of a procedure, it is not unusual for children to persist in such play after the event, as they cognitively and emotionally process and work through the experience.

The concept of psychological preparation with planned coping takes on new importance in the context of what we are learning about the foundation of experiences that become overwhelming and can lead to post-traumatic stress disorder (PTSD). Goleman (1995) summarizes PTSD as resulting from situations in which a person feels overwhelmed; perceives no choice, no power, no chance to escape; and which exceed one's coping resources. When these perceptions of a situation concur, there is a transition from cortical (analytical) thinking to responding from the more primitive brain centers, leading to the release of neurochemicals that serve to more deeply etch the memory and fight-or-flight responses. Planning and rehearsing coping may not change the fact that the stressor can't be avoided, but can contribute to a sense of having the skills to cope effectively, having certain choices, and being able to receive support. This, combined with new knowledge of the long-term impact of repeated stressors on brain development (Anand and Scalzo 2000; Goleman 1995; Rothschild 2000; Tupler and DeBellis 2006), highlights the importance of bolstering infants, toddlers, and their parents in selecting active and optimal coping strategies.

When Parents Are Not Available

When parents are unavailable, provision of appropriately gratifying social and play interactions becomes a necessary staff responsibility that should be considered as integral a part of the infant's care as maintenance of adequate hydration and nutrition. Although staff can never replace parents, they can facilitate normal patterns of trust, pleasure, motivation, and cognitive development. A limited number of caregivers, primary nursing with consistent patterns and timing of care, primary child life care, and inviolable uninterrupted time for play and affective give and take can encourage attachment, predictability, and interaction. These considerations are important for all young hospitalized children and are paramount for those whose hospital care will be extended and/or repeated.

In summary, play that is preventive aims at creating as normal and optimizing an environment as the hospital allows, supporting meaningful social relationships that foster healthy emotional development. Whether hospital experience is brief, extended, repeated, or occurs in an outpatient clinic or at home, provision of play as described above enriches the child's and the family's experience, comfort, and involvement.

PLAY THAT IS PRIMARILY REMEDIAL

The hospital environment is unique in its perpetual activity, frequent disruptions to sleeping babies, frequent uncomfortable events, use of sophisticated equipment, and large numbers and changes of caregivers. These deviations from the wide range of normal infant environments frequently elicit readily observable developmental disturbances. For children too young for verbal explanations, play can be individually focused to address each individual baby's particular issues. Play that is issue-specific and remedial is typically adult-initiated and structured (rather than child-initiated). It combines the caregiver's perceptions of the infant's strengths and vulnerabilities; the family's ability to be present and engaged; medical and social history; developmental capabilities; level of initiative and expressiveness; and recognition of one or several outstanding social-emotional and developmental challenges, obstacles, disruptions, or disturbances. Rhythmicity, issues related to social interaction, and problems created by the medical environment are common problems readily addressed through play.

Early Rhythmicity

In adequate home environments, most infants and toddlers experience encouragement to conform to predictable sleep/wake/mealtime/playtime patterns. Ideally, parents respond fairly quickly and contingently to the infant's distress, and the parents' sense of efficacy and enjoyment of the infant increases as the infant rewards them with signs of pleasure and enjoyment. Parents typically learn to interpret their infant's preverbal cues and respond to these consistently. Not only do parents provide much pleasurable, intimate contact but they also protect and minimize inappropriate or overwhelming stimulation. With support from responsive parents, babies learn self-regulation and use their newfound skills to adapt to the rhythms of the home environment and to make themselves available for satisfying interactions with their world.

Encouraging responsive care and rhythmicity in the form of predictable daily sleep, wake, play, and care patterns is both vital and a multidisciplinary challenge in the health care setting (Liakopoulou et al. 1983). When hospitalized or chronically ill, infants and toddlers may experience disruptions from any given state due to internal factors (such as side effects of medication, variations in levels of pain, intermittent fevers, increased need for respiratory support) that pose obstacles to establishing a basic capacity for self-regulation. When infants also are biologically challenged by sensory sensitivity, difficulties processing sensory input, or difficulties using their bodies to respond to sensory input (Greenspan and Wieder 1998), the obstacles are compounded. Primary nurses can serve as orchestrators with parents of creating a schedule for coordinating the infant's essential patterns and sensory challenges with what is known of the procedures and rehabilitation interventions the child is likely to require, the timing of hospital routines such as rounds, and the timing of the presence of the infant's family, child life, or other primary caregivers for social-emotional-developmental nurturing. If parents are not consistently available, this level of care is extremely difficult to realize without concerted effort and commitment on the part of staff, as well as vigilant gate-keeping on the part of the nurses. Even for infants being cared for as outpatients, frequent clinic visits and changing home-care nurses can disrupt the rhythms of the entire household. Well-intentioned care may not succeed if the infant's sensory preferences and limitations are not articulated to those interacting with him. Planning play and/or nurturing as a responsive and routinely available part of the infant's day should be a required part of each child's care plan.

Antonio has spent the first six months of his life in the pediatric intensive care unit. He receives his nutrition through a gastrostomy tube. Frequent and relatively sudden needs for his tracheostomy to be suctioned and for his vital signs to be taken have left him with few events to distinguish day from night or to have full, restful sleep. His primary nurse has taken great care to note when he seems most likely to want to be alert and to note if there is a time of day when he seems most "out of sorts" and in need of a nap. On that basis, she has altered his care, recommending grouping of care just before an ideal sleep time, and recommending times to avoid disliked care. The unit's child life specialist and physical therapist have adjusted their schedules as much as feasible, to match the times he is most likely to be alert and receptive to social interaction and play.

Discomfort in Social Interaction

Problems in the infant's response to social interaction may occur, even in instances in which the best efforts have been made to support and incorporate parents, to promote a rhythmic and predictable day, and to provide familiar and nurturing primary caregivers. Evidence of withdrawal from social interaction may become observable as early as the first several weeks of life (Brazelton and Nugent 1995; Brazelton and Sparrow 2006; Greenspan, DeGangi, and Wieder 2001: Nugent et al. 2007). Demonstrations of insecure attachment, including atypical stranger anxiety, have been described in the classic writings of Bowlby (1982) and Ainsworth and colleagues (Ainsworth et al. 1978). More recently, Lubit, Maldonado-Duran, Helmig, and Lartigue (2006) discuss the relationship of care by simultaneous or sequential multiple caregivers (an obvious parallel to hospital care) to the precursors of attachment disorders.

Withdrawal

Physical withdrawal (e.g., arching the back or pulling back limbs) or social withdrawal (e.g., gaze aversion, "shutting down" and going to sleep, or avoidance of social interactions) may result either from compromised innate capacities for processing stimuli (Brazelton 1976; Brazelton and Nugent 1995; Greenspan and Wieder 1998; Greenspan, DeGangi, and Wieder 2001) or from overwhelmingly uncomfortable environmental and physical stimuli (Greenspan and Porges 1984; Greenspan, DeGangi, and Wieder 2001). Parents and staff may feel unsure about how to interact with and engage a sick infant or may feel that the infant is better off without them.

When a young infant shows signs of withdrawal, it is important to first determine a form of physical or social interaction that the infant can comfortably tolerate. For example, when direct gaze is too uncomfortable for an infant, creating a safe distance with unbreakable mirrors and toys held in the infant's line of vision in order to include the caregiver's face may be useful in facilitating eye contact. Although interesting and varied toys contribute to optimizing the infant's interest and attention, they are secondary to the pleasurable human interaction that they can facilitate. Initially, the infant may tolerate input to only one sensory system at a time, with a gradual incorporation of additional simultaneous sensory input. If social withdrawal is in response to painful procedures, it is important to provide more pleasurable interaction, including pleasant touch if the child is receptive, to counterbalance the negative stimulation the child is receiving. Predictable play and social interaction time, designated procedure times, and primary caregiving may increase predictability and therefore the infant's ability to enjoy social interaction.

Older babies and toddlers may avert their gaze even while engaged in social interaction. This is most commonly observed in babies with lengthy or frequent hospitalizations, notably in those who are "floor favorites," and is typically an indication of social overstimulation from which the child cannot otherwise escape. Unfortunately, these cues are often ignored. In essence, promoting this behavior encourages overadapted responses, in which babies are satisfying the adults around them without letting their own needs be clearly known. Many of the babies who display this form of gaze aversion are so frequently (but briefly) greeted and distracted from their own self-motivated play and attention that they also appear to "learn" to have a problematically decreased attention span. This may interfere with the acquisition of developmental skills of which they would otherwise be capable. Intervention includes provision of regular, extended play periods during which caregivers are in proximity to respond to the child's cues, but do not unnecessarily interrupt any self-motivated play, and act to protect the child's play from unnecessary interruption. This may require requesting that other children's parents and hospital staff stay at least 15 minutes (Parmalee, cited in Goldberger 1987), or preferably, interact at some other time. Most family visits of any length are typically in the best interest of the child and merit support.

Expressions of Insecure Attachment

Infant-parent attachments that were insecure before hospitalization, as well as those weakened as a result of hospitalization, may be demonstrated by emotional detachment or by indiscriminate clinging to any available caregiver (Ainsworth 1962; Lubit et al. 2006). Although this behavior may be functional for infants with extended hospital stays, it is generally highly maladaptive and precludes the formation of a secure attachment with a primary caregiver. Gratifying contact with a few designated nurturers other than parents is the optimal hospital route of care. Toys may be used to facilitate eye contact with interaction, which encourages the infant's acknowledgment of the nurturing adult. Transitional objects may be encouraged or even created (e.g., a toy that is always placed with an infant or toddler immediately after nurturing) to assist the infant in having a continued sense of being nurtured. Numerous extraneous handlers and brief interactions should be actively discouraged. It is important to employ thoughtful decision-making about the future continuity of any relationship that may develop when considering using students and volunteers to interact with infants and toddlers in the health care setting.

Stranger Anxiety and Separation Anxiety

Caution during encounters with unfamiliar adults and marked anxiety when separated from the family appear in the second half of the first year and persist through toddlerhood. Natural fears of strangers at this age are confirmed when strangers are often involved in painful procedures. Separation from parents may appear permanent to toddlers and may be experienced as punishment or abandonment.

When stranger anxiety is the initial concern (e.g., the baby cries when "strangers" enter the room, whether or not the parent is in proximity), emotional care through play may include making contact with the child from whatever distance is comfortable. For example, blowing bubbles from across the room, playing peek-a-boo, rolling balls or trucks to the baby, or playing with an interesting toy in the infant's line of vision but from a "safe" distance are all means of interacting without immediate contact. The goal is to increase the infant's sense of safety and comfort so that he or she can return the ball or truck to the hospital caregiver and eventually feel safe while in closer contact with a hospital "stranger."

When separation from family and home is the predominant problem, play of a more symbolic nature is ideal. Simple symbolic play may include peek-a-boo games in any creative form; language of "going and coming back again" in play with bubbles, balls, cars, and whatever else is available; simple hiding-and-finding games (e.g., baby bear looking for mommy bear and/or daddy bear; finding the shapes inside sorting toys; "little car" looking for his "big car"). Much comforting and searching around the hospital unit may be required before the infant can engage in any form of symbolic play. Ideally this play should be carried out by a staff person who will be able to remain available to the child or facilitate the transition to the next caregiver to avoid repeating the experience of abandonment. Play that addresses separation anxiety is likely to need to be repeated frequently throughout hospitalization.

Separation from Familiar Environment

Any change in location is a consideration of primary importance to babies who have spent unusually extended times in intensive or acute care and are approaching discharge to a chronic care facility. These children may have experienced a paucity of "excursions" (e.g., only to radiology or to the operating room) as compared with children who have lived at home and have experienced social visits as well as trips to the supermarket. They are likely to have had some sort of relationships, many superficial rather than strong and specific, with vast numbers of caregivers and to the unit as a whole, but few, if any, of these people may be available to ease the transition. It is useful to prepare a toddler capable of receptive language or ability to attend to symbolic play by taking a doll or a favorite stuffed animal on a ride, showing that doll a new bed, and playing with a new group of nurses. Visiting another unit within the hospital to see another place that "children sleep" can also help. A photograph album or videotape of familiar sights and people of the current hospital unit also may help ease the transition, and can be used in the future to help the child know his or her history. Conversely, for hospital units accepting transfers and therapists working with toddlers transitioning to foster care, albums and videos can help give words to an important experience, particularly when the toddler's own ability to do so is limited.

Andre was transferred from one teaching hospital to another for a rare specialty surgery. He had been a unit favorite. In nearly three years he had spent just weeks on two or three occasions at home. His transfer information described him as "a sad little guy" with limited affective expression and no recognizable language. Once in the new hospital, he was almost immediately rushed into surgery, with no chance for any form of preparation, and was mute and avoided all eye contact while initially recovering. His primary child life specialist sat at a safe distance (judged by his ability to glance at her) and told the story of "the little boy who went from one hospital to another. At one hospital he knew lots and lots of people and in the new hospital he didn't know anyone at all." He nodded yes on subsequent days to the question of whether he wanted to hear the story of the little boy; he tolerated little variation from the key theme. After a fairly brief time, this story became a tool for other staff. For example, he was initially resistant to interaction with the physical therapist. When in her presence he was asked if he wanted to hear the story of the other little boy whom the child life specialist and the physical therapist both knew who came to their hospital and who got to know them, he perked up and nodded and tolerated the physical therapist's gentle interactions.

Problems Created by the Medical Environment

Among the problems specific to the hospital are those created by the process of medical care. Hospitals are unique in their great number of caregivers. The majority of these caregivers typically convey genuine affection for children; nevertheless, they will also require patients' passivity, may impose discomfort, and are likely to discourage normal exploration (IVs cannot be mouthed or waved in the air).

Fortunately for many young children, after the stress of admission and initial procedures, parental support and genuine caring on the part of staff decreases these difficulties. However, the following is a brief listing of some of the situations and interventions most typical of hospitals.

Enforced Passivity

In few settings would adults want or expect a child to remain passive while an adult is inflicting pain. Indeed, preschoolers are being taught about private parts of their bodies and to "say no." Parents discovered to be using four-quadrant restraints on their child at home no doubt would be considered abusive, as would parents severely restricting their child from moving around and freely exploring his or her environment. Although such constraints are sometimes unavoidable in the process of sustaining and improving children's health, adequate staffing to ensure as much supervised time for playing freely without restraints and with adequate nurturing helps to ameliorate the effects of such constraints. As always, parents' presence and involvement offer greatest potential in compensating for this sort of passivity. While restrained, a variety of toys fastened securely and safely to enable the baby's active manipulation with hands and feet increases the opportunity for normal exploration. When passivity has been learned, it is ideal to respond to the infant's slightest cues and provide several options for pleasurable play that require increasing motivation (e.g., appropriately responsive toys within immediate reach gradually moved in subsequent play sessions so that the infant must work a bit more to acquire them). This will reinforce the infant's role as active and initiating.

Margarita has grown up tethered to an IV pole that delivers nutrition to her bloodstream. Despite the caring staff and her parents' regular evening visits, her frequent abdominal surgeries have meant that in the past she has been flat on her back or supported on pillows in a semi-upright position. Now she has all the skills in place to sit, shift her balance to pick up a toy, and regain her balance. However, she sits and smiles at the new and interesting toy, with no apparent expectation to achieve her goal with autonomy. However, she is pleased for others to offer it to her. Goals include placing toys close to her initially and gradually moving them a bit further so that she develops that part of her self-concept from intrinsically motivated activities.

Another form of passivity is when toddlers can only watch what others can do, but cannot participate themselves. They may see others whose activity is unrestricted, children breathing without being tethered to hosing like they are, or siblings eating a normal diet. Play with toys that are facsimiles or that use similar equipment may help normalize the toddler's experience.

Medical Equipment Incorporated in Body Image

When infants and toddlers have grown up with such medical equipment as IVs, ostomies, gastrostomy tubes, and tracheostomies, they may have incorporated these into their body image just as another child would learn that he or she has hands, feet, and ears. Certainly families, health care providers, and even strangers have paid enough attention to these appliances. When equipment will no longer be used, young children may seem to mourn its loss. Deliberately planned play that incorporates rehearsal and practice immediately before the event may help prepare a toddler for this change.

Henry has had a colostomy since right after birth. Right around his first birthday, his family was delighted to learn that he had grown enough for the ends of his colon to be reattached and placed back in his abdomen. He would be a "regular" boy! However, from Henry's position this wasn't going to be the same joyful experience. In addition to the incisional pain, he would feel stool pass through his lower GI tract for the first time. Stools would feel caustic to his unaccustomed skin, and adults would perform a new and irritating cleansing process on a part of his body that had previously received little attention. Worst of all, Henry has always had a bag attached to his belly. The bag is the focus of much attention: It must be cleaned and changed, and care taken that it stays in place. One could wonder, how is it different for Henry to lose his colostomy than it would be to lose, say, his hair or his toes? He has just gotten adept at naming his body parts and his colostomy has been an important one.

Play for Henry involved giving a doll anesthesia, putting a bandage or Band-Aid over the site of his stoma, and waving "bye-bye" to the doll-sized imitation ostomy bags. Further play focused on washing the doll's bottom.

Nonetheless, after surgery Henry seemed stunned. He seemed to want to reenact the doll anesthesia and then saying "bye-bye" repeatedly the first day before moving on to other play. Every morning he began his play with the health care materials, but for less time each day before moving on to other activities. During play he became more active in being the one to say "bye-bye" to the ostomy bag and initiate taking it off and putting it into the wastebasket.

Preparation for Surgical Experiences and Medical Play

If a young infant, or the primary caregiver, has already experienced overwhelming procedures, before good preparation for a new procedure can take place, often the child needs to replay the past difficult time in a new, calm, and "safe" context. If a 10-month-old infant crawls around the room to avoid the doctors' surgical masks as well as the child's mask for anesthesia induction, it is a sign that the infant may benefit from first observing, then ideally participating, in playing through the past experience while adults vocalize reassurance along with acknowledgement of the difficult feelings associated with the experience. At times this must happen from quite a distance.

At just 15 months of age, Jonathan was already suspected to have Crohn's disease. He had been held down for numerous blood tests and examinations prior to admission. On admission he screamed in terror when anyone entered his room and fought even the simplest care, such as routine checking of vital signs. Despite the array of toys in her arms, the child life specialist working on that unit was no less of a threat. She couldn't cross the threshold. However, as she sat on the floor just outside the doorway and first engaged in routine play with simple items then switched to the more interesting but anxiety-provoking doll and medical equipment, Jonathan was transfixed. As long as she didn't attempt to make eye contact, he drank in the repeated confirmations of "the doll's" past struggles. He listened with apparent caution as the child life specialist made strong statements about how it was our job to make it different this time, to make it easier. By the end of the week the child life specialist could play near his bed and by the middle of the next week he was an active participant. His mother "practiced" with him just before even the very routine procedures.

Even "simple," community-based care can change a young child's memory.

Shiloh, at 22 months, had little expressive language. For nearly a full day after a fall, his parents and neighbors wondered if Shiloh had sustained a fracture to his arm, even though his fingers still moved. To Shiloh's great distress, he was helpless to stop those neighbors with medical training who repeatedly wanted to palpate the site. By the time the community consensus was that his arm was likely fractured and needed to be X-rayed, Shiloh was already extremely overwhelmed by the repeated pain and numbers of people approaching. His mother said that she thought they were in for a huge struggle as Shiloh already became very distressed and fought even routine visits to their kindly pediatrician. One neighbor familiar with health care play suggested that they play about the unfolding events as there likely would be X-rays and casting at the emergency center that would go much more easily if Shiloh cooperated as much as he could. They used a flexible cloth doll and played about people touching the doll's arm so they could take a good, big picture with a big camera. The doll might say "Ouch!" when they put his arm just the right way, but they would be careful and it would be okay. As it was a likely stress point, Shiloh was encouraged to move the doll's arm very gently, and then even more gently, and yet even more gently, even though the doll was saying "Ouch." They also showed the doll how to "blow the feelings away" onto a glitter-and-star-filled "magic wand" tube, doubly useful as it gave his devoted 16-year-old sister a role (holding the wand and helping him blow) and a way to be helpful. Then they played about a big hard Band-Aid, much bigger and harder than any the doll had ever seen before. They put wet gauze on the doll and talked about how the Band-Aid would be wet at first, then get warm, and then get very hard. At the emergency center, Shiloh did everything as it had been practiced, including calmly saying "Ouch" when his arm was positioned.

Several days later, toting cast, Shiloh and his mom visited the neighbor who had played with him. The neighbor moved to kiss Shiloh's cast and he suddenly withdrew his arm. He was still fearful of being touched or even approached. His mother immediately responded, "You didn't kiss the doll first!" Shiloh had set rules now about how to approach his arm.

Although this was not a defining or life-threatening experience for Shiloh, it set the foundation for future similar situations. This is obvious in the immediate, as the cast would need to be removed. Again the family used the doll to practice for the loud and frightening cast-cutter, and it went quite smoothly. Shiloh cried vigorously but allowed his arm to be handled and otherwise didn't protract his distress. We expect that these two mastered experiences will influence Shiloh's self-concept and approach to more routine health care contacts.

One provision for infants and toddlers who have been overwhelmed by medical experiences is the availability of "general health care play," where parents and staff can observe, provide input, and note if the child's play over time begins to become calmer, or if it remains tinged with tension.

At age 11 months, Amber's play with syringes initially was agitated and full of approach-withdrawal. Although her treatment dictated the placement of a deeper IV line through which she now received medications and had her blood taken for tests, the memories of past overwhelming and difficult experiences were strong. She seemed to be most interested when she witnessed a slightly older, more comfortable child at play with the feared items. Eventually she picked up a needleless syringe and repeatedly pushed and withdrew the plunger. Although she remained wary, she observed the other children and began to explore other familiar equipment as well.

STRATEGIES FOR PROVIDING SUPPORTIVE PLAY

In order to be safe and worthwhile, play materials need careful maintenance and supervision. They should be cleaned between uses and checked carefully for small, sharp, or broken parts. Materials should be stored in an organized and safe manner. Distribution of toys for use by patients in their cribs should occur regularly and with awareness of each child's abilities, preferences, and needs. Patients confined to cribs must be provided for just as thoroughly as those who can enjoy a supervised group play session. If toys are to stay in useful, unbroken shape, be cleaned between use according to infection control standards, and be delivered to patients with a keen "match" for emotional and developmental needs and interests, there must be someone whose job includes that function. Although students and volunteers can greatly enrich a patient's experience, it is important that volunteers and students be supervised by the unit's consistent caregivers. It is important that the volunteers are well versed in all aspects of young children's social-emotional development, particularly in regard to responses to receiving health care, as well as having an overview of typical child development and infants' and toddlers' capacities for understanding. Although by no means the sole providers of diversion, nurturing, or supervision of volunteers and students, child life specialists or similar play specialists are typically the only professionals whose role focuses on children's and families' emotional adjustment and well-being (Bolig 1984). Busy nursing and medical staff are not likely to have the time or the training to provide for the play needs of all inpatients on an active pediatric unit. Adequate staffing is required to provide timely and meaningful interaction. Ongoing goals, plans, and assessments should be an integral part of the emotional developmental care of young children in hospitals.

Because not all children who can benefit from playing about their health care experiences are able to have those needs met and all of their concerns addressed while they are still within the health care setting, it is essential that those providing therapeutic care in the community be aware of the potential for health care experiences to impact young children's lives. The effects of very young children's experiences with health care on their development may not be readily apparent, and professionals must be alert for representations in children's play, combined with parental report. At times it may require research into the medical experiences of the child to increase understanding of key components and to gain insight on what the child likely encountered. As illustrated in this chapter, providing young children with the opportunities to "play through" their experiences can increase their understanding, support optimal development, and provide a positive foundation for future medical experiences and challenging life events.

CONCLUSION

Infants and toddlers are acknowledged to be vulnerable to the long-term effects of hospitalization. Play in its various forms should be systematically and deliberately planned, conducted, and observed in order to address each child's unique sensitivities and the specific developmental and emotional experiences of hospitalized infants and toddlers and their families. Such play has the potential to both prevent and remediate the developmental and emotional effects of hospitalization. One challenge is to ensure that staffing is realistically adequate to provide timely and individualized care. Ideally, future research will help to delineate the areas of specific risk and evaluate the benefits of developmental support to very young children in hospitals.

NOTES

1. Ideas included in this article are a result of close collaboration with Belinda Ledbetter, BA, Early Head Start Specialist, Rural Utah Child Development Head

Start. Correspondence should be addressed to Joy Goldberger, MS, CCLS, Child Life Department, 174 Blalock, The Johns Hopkins Children's Center, 600 N. Wolfe St., Baltimore, MD 21287-4174.

2. A child life specialist is a professional with a background in child development and formal training in using play to recognize, predict, and prevent the potential for obvious and subtle signs of social-emotional distress, and to support and enhance development and adjustment. A child life specialist understands the range of responses to health care settings and the nature of health care procedures and their potential to pose a threat to children and their parents at different developmental stages, as well as posing threats to parents' ability to cope. This person should be prepared to help parents recognize and deal with signs of stress in their children, as well as be able to support them in being playful, loving, and physically comforting with their children. A child life specialist should be aware of individual patient needs in terms of diagnosis, likelihood and nature of other procedures, or challenges that lie ahead for each infant and family, as well as the family's overall adjustment.

REFERENCES

Ainsworth, M. D. 1962. The effects of maternal deprivation: A review of findings and controversy in the context of research strategy. In *Deprivation of maternal care.* Geneva: World Health Organization.

Ainsworth, M. D. S., M. C. Blehar, E. Waters, and S. Wall. 1978. *Patterns of attachment.* Hillsdale, NJ: Erlbaum.

American Academy of Pediatrics Committee on Hospital Care. 2006. Child life services. *Pediatrics* 118:1757–1763.

Anand, K. J. S., and F. M. Scalzo. 2000. Can adverse neonatal experiences alter brain development and subsequent behavior? *Biology of the Neonate* 77:69–82.

Bolig, R. 1984. Play in hospital settings. In *Child's play: Developmental and applied,* ed. T. D. Yawkey and A. D. Pellegrini, 323–345. Hillsdale, NJ: Erlbaum.

Bolig, R., D. Fernie, and E. Klein. 1986. Unstructured play in hospital settings. *Children's Health Care: Journal of the Association for the Care of Children's Health* 15:101–107.

Bowlby, J. 1982. Attachment and loss: retrospect and prospect. *American Journal of Orthopsychiatry* 52:664–678.

Bowlby, J., J. Robertson, and D. Rosenbluth. 1952. A two-year-old goes to the hospital. *Psychoanalytic Study of the Child* 7:82–94.

Brazelton, T. B. 1976. Emotional needs of children in health care settings. *Clinical Proceedings of the Children's Hospital National Medical Center* 32:157–166.

Brazelton, T. B., and S. I. Greenspan. 2000. *The irreducible needs of children: What every child must have to grow, learn, and flourish.* Cambridge, MA: Perseus.

Brazelton, T. B., and J. K. Nugent. 1995. *The Neonatal Behavioral Assessment Scale.* Cambridge, MA: Mac Keith.

Brazelton, T. B., and J. D. Sparrow. 2006. *Touchpoints birth to three: Your child's emotional and behavioral development.* Cambridge, MA: Da Capo.

Douglas, J. W. B. 1975. Early hospital admissions and later disturbances of behavior and learning. *Developmental Medicine and Child Neurology* 17:456–480.

Engel, G., and F. Reichsman. 1956. Spontaneous and experimentally induced depression in an infant with a gastric fistula. *Journal of the American Psychoanalytic Association* 4:428–453.

Engel, G., F. Reichsman, V. Harway, and D. W. Hess. 1974. Follow-up study of an infant with gastric fistula and depression: VI. Infant feeding and behavior as a mother 19 years later. *Psychosomatic Medicine* 36:459.

Erikson, E. H. 1963. *Childhood and society.* Rev. ed. New York: Norton.

Fivush, R. 1998. Children's recollections of traumatic and nontraumatic events. *Development and Psychopathology* 10:699–716.

Freud, A. 1952. The role of bodily illness in the mental life of children. *Psychoanalytic Study of the Child* 7:69–81.

Freud, A., and D. Burlingham. 1944. *The writings of Anna Freud*, vol. 3, *Infants without families: Reports on the Hampstead Nurseries, 1939–1945.* New York: International Universities Press, 1973.

Gaensbauer, T. J. 1995. Trauma in the preverbal period: Symptoms, memories, and developmental impact. *Psychoanalytic Study of the Child* 50:122–149.

———. 2000. Psychotherapeutic treatment of traumatized infants and toddlers: A case report. *Clinical Child Psychology and Psychiatry* 5:373–385.

———. 2002. Representations of trauma in infancy: Clinical and theoretical implications for the understanding of early memory. *Infant Mental Health Journal* 23:259–277.

———. 2004. Telling their stories: Representation and reenactment of traumatic experiences occurring in the first year of life. *Journal of Zero to Three: National Center for Infants, Toddlers, and Families* 24:25–31.

Gaensbauer, T., I. Chatoor, M. Drell, D. Siegel, and C. H. Zeanah. 1995. Traumatic loss in a one-year-old girl. *Journal of the American Academy of Child and Adolescent Psychiatry* 34:520–528.

Gaynard, L., J. Wolfer, J. Goldberger, R. Thompson, L. Redburn, and L. Laidley. 1990. *Psychosocial care of children in hospitals: Clinical Practice Manual from the ACCH Child Life Research Project.* Washington, DC: Association for the Care of Children's Health.

Goldberger, J. 1987. Infants on acute care hospital units: Issues in stimulation and intervention. In *Pediatric Round Table 13: Infant stimulation*, ed. B. Lester and E. Tronick, 111–121. Skillman, NJ: Johnson & Johnson.

———. 1990. Lengthy or repeated hospitalization in infancy: Issues in stimulation and intervention. *Clinics in Perinatology* 17:197–206.

Goldberger, J., and J. Wolfer. 1991. An approach for identifying potential threats to development in hospitalized infants and toddlers. *Infants and Young Children* 3:74–83.

Goleman, D. 1995. *Emotional intelligence.* New York: Bantam.

Gottfried, A. E. 1985. Intrinsic motivation for play. In *Pediatric Round Table 11: Play interactions: The role of toys and parental involvement in children's development*, ed. C. Brown and A. W. Gottfried, 45–52. Skillman, NJ: Johnson & Johnson.

Gottfried, A. W. 1985. The relationships of play materials and parental involvement to young children's development. In *Pediatric Round Table 11: Play interactions: The role of toys and parental involvement in children's development,* ed. C. Brown and A. W. Gottfried, 181–185. Skillman, NJ: Johnson & Johnson.

Green, M., and A. Solnit. 1964. Reactions to the threatened loss of a child: A vulnerable child syndrome. *Pediatrics* 34:58–66.

Greenspan, S. 1988. Fostering emotional and social development in infants with disabilities. *Zero to Three: The Journal of the National Center for Clinical Infant Programs* 9 (1): 8–17.

———. 1995. Monitoring social and emotional development of young children. In *Behavioral and developmental pediatrics: A handbook for primary care.* Boston: Little, Brown.

Greenspan, S., G. DeGangi, and S. Wieder. 2001. *The Functional Emotional Assessment Scale (FEAS) for infancy and early childhood: Clinical and research applications.* 2nd ed. Bethesda, MD: International Council on Developmental and Learning Disorders.

Greenspan, S., and S. Porges. 1984. Psychopathology in infancy and early childhood: Clinical perspectives on the organization of sensory and affective thematic experience. *Child Development* 55:49–70.

Greenspan, S., and S. Wieder. 1998. *The child with special needs: Encouraging intellectual and emotional development.* Cambridge, MA: Perseus.

Jones, C. L. 1979. Criteria for evaluating infant environments in hospitals. *Journal of the Association for the Care of Children in Hospitals* 7:3–11.

Lazarus, R., and S. Folkman. 1984. *Stress, appraisal, and coping.* New York: Springer.

Liakopoulou, M., A. Patterson, S. Samaraweera, and L. Finnegan. 1983. Developmental interventions in infancy during lengthy hospitalization. *Journal of Developmental and Behavioral Pediatrics* 4:213–217.

Lubit, R., J. M. Maldonado-Duran, L. Helmig, and T. Lartigue. August 2, 2006. Child abuse and neglect: Reactive attachment disorder. http://www.emedicine.com:80/ped/topic2646.htm (accessed July 22, 2007).

Maki, P., H. Hakko, M. Joukamaa, E. Laara, M. Isohanni, and J. Veijola. 2003. Parental separation at birth and criminal behaviour in adulthood: A long-term follow-up of the Finnish Christmas Seal Home Children. *Social Psychiatry and Psychiatric Epidemiology* 38:354–359.

Meijer, A. 1985. Hospitalization in infancy as a long-term at-risk indicator. In *The at-risk infant: Psycho/socio/medical aspects,* ed. S. Harel and N. Anastasiow, 275–284. Baltimore: Brookes.

Minde, K. 2000. Prematurity and serious medical conditions in infancy: Implications for development, behavior, and intervention. In *Handbook of infant mental health,* ed. C. Zeanah. New York: Guilford.

Newcombe, N., and N. A. Fox. 1994. Infantile amnesia: Through a glass darkly. *Child Development* 65:31–40.

Nugent, J. K., C. H. Keefer, S. Minear, L. C. Johnson, and Y. Blanchard. 2007. *Understanding newborn behavior and early relationships: The Newborn Behavioral Observations (NBO) system handbook.* Baltimore: Brookes.

Peterson, C., and B. Parsons. 2005. Interviewing former one- and two-year-olds about medical emergencies five years later. *Law and Human Behavior* 29:743–754.

Peterson, C., and R. Rideout. 1998. Memory for medical emergencies experienced by one- and two-year-olds. *Developmental Psychology* 34:1059–1072.

Petrillo, M., and S. Sanger. 1980. *Emotional care of hospitalized children*. Philadelphia: Lippincott.

Piaget, J. 1962. *Play, dreams, and imitation in childhood*. New York: Norton.

Porter, F. L., R. E. Grunau, and K. J. S. Anand. 1999. Long-term effects of pain in infants. *Developmental and Behavioral Pediatrics* 20:253–261.

Provence, S., and R. C. Lipton. 1962. *Infants in institutions*. New York: International Universities Press.

Quinton, D., and M. Rutter. 1976. Early hospital admissions and later disturbances of behavior: An attempted replication of Douglas' findings. *Developmental Medicine and Child Neurology* 18:447–459.

Robertson, J. 1958. *Young children in hospitals*. New York: Basic.

Rothschild, B. 2000. *The body remembers: The psychophysiology of trauma and trauma treatment*. New York: Norton.

Rouse, K. A. G. 1998. Infant and toddler resilience. *Early Childhood Education Journal* 26:47–52.

Rovee-Collier, C. 1990. The "memory system" of prelinguistic infants. *Annals of the New York Academy of Sciences* 608:517–542.

———. 1993. The capacity for long-term memory in infancy. *Current Directions in Psychological Science* 2:130–135.

———. 1999. The development of infant memory. *Current Directions in Psychological Science* 8:80–85.

Rutter, M. 1981. *Maternal deprivation reassessed*. Middlesex, UK: Penguin.

———. 1987. Psychosocial resilience and protective mechanisms. *American Journal of Orthopsychiatry* 57:316–331.

———. 1999. Resilience concepts and findings: Implications for family therapy. *Journal of Family Therapy* 21:119–144.

Rutter, M., E. Colvert, J. Kreppner, C. Beckett, J. Castle, C. Groothues, A. Hawkins, T. G. O'Connor, S. E. Stevens, and E. J. S. Sonuga-Barke. 2007. Early adolescent outcomes for institutionally deprived and non-deprived adoptees. I: Disinhibited attachment. *Journal of Child Psychology and Psychiatry* 48:17–30.

Spitz, R. 1945. Hospitalism: An inquiry into the genesis of psychiatric conditions in early childhood. *Psychoanalytic Study of the Child* 1:53–74.

Stashinko, E. E., and J. Goldberger. 1998. Test or trauma? The voiding cystourethrogram experience of young children. *Issues in Comprehensive Pediatric Nursing* 21:85–96.

Terr, L. C., J. .M. Deeney, M. Drell, J. W. Dodson, T. J. Gaensbauer, H. Massie, K. Minde, G. Stewart, S. Teal, and N. C. Winters. 2006. Playful moments in psychotherapy. *Journal of the American Academy of Child and Adolescent Psychiatry* 45:604–613.

Thompson, R., and G. Stanford. 1981. *Child life in hospitals: Theory and practice*. Springfield, IL: Thomas.

Tupler, L. A., and M. D. DeBellis. 2006. Segmented hippocampal volume in children and adolescents with posttraumatic stress disorder. *Biological Psychiatry* 59:523–529.

Wachs, T. 1985. Home stimulation and cognitive development. In *Pediatric Round Table 11: Play interactions: The role of toys and parental involvement in children's development*, ed. C. Brown and A. W. Gottfried, 142–152. Skillman, NJ: Johnson & Johnson.

Wagner, N., and K. McCue. 1987. Collaborative approaches to research with hospitalized infants. Paper presented at the annual meetings of the Association for the Care of Children's Health, Halifax, Nova Scotia, Canada, May.

Williamson, G. G. 1988. Motor control as a resource for adaptive coping. *Zero to Three: Journal of the National Center for Clinical Infant Programs* 9 (1): 1–7.

Wolfer, J., L. Gaynard, J. Goldberger, L. Laidley, and R. Thompson. 1988. An experimental evaluation of a model child life program. *Children's Health Care* 16 (4): 244–254.

Wolfer, J., and M. Visintainer. 1975. Pediatric surgical patients and parents' stress response and adjustment. *Nursing Research* 24:244–255.

———. 1979. Prehospital psychological preparation for tonsillectomy patients: Effects on children's and parents' adjustment. *Pediatrics* 64:646–655.

Zeitlin, S., and G. G. Williamson. 1994. *Coping in young children: Early intervention practices to enhance adaptive behavior and resilience.* Baltimore: Brookes.

11

Watch, Wait, and Wonder: Infants as Agents of Change in a Play-Based Approach to Mother-Infant Psychotherapy

Mirek Lojkasek, Elisabeth Muir, and Nancy J. Cohen

Watch, Wait, and Wonder is an infant-led parental psychotherapeutic approach that specifically and directly uses the spontaneous activity of the child in a free play format to enhance parental sensitivity and responsiveness; the child's sense of self, self-efficacy, and emotion regulation; and the mother-child attachment relationship. This approach provides space for the child and parent to work through developmental and relational struggles through play. Important to the process is engaging the parent to be reflective about the child's inner world of feelings, thoughts, and desires, and by so doing come to recognize the separate self of the infant and gain an understanding of the parent's own emotional responses to the child. It is the central role of the child in the intervention that differentiates Watch, Wait, and Wonder from other interventions, which focus primarily on the more verbal partner, the parent. Research indicates that WWW is applicable to a range of infants and young children with relational, behavioral, regulatory, and developmental problems. In this chapter, Watch, Wait, and Wonder is described and theoretical and technical aspects are illustrated through a case presentation.[1]

BASIC STATEMENT OF THE PROBLEM

Infants present at clinics with difficulties in eating and sleeping, irritability, fussiness, and difficulty being soothed. They have tantrums, aggression, high activity levels, and sometimes put themselves in danger (e.g., through recklessness and indiscriminate friendliness). These all can be signs of separation anxiety manifesting an attachment disturbance. Mothers report being distressed, feeling disconnected, not feeling bonded, and sometimes fear they will harm their child. They also report an inability to play with or enjoy their child and/or feelings of depression or anxiety about their relationship with their child. Often multiple problems are evident, as is the case in the following example.

"He's not been sleeping for the past 11 months," reported the exhausted, distraught mother of 12-month-old Jordan. "Ever since he was born, he doesn't know the meaning of sleep. I couldn't get him to sleep during the day or night; I was getting ready to call the orphanage. I reached a point where I could not go into his room anymore at night because he was making me very angry. You put out so much for him and he is not a cuddly baby, a very affectionate baby, he wants you to pick him up but he doesn't cuddle in, he wants to use you, he never cuddled. I almost feel like 'I am giving you so much, buddy, and you never give anything back.' The other day he spent the whole day screaming, he hadn't napped, and I just reached a point where I put him in his room and said I don't care if you scream, and I listened to him scream and scream and I went and sat in the car and I thought about just driving away."

Not only did Jordan display his distress by being unable to settle and relax in his sleep, often waking up five to six times a night, but observation revealed a toddler who rarely glanced at or approached his mother. When he played it was with his back turned to her. His play was unfocused and scattered and he seemed unable to stay with any one toy. Instead he often stumbled around the room, and when he did approach his mother it was incomplete, as he half climbed on her lap then turned away, seeming to give up. Jordan showed little eye contact and did not easily seek out his mother, and there was little doubt that this in turn caused her great distress. Jordan's father observed, "I could feel that the relationship between them was deteriorating. I was concerned." Developmentally, Jordan seemed not to have achieved age-appropriate levels of being able to be calm and attentive, to engage and relate, and to show curiosity and explore his world.

This mother and her toddler represent the considerable distress that is often observed when mothers present with young children. Jordan's mother viewed the difficulties as primarily lying in Jordan, as if he was doing something to her, and she was angry with him. She wanted the therapist to fix Jordan. Of great concern was the degree to which their difficulties were impacting their attachment. There appeared to be little relaxation and sense of security in their relationship. In such circumstances it is difficult for the mother to respond sensitively and for a secure attachment to develop. In turn, the infant's response can be considerable distress and anger, what Bowlby (1969) aptly labelled as protest. Protest signals a need to reestablish a connection. If it fails, as is often evident in chronic situations, symptoms emerge in both mother and child and in their relationship. These symptoms include conflict and often withdrawal or detachment from the relationship. This may also be underpinned by depressive symptoms like despair and hopelessness.

What approaches are available to us to strengthen this dyad and their very fragile attachment relationship? Traditional play therapy has focused on the child. The therapeutic work would center on the relationship between the child and the therapist, where it was felt that the child would reenact relational problems in transference. Alternatively, in the infant mental health field, the emphasis has been on the more verbal partner in the infant-mother dyad, typically the mother (Lojkasek, Cohen, and Muir 1994). With Jordan and his mother, the origin of the difficulties may be due to his mother's developmental history of loss, neglect, or trauma; her lack of knowledge and skill; or it may be his temperament that predisposes him to difficulties in sleeping and relating. The problems that have emerged appear relational in nature—a mother who feels persecuted by a difficult baby and a toddler who connects in a very restricted way to his mother. There are two people who are distressed, a mother whose attachment is already compromised and an infant whose attachment is being compromised; both require therapeutic help.

In this chapter we describe a method of working psychotherapeutically in a relational way with young children and their mothers. Watch, Wait, and Wonder (WWW) stems from our efforts to find ways both to fully involve young children as agents of change in their own treatment and to enable mothers to directly work with their children. WWW intervenes at a behavioral and experiential level, and promotes parental reflective functioning and sometimes insight. Central to WWW is the belief that it is essential not to intervene in ways that might come between a mother and her young child. This is especially important when the mother-child relationship is already fragile and under stress.

While acknowledging that the relationship between mother and infant is influenced by the marital relationship, biological factors, and the wider social cultural milieu, the focus in this chapter will be on what emerges between mother and child in their relationship. This does not imply that the clinician should not consider the wider influences when indicated.

Although in this chapter we focus on the infant-mother relationship, it is important to keep in mind that we use this infant-led approach with fathers and other caregivers as well (e.g., foster parents/grandparents). Moreover, Watch, Wait, and Wonder has been successfully adapted to work with older children.

THEORETICAL ROOTS OF WATCH, WAIT, AND WONDER

Attachment

Attachment theory and research have played a significant role in the last 30 years in the identification of relational mechanisms that both contribute to and interfere with the mother-infant attachment relationship (Ainsworth et al. 1978; Bowlby 1969, 1973, 1980, 1988; Bretherton 1985; Goldberg 2000; Thompson 1999). Knowledge of these mechanisms can inform intervention. At a basic level, attachment theory and research provides a rationale for a relational approach to early problems, which is the basis of Watch, Wait, and Wonder. The body of work has made it clear that children are predisposed to strive for a relational connection and that disruptions to that process can create significant distress and impact development.

Bowlby (1969) described attachment as a biologically based behavioral system that under conditions of threat enables the infant to gain safety by seeking proximity to the mother. On a psychological level, attachment functions to reduce distress and maintain a sense of felt security. It is in the context of a secure attachment relationship that the infant is able to explore and learn about his or her relationships and the world. Novelty and challenges can be viewed from a point of curiosity rather than as a threat when the infant feels secure, knowing that the mother can be sought when in need (Byng-Hall 1995). Difficulties between infant and mother can be explored when there is a confidence that to do so will not threaten their relationship.

We have learned from attachment research that secure attachment develops in a relationship with a mother who can perceive her infant's signals accurately and respond to them sensitively. She can display affection, accept her infant's behavior and feelings, and be physically and emotionally accessible and available with responses that are consistent and predictable (Ainsworth et al. 1978; Goldberg 2000). It is not necessary that a mother respond always in this way but rather that the balance of her behavior be toward sensitive responsiveness, what Winnicott (1976d) called "good enough" mothering. Alternately, infants who are not securely attached have mothers who may be dismissive of their emotional bids or provide minimal, inconsistent, and unpredictable care, and who may be frightening to or frightened by their infants (Main and Hesse 1990; Thompson 1999; van IJzendoorn, Schuengel, and Bakersmans-Kranenberg 1999).

Attachment has been related to growth of important psychological functions, such as engaging and relating, exploration and initiative, curiosity, emotion regulation, and reflective capacities (Ainsworth et al. 1978; Cassidy 1994; Goldberg 2000). These abilities, in turn, influence the infant's competence and subsequent relationships with peers and others. Alternately, insecure attachment has been linked to social, emotional, and behavioral problems (Belsky and Nezworski 1988; Goldberg 2000; Greenberg et al. 1993; van IJzendoorn and Bakersmans-Kranenberg 1996; van IJzendoorn, Schuengel, and Bakersmans-Kranenburg 1999). Long-term sequelae of attachment security have now been documented into adulthood (Sroufe et al. 2005), although this research is not without controversy (Kagan 1984).

It is thought that through repeated interactions, infants form attachment representations or internal working models of self in relation to others. Internal working models (IWMs) include perceptions, thoughts, feelings, beliefs, and assumptions, which guide attention to the processing of attachment experiences, and attachment behavior (Bowlby 1980; Main, Kaplan, and Cassidy 1985). At a basic level, IWMs allow the infant to predict the mother's likely behavior when the infant is distressed, in danger, and in need of protection, comfort, and support. Securely attached infants develop IWMs of their mothers as physically and emotionally available and sensitively responsive, and IWMs of themselves as worthy of love and care. This allows them to tolerate distress and cope better.

There is research now that suggests that IWMs are transmitted across generations (Benoit and Parker 1994; Fonagy, Steele, and Steele 1991). Although research continues to search for the exact mechanism, intergenerational transmission is thought to occur through interaction between the mother and infant. This suggests that interventions that focus on the infant-mother relationship might impact upon this intergenerational transmission of attachment. Furthermore, being able to recall and come to accept early attachment experiences and the emotions associated with those experiences appears to free the mother to be more sensitive and responsive to the infant (Main, Kaplan, and Cassidy 1985). A therapeutic component of Watch, Wait, and Wonder is to provide opportunities for the mother to examine her IWMs and how they influence her relationship with her infant.

The idea that infants are biologically motivated to establish attachments suggests that interventions can make use of this, creating a therapeutic space where obstacles to the infant's tendency to seek physical and emotional proximity are reduced and allowing corrective emotional experiences to take place. Watch, Wait, and Wonder aims to increase maternal sensitivity and responsiveness, and to reduce those qualities of the relationship that lead to insecurity. Once a sense of security is on the way to being established between the infant and mother, the two are more likely to begin to explore the difficulties in their relationship. The secure base of the relationship becomes a safe context where they can explore what went wrong in the first place. The therapist also functions as a secure base from where the dyad can safely explore their difficulties.

Infants use the security of their attachment to explore the social and physical world, which promotes the development of a sense of self. Relationship problems in infancy can then be understood as emerging when a compromise occurs in the relational connection between the mother and infant. This compromise is an attempt on the part of the infant to find a way to fit in with the mother and affects the infant's self-differentiation and exploration of a potential self. The relationship between attachment and the development of a self can be understood using the concepts of holding and containing.

Holding

According to Winnicott (1976a, 1976b, 1976d), an essential aspect of maternal sensitivity and responsiveness is the good-enough mother's capacity to "hold" her infant. This requires of the mother that she relate to her infant in two ways. One of these maternal functions involves her capacity to meet the infant's *spontaneous gesture*, one that comes from within the infant, with her own reciprocal gesture. Winnicott suggests that it is of critical importance in mother-infant interaction that the infant give the signal guiding the mother toward her or his needs. This requires the mother to create the conditions in which the infant can take the initiative. The second function, and of equal importance, is the mother's nonintrusive, nonimpinging, and essentially noninteractive presence. This maternal function depends on her capacity, at times, to not actively engage the infant in play or interaction, but to remain quietly observing the infant playing alone in her attentive presence.

Winnicott (1976c) suggests that these maternal functions meet the infant's need for "going on being" without impingements, where the infant can experience his or her true self. Since we think that there is not a fixed true self, but rather a range of potentialities that may or may not develop depending on environmental influences and responses, we will refer to this as a potential self (R. Muir and E. Muir 1992). This potential self is fostered through experiences of continuity of self, the infant thus acquiring in his or her own way and at his or her own pace a sense of a personal and physical psychic reality. It is only when the infant is alone in the presence of someone that he or she can discover his personal life.

> When alone [with someone], the infant is able to do the equivalent of what in an adult world would be called relaxing. The infant is able to become unintegrated, to flounder, to be in a state in which there is no orientation, to be able to exist for a time without being either a reactor to an external impingement or an active person with a direction of interest or movement. [Given this state of affairs,] in the course of time, there arrives a sensation or impulse. In this setting the sensation or impulse will feel real and be truly a personal experience. [For this to occur,] it is essential that there is someone present although without making demands. (Winnicott 1976a, 34)

Any threat to this "going on being" creates an anxiety and leads to a state of reactivity rather than simply being. Winnicott (1976b) suggests that impingements on "going on being" lead to a false life built on reactions to stimuli. The attentive and responsive presence of the mother, coupled with allowing her infant space in which to discover herself or himself in the world, would appear to meet the necessary conditions for a secure attachment. Thus, we suggest that Winnicott's description of the two aspects of holding can also be related to the functioning of a mother who is sensitive, accessible, and contingently responsive—that is, a mother who can foster a secure attachment. We infer that a mother who is unable to hold her infant in these ways would tend to be inaccessible, unresponsive, intrusive, and noncontingently responsive. Underlying these interactions are mental processes that either enable or interfere with a mother's capacity to hold her infant. It has been our observation that mothers are able to hold in Winnicott's sense if they can tolerate the feelings, both in themselves and in their infant, that emerge in the interaction with the infant.

Containing

Bion (1959, 1962) suggests that the "containing" mother is one who can tolerate what is evoked in her by the infant's behavior and remain engaged with and accept the infant's behavior and feelings. Containing reflects the mental processes that we understand to be involved in how the mother is to be able to hold her and her infant's affects. She can think and convey, through her behavior and emotional response, that the feelings are bearable, meaningful, and not destructive. It is important to clarify that containing does not mean to be cut off and therefore holding back feelings but rather to be able to fully experience those feelings and to reflect upon them rather than act on them. This can entail at times acceptance of disturbing, extreme, and provocative actions and feelings directed toward her and not responding in kind. If her baby is showing curiosity and moving away from her she might experience it as rejection but able to reflect on her feelings and appreciate the baby's adventurousness. She will recognize these behaviors more as communications about the infant and less as criticisms of her. She will less likely be compelled to interfere with her infant's spontaneity, need for her, or need to become engrossed in activity away from her.

The mother whose infant hits her in anger recognizes that the anger is part of all relationships and that the infant is not "bad like his father," for example. She does not respond by hitting the infant to "teach her a lesson." In a containing response, the mother sets a limit around hitting but also remains engaged, attempting to acknowledge and understand the anger. She is aware that it is *the infant's* pain, not necessarily an accusation, not an attack on her, and certainly not something that will destroy her. She helps the infant calm and soothe, to regulate his or her emotional experience, but in such a way that it is still experienced in a manageable manner. The effect for the child is a sense of being understood rather than overwhelmed, where the child might otherwise be left feeling "when I feel angry, I am so bad that

I frighten my mother." When the dyad remains engaged in this way there is greater communication around the meaning of anger. The infant integrates that anger can be useful, informative, and expressed in ways that are heard by important others rather than becoming repressed, an unacknowledged part of herself or himself necessary to maintain a sense of security in the relationship. Thus, the infant's need to explore her or his own affects and test her or his ability to affect the environment is met in these contained interactions with the mother.

The Non-Containing Mother

In clinical presentation, an infant's symptoms usually indicate a breakdown in maternal sensitivity and responsiveness due to the mother's inability to function as a container for her infant's emotional state of mind. The angry mother strikes her infant; the mother afraid of her child's exploration keeps the child close. It is important to be aware that non-containing moments do not only happen around negative emotionally charged experiences. Closeness and physical contact may be met with blocking of access or pushing the child away, in a mother for whom closeness evokes anxiety. Joyful, playful moments too may trigger anger for the mother around what she did not get from her own mother. This inability is related to her internal representations of relationships, which distort her perceptions of her infant, including the infant's affectivity and motivation.

Like many contemporary clinicians, we think that one way difficulties in the relationship between mother and infant arise is when the infant's attachment needs and developmental strivings or challenges become powerful activators of the mother's disowned feelings related to her own unrequited attachment needs—what Fraiberg, Adelson, and Shapiro (1987) called "ghosts in the nursery." This mother must defend herself against the grief and rage over what she did not get from her own mother, which is evoked by her interaction with her infant. In a problematic mother-infant relationship, instead of viewing her infant's activity as her or his own unique way of communicating needs and capacities, the mother interprets her or his gestures according to her own representational world. This takes an interactional form between her and her infant. She might infer a negative motivation from an ordinary attempt to master the environment or to gain access to her. She might also *not* see certain capacities and attribute to the infant inappropriate characteristics. Her own behavior will unconsciously evoke the required behaviors in her infant, who is pulled increasingly into accommodating his or her activity to fit the mother's representations. Dependent on the mother for survival, for basic care and nurturance, and with little scope or capacity to counter her expectations, the infant has no choice but to conform. The infant's potential self is subjugated to the demands of the mother's representational world.

Infant characteristics can also contribute to relational difficulties—for example, an infant who is hypersensitive to touch and as a result moves away when touched by the mother. Any mother would feel unwanted and distressed if her infant seemed repelled by her touch. However, such situations are often not so straightforward and require that the mother be "sensitized" by her own history. If the mother comes from a history of rejection, she may feel rejected and wounded by her infant's unresponsiveness and turn away from the infant—resulting, over time, in the infant also turning away. Now the infant is contributing directly to the relational difficulty not only because of a developmental challenge but also because of his or her adaptation to his mother's rejection. By the time we see children in our clinic, which can be as early as eight months, such patterns are evident, and it is often difficult and rarely helpful to tease apart individual contributions. These patterns in relating have yet to be fully internalized by the infant and thus there is great opportunity for change.

In all of these situations, whether the infant's constitutional endowment, the infant's temperament, or the mother's own contributions are the most significant, the net result is that the infant's signals are misunderstood or ignored. This usually leads to a mounting distress in the infant that is experienced by the perplexed mother as overwhelming, rejecting, or even frightening. This relational distress has an impact on the developing attachment of the infant to the mother. Ogden suggests that through seeing only certain behaviors or aspects of her infant, the mother is essentially saying to the infant, "You be this way or else . . . you will cease to exist in my eyes" (Ogden 1991, 16). This obviously restricts and distorts the development of the infant's self. It also interferes with the development of a secure attachment. In fact, it actually threatens the attachment, since the injunction carries with it the threat of abandonment.

The dilemma for the infant is insurmountable. If the infant is himself or herself, the infant loses the mother; if the infant loses the mother, the infant loses himself or herself. Ironically, in this way, if the infant keeps the mother, the infant loses himself or herself. The outcome of this kind of experience is separation anxiety, preventing the infant and mother from achieving a comfortable fit and thus a confident emotional connection. What emerges is the symptomatic behavior we often see in our practice that reflects, and is often a metaphor for, the struggle between them. The therapeutic work in this case must include a process of disentangling the mother and infant relationship from those influences that impact on the infant's attachment security and development. We have found that this disentangling work proceeds optimally when we work directly with the relationship.

OVERVIEW OF WATCH, WAIT, AND WONDER

Watch, Wait, and Wonder began as series of instructions to mothers to practice at home with their infants as part of integrated mental health intervention in Milwaukee (Johnson, Dowling, and Wesner 1980; Wesner, Dowling, and Johnson 1982). It was Elisabeth Muir and her colleagues in Dunedin, New Zealand (E. Muir, Stupples, and Guy 1990), and then in Toronto (E. Muir, Lojkasek, and Cohen 1999) that adapted this program into a psychotherapeutic approach. Research on the method was conducted at the Hincks-Dellcrest Centre in Toronto.

As the theoretical discussion illustrates, we view problems of early childhood as relational in nature, in that the problem is seen as lying not necessarily only in the caregiver or in the infant but rather in the relationship between them. In WWW we are less interested in individual contributions and more focused on what emerges between mother and infant in their relationship. When we speak of the mother's or the child's contribution to the problem, we are not implying that either the mother or the child carries blame, rather that the process between them and the resulting difficulties are complex and go beyond simplistic explanations (e.g., difficult temperament). At minimum, both contributions need to be recognized so that problems can be observed as they emerge in the relationship. We believe this is understood but not always incorporated in practice.

Although the infant is present in most relational therapies, in WWW he is involved not only to help the mother become aware of her distortions, but also to provide both the infant and the mother with an opportunity to directly resolve difficulties that have developed over time. This inclusion of the infant as part of the therapeutic work is consistent with the current view of infants as active contributors to their relationships and to their own developmental growth. Even in situations where we believe that infant characteristics have contributed minimally compared to the mother's role in their problems, it is important to include the infant in the therapeutic process. The infant, while not contributing significantly to the problematic interaction, can be engaged in a therapeutic manner.

WWW is dyadic in nature, and typically one parent is seen with the infant. This is the parent who is the most distressed and therefore motivated to change—typically, in our experience, the mother. WWW sessions are divided into two parts, the first being an infant-led activity where the mother is instructed to join her infant on the floor in the play space. She is to observe and be interested (i.e., emotionally engaged) in her infant and the infant's activities, but to respond only at her or his initiative, which in Winnicott's (1976c) terms, is to meet the infant's "spontaneous gesture" with her own reciprocal gesture. We also ask her that when the infant does not initiate but is playing independently, she not actively engage in play or interaction but remain quiet and observe the infant playing in her attentive presence, to be essentially present and engaged with the infant's activities, but nonintrusive, nonimpinging and when required essentially noninteractive. In essence, the instructions ask the mother to take a position of being sensitive and responsive toward her infant's signals as specified by attachment theory and research. Another way to think about WWW is that we ask the mother to be attentively present and responsive from moment to moment as a therapist might be with an adult patient.

Although it is difficult in practice, over time this new way of engaging in WWW provides a different kind of relational experience, one where the infant feels more secure and both mother and child enjoy a newfound, pleasurable relatedness. The first effect of WWW is to enhance the mother-child connection and increase a sense of security in the relationship by virtue of her attentive physical presence and gaze. The mother is not just sitting there but is actively engaged with her infant's activity. This newfound sense of security in the relationship with the mother provides an opportunity for the infant to take initiative and directly attempt to resolve an area of concern. For example, an infant denied physical contact by the mother might seek physical contact. It is only when the infant begins to feel secure that he or she begins to be curious in exploring the relationship with the mother and the world in new ways.

Invariably, the infant will introduce his or her relational and developmental concerns, and the mother may become intrusive, unresponsive, or punitive. It is at these moments that the mother experiences difficulty holding and containing and therefore responding sensitively to what the infant shows. In the session this would be evident in the mother's difficulty in following her infant's lead. Such interactional moments evoke considerable feeling and provide an opportunity for the mother and therapist to examine the difficulties that emerge for the mother.

In the second half of the session, a discussion between the mother and therapist about her observations of the infant-led activity takes place. This allows her to examine not only her observations but any worries she has about following her child's lead, which are closely related to her having trouble sensitively responding to her infant's cues. The discussion allows the mother to begin to reflect on her infant's inner world of thoughts and feelings, and begin to differentiate them from her own.

The role of the therapist in WWW differs from other approaches where the therapist is more directive. In WWW, the therapist provides a secure base for the mother and child through a supportive reflective presence. The therapist neither models nor instructs the mother on how to respond, beyond the basic instructions to follow her infant's lead, nor does the therapist interpret the child's or the mother's behavior. Instead the therapist becomes curious about what takes place between the mother and child. The therapist facilitates the mother's observation and reflection of her child's behavior, their interaction, and their inner world of thoughts and feelings. The therapist takes a nonexpert position regarding her child and their relationship and joins the mother initially in not knowing but discovering and learning over time together, all the while emotionally supporting the mother so that she is not overwhelmed by anxiety. In this way, the therapist follows the lead of the mother and provides a containing secure base function in the same way that the mother is asked to follow her child's lead. The aim is to help the mother increasingly use the relationship with her child and her own inner differentiated experience to decide how to respond to her infant.

WWW aims to increase the mother's tolerance of the ambiguity often inherent in mothering and her capacity to think about rather than to act on her impulses. While such a process can be difficult, when it is well contained by a supportive therapist sensitive to the mother's level of anxiety, the effect is greater internalized maternal competence and self-reliance. While attending to the therapeutic relationship with the mother is an important part of treatment, care is taken to focus the work primarily on the mother-infant dyad, where the most important potential for change lies.

WATCH, WAIT, AND WONDER IN PRACTICE

In this section we will describe the practice of WWW using a case study. We begin by describing the assessment phase and provide background information and observations of a mother and son dyad that sought help at our clinic. We then describe one WWW session in depth. We chose a one-session example so that the reader can see how the infant-led activity informs the process of discussion.

Assessment

The assessment consists of establishing a therapeutic alliance with mother and child, gathering relevant information on central concerns, their history, attempts at solution, developmental and family history, and parental attachment history. As part of the assessment we observe the mother and child in considerable detail when we first meet (how they manage a new situation and person) and in free play format. In addition, the child's developmental functioning is assessed through observation, and if necessary, psychological testing. If there are two parents, each would be seen alone with the child with each area assessed for each dyad, and the family would be observed together. The quality of the relationship between the adult couple is also explored. Observations focus on how the dyads connect, their boundaries and limit setting, their initiative and autonomy, how they express and respond to feelings, their acceptance of personality characteristics, how they validate and affirm their child, and how they negotiate independent and at times contradictory needs. These observations help us understand the mother-child relationship and independent functioning of both partners.

Kyle and Anne

Anne, a single 30-year-old mother, and her 24-month-old son, Kyle, were referred by Child Protective Services. Anne grew up in a large family. She reported having to fend for herself from an early age and being a rebellious teenager. Getting into trouble by being independent was a salient theme for Anne in her earlier life. Another significant factor in this case is that Kyle's father had sexually abused Kyle's siblings, Anne's children from a previous relationship, before Kyle was born. He had not lived with Anne for many years and had never met Kyle. However, Anne feared that he might follow through with his threats to kidnap Kyle. The older siblings were living in foster care.

Our observations revealed that Kyle was a robust 24-month-old boy who was functioning developmentally within the normal range. He was curious and actively played and explored, particularly enjoying gross motor play. Kyle tended to be scattered and unfocused in his play, going from activity to activity without elaborating play themes as we would expect for a child of his age. Kyle seemed overfriendly toward the therapist, which stood in marked contrast to his tendency to avoid his mother, sometimes ignoring her requests.

Anne described feeling that she had difficulty understanding and responding to Kyle's emotional needs and did not feel confident as a mother. Anne's pregnancy and first year with Kyle were considered easy and remembered positively. Difficulties for the dyad emerged as Kyle began to show some independence through exploration, which made Anne anxious. Kyle seemed to need much supervision around his curiosity as he could at times put himself in danger, for example, opening a hot oven door. Anne was particularly anxious about his unpredictable aggressive behavior. For instance, he would suddenly grab and squeeze her face or hit her. Kyle often tested limits, and Anne found it difficult to follow through with consequences. This conflict in their relationship resulted in Anne feeling anxious about Kyle's growing independence.

Anne had difficulty setting limits with Kyle and at times he refused to listen. During the free play assessment, when they played together, Anne often took the lead and could be intrusive even when Kyle signaled distress at her intrusion. Many of their games took on an aggressive and frightening quality, with Anne poking, tickling, chasing, and playing "I'm gonna get you." These games were initially exciting but often led to distress and anger toward Anne. When Kyle displayed curiosity in some toy, Anne would typically distract him or intrude with her own agenda. Sometimes Anne looked frightened at what he might "get into" in his play. However, there were also positive and pleasurable moments in their interaction. Furthermore, when Kyle was distressed he went to his mother, who provided him with comfort and support, and soothed his distress.

Anne's comment to us of not understanding Kyle's behavior was an important marker for suitability for WWW. The method was recommended to help Anne gain a better understanding of Kyle's behavior by becoming more informed about his inner world and how what he might be thinking and feeling affected her own thoughts and feelings. We also explained that Kyle too needed an opportunity to express his concerns and feelings through play in the presence of his mother.

Infant-Led Activity

WWW takes place in weekly sessions typically one hour in length. There may be as few as 8 sessions, but usually dyads are seen for 18 sessions over 6 months. Mothers who have had a history of trauma often require more than 18 sessions in their work with their children. The mother is told that the therapist will give an initial set of instructions but that the therapist will not give suggestions on how she and the child are to interact or provide advice typical of other professionals. The therapist communicates confidence that the mother and child will find their own optimal way of engaging and resolve their difficulties by coming to understand each other better. It is through the understanding gained through reflection on her infant's behavior and inner life that the mother will learn what approach will be effective with the infant when managing parental difficulties and decisions outside of the session. Similarly, it is explained that the child will have an opportunity through play and activity to communicate about, and attempt to work through, his relational and developmental struggles. It will be the mother's job, with the help of a supportive therapist, to explore her understanding of her child, rather than relying on the therapist.

A heavy plastic mat with pillows or a beanbag delineates the WWW space for comfortable sitting and playing with toys, which are arranged in the same order every week. Both toys that can be manipulated and constructed as well as representational toys (e.g., dinosaurs, house, and family figures) are included. A variety of toys are included to provide an opportunity for the child to explore emotional and relational themes that are of central concern. The mother is given instructions at the onset of treatment for the Watch, Wait, and Wonder activity. We do not call it play because many children particularly at the beginning may spend the time sitting on the mother's lap, lounging, and being fretful or unable to play. Calling it play instead of activity conveys an expectation that he must play.

In WWW the instructions given to the mother are provided to help her take a holding and containing stance toward her infant. The specific instructions for the play/activity part are as follows:

> I would like you to get down on the floor and follow your child's lead. Be sure to respond to your child's initiatives but be careful not to initiate or direct the activity in any way. Allow your child to explore, play, or hang out, and keep in mind that whatever he [she] wants to do is okay. Remember to Watch, Wait, and Wonder.

The therapist explains that this is a time for mother and child and that the therapist will be present but not interactive. The therapist sits off to the side, not interfering or intruding, but quietly observing and being curious about what is unfolding between the mother and child. In this stance the therapist provides a reassuring holding and containing presence to the mother, who often finds the process initially challenging. While the therapist does not advise the mother, she or he communicates that they are working on this together, enabling the mother greater tolerance of the uncertainty inherent in this process. Much of the interaction is to provide a secure base for the dyad, through interest and curiosity in their activity and a supportive validating presence for the mother.

These are specific instructions to create a therapeutic space where the infant more fully and actively participates in therapy. Mothers have to play many roles in their children's lives including being playmates, teachers, and limit setters; they cannot solely follow their child's lead. While it is important to be aware that we do not view these instructions as suggestions for optimal parental behavior, we view this way of being with a child as important in daily life and as an antidote to the current societal focus on activity over being together.

Kyle and Anne during the Infant-Led Activity

In the very first WWW session, as the instructions are being given to Anne, Kyle brings up a primary issue related to the presenting problems. Kyle and Anne's first WWW session followed five meetings where assessment information was gathered. The room and therapist are therefore familiar, which lets us know that the issues that emerge are compelling for the dyad and not a reaction to meeting the therapist for the first time. Even before his mother sits on the floor signaling her readiness to participate, Kyle moves to play with the anatomically correct male and female baby dolls. Once she is on the floor he pulls at the doll's diaper and looks at his mother. She, in turn, stares back, looking a little surprised. Kyle picks up a block, looks at it, and then quickly stands up, completes a 360-degree turn, and sits backward into his mother's lap. Here he sits for most of the play/activity time, occasionally reaching out for toys from his mother's lap. His mother envelops him in her arms and often touches, strokes, and kisses him. She is clearly not following his lead, as he has not signaled a need for affection.

As the session progresses, Kyle continues to stay in his mother's lap, picking up two blocks and holding them together, looking at them. His mother rubs his leg as if to draw his attention to her. He looks ahead and there is little eye contact between mother and son. Kyle then picks up a family doll but this activity is quickly taken over by his mother, who holds them out in front of his face and asks him to label them. Kyle peers over this barricade of family dolls to look at the baby dolls on the floor that he was interested in earlier but then looks away and picks up another family doll. His mother asks him questions about the dolls ("Who is that?") and then takes the mother doll from him and pushes it up against his nose. Kyle protests and then becomes listless and yawns. Up to this point Kyle had made several attempts to get up from his mother's lap. As he tried to lift himself up his mother wrapped her hands around him seeming to block his attempts, resulting in Kyle staying put.

In his mom's lap, Kyle finally reaches forward, picks up the baby doll he had been interested in, and starts to look under the diaper. His mother quickly takes over and distracts him from pulling off the diaper. She points out the doll's toes and bellybutton and asks him to name body parts. She tells Kyle, with an edge of anger in her voice, that the doll will get a cold and that they should put the diaper on. She points to the toes again and as he tugs at the diaper, she points to the belly asking him "What is this?" Kyle says "Blah" and lets the doll roll off his lap onto the floor. He then picks up a truck and aimlessly spins one of its wheels.

A minute later Kyle again picks up the baby doll. His mother takes hold of the doll's legs. Kyle lets the doll go. His mother stands the doll on its legs facing Kyle and just out of his reach. Kyle reaches forward and tugs on the diaper; he seems dispirited and listless. He lets it drop and as he does so, his mother tells him angrily that the doll will get a cold. She retrieves the other doll and diaper and starts to put it back on the doll asking Kyle if he can do it. Kyle reaches and takes the diaper off and says "Wow" noticing the boy's genitals. His mother wants him to put the diaper on, that the baby will be cold, and Kyle draws back recoiling and makes a roaring assertive sound. His mother says, "I think you're grouchy. Are you grouchy?" Kyle just sits there on his mother's lap not responding to her or exploring.

A minute later Kyle looks up at his mother, then rather feebly pulls at the diaper of the baby doll, and then quite spontaneously draws back placing his hands in his lap. Kyle now appears trapped in his mother's lap, yawning, looking around; he picks his nose. His mother tickles him. Kyle remains slumped in her lap making whining fretful noises. She puts both of her arms tightly around him leaving only one arm free. At one point he turns toward her, then reaches out and puts his arms around her neck, but pulls back quickly. She hugs him and he sits there staring. Kyle appears to have taken on his mother's prohibition, inhibiting his spontaneous activity. He becomes fretful and angry and then listless and passive. In her facial expressions, Anne's verbal injunctions and her body posture, Anne's anxious control and irritability is palpable.

We now have a clearer idea about the area of Kyle's curiosity that evokes his mother's intrusiveness. Anne appears to be anxious about Kyle's sexual curiosity. It is a central premise in WWW that when a mother fails to follow her child's lead it is because of anxiety evoked by the infant's behavior related to their history as well as the mother's developmental past. WWW differs from many interventions here in that space is created for the concern to emerge. As Kyle explores, Anne experiences difficulty containing her anxiety and she quickly interferes with his initiatives. While Kyle initially protests, he eventually gives up, becoming listless, passive, and sad. Kyle appears to be caught in the "You be this way or else . . . you will cease to exist in my eyes" dilemma described by Ogden (1991). The effect is emotional disconnection, and Kyle's suppression of an aspect of his curiosity. The way Kyle raises the issue persistently suggests that there is growing concern in this area of his development.

Since this is occurring in the moment and is emotionally alive in session it is possible that Anne may bring up her concerns about Kyle's behavior during the discussion. Unlike other therapies, in WWW the therapist does not lead the mother toward the therapist's focus or concern but waits for the mother to raise a worry in her description of her observations of the activity in the session. In other words, the therapist follows the mother's lead. In our experience, raising a concern before the mother is emotionally aware and ready to discuss it often results in the mother's not recalling, minimizing, or dismissing the observations. When the mother is ready and emotionally motivated, she will explore the area of concern.

During the process the therapist does not interpret Kyle's behavior nor reassure his mother that Kyle was just being curious in sexual differences like all children his age. Nor does the therapist end the activity time prematurely because "nothing seems to be happening" and simply sitting together in this way provokes anxiety for all. The therapist does, however, provide a reassuring presence for the mother primarily through nonverbal gestures.

Observation and Discussion

The observation and discussion component in WWW has basically two functions. In earlier work (E. Muir, Stupples, and Guy 1990), the inclusion of the discussion was stimulated by the realization that mothers could become anxious when asked to follow the infant's lead. The discussion, as a debriefing, was intended to address this anxiety. The discussion also provides an invaluable opportunity to stimulate the mother's capacity to reflect on her child's inner world, her own inner world, and their relationship as it occurred in vivo in the session. Research on reflective capacity has increasingly supported the idea that the mother's ability to think about her infant as a separate person with her or his own wishes, desires, thoughts, and feelings is important for the formation of a secure attachment and other developmental functions such as emotion regulation (Fonagy et al. 2002). Learning to reflect is a process. It is not unusual that such a discussion involves periods of silence as the mother struggles to put what she observed into words.

The close proximity of the discussion to the play activity ensures that feelings are close to surface and available to reflection in a powerful and emotionally alive therapeutic manner. The mother is often aware of the feelings that accompanied something that happened in the session that evoked anxiety. Those feelings are more likely to be available for her to experience and understand in a containing relationship with the therapist, and therefore restructured and integrated in a manageable manner by the mother. Such integration allows the mother to more clearly differentiate her own anxiety from the behavior of the infant and, over time, to respond in a more containing manner toward him. In the discussion the mother is asked the following questions in sequence:

> What did you observe? What do you think was going on for your child? (And, specifically with regard to an observation event:) What was your child thinking and feeling? What was the play about? What did you experience (with regard to the event), think about, and feel?

We refer to these questions as relational questions in that they focus the mother on reflecting back and forth between her infant's and her own behavior and experience. The basic process would entail the mother describing several observations but often selecting one that is salient for the mother. This event would be explored in detail by getting a full description and asking the mother about the child's experience and then her own. Again, during the discussion as in the play activity, the therapist does not instruct, give advice, or interpret the child's play or activity. The therapist is sensitive and responsive to the mother, allowing for discussion and elaboration of her own observations, thoughts, and feelings. Together they focus on understanding the relational and developmental issues that the infant and mother are trying to master, focusing on the inevitable problems the mother experiences in following her child's lead.

Anne Discusses Her Observations

In the case of Anne and Kyle, Anne discusses a number of events, but clearly Kyle's curiosity about what lies under the diaper is a central concern. Below is a part of a transcript where Anne finally brings up her worries about Kyle's curiosity about what is under the diaper.

T: Can you talk about what you observed?

M: [*long pause*] . . .Okay, I wasn't sure I wanted to say anything about this, but I will because it's something that kind of bugs me. It really bugs me when he picks up those dolls and the first thing he does is take off their diapers. I find it difficult, I guess, because of what happened with my other kids. He takes off the diaper and he obviously knows the boys from the girls and the boy doll's a bigger thrill than the girl doll because it's the same as him but I don't know how to deal with it. I guess when the older kids were young I didn't notice it, it was something natural so it wasn't something that needed to be dealt with, but now it bugs me.

T: Tell me what bothers you about it?

M: I just wonder how much is like . . . What's the borderline? What's normal and what's not?

T: What did it feel like to you?

M: I don't like it when he does it!

T: So it doesn't feel right?

M: No!

T: What do you think it says about him, what was going on for him?

M: Look, I'm sure he's just being curious, but I'm uncomfortable with his curiosity. I know it's stupid saying that.

T: No! I'm glad you brought it up. It's a concern many mothers have and I think it's a hard thing to talk about. And I think you also made a connection with what happened to your other kids. [*Therapist provides supportive presence.*]

M: Yeah, well, I think because I was unaware of it happening with the older kids I'm supersensitive to it now. I think the older kids may have exhibited sexual behavior that wasn't ordinary behavior for their age but I don't know what's okay—you know, I don't know what's normal. So they may have been exhibiting all kinds of behavior that I thought was normal. Like I had no idea what was going on and it was a shock to find out. So now I'm trying to be really sensitive and really watch things like that with him. I guess not because I'm afraid that he's been sexually abused because he hasn't been, but, and I feel this is a real stupid thing, but because his father was the older kids' abuser . . . and I guess that's why it bugs me.

T: So you're worried, there's some concern about Kyle being like his dad?

M: Yes. If he's taking off the dolls' diapers my first thought isn't "Oh, he's curious." My first thought is "Don't do that!"

T: What are the feelings when that happens?

M: I think . . . it's fear.

T: Let me pull this together a little. When you observe that Kyle undresses the dolls, you get a little scared because it brings up those feelings about Kyle's dad and what Kyle's dad did. In a way there's a bit of a conflict in you. On the one hand you understand it is most likely curiosity that any child would show, yet at the same time, you're afraid because you wonder how much he is like his dad.

M: Yeah, yeah! And I guess it scares me too because I didn't know what was normal, there's no clean lines between what's normal and what's abnormal when it comes to that. I don't want to stunt his normal curiosity. And I don't want him to think. "Oh, Mom says I shouldn't do it, so I want to do it!"

T: It would backfire?

M: Yeah. But I want it to be a healthy medium.

T: It's an important struggle, and is extra-complicated for you because of Kyle's dad. It raises an important question you might want to think about—whether, at times, it's difficult for you to separate out Kyle's father from Kyle. So it's hard sometimes to look at Kyle when he does something like taking off the diaper, without thinking about his dad, without that coming up.

M: Yes. And to be quite honest it's when he does anything, anything that exhibits sexual curiosity, and I think back about what happened. I don't think I should feel that way. I don't think I should feel it's scary.

T: So what I think we can attend to in the next little while is, first of all, when those feelings come out to talk about them, and second, whenever it feels that Kyle reminds you of his dad or triggers those memories, we talk about that and we try to understand that and see if we can separate them a little bit.

This case example demonstrates the powerful process of WWW as it unfolds in session. In the infant-led activity the child brings to the mother's attention an area of difficulty related to their attachment and autonomy. In the case of Kyle's curiosity, Anne experienced considerable difficulty containing her anxiety and she acted on her feelings by becoming intrusive and changing the play. She no longer was able to follow Kyle's lead and in a sense "converse" with him through play about his curiosity. The effect was that Kyle lost initiative and increasingly became fussy and angry and eventually listless and apathetic. At that point, both Anne and Kyle seemed stuck. In this session we identified an important relational difficulty around Kyle's curiosity and autonomy. Kyle's protests tell us that he has not yet given up, but the eventual apathy and loss of curiosity was of considerable concern. It is not surprising that there is anger and aggression in the relationship.

The discussion revealed the difficulties in containing that emerged for Anne. Her willingness to speak about her fears in spite of feeling silly reveals a strength in Anne. Although she understands, on the one hand, that Kyle is "just being curious," on the other hand she cannot help but worry that he may have characteristics similar to his biological father. This is a problem of differentiation, as Anne confuses her own anxieties with Kyle's behavior. The therapist invites her to begin to attend to this in session. Anne has become more aware of how her fears impact her connection with Kyle and his initiative.

It is this relational link, which directly involves the infant, that is critical in WWW. This link might have not emerged if the space was not created where Anne and Kyle engaged only with each other in the presence of an attentive but essentially noninteractive therapist. While Anne has had worries about Kyle being like his dad, she was not aware of how the worry was enacted in their interaction. Furthermore, this discovery she had made, though facilitated by the therapist, was her own, leaving her with a sense that she could puzzle out what made her anxious about Kyle's behavior. As Anne began to differentiate her own fears from Kyle's normal developmental strivings, she was better able to respond to his curiosity just as curiosity.

Though not illustrated above, the discussion segment is also an opportunity for some mothers to make links between the past and present and to explore intergenerational influences on mothering behavior. Such explorations, however, are not essential, as change can happen for dyads even where the mother stays at the level of making observations and reflecting on her infant's and her own inner life. In Anne's case, she eventually went on to discuss how she and her mother were unable to talk about sexual curiosity and how in a way she was now repeating this with Kyle.

In the first session Kyle appeared to have taken on his mother's prohibitions, losing initiative and curiosity. Over the next few sessions, as Anne became more comfortable with his curiosity in general and provided a holding and containing presence, Kyle began to explore more away from his mother, using her as a secure base. As his mother responded with encouragement he began to practice greater autonomy. Kyle's experience of being curious in the presence of an attentive, encouraging mother is an important part of the therapeutic process. We can hypothesize that he began, through the process, to develop a new inner working model of his relationship, one where it is safe to be curious and explore. Such a process takes time. In part, Anne increasingly was able to provide a containing presence with the support of an attentive therapist. She knew that concerns could be discussed and understood and that the therapist was present to help contain the distressing aspects of the emotional experience that emerged. This seemed to us to allow Anne to be increasingly attentive and nonintrusive in spite of conflicting feelings.

While the discussion between Anne and the therapist was an important part of the process, the new interactive experience that emerged over time between Anne and Kyle was just as important. As therapists we can often get caught up in the discussion part of the work.

RESEARCH

We have completed a study (Cohen et al. 1999; Cohen et al. 2002) comparing WWW to the more traditional Psychodynamic Infant Parent Psychotherapy (PIPP), initially introduced by Selma Fraiberg. PIPP is often used in clinical settings and has been well established in the empirical literature (Cramer et al. 1990; Lieberman, Weston, and Pawl 1991). The focus in PIPP is on the mother's understanding of how early attachment experiences influence her relationship with her infant, as well as on the transference relationship the mother experiences with the therapist. Like WWW, this approach also includes the infant around play and activity on the floor. In this case the therapist and mother sit on the floor together observing the baby and discussing whatever may emerge, which may or may not be related to something happening in the session. This approach differs from WWW in that there is no specific instruction for the mother to follow her child's lead while the therapist looks on. While infants in the PIPP approach can play out difficulties in relating, the time and space for this type of activity is not provided consistently. Also, while both WWW and PIPP encourage parental reflective capacity, the therapist in PIPP also provides guidance and makes observations and interpretations. It is important to point out that the differences between the two approaches are subtle and both are very congruent with attachment theory. Our aim here is not to argue that one treatment is better than the other because we do believe both are effective. However, the differences between the two approaches, as subtle as they may be, allow us to test for contributors of the infant taking the lead in the presence of an observing mother to treatment effectiveness and inform practice.

We would expect that both approaches would be effective in reducing symptoms and that mothers in both groups would display greater sensitivity and responsiveness at the end of treatment. However, consistent with our ideas about greater involvement of the infant as an active contributor, we expected that WWW group infants would display better functioning at the end of therapy. Furthermore, given the emphasis on empowering the mother in understanding and being the expert on her own infant, we expected that mothers in WWW would feel greater confidence in their role as parents.

Sixty-seven 10- to 30-month-old infants and their mothers participated in this study. Infants in the study presented with a wide range of multiple behavioral (e.g., aggression, temper tantrums), emotional (e.g., separation anxiety), and regulatory symptoms (e.g., sleeping and feeding problems). Problems were long-standing, often beginning in the infant's earliest months of life. Mothers were from a wide range of SES and educational backgrounds. Dyads were assigned randomly to either WWW or PIPP, and extensive assessments were conducted pre and post treatment and at a six-month follow-up, providing an additional set of controls for changes over time. Treatment was relatively brief, taking place, on the average, over a five-month period consisting of 14 one-hour sessions.

Our research demonstrated that both WWW and PIPP were very effective in reducing infant presenting problems, and parenting stress. As well, at the end of treatment we observed significantly greater interactional reciprocity and reduced conflict in mother-infant dyads in both groups. Therefore, mother-infant dyads in both groups displayed increased sensitivity and responsiveness and greater relational harmony, associated with developing secure attachment in both groups. However, one-third of the infants in the WWW group shifted toward a more organized or secure attachment as assessed in the Strange Situation (Ainsworth et al., 1978) and only one-tenth in the PIPP group did so.

As we anticipated, at the end of treatment, only infants in the WWW group showed gains in their functioning as assessed by their developmental ability (i.e., scores on the Bayley scales) and emotion regulation. Furthermore, at the end of treatment mothers of children in the WWW group were significantly more likely to report greater satisfaction and efficacy in their mothering than mothers in the PIPP group. Mothers in the WWW group were also more likely to report significantly lowered symptoms of depression compared to mothers in the PIPP group, which we believed to reflect an increased sense of competence and effectiveness in their mothering. We interpreted the differential findings as reflecting the subtle differences between WWW and IPP in that in WWW the infants had greater opportunity for involvement in the therapeutic process and could actively participate in their own relief of distress. As well, the findings suggested that the active reflective process that emphasizes helping the mother become the expert on her infant may ultimately leave her feeling more confident. It is important to point out that mothers in both groups reported feeling significantly more confident and effective in their mothering over time, but greater gains were made by WWW mothers.

When followed at six months post treatment, both groups maintained their gains or made additional improvements. Also by this point the PIPP infants appeared to have "caught up" in developmental functioning and emotion regulation and attachment security. We concluded that both interventions were of lasting benefit to mother-infant dyads. Nevertheless, the more rapid gains in functioning made by infants in WWW suggest that these infants likely were functioning developmentally on track earlier than the infants in the PIPP group. Given that functioning is important to everyday well-being, our data highlights the importance of including infants directly in their treatment.

CONCLUSION

In this chapter we described an infant-led psychotherapeutic approach called Watch, Wait, and Wonder and discussed the importance and ways of directly including infants in their treatment. WWW is an uncommon approach that allows for the infant to take the lead and guide the adult toward a deeper understanding of his world. WWW aims to intervene in a way that fosters the development of a strong, secure relational connection. This strong relational connection facilitates the infant's initiative, exploration, and the differentiation of his or her potential self and sense of self-efficacy. As attachment and autonomy are established, the dyad becomes more secure in negotiation of needs in the mother-child relationship. Furthermore, WWW creates a space for the mother to observe and reflect on her infant's inner experience, to reflect on her infant as an individual with his or her own feelings, thoughts, needs, and desires. The process helps the mother attend to and accurately perceive her infant's cues without distortions, and to "unhook" the relationship from past relational influences, "ghosts in the nursery," fostering feelings of expertise and a sense of efficacy.

NOTE

1. We are grateful to Susan Mockler and Richard Krogh for their helpful comments on drafts of this chapter. Send correspondence or requests for further information, including training, to Dr. Mirek Lojkasek, 114 Maitland St., Toronto, Ontario, M4Y 1E1, Canada, or E-mail mlojkasek@hincksdellcrest.org.

REFERENCES

Ainsworth, M. D. S., M. C. Blehar, E. Waters, and S. Wall. 1978. *Patterns of attachment: A psychological study of the Strange Situation.* Hillsdale, NJ: Erlbaum.
Belsky, J., and T. Nezworski, eds. 1988. *Clinical implications of attachment.* Hillsdale, NJ: Erlbaum.

Benoit, D., and K. Parker. 1994. Stability and transmission of attachment across three generations. *Child Development* 65:1444–1456.

Bion, W. 1959. Attacks on linking. *International Journal of Psychoanalysis* 40:308–315.

———. 1962. *Learning from experience.* New York: Basic.

Bowlby, J. 1969. *Attachment and loss,* vol. 1, *Attachment.* New York: Basic.

———. 1973. *Attachment and loss,* vol. 2, *Separation.* New York: Basic.

———. 1980. *Attachment and loss,* vol. 3, *Loss, sadness, and depression.* New York: Basic.

———. 1988. *A secure base: Parent-child attachment and healthy human development.* New York: Basic.

Bretherton, I. 1985. Attachment theory: Retrospect and prospect. In *Growing points of attachment theory and research. Monographs of the Society for Research in Child Development* 50 (1–2, serial no. 209), ed. I. Bretherton and E. Waters, 3–35.

Byng-Hall, J. 1995. *Rewriting family scripts: Improvisation and systems change.* New York: Guilford.

Cassidy, J. 1994. Emotion regulation: Influences of attachment relationships. In *The Development of Emotion Regulation: Biological and Behavioural Considerations. Monographs of the Society for Research in Child Development* 59 (2–3, serial no. 240), ed. N. Fox, 226–249.

Cohen, N. J., M. Lojkasek, E. Muir, R. Muir, and C. J. Parker. 2002. Six-month follow-up of two mother-infant psychotherapies: Convergence of therapeutic outcomes. *Infant Mental Health Journal* 23:361–380.

Cohen, N. J., E. Muir, M. Lojkasek, R. Muir, C. J. Parker, M. B. Barwick, and M. Brown. 1999. Watch, Wait, and Wonder: Testing the effectiveness of a new approach to mother-infant psychotherapy. *Infant Mental Health Journal* 20:429–451.

Cramer, B., C. Robert-Tissot, D. D. Stern, S. Serpa-Rusconi, G. B. De Muralt, F. Palacio-Espasa, J. Bachman, D. Knauer, C. Berney, and U. D'Arcis. 1990. Outcome evaluation in brief mother-infant psychotherapy: A preliminary report. *Infant Mental Health Journal* 11:278–300.

De Wolff, M., and M. H. van IJzendoorn. 1997. Sensitivity and attachment: A meta-analysis on parental antecedents of infant attachment. *Child Development* 571–591.

Fonagy, P., G. Gergely, E. L. Jurist, and M. Target. 2002. *Affect regulation, mentalization, and the development of the self.* New York: Other Press.

Fonagy, P., H. Steele, and M. Steele. 1991. Maternal representations of attachment during pregnancy predict the organization of infant-mother attachment at one year of age. *Child Development* 62:891–905.

Fraiberg, S., E. Adelson, and V. Shapiro. 1987. Ghosts in the nursery: A psychoanalytic approach to the problems of impaired infant-mother relationships. In *Selected writings of Selma Fraiberg,* ed. L. Fraiberg, 100–136. Columbus: Ohio State University Press.

Goldberg, S. 2000. *Attachment and development.* London: Arnold.

Greenberg, M. T., M. L. Speltz, M. DeKlyen, and M. C. Endriga. 1993. The role of attachment in early development of disruptive problems. *Development and Psychopathology* 3:413–430.

Johnson, F. K., J. Dowling, and D. Wesner. 1980. Notes in infant psychotherapy. *Infant Mental Health Journal* 1:19–33.

Kagan, J. 1984. *The nature of the child.* New York: Basic.

Klein, M. 1932. *The psychoanalysis of children.* London: Hogarth, 1975.

———. 1946. Notes on some schizoid mechanisms. *International Journal of Psychoanalysis* 27:99–110.

Lieberman, A. F., D. R. Weston, and J. H. Pawl. 1991. Preventive intervention and outcome with anxiously attached dyads. *Child Development* 62:199–209.

Lojkasek, M., N. Cohen, and E. Muir. 1994. Where is the infant in infant intervention? A review of the literature on changing troubled mother-infant relationships. *Psychotherapy* 31:208–220.

Main, M., and E. Hesse. 1990. Parents' unresolved traumatic experiences are related to infant disorganized attachment status: Is frightened and/or frightening parental behaviour the linking mechanism? In *Attachment in the preschool years: Theory, research, and intervention,* ed. M. T. Greenberg, D. Cicchetti, and E. M. Cummings. Chicago: University of Chicago Press.

Main, M., N. Kaplan, and J. Cassidy. 1985. Security in infancy, childhood, and adulthood: A move to the level of representation. In *Growing points of attachment theory and research. Monographs of the Society for Research in Child Development* 50, ed. I. Bretherton and E. Waters, 66–104.

Muir, E., M. Lojkasek, and N. Cohen. 1999. *Watch, Wait, and Wonder: A manual describing a dyadic infant-led approach to problems in infancy and early childhood.* Toronto: Hincks–Dellcrest Institute.

Muir, E., A. Stupples, and A. D. Guy. 1990. Mother-toddler psychotherapy and change patterns of attachment: Some pilot observations. Manuscript.

Muir, R., and E. Muir. 1992. True self, core self, or potential self. Symposium presented at the meeting of the World Association for Infant Psychiatry and Allied Disciplines, Chicago.

Ogden, T. 1991. *Projective identification and psychotherapeutic technique.* Northvale, NJ: Jason Aronson.

Sroufe, L. A., B. Egeland, E. A. Carlson, and W. A. Collins. 2005. *The development of the person.* New York: Guilford.

Thompson, R.A. 1999. Early attachment and later development. In *Handbook of attachment,* ed. J. Cassidy and P. R. Shaver, 265-286. New York: Guilford.

van IJzendoorn, M. H. 1995. Adult attachment representations, parental responsiveness, and infant attachment: A meta-analysis on the predictive validity of the Adult Attachment Interview. *Psychological Bulletin* 177:387–403.

van IJzendoorn, M. H., and M. Bakersmans-Kranenburg. 1996. Attachment representations in mothers, fathers, adolescents, and clinical groups: A meta-analytic search for normative data. *Journal of Clinical and Consulting Psychology* 64:8–21.

van IJzendoorn, M. H., C. Schuengel, and M. J. Bakersmans-Kranenburg. 1999. Disorganized attachment in early childhood: Meta-analyses of precursors, concomitants, and sequelae. *Development and Psychopathology* 11:225–249.

Wesner, D., J. Dowling, and F. Johnson. 1982. What is maternal-infant intervention? The role of infant psychotherapy. *Psychiatry* 45:307–315.

Winnicott, D. W. 1976a. The capacity to be alone. In *The maturational processes and the facilitating environment.* 3rd ed. London: Hogarth.

———. 1976b. Ego distortion in terms of true and false self. In *The maturational processes and the facilitating environment.* 3rd ed. London: Hogarth.

———. 1976c. Ego integration in child development. In *The maturational processes and the facilitating environment.* 3rd ed. London: Hogarth.

———. 1976d. The theory of the parent-infant relationship. In *The maturational processes and the facilitating environment.* 3rd ed. London: Hogarth.

12

Transdisciplinary Play-Based Intervention with Young Children with Disabilities

Toni W. Linder, Keri Linas, and Kim Stokka

BASIC RATIONALE AND THEORY

Play is the universal language of children (Klein, Wirth, and Linas 2003). Through play, children spontaneously relate their interests, desires, emotions, and thoughts. Most children play without encouragement, because play is enjoyable and therefore self-motivating. As children develop the ability to think symbolically, they use gestures, actions, and language to represent their understanding of the world. They demonstrate how they feel, their understanding of relationships and conceptualization of time, space, and various concepts. Through play, children experiment with various actions and consequences, and use their imaginations to create new realities. Play provides a means for practicing skills, experimenting with new abilities, and acquiring insight into self and others. Because play is such a powerful medium, it presents a dynamic venue for both assessment and intervention. Play therapists understand this perspective. However, what this chapter outlines is a systemic change for providing mental health services to children under the age of three. The transdisciplinary approach outlined and illustrated below introduces this concept. To fully comprehend this approach, additional cross-disciplinary and developmental training is imperative.

A Transdisciplinary View

Current models of development (Sameroff and MacKenzie 2003; Shonkoff and Phillips 2000) emphasize the transdisciplinary nature of development. Biological, psychological, social, and cultural influences come together to provide an internal emotional framework from which the child views the world. In other words, the social-emotional domain is highly influenced by, as well as having an impact on, all areas of development. For example, the child who has been physically abused and/or neglected may demonstrate extreme withdrawal or extreme aggression. This same child may also demonstrate delayed or disordered language, hypersensitivity to touch, and cognitive delays, as emotional issues have an impact on other areas of development. On the other hand, delays in development that exist concurrent with abuse may compound the emotional issues exhibited by a child (Bronson 2000; Charney 1993). For example, the child who has limited language and cognitive skills may express intentions and frustrations through screaming, crying, or acting out, thus influencing his or her social and emotional skills. The caregiver's frustration may increase as she or he seeks to understand or soothe the child. Attention to the social-emotional area in isolation may not result in the desired therapeutic outcomes. Traditional play therapy techniques or behavioral approaches may not give the child the needed communicative strategies to accomplish desired goals or meet his or her needs. Play interventions that are responsive to the child's overall developmental needs require a comprehensive understanding of all developmental domains.

The purpose of this chapter is to illustrate how play-based developmental intervention with a child can evaluate the cross-disciplinary influences of development and provide a basis for planning holistic intervention. Intervention to address emotional concerns may very well be a complicated issue, with many developmental components involved. Rather than assess and address each in isolation, a comprehensive approach may be more effective than traditional approaches to play therapy because the child's social-emotional health does not develop in isolation from the other domains of development. Transdisciplinary Play-Based Assessment (TPBA) (Linder 1993a, forthcoming-a) and Transdisciplinary Play-Based Intervention (TPBI) (Linder 1993b, forthcoming-b) are holistic processes meant to address the interrelated nature of development.

TPBA is a team approach that provides a foundation for understanding the issues affecting the child's development. Rather than have various disciplines independently assess developmental concerns, the transdisciplinary team examines the child in combination. Play sessions, in combination with information on the child's biological, developmental, and social history, provide an overview of the child's current developmental status across the domains of cognitive, communication, sensorimotor, and emotional and social development. Information is gathered from primary caretakers to design a motivating play environment and assess areas of concern to the family. TPBA involves observing the child in play with parents and other significant adults, siblings, or peers, as well as a "play facilitator." A primary intention of the transdisciplinary approach to therapy is to help parents have playful and positive parent-child interactions, not to make them into therapists. Observations may be done in one or more sessions, in a center and/or home and community sites. Observational guidelines are provided (Linder, forthcoming-a) to help focus attention on specific behaviors and skills. Age tables are also provided to help professionals view behaviors within a developmental context. TPBA age tables are designed for use with children who are functioning below the developmental age of six, although observational guidelines can be used with older children who are developmentally below age six. In combination, observation guidelines and age tables across the developmental domains provide a keystone for determining both a baseline level of performance and a means of hypothesizing causal relationships across domains. Development is complex and certainly not easy to decipher. Looking at the child as a whole, however, is a first step to the creation of an effective, comprehensive plan for intervention.

Interrelationships

Each of the four domains in TPBA addresses seven subcategories of development. Table 12.1 depicts the definitions of the subcategories in the area of Emotional and Social Development. These are the areas most commonly addressed in a play assessment focused on social-emotional development or behavioral interactions. Observational information from these subcategories contributes to obtaining an accurate, holistic picture of what may be influencing emotional development and social behaviors. Tables 12.2, 12.3, and 12.4, respectively, illustrate each of the subcategories for sensorimotor development, language and communication, and cognitive development and the relationship of these subcategories to emotional and social development. A quick survey of these tables points out the interconnectedness of the various subcomponents of development to the child's overall emotional and social status.

As can be seen by examining the previous tables, the area of emotional and social development is greatly influenced by, as well as having an impact on, other areas of development. The first essential principle of TPBA is appreciating the interrelationship of behaviors across all domains. In fact, if only emotional health and social interactions are assessed, the potential exists for misdiagnosis and inappropriate or insufficient treatment.

Thus another critical element of TPBA is the involvement of professional team members with specific expertise who are capable of imparting their knowledge and skills to ensure a holistic view of the child. Without the input of multiple disciplines, there is an increased chance of obtaining an inaccurate perspective of the child's needs (Linder, forthcoming-a). Approaching the child's developmental concerns through an integrative perspective increases the potential for successful intervention (Weatherston, Ribaudo, and Glovak 2002).

Table 12.1.   TPBA/TPBI Emotional and Social Subcategories

Emotional and Social Subcategory	Description of Subcategory
Emotional Expression	Communication of reactions, feelings, or intentions to others through facial patterns, muscle tension, body posture and position of extremities, movements, gestures, and words (includes overall disposition)
Emotional Style	Typical affective response to different situations, including elements of temperament, such as approach or withdrawal to new stimuli and adaptability to change
State and Emotional Regulation	Ability to regulate physiological states of awareness (sleeping, crying, etc.) and control emotional reactions to both internal and external stimuli, including being able to inhibit impulsive actions and emotions and to self-calm
Behavioral Regulation	Ability to control impulses, monitor one's actions and interactions, and respond within the parameters of culturally accepted behavior, including compliance with adult requests, self-control over behaviors perceived as wrong, and use of social conventions
Sense of Self	Understanding of self as a separate person capable of having an effect on the environment, including desire to accomplish goals and feel independent and competent
Emotional Themes of Play	Expression of inner feelings, worries, fears, and traumas through the actions of play, including through the dramatic representations of self or dolls
Social Relations	Ability to attend to social aspects of play, to read cues, to interpret and communicate social information, to get along with others and avoid negativity and conflict with others (including parents, strangers, siblings, and peers) within isolated, parallel, associative, cooperative, or complementary roles in play interactions

PLAY INTERVENTION PROCESS

The following discussion introduces how social and emotional intervention can integrate in a modified play therapy model, an early intervention model, and an infant mental health model.

Shift in Philosophy

Traditional approaches to play therapy have been categorized as "individual psychotherapies," in which the child is seen alone by the therapist. These approaches would include psychoanalytic or psychodynamic theory,

Table 12.2. TPBA/TPBI Sensorimotor Subcategories: Relationship to Emotional and Social Behaviors

Sensorimotor Subcategory	Description of Subcategory	Relationship to Emotional Development and Social Interactions
Functions Underlying Movement	Automatic postural reactions (e.g., balance), muscle tone, ability to move body parts independently	If a child has high or low tone, it may be difficult for the child to orient to others. Others may also respond negatively to the child's inability to respond or orient easily.
Gross Motor Activity	Areas related to large motor actions and positions including child's preference for gross motor activity, quality of movement, level of independence, ability to assume and maintain developmental positions, effectiveness and efficiency of gross motor actions, coordinated use of two body sides, and ability to move from one play activity to another	Children are emotionally influenced by their motor skills compared to other children. Inability to do basic motor tasks may influence self-concept, motivation to perform motor tasks, and desire to interact with others in motor activities.
Arm and Hand Use	Areas related to upper extremity skills and eye-hand coordination including child's preference for fine motor activity, level of independence, effectiveness and efficiency of reach, hand and finger use, grasp, in-hand manipulation, and release	As with gross motor tasks, children who have difficulty with fine motor tasks may avoid activities such as puzzles, drawing, writing, and other activities involving skill with fingers, hands, and arms. If these are group activities, the child may withdraw or resist participation.
Motor Planning	Ability to figure out how to perform actions, use toys or equipment, and move through space under various conditions including modeling, verbal command, and self-initiated activity	Children who have difficulty understanding where their body is in space, how to plan and coordinate movements through space, and follow directions related to motor movements may avoid social interactions that will display their deficiencies.

(continued)

Table 12.2. (*continued*)

Sensorimotor Subcategory	Description of Subcategory	Relationship to Emotional Development and Social Interactions
Modulation of Sensation	Areas related to child's reactions to sensation, including preference or avoidance of toys, space, and playmates; the match between reactions and the intensity of experiences; and the match between child's general level of activity and the demands of the situation	Children who are easily overstimulated by one or more senses may avoid interaction that involves that stimulation. Children who are sensory-seeking may be overactive or interactive, thus "turning off" adults and peers in social situations. For example, children who have difficulty moderating touch may avoid contact with others. Children who find sounds overwhelming may avoid noisy situations, including group speech interactions. Children who are hypersensitive to smell or taste may engage in inappropriate activities with others in order to use these senses. Children who seek extra stimulation through smell, taste, touch, pressure, movement, vision, or hearing may be irritating to others as a result of unusual or intense behavioral interactions.

| Motor Contributions to Self-Care Activities | Performance on common daily activities requiring motor skill including ball games and other gross motor play (e.g., tricycle, swing); drawing, coloring, cutting with scissors and other preacademic tasks; using toys and blocks; eating with utensils; and performing basic dressing tasks | Children who are not able to perform basic self-care tasks are perceived by peers and adults as more immature than their peers. They may be treated as if they are developmentally younger. |
| Vision | Ability to attend, localize, and respond to visual stimuli in the environment | Children who do not see or have impaired vision may not see others' facial expressions, respond to others' subtle gestures or body movements, or move easily through their environment. They may, consequently, not respond to social or emotional cues, may respond inappropriately, or may demonstrate behaviors related to lack of vision rather than intention (e.g., bumping into others). |

Table 12.3. TPBA/TPBI Communication Subcategories: Relationship to Emotional and Social Development

Communication Subcategory	Description of Subcategory	Relationship to Emotional Development and Social Interactions
Language Comprehension	Ability to understand, process, and respond to language including vocabulary and concept, questions, grammatical structures, and requests	Inability to comprehend what another is saying may lead to withdrawal, ignoring others, or inaccurate responses due to misinterpretation.
Language Expression	Ability to use language in any modality to express thoughts and feelings, relate events, and to ask and answer questions	Children who cannot express their feelings and ideas may resort to behavioral means of expression. Their desires, frustrations, or anxieties may be expressed through crying, screaming, hitting, kicking or biting, or other negative behaviors.
Pragmatics	Ability to use nonverbal and verbal for different purposes in different social contexts including responding to language, using greetings, taking turns, maintaining a topic, and exchanging and clarifying information	Children who do not understand how to initiate, maintain, or terminate conversations appropriately within different social situations may have difficult or inappropriate social interactions.
Articulation and Phonology	Areas related to the ability to produce the sounds (articulation) and represent the sound system (phonology) of their language	Children who are not easily understood may be avoided by others. On the other hand, children who try to make themselves understood but become frustrated may give up or avoid social interactions that result in not being understood.
Voice	Areas related to the quality of speech, including pitch, loudness, and quality, as well as speech rate	Children with an unusual voice may avoid social interaction for fear of being made fun of.

Fluency	Ability to produce easy, smooth speech.	Children who stutter or have difficulty producing fluent speech may avoid interaction, or begin interaction but quickly turn away when others ask them for clarification or try to complete their intended speech.
Oral Mechanism	Areas related to the structure and function factors of the oral mechanism, including the articulators and oral and nasal cavities	Children who have difficulty with imitation of sounds or production of new words may resist interaction with others. Children with oral motor problems or oral structural deformities may also be avoided by other children.
Hearing	Areas related to acuity and to the ability to attend, localize, and respond to voices and sounds in the environment	Children who have hearing loss may not always respond to others, their speech may be delayed, or they may use alternative forms of communication. It may be difficult for adults and peers to maintain conversation or interaction with children with hearing loss.

Table 12.4. TPBA/TPBI Cognitive Subcategories: Relationship to Emotional and Social Development

Cognitive Subcategory	Description of Subcategory	Relationship to Emotional Development and Social Interactions
Attention	Ability to select stimuli, focus on the stimuli; sustain concentration, shift focus, and ignore distractions	Children who have difficulty attending to social cues, giving eye contact, and shifting gaze appropriately between people and objects to obtain social information often have difficulty with social interaction. These characteristics may be diagnostically relevant (e.g., autism, ADD) or provide insight into temperament or self-concept.
Memory	Ability to recognize, recall, or reconstruct routines, skills, concepts, and events after short-term and/or long-term delays	Lack of ability to recall people, information or events, unusual memory abilities, or selective memory influences social interactions and can be diagnostically relevant.
Problem-Solving	Ability to understand causal relationships and to independently organize and sequence thoughts and actions toward a goal in a timely process, to monitor progress, to make modifications as needed, and to generalize what is learned to new situations	Understanding of social cause-and-effect and ability to apply social problem-solving is an important social skill. Inability to apply or generalize social problem-solving may be diagnostically relevant.

Social Cognition	Ability to infer social causes from consequences, to understand the thinking and intentions of others, and to differentiate intention from accident	Understanding how others think and feel is critical to empathy and social responsiveness. Reduced social cognition greatly influences social interactions.
Complexity of Play	The highest level and predominant type of play exhibited, including sensory motor play, functional/relational play, construction, dramatic play, and games with rules	The type of play, variety of actions, and symbolic representation demonstrated by the child provide insights into developmental level, thought patterns, and emotional concerns.
Science and Math Concepts	Ability to recognize or recall personal or conceptual information related to people, objects, events, categories, characteristics, and numeracy concepts	How the child labels, classifies, categorizes, and assigns meaning to information, events, and feelings is an important indicator of perspective and worldview.
Emerging Literacy	Understanding and use of books, pictures and story comprehension, story-reading behaviors, phonemic awareness, letter recognition, word recognition, drawing, and writing	Selection of books, interpretation of meaning, projection of characters, and narrative creation all demonstrate emotional and self-understanding.

child-centered, cognitive, and behavioral approaches (see Schaefer 2003 for a comprehensive overview). A second approach has been systemic, where the family is seen by the therapist under the expectation that change in the family will result in a "cure" or change in the child (see Nichols and Schwartz 2004 for a comprehensive overview). Although these traditional approaches are widely practiced and accepted, there is an increasing awareness of the need for an integrative model to serve the needs of young children and families. For example, more recent approaches such as Eco-systemic Play Therapy (O'Connor 2000; also see chapter 5 in this volume) have worked to enlarge the sphere of intervention to include assessment and intervention at the child, family, and school levels.

Results of federal legislation, research, and theory are also contributing to a changing approach to therapy for young children. There is a recognized need for a paradigm shift integrating the fields of infant mental health and early intervention for children with emotional needs (Foley and Hochman 2006). Particularly for children under the age of three, advocated early intervention practices include (1) serving children within the context of the family and community by providing intervention in natural environments; (2) embedding intervention targets into daily activities and play routines; (3) integrating therapies into holistic approaches; and (4) using child-directed, adult-mediated intervention (Sandall, McLean, and Smith 2000; Smith et al. 2002; Wolery and Bailey 2002). These principles are also appropriate for infant mental health interventions and early childhood play therapy. The application of these principles for children with social-emotional needs is outlined in the following sections.

Natural Environments

The 1997 Amendments to Public Law 105-17 (the Individuals with Disabilities Education Act [IDEA]) emphasized providing services for children with special needs in natural environments, including home and community settings along with children without disabilities. The Individuals with Disabilities Educational Improvement Act of 2004 (IDEIA) further emphasizes these principles. Young children with social and emotional concerns are eligible under Part C of IDEIA, and therefore the regulations of this law apply to these children.

The concept of "natural environments" has evolved from initially being interpreted as a location for services to include the focus and method of service delivery (Childress 2004; Dunst, Bruder, Trivette, et al. 2001; Dunst, Trivette, Humphries, et al. 2001; Jung 2003). Based on bioecological theory (Bronfenbrenner 1979), activity theory (Vygotsky 1978), social learning theory (Bandura 1971), family systems theory (Dunst and Trivette 1988; Whitechurch and Constantine 1993), and transactional theory (Sameroff and Chandler 1975), intervention in natural environments includes help-ing children to learn in everyday life situations with family and community members who incorporate learning into daily activity settings using contex-tualized learning and "situated practice" (Dunst, Trivette, Humphries et al. 2001). For young children with emotional and social concerns, this often means educating and supporting families and other caregivers in how and *why* changes in interaction patterns will benefit the child and family. Sup-port may involve a variety of approaches, including counseling, consulta-tion, coaching, or directive teaching.

Child-Directed, Interest-Based Intervention

Research has demonstrated several key aspects to maximizing the learn-ing process for children: (1) self-initiated and self-directed problem solv-ing (Dunst, Bruder, Trivette, et al. 2001; Dunst, Herter, and Shields 2000; Odom et al. 2000); (2) active participation or engagement on the part of the child (Bernheimer, Gallimore, and Weisner 1990; Campbell 2004; Dunst, Bruder, Trivette et al. 2001); and (3) mastery motivation (Emde and Robinson 2000; Keilty and Freund 2004; Shonkoff and Phillips 2000). These three elements are foundations for TPBA and allow the team to ob-serve factors that will contribute to the child's learning and development. Moving into intervention, these same factors are fundamental to the thera-peutic process. Intervention should involve something that the child wants to do and that is motivating. Almost any activity can be motivating if play is involved and it is well facilitated. Particularly for children with more severe disabilities, internal motivation may be lacking and adult encouragement and support may be needed to encourage engagement.

Not all children have the same interests, nor are they motivated by the same challenges. Play with objects, people, or movement offer varying levels of motivation to different children (Morgan, MacTurk, and Hrncir 1995). When children are interested, their attention is more focused; when they are more focused, they can become more engaged; and when they are engaged, they are motivated to interact, communicate, and learn. Therefore, individualizing materials, activities, and interaction patterns for each child is essential.

Embedded Therapy Goals

Embedding is defined as "a procedure in which children are given op-portunities to practice individual goals and objectives that are included within an activity or event in a manner that expands, modifies, or adapts the activity/event while remaining meaningful and interesting to children" (Bricker, Pretti-Frontczak, and McComas 1998, 73). Moving intervention into activities, routines, and settings that the child encounters on a regular basis affords an opportunity for practice and generalization of skills across functional experiences (Cook 2004; Dunst, Bruder, Trivette, et al. 2001; Dunst, Trivette, Humphries, et al. 2001; Jung 2003; Raab and Dunst 2004; Raver 2003). Rather than depending on "treatment" that lasts for minutes or hours, embedding skills and processes in naturally occurring events throughout the day provides ongoing intervention. Multiple opportunities across different settings are needed for the child to experience the phases of learning: acquisition, fluency, maintenance, and generalization (Keilty and Freund 2004; Wolery 2000). Throughout the child's day literally thousands of experiences, intentional or incidental, can become learning or practice opportunities (Dunst, Bruder, Trivette, et al. 2001). Understanding that every experience presents a learning opportunity is the key to embedding therapeutic goals.

Skills from all areas of development are required for emotional security and stability, successful play, positive social interactions, and effective participation in activities and routines. Embedding skills or processes to be addressed in intervention requires conscious thought and planning. For example, taking a bath can be fun for the child and parent and can also be a learning experience and provide therapeutic support for emotional and social development, as well as other areas of development. The toddler can practice balance and transition skills by picking up tub toys from the floor and throwing them in the tub. This becomes a social activity when turn taking with the parent is involved. Once in the tub, playing with the water, bath foam, or bubbles engenders emotions that can be channeled into social games or various problem-solving activities. The adult reflects feelings, presents challenges, models language and communication, and encourages exploration.

To maximize the potential for therapeutic support, however, it is essential to understand developmental processes and sequences, use effective interaction patterns to support mastery motivation, and make adaptations that can increase participation (Campbell 2004; Dunst, Bruder, Trivette, et al. 2001; Keilty and Freund 2004). If parents do not naturally possess the necessary knowledge and skills, the professional needs to provide the support to help them gain understanding and expertise. Many young children may have social and emotional concerns that are partially a result of ineffective caregiver-child interaction patterns. One of the partners in the interaction may not be reading, responding to, or interpreting the other's actions and communicative intentions (Rosenberg and Robinson 1988). This is particularly true for young children with disabilities, whose muscle tone, eye contact, facial expressions, and communication patterns may differ from those of typically developing children, and thus, their emotional and/or social cues may be missed or misinterpreted (Huebner and Thomas

1995). With professional support, parent-child interactions throughout the day can be enhanced, resulting in improved developmental outcomes for the child and increased self-confidence for the parent.

Adult-Mediated Intervention

In addition to thinking about therapy in everyday learning environments, the natural environments concept also encompasses learning through contexts of natural interactions (Dunst, Bruder, Trivette, et al. 2001). The adult is not directing the child, but rather mediating the child's learning through a variety of indirect approaches. The traditional pattern of "working" with the child and family has consisted of the professional providing direct time with the child and indirect time with the family, merely updating them, verbally or in writing, on what was done and what follow-up they should do at home. If the child is not making adequate progress, the family or professional may request an increase in frequency, intensity, and/or duration of intervention, which typically means more of the professional's time in visits or sessions (Rush, Shelden, and Hanft 2003). However, such an increase in the professional's time does not guarantee developmental progress (Dunst, Trivette, Humphries et al. 2000; McWilliam 2000). The most effective way to increase frequency, intensity, and duration of intervention is to address developmental issues throughout all of the experiences of the child's day (Dunst, Bruder, Trivette et al. 2001; Dunst, Trivette, Humphries, et al. 2001), through interactions with the significant people in the child's life. As a result, the traditional role of professionals is shifting.

Although the model of adult-directed therapy is still prevalent, the early intervention and infant mental health programs are moving toward a more family-centered, child-directed model where professionals play a consultative role with the persons who interact with children in home, child care, school, and community settings. The professional is becoming a coach, a consultant, and a collaborative partner in the intervention process. The goal is to help those who interact with the child on a continuous basis understand how best to support the child's learning and development. This involves ongoing discussion with the important adults in the child's life to examine, reflect upon, and refine their knowledge and skills (Greenspan and Wieder 2003; Flaherty 1999; Rush, Shelden, and Hanft 2003).

A continuum from child-initiated to adult-directed or blended practices is needed, depending on the developmental level of the child, the goals of intervention, and the amount of support the child and family need (Dunst, Trivette, Humphries, et al. 2001; Kaiser and Hancock 2003). The professional helps identify what the goals are for a specific context, what is currently happening, and how this can potentially be modified. Sameroff and MacKenzie (2003) define the transactional model that has evolved over 25 years and supports the interaction between the child and parent. This model focuses on the "three Rs" of intervention: (1) remediation, in which efforts are focused on improving aspects of the child's development; (2) redefinition, which is directed toward helping parents redefine the way they perceive their child; and (3) reeducation, or improving the knowledge and skills of the family. These elements are now included in the role of the professional, who may engage in joint problem-solving, model or demonstrate, observe, encourage self-reflection, give feedback, and provide information or resources. The relationship is one of nonjudgmental supportive collaboration (Rush, Shelden, and Hanft 2003). This is a major shift in philosophy and practice for professionals from disciplines rooted in the deficit model, and many professionals will require additional training and supervision to adequately make the transition to this new role (McBride and Peterson 1997; Wesley, Buysse, and Skinner 2001). *Transdisciplinary Play-Based Intervention 2* (Linder, forthcoming) provides principles, practices, and examples of how professionals can work with families to support their learning and practice.

In addition, professional roles are being expanded to include providing for informational, material, and emotional support needs. First, informational support may be needed, including information about diagnoses or issues related to the child's functioning, child development sequences and expectations, services and resources, and/or intervention strategies. Second, professionals may also need to help families access materials or service supports in order to meet basic needs, to find or adapt needed equipment or materials, and/or to access resources or financial assistance. Finally, providing emotional support is of fundamental significance (Guralnick 1997; McWilliam and Scott 2001). Parent counseling or support groups are one method for helping parents with specialized needs, such as groups for parents of children with a diagnosis of regulatory dysfunction, bipolar disorder, or autism.

Another important role for professionals in early intervention is to help the adults in the child's life adapt to the home, school, and community environments so as to increase the child's potential to participate as independently as possible in a broad range of activities across many natural settings (Campbell 2004). Arranging accommodations or making adaptations within natural environments is one way to assist the child in participating more fully and more independently in everyday activities and routines. For example, children who have social or emotional problems related to lack of ability to communicate with others may benefit from augmentative techniques, such as picture schedules, or assistive communication devices—for instance, switch- or computer-activated devises.

With children, professionals in early intervention or infant mental health play the role of emotional mediator and facilitator of social interaction and of the learning process. With families, these same professionals are playing more of a role as collaborator, coach, or consultant. Both approaches are an attempt to empower the children and families to assume a greater role in their own learning, to attain autonomy, and to feel confident and successful in their efforts. The professional supports the family in meeting their priorities and the child's needs through integration of information from all areas of development and consults with the family on how to foster development within the context of their everyday life (Childress 2004). Parent-mediated intervention results in an increase of frequency, duration, and intensity of intervention for the child, resulting in more effective intervention outcomes for both the child and family (McWilliam and Scott 2001; Raab and Dunst 2004).

Integrated, Holistic Therapy

Although Transdisciplinary Play-Based Intervention integrates information from all disciplines, a single professional plays a primary therapist role. This enables the child and family to develop a relationship with one person (Dinnebell, Hale, and Rule 1999). Families who experience this model over time prefer the model over more fragmented approaches involving seeing a variety of therapists (McWilliam and Scott 2001). As no one professional has all of the "answers," or training, input from various disciplines is needed to address all of the issues related to each child and family. A transdisciplinary approach with a primary therapist requires continuous discussion, consultation, and support from all team members. When necessary, team members assist the primary provider to impart needed information or strategies.

Specific Intervention Strategies

Although many approaches for intervention exist on the continuum from very structured and adult-controlled to unstructured and totally child-directed, typically a range of strategies is needed. State-of-the-art approaches recommend the "System of Least Prompts" (Grisham-Brown, Pretti-Frontczak, Hemmeter, and Fidgley 2002; Wolery 2000) being used to scaffold the child into higher levels of behavior and development. Least prompts are approaches that maximize the child's efforts and minimize the adult's supports. For example, to help the child communicate how he feels, the adult might use a gesture or sign to signal the emotion, provide a choice of two words or picture cues, comment on the child's actions or facial expression, or give the child a physical means of expressing emotion.

The least supports approach requires the child to use thinking first, then listening and watching, with scaffolded assistance prior to physical help.

Functional practice is also important to gain mastery and a sense of accomplishment (Keilty and Freund 2004) and should be included at every opportunity. For example, practice in turn-taking can be done when eating pieces of cereal at breakfast, when pushing sound-making buttons on toys, during peek-a-boo games, when singing songs, and when talking. The more frequently a skill is used and the more settings in which it is employed, the more fluid will be the use of the skill and the more easily it will be generalized (Wolery 2000).

Strategies that build on the theories of Piaget, Vygotsky, Bandura, Bruner, and others all emphasize the importance of a moderate challenge (not too high or too low a level), the need to capitalize on the child's interests and internal motivation, the necessity for active participation and self-direction, the value of meaningful practice, the critical role of social models, and emotional support for learning. These are all strategies that are incorporated into the TPBI process.

CASE ILLUSTRATION

Background Information

Ameera is a two-year-old girl who was initially referred for a play assessment by her parents due to frequent tantrums, lack of social interaction, and minimal communication. She was born in the United States where the family had been living for the last eight years. Ameera's parents were originally from Pakistan and were raised speaking both Urdu and English, although they primarily spoke to Ameera in English. The family had moved three times in the last four years because of her father's work demands. His job required frequent traveling and he often spent long periods away from Ameera and his wife. Additionally, the family had been religious in Pakistan but had not been reconnected with the Muslim community after their move. Ameera's parents requested assistance finding religious and cultural resources.

Ameera's parents were concerned because she had not met developmental milestones. She sat independently at 9 months, walked at 15 months, and started using one-word phrases at 20 months. Ameera suffered from Gastroesophageal Reflux Disease (GERD), which was not resolved until Ameera was 18 months. Ameera had repeated otitis media (ear infections) throughout infancy and received bilateral pressure equalization (PE) tubes at 22 months because of the chronic otitis media. Her hearing had been recently tested and was found to be within normal limits. According to her mother, Ameera's pediatrician had recently reported that Ameera's body mass index was reduced. The family had been referred to a nutritionist to increase Ameera's daily caloric intake.

Ameera's parents were struggling to understand and help Ameera. They were exhausted because Ameera was constantly "on the go." Her sleep was dysregulated. She had difficulties falling and remaining asleep and would wake several times in the night. Ameera refused to take naps during the day even though she appeared tired to her mother and became particularly cranky at such times. She enjoyed physical games and activities, reaching for objects, picking up small objects, lifting, pushing, and pulling heavy objects. However, her mom described her as "awkward" and she frequently fell. She resisted being wrapped in a towel and was picky about what clothes she wore. Ameera also had difficulty with change. When her routine was altered, she cried, screamed, and kicked.

Her parents also had concerns about Ameera's behavior at day care. She had on several occasions bit teachers and peers. She also did not seem to notice the other children at her day care. Her play was solitary and she seemed to be more interested in the toys than in the other children in the room. Her teachers said that she primarily liked to play in the sensory table with water. Most activities needed to be structured to help Ameera participate in a meaningful way. For example, Ameera struggled to participate in group activities such as snack time or good-bye songs. During snack, Ameera sat in her chair with her fingers in her mouth, her nose, or her neighbor's hair. While the other children helped the day care provider wash the table, Ameera mouthed the sponge or played with the water. The other children had begun using small paper cups, but Ameera requested her bottle through pointing. The teacher usually had to seat Ameera next to her with frequent hands-on prompts to help Ameera pay attention.

Ameera's day care providers suggested she was not completing or participating in age-appropriate self-help tasks and at times did not appear to understand the sequence of how to perform these self-help tasks. Even though other children followed directions to gather their sleeping bag from their cubbies, or to "go get their coats and mittens," Ameera stood and waited for someone to help her. She did not observe or imitate her peers when they completed these directions.

In response to the parents' and teachers' reports, the team felt it was important to look at the complexity of Ameera's play, level of language and communication, social interactions, state and emotional regulation, sensory processing, motor planning, and behavior regulation. They planned to observe her as a team in a play session, as well as have a team member observe her at home and at her child care center.

Phase I: Play Assessment

The play assessment team consisted of an educational psychologist, a social worker, a clinical psychologist, a speech and language pathologist, and an occupational therapist. Additional team members included Ameera's parents and the child care provider. The team decided Ameera would begin playing with her parents in the playroom while the play facilitator sat quietly in the room to give Ameera a chance to warm up to the new environment and the strangers. The playroom was equipped with an eyeball camera that was streamed to a small conference room where the remaining team members could observe in vivo Ameera's play and parent-child interactions.

Ameera was somewhat shy when she entered the playroom and clung to her mother as she looked around. Once Ameera felt settled, she became interested in the toys and quickly began to play. She started with water play, pouring from a cup, but shifted to other toys when she couldn't figure out how to remove a hinged lid from a pot. During the session she played with cars, dolls, a telephone, bubbles, beans, and books. She played with her mother, her father, and a play facilitator over the course of an hour. She was active, vocal, and interested in all activities, but flitted from toy to toy. She became upset and screamed when she was told by her mother to put the beans away.

During the course of the hour, she was observed to do repetitive play with sensory activities such as the bubbles and minimal functional play with toys such as the telephone. Her play was limited to one to two actions after which she would either repeat the sequence again or find another activity. When challenged by a toy, Ameera gave up immediately and did not request assistance with eye gaze, gesture, or vocalization. When she did achieve success, such as when she put a toy ring on a pole, she did not demonstrate a sense of pride or a desire to share her accomplishment. She communicated primarily with grunts, vowel sounds, and single consonant–vowel syllables, occasionally imitating a word that was said by an adult, although without accurate pronunciation.

Ameera frequently was observed to bump into objects and trip over toys or the short carpet. When she shifted her weight from one side to another, she often lost her balance. She demonstrated characteristics of low muscle tone as seen by her curved back as she sat, need for external supports, such as leaning on the table, locking her knees when standing and walking, and sitting in a "W-sit" (sitting with the legs in the shape of a "W" to provide a wide base for support). In addition, she used an immature grasp, raking the beans rather than using a pincer grasp (forefinger and thumb).

At one point during the assessment, Ameera needed to have her diaper changed. Her mother suggested that changing the diaper would likely cause a tantrum and the team suggested she proceed with the diaper change so that they could see Ameera's behavior, her response to control, and her strategies for self-soothing. True to her mother's prediction, Ameera screamed, kicked, arched her back, and threw herself backward. This behavior persisted until she was distracted with a new, interesting toy brought to her attention by the play facilitator while her mother continued to change her diaper. Her mother and child care provider commented that this was a "mild" tantrum, as her tantrums usually were more intense and longer lasting. They also noted that although her play during the session was typical of what they saw at home and at child care, her behavior overall was better than usual, as her crying was typically more frequent. They felt the new environment with many new toys was motivating to her. This view was supported at the end of the session, when she had a major meltdown and pointed back to the playroom.

During the debriefing with the parents following the assessment, the team communicated their observations of Ameera and determined that while she was referred primarily for mental health concerns, other areas of development were having an impact on her overall functioning. They reviewed portions of the videotape and noted areas where she was ready for higher level skills that would, in turn, influence her behavior and social interaction. With input from her parents and child care provider, the team summarized the developmental areas that were having an impact on her emotional, social, and behavioral development. For example, Ameera's lack of ability to use words was inhibiting her ability to communicate her needs and desires, and resulted in her using forceful actions and intense vocalizations instead. Her limited focus on others' thoughts, intentions, and feelings limited her social interactions, and at the same time kept her from learning through imitation. Low muscle tone and difficulty with motor planning contributed to her low mastery motivation and also made trying new action sequences challenging. When she did try something and was unsuccessful, she either gave up or became extremely frustrated. When this happened, Ameera's lack of ability to self-soothe led her to demand attention and made it difficult for others to regulate her behavior. Her difficulty with self-calming also influenced her nighttime sleep patterns, and lack of sleep contributed to her irritable temperament and low frustration tolerance. Attention to all of these areas in combination would most likely lead to improvement in her emotional, social, and behavioral development.

Phase II: Intervention Planning

In contrast to traditional methods of early childhood intervention, in which the child and family are required to make separate appointments to receive play therapy for emotional concerns, speech therapy for communication concerns, and occupational therapy for motor concerns, the transdisciplinary intervention appoints one professional as the lead facilitator who will carry out the interventions planned and created by the team. For Ameera, the team determined the clinical psychologist would be the professional who would have direct contact with the child and family. Each team member would provide consultation and support to the psychologist to help embed their specific interventions into the play and family activities. The team would meet biweekly to review Ameera's progress and address intervention concerns.

During the initial intervention planning meeting, the team built upon the assessment summary discussion and established four functional targets for intervention. For each, they noted how they would determine that the intervention had been successful. In the spirit of the transdisciplinary approach, the team dialogued about how related areas would be addressed simultaneously. In order for the interventions to occur within the natural environment of the child and family, the team listed priority times of the day, routines, or activities when the interventions could be implemented as well as specific adult-directed strategies and environmental modifications that would facilitate accomplishing the targeted goals. The team then discussed the details of these approaches with the family and other caregivers, providing specific examples of how each technique might be used in different situations and activities throughout the day.

Building on the family priorities, the team identified decreasing behavioral outbursts, improving social and communicative interactions, and increasing the fluidity of Ameera's gross motor movements as the first desired outcomes of intervention. They connected the family to a Shia Muslim mosque and an Islamic cultural center, as requested, and also offered to consult with the religious community about working with Ameera during her religious education.

Phase III: Intervention

The professionals were members of a Part C Early Intervention (EI) team. Adhering to the family-focused and natural-environment emphasis of Part C, the interventions were carried out in Ameera's home with her parents. The following interventions, however, could have been carried out in a variety of settings. Due to the parents' priorities, the clinical psychologist was designated as the lead facilitator to accomplish the family and team goals. Rather than meeting in isolation with either the parents for couples counseling or with Ameera alone for play therapy, the clinical psychologist worked with Ameera and her parents *together* (her mother or, when her father was in town, both parents) during the play therapy. The following strategies were used to accomplish the established goals. Although outlined by the intervention target below, the strategies were addressed in an integrated fashion during therapy.

(1) Ameera will initiate and maintain a social interaction through two turns, during a meal, playtime, and a school activity, using words and gestures, each day for a week.

During the play therapy, the therapist modeled for Ameera's parents how to use exaggerated visual physical cues with wait time to help capture Ameera's attention, develop turn taking, and sustain her interactions. The therapist explained that it was important to demonstrate that the adult was anticipating Ameera's response. Rather than giving the parents rote instruction or paperwork, the therapist modeled and involved the parents in turn-taking games that required interaction, such as playing ball or blowing bubbles. The therapist suggested additional home and school games they could use such as a swing or playground teeter totter (or any kind of physical activity which would require an adult support). The therapist modeled taking a turn, pausing, and providing wait time for Ameera to request the therapist to make an action. Following the wait time, a physical gesture such as open arms was added, and then, if Ameera did not respond with a request for action, the therapist used a verbal prompt to facilitate the interaction. Additionally, the therapist marked the turns by verbalizing "my turn," "your turn." The therapist provided playtime for Ameera and her parents to practice these skills during the session. The skills learned during the session were then practiced during the specified routines that the family and team had previously determined. Problem-solving with the parents occurred at each session to revise and expand strategies as needed. The result of this intervention helped Ameera to take turns in her play interactions and to begin initiating play with others, as opposed to waiting for them to initiate an interaction with her. Language was modeled to encourage imitation and then initiation of comments, such as "my turn." Including her parents in the games also modeled for them the process they could use at home.

2) Ameera will be able to plan and carry out a sequence toward her desired goal a minimum of four times during each day for one week.

To accomplish this goal, the therapist continued to work with Ameera and her parents during playtime. Through consultation with the educational psychologist, the team determined that to help Ameera carry out a particular sequence toward a desired goal, the first step would be to encourage Ameera to extend her play. Initially, it was necessary for the therapist to model new and expanded routines within her current play. For example, when Ameera dumped the beans on the floor, the therapist picked beans up and placed them in a cup. Once Ameera placed the beans in the cup the therapist added one additional step such as stirring the beans in the cup. The therapist used simple language to describe what she and Ameera were doing to help Ameera build vocabulary. The next step was to encourage

Ameera to plan what she wanted to do using words. This also prompted her to think of a goal and a next step in her play and interactions with others. To encourage interaction with new toys and to prevent perseveration, the therapist brought new materials to Ameera's attention while removing the items that became a preoccupation. The therapist then demonstrated how extending Ameera's sequence of actions could be accomplished while sharing a book at home. For example, the therapist showed the parents how to encourage taking turns with pointing to pictures, labeling pictures, turning pages, making animal sounds, and so on. Once Ameera responded, her parents immediately gave her feedback, such as "*Yes*, that is a bear!" Ameera smiled and repeated, "Bear!"

3) Ameera will spontaneously verbalize two- to three-word sentences at home and during a school activity to get needs met at least ten times during each day for one week.

For this goal the therapist coached her parents to continue verbally labeling items while pointing to them or holding them next to their mouth during daily routines such as mealtime, bath time, or driving in the car. They were instructed to point out and name new and interesting objects without using long sentences, so that Ameera had an easier time connecting the word to the objects or actions being talked about.

During the play sessions Ameera and her family also learned how to play the "Wait, Wait, Tell Me" game. This game involved creating situations where Ameera needed to communicate with the therapist or her parents. The adults placed desired toys or materials out of her reach in order to require Ameera to communicate with others. When Ameera provided a sound, or a verbal approximation of the word, the therapist provided the whole word using exaggerated positive affect, and provided the toy. Ameera's parents had wondered if by assuming that Ameera was using a word, they would actually prevent her language from developing because they might be incorrect. The psychologist, after consulting with the speech and language pathologist, explained that by mirroring Ameera's word approximations, Ameera would hear the word and also begin learning that her sounds have meaning and impact. This would provide a natural motivating reinforcement to continue initiating words or sounds directed toward others.

The family was encouraged to continue with their bedtime routine of reading to Ameera. The speech and language pathologist suggested that the psychologist explain to the parents how to focus on specific aspects that would encourage Ameera's language, thinking, and conceptual skills. For example, taking turns talking about what was on the page (social interaction). Or talking about what was happening in the page (action words); describing and labeling aspects on the page (vocabulary development); talking about what would happen next (sequencing). The therapist modeled how to share a story with Ameera so as to keep the reading fun, rather than "therapeutic."

4) Given preparation and support, Ameera will tolerate shifts from one activity to another without behavioral outbursts.

For many two-year-olds, shifting activities and transitions can be about control. However, the occupational therapist suggested that for Ameera it might also be related to difficulty integrating sensory information. Ameera enjoyed predictable, repetitive sensory activities. When asked to shift, the therapist explained, Ameera needed to stop something that was pleasurable to engage in an unknown. This was daunting to her, and rather than confront the unknown, Ameera fought to maintain control of the pleasurable experience. The clinical psychologist and the occupational therapist concluded that regardless of the etiology of the difficulties, transitioning would be easier for Ameera if she felt a degree of control and independence. The psychologist asked the parents to think of two goals they wished to accomplish that often became problematic and to think of options for Ameera to choose from about how these two tasks could be accomplished. Her parents suggested brushing her teeth and going to the store. They thought of having Ameera choose which toothbrush she wanted to use. The therapist added that Ameera could have the choice of which toothpaste, and whether she wanted to have the parents sing a song or count while she brushed.

The parents quickly surmised that this tactic could be used for any activity such as going to the grocery store. They came back to the following session and said they had offered the choice of helping to find the cereal or the coffee and Ameera was elated. Anticipating that not all grocery store visits would make Ameera "elated," the psychologist suggested using visual pictures from coupons or the newspaper of what she was to look for. If she had a meaningful role in an activity, she would be less likely to become distressed and have a tantrum. Similar strategies of offering choices helped with Ameera's reluctance to go to sleep. For example, her parents asked Ameera, "Do you want to sleep with your bear or your stuffed dog?" Or "Do you want to read one book or two?" Once the routine was established, the therapist encouraged the family to maintain it.

The team also thought that it would beneficial for Ameera and her family to implement a picture schedule at home for certain daily routines such as bedtime and going to day care. The picture schedule would help Ameera comprehend what was happening next, would facilitate Ameera's ability to transition from one activity to the next, and would help her complete activities independently. Using the same vocabulary each time the step was implemented would help Ameera become familiar with the routine. A picture schedule could be used for times of the day when the schedule was inconsistent to help Ameera know what to expect. The schedule at school would be time-based, with pictures showing the next activity. While the picture schedule at home would include both predictable time-based routines, such as meals, it would also include adaptable pictures that could be added as needed (such as a picture of the grocery store). Taking pictures of Ameera engaged in daily activities and then sliding them into pockets would serve as a simple way to show Ameera what was coming next. If for some reason the schedule changed, the pictures could also be changed and her parents could explain to Ameera that the schedule has changed. When possible, Ameera could choose the order of the activities at home.

CONCLUSION AND FUTURE DIRECTIONS

A paradigm shift is needed to create a systemic change in how practitioners intervene with families and very young children. The research clearly states the importance of early intervention efforts. Current research has shown that the roots of many psychological disorders may be identified before the age of five (Costello, Foley, and Angold 2006; Shaw et al. 2001). Recent estimates indicate that up to half of all psychiatric disorders might have been prevented with effective early intervention treatment (Dietz et al. 1997; Kim-Cohen et al. 2003). Though the research exists to support early intervention efforts, the practice of integrating efforts has yet to reach many practitioners working with very young children and their families.

The transdisciplinary approach to intervention may be initially challenging for many mental health centers and clinics that are not set up with teams representing multiple disciplines. One of the challenges of the current system is that infant mental health and the Part C system are still viewed as disparate entities and separate approaches to intervention. The integration of these two systems is crucial to establish best practice for treating children under the age of five. While both disciplines of education and psychology deem early intervention practice important in the future development of resilient children, each field continues to operate in its own frame of reference. Not only do mental health professionals typically operate in isolation, they are most often trained with a very specific psychological focus. Beyond a few courses in child development or lifespan development, most mental health practitioners have not had adequate training on how to intervene with very young children. Similarly, many early interventionists working in the Part C system have not been adequately trained to intervene with children who are experiencing mental health problems at a young age.

Play therapists are in an ideal situation to provide a link between children with disabilities who are involved in the Part C system and families involved in the infant mental health system. Expanding the concept of mental health treatment for very young children to take a holistic perspective is a direction for the future. A comprehensive, transdisciplinary approach is necessary both at the assessment and intervention level for children age five and under. As discussed in this chapter, families and children benefit from one provider addressing multiple domains of development. Instead of therapy provided by a speech therapist, occupational therapist, and psychologist, the play therapist can be the primary practitioner working with a family to address all domains of child development. With one person as the primary therapist or facilitator for the child, an attachment with the child and family through consistent, ongoing intervention can be formed, a critical aspect of therapy. The knowledge and expertise of a team of professionals who provide education, consultation, and support on strategies for various areas of child development, enables the team to more fully address all of the child's needs.

Perhaps even more importantly, the play therapist consults and collaborates with the child's parents so that the intervention efforts extend far beyond the time spent with the interventionist or play therapist. Schore (2000) notes that all psychopathology stems from challenges encountered with attachment. Researchers believe that building relationships with caregivers may be the single most important task of infancy and that failure to accomplish this task constitutes the most significant threat to healthy development (Fenichel 2002). Parents and primary caregivers have a major role in shaping the behavior and psychology of children (Polan and Hofer 1999), in addition to building the foundations for successful social skills and academic learning. Brain development is directly related to interactive experiences (Schore 1994). Similarly, only through nurturing experience can the brain realize its full potential (Cicchetti and Tucker 1994; Thomas et al. 1997). The contribution of parents and primary caregivers to the lifespan development of a child cannot be underestimated.

Transdisciplinary play-based intervention provides a framework for practitioners from the fields of education and psychology to unite in an effort to provide best practice in intervening with very young children and their families. Success is more likely when cross-disciplinary professional development opportunities are available for practitioners in the fields of psychology and early childhood development. Transdisciplinary training and support enables families to benefit from an array of services provided by a single individual with whom they can develop a trusting relationship. Systemic change can occur when family members are empowered to provide the primary scaffolding through which their children learn and grow, supported by a team of professionals who encourage and support both the child's and the family's development.

REFERENCES

Bandura, A. 1971. *Social learning theory*. New York: General Learning Press.

Bernheimer, L. P., R. Gallimore, and T. S. Weisner. 1990. Ecocultural theory as a context for the individual family service plan. *Journal of Early Intervention* 14:219–233.

Bricker, D., K. L. Pretti-Frontczak, and N. R. McComas. 1998. *An activity-based approach to early intervention*. 2nd ed. Baltimore: Brookes.

Bronfenbrenner, U. 1979. *The ecology of human development: Experiments by nature and design*. Cambridge, MA: Harvard University Press.

Bronson, M. B. 2000. *Self-regulation in early childhood: Nature and nurture*. New York: Guilford.

Campbell, P. H. 2004. Participation-based services. *Young Exceptional Children* 8 (1): 20–29.

Charney, D. 1993. Psychobiologic mechanisms of posttraumatic stress disorder. *Archives of General Psychiatry* 50:294–305.

Childress, D. C. 2004. Special instruction and natural environments: Best practices in early intervention. *Infants and Young Children* 17 (2): 162–170.

Cicchetti, D., and D. Tucker. 1994. Development and self-regulatory structures of the mind. *Development and Psychopathology* 6:533–549.

Cook, R. J. 2004. Embedding assessment of young children into routines of inclusive settings: A systematic planning approach. *Young Exceptional Children* 7 (3): 2–11.

Costello, E., D. L. Foley, and A. Angold. 2006. Ten-year research update review: The epidemiology of child and adolescent psychiatric disorders. II. Developmental epidemiology. *Journal of the American Academy of Child and Adolescent Psychiatry* 45 (1): 8–25.

Dietz, K., J. V. Lavigne, R. Arend, and D. Rosenbaum. 1997. Relation between intelligence and psychopathology among preschoolers. *Journal of Clinical Child Psychology* 26 (1): 99–107.

Dinnebell, L. A., L. Hale, and S. Rule. 1999. Early intervention program practices that support collaboration. *Topics in Early Childhood Special Education* 19 (4): 225–235.

Dunst, C. J., M. B. Bruder, C. M. Trivette, D. Hamby, M. Raab, and M. McLean. 2001. Characteristics and consequences of everyday natural learning opportunities. *Topics in Early Childhood Special Education* 21 (2): 68–92.

Dunst, C. J., S. Herter, and H. Shields. 2000. Interest-based natural learning opportunities. *Young Exceptional Child Monograph Series No. 2*, 37–48.

Dunst, C. J., and C. M. Trivette. 1988. A family systems model of early intervention with handicapped and developmentally at-risk children. In *Parent education as early childhood intervention: Emerging direction in theory, research, and practice*, ed. D. Powell. Norwood, NJ: Ablex.

Dunst, C. J., C. M. Trivette, T. Humphries, M. Raab, and N. Roper. 2001. Contrasting approaches to natural learning environment interventions. *Infants and Young Children* 14 (2): 48–63.

Emde, R., and Robinson, J. 2000. Guiding principles for a theory of early intervention: A developmental-psychoanalytic perspective. In *Handbook of early childhood intervention*. 2nd ed., J. P. Shonkoff and S. J. Meisels, 160–178.

Fenichel, E. 2002. Relationships at risk: The policy environment as a context for infant development. *Infants and Young Children* 15 (2): 49–56.

Flaherty, J. 1999. *Coaching: Evoking excellence in others.* Boston: Butterworth Heinemann.

Foley, G. M., and J. D. Hochman. 2006. *Mental health in early intervention: Achieving unity in principles and practice.* Baltimore: Brookes.

Greenspan, S. I., and S. Wieder. 2003. Infant and early childhood mental health: A comprehensive developmental approach to assessment and intervention. *Zero to Three* 24 (1): 6–13.

Grisham-Brown, J., K. Pretti-Frontczak, M. L. Hemmeter, and R. Fidgley. 2002. Teaching IEP goals and objectives in the context of classroom routines and activities. *Young Exceptional Children* 6 (1): 18–27.

Guralnick, M. J. 1997. The effectiveness of early intervention: Directions for second generation research. In *The effectiveness of early intervention,* ed. M. J. Guralnick, 3–20. Baltimore: Brookes.

Huebner, R., and K. R. Thomas. 1995. The relationship between attachment, psychopathology, and childhood disability. *Rehabilitarian Psychology* 40 (2): 111–124.

Jung, L. A. 2003. More is better: Maximizing learning opportunities. *Young Exceptional Children* 6 (3): 21–26.

Kaiser, A. P., and T. B. Hancock. 2003. Teaching parents new skills to support their young children's development. *Infants and Young Children* 16 (1): 9–21.

Keilty, B., and M. Freund. 2004. Mastery motivation: A framework for considering the "how" of infant and toddler learning. *Young Exceptional Children* 8 (1): 2–10.

Kim-Cohen, J., A. Caspi, T. E. Moffitt, H. Harrington, B. J. Milne, and R. Poulton. 2003. Prior juvenile diagnoses in adults with mental disorder. *Archives of General Psychiatry* 60:709–717.

Klein, T. P., D. Wirth, and K. Linas. 2003. Play: Children's context for development. Young Children 58:38–45.

Linder, T. W. 1993a. *Transdisciplinary play-based assessment: A functional approach to working with young children.* Baltimore: Brookes.

———. 1993b. *Transdisciplinary play-based intervention.* Baltimore: Brookes.

———. Forthcoming-a. *Transdisciplinary play-based assessment.* 2nd ed. Baltimore: Brookes.

———. Forthcoming-b. *Transdisciplinary play-based intervention.* 2nd ed. Baltimore: Brookes.

McBride, S. L., and C. Peterson. 1997. Home-based early intervention with families of children with disabilities: Who is doing what? *Topics in Early Childhood Special Education* 17 (2): 209–233.

McWilliam, R. A. 2000. It's only natural to have early intervention in the environments where it's needed. In *Young Exceptional Children Monograph Series No. 2,* ed. S. Sandall and M. Ostrosky, 17–26. Denver: Division for the Council for Exceptional Children.

McWilliam, R. A., and S. Scott. 2001. A support approach to early intervention: A three-part framework. *Infants and Young Children* 13 (4): 55–66.

Morgan, G., R. MacTurk, and E. Hrncir. 1995. Mastery motivation: Overview, definitions, and conceptual issues. In *Mastery motivation: Origins, conceptualizations, and applications,* ed. R. H. MacTurk and G. A. Morgan, 1–18. Norwood, NJ: Ablex.

Nichols, M. P., and R. C. Schwartz. 2004. *Family therapy concepts and methods*. 6th ed. Boston: Pearson.

O'Connor, K. J. 2000. *The play therapy primer*. 2nd ed. New York: Wiley.

Odom, S. L., P. C. Favazza, W. H. Brown, and E. M. Horn. 2000. Approaches to understanding the ecology of early childhood environments for children with disabilities. In *Behavioral observation: Technology and applications in developmental disabilities*, ed. T. Thompson, D. Felce, and F. Symons, 193–214. Baltimore: Brookes.

Polan, H., and M. A. Hofer. 1999. Psychobiological origins of infant attachment and separation responses. In *Handbook of attachment: Theory, research, and clinical applications*, ed. J. S. Cassidy. New York: Guilford.

Raab, M., and C. J. Dunst. 2004. Early intervention practitioner approaches to natural and environment interventions. *Journal of Early Intervention* 27 (1): 15–26.

Raver, S. 2003. Keeping track: Using routine instruction and monitoring. *Young Exceptional Children* 6 (3): 12–20.

Rosenberg, S., and C. C. Robinson. 1988. Interactions of parents with their young handicapped children. In *Early intervention for infants and children with handicaps: An empirical base*, ed. S. K. Odom, 159–177. Baltimore: Brookes.

Rush, D. D., M. L. Shelden, and B. E. Hanft. 2003. Coaching families and colleagues: A process for collaboration in natural settings. *Infants and Young Children* 16 (1): 33–47.

Sameroff, A. J., and M. Chandler. 1975. Reproductive risk and the continuum of caretaking casualty. In *Review of child development research*, ed. F. D. Horowitz, M. Hetherington, S. Scarr-Salapatek, and G. Siegel. Chicago: University of Chicago Press.

Sameroff, A. J., and M. J. MacKenzie. 2003. A quarter-century of the transactional model: How have things changed? *Zero to Three* 24 (1): 14–22.

Sandall, S., M. McLean, and B. Smith. 2000. *DEC recommended practices in early intervention/early childhood special education*, 29–37. Arlington, VA: Council for Exceptional Children.

Schaefer, C. E., ed. 2003. *Foundations of play therapy*. New York: Wiley.

Schore, A. 1994. *Affect regulation and the origin of the self: The neurobiology of emotional development*. Mahwah, NJ: Erlbaum.

———. 2000. Parent-infant communication and the neurobiology of emotional development. Paper presented at the Head Start National Research Conference, Washington, DC, June 28–July 1.

Shaw, D., E. B. Owens, J. Giovannelli, and E. B. Winslow. 2001. Infant and toddler pathways leading to early externalizing disorders. *Journal of the American Academy of Child and Adolescent Psychiatry* 40 (1): 36–43.

Shonkoff, J., and D. Phillips, eds. 2000. *From neurons to neighborhoods: The science of early childhood development*. Washington, DC: National Academy Press.

Smith, B. J., P. Strain, P. Snyder, S. Sandall, M. McLean, A. B. Ramsey, and W. C. Sumi. 2002. DEC recommended practices: A review of nine years of EI/ECSE research literature. *Journal of Early Intervention* 25 (2): 108–119.

Thomas, D., E. Whitaker, C. D. Crow, V. Little, L. Love, M. S. Lykins, and M. Letterman. 1997. Event-related potential variability as a measure of information storage in infant development. *Developmental Neuropsychology* 13:205–232.

Vygotsky, L. 1978. *Mind in society: The development of higher psychological processes.* Cambridge, MA: Harvard University Press.

Weatherston, D. J., J. Ribaudo, and S. Glovak. 2002. Becoming whole: Combining infant mental health and occupational therapy on behalf of a toddler with sensory integration difficulties and his family. *Infants and Young Children* 15 (1): 19–28.

Wesley, P. W., V. Buysse, and D. Skinner. 2001. Early interventionists' perspectives on professional comfort as consultants. *Journal of Early Intervention* 24 (2): 112–128.

Whitechurch, G. G., and L. L. Constantine. 1993. Systems theory. In *Sourcebook of family theories and methods: A contextual approach*, ed. P. G. Boss, W. J. Doherty, R. LaRossa, W. R. Schumm, and S. K. Steinmentz. New York: Plenum.

Wolery, M. 2000. Recommended practices in child-focused interventions. In *DEC recommended practices in early intervention/early childhood special education*, ed. S. Sandall, M. McLean, and B. Smith, 29–37. Arlington, VA: Council for Exceptional Children.

Wolery, M., and D. Bailey. 2002. Early childhood special education research. *Journal of Early Intervention* 25 (2): 88–99.

13

Dyadic Play Therapy for Homeless Parents and Children

Ruth P. Newton

Just as cigarettes, alcohol, and drugs are known teratogens for a developing fetus, homelessness may have an equally disturbing effect on a developing child. Homelessness flies in the face of well-established principles that children need stability, safety, routine, and opportunities to learn and explore within parental environments that are sensitive and reliable. In a very young child, the weight and impact of homelessness can compromise all developmental systems, particularly if it occurs within sensitive periods of brain development. The impact is even more dire if the parents of this child no longer have the ability to provide adequate care, encouragement, and protection due to lack of resources and support. The unique circumstances experienced by a homeless family challenges intervention planning, as there are wide differences between a child who has always been housed and for the first time is homeless and a child who is born into homelessness to a mother who has been homeless for many years.

This chapter will focus on the dyadic therapy interventions done through Child and Family Mental Health Services at a large homeless rehabilitation center (St. Vincent de Paul Village) in downtown San Diego. Child and Family Mental Health Services has a specific program for pregnant women and children from birth to age five and their families called Project SAFECHILD. SAFECHILD programming includes designed-for-homeless "Mommy and Me" classes, 0–5 Parent Education classes, developmental screenings, formal assessments, parent-child dyadic play therapy, and individual parent and family therapy interventions. What may or may not be similar to other clinics working with homeless children and their families is the multilevel treatment approach occurring within SAFECHILD, which is nested within the larger Village programming focused on homeless rehabilitation. Thus all dyadic play therapies are occurring simultaneously with other levels of care. To help the reader build an adequate context to evaluate the purpose, goals, and outcomes for dyadic play therapy in a homeless population, it is necessary to give a brief overview of the setting and levels of care.

St. Vincent de Paul Village (SVdPV) houses approximately 850 people per night. On any given night, approximately 65 families are housed, including 150 to 190 children of which 38–40 percent are under five years of age. Eighty-five percent of the families are headed by a single mother. Rehabilitation services offered include career and education, mental health assessment and intervention, chemical dependency, on-site licensed childcare, on-site medical and dental care, and case management for residents who decide to advance to long-term programming allowing a two-year housing stay. It is quite literally a village.

Young children age birth to five and their families entering the village have some commonalities within uniquely differing family systems. Specifically, upon entry, a young homeless child often has broken sleep and eating routines, may have moved multiple times since birth, has few to no toys or educational materials, may have obvious speech and language delays, may have lived in and slept in strollers for long periods, has a poor diet and prolonged bottle use, has had little to no play, may be dirty, is easily distressed, and has a stressed parent who cannot easily soothe the child. Data last analyzed show that the average age of 217 children formally evaluated was two, and these children had moved on average four times since their birth. Of these children, 93 were infants under 18 months of age who had moved an average of three times since birth. The mother's educational level was approximately 11th grade. The majority of the mothers were unmarried and without a partner. Mothers had birthed more children (average four) than were with her at evaluation, losing at least one child (range zero to seven) to Child Protective Services, foster placement, and/or adoption. Seventy-three percent of the children evaluated in the past three years had speech delays. Many had motor delays from living in strollers. Many of these motor delays improved dramatically with increased floortime provided in our on-site childcare program.

Because of the critical developmental period for brain growth and development (pregnancy to three years of age), which is dependent upon the quality of the care experienced during pregnancy and given by the primary attachment figure after birth, the unique stresses of a homeless mother can severely affect a young child's development. What is common in the homeless mothers of young children seen to date is their own emotional dysregulation. Most mothers were not well parented themselves. Chronic emotional dysregulation in a primary caregiver is well known to severely impact a child's development; therefore we conceptualize all parent-child dyadic interventions using attachment theory (Ainsworth et al. 1978;

Bowlby 1969; Hesse and Main 2000; Main and Solomon 1990), affect regulation theory (Schore 1994), and the unique culture of the homeless (Payne, DeVol, and Dreussi Smith 2001).

BASIC RATIONALE AND THEORY

Attachment

Longitudinal research following children whose attachment tie to their parents was determined in early childhood clearly shows that the quality of the parent-child relationship can affect ongoing development. In a longitudinal study spanning 30 years, Alan Sroufe and his colleagues (2005) have shown that children who have sensitive and responsive parents who support their needs for exploration and protection arrive into adulthood secure. Secure children have been found to be more cooperative, have greater interests in task mastery, have more friends, and have greater emotional regulation. The child's attachment bond to the primary caregiver is considered to be a biological system shaped by evolution to increase infant survival (Bowlby 1969, 1988). Common attachment behaviors, including crying, smiling, and clinging, serve to keep the child in close proximity to the caregiver for protection. A newborn is rarely a few feet from a caregiver; however, as children develop, wider concentric circles of movement away from the caregiver for exploration with returns to the caregiver for protection, safety, or refueling are seen. When stressed, afraid, or in need of nurturance, a young child returns to the caregiver for soothing and care. Once soothed and nurtured, the child returns to the developmental tasks of play and exploration. This rhythmic movement is natural, biological, and intrinsic to growth and development. The quality of the attachment bond is dependent upon the parent's sensitivity to the child's needs, particularly over the first year of life.

For the homeless parent and child, this natural movement can be greatly misshapen and distorted due to a lack of safe spaces, prolonged stress, vigilance, and lack of resources available to the dyad. Many homeless mothers are also trying to care for multiple children while trying to find or create a stable life. This becomes particularly difficult if the mother's education level is low, requiring her to complete her education in order to find adequately paying work to support her family. Stressed mothers generally have difficulty providing sensitive caregiving to their children, as survival concerns preempt caregiving. We find at SVdPV that homeless dyads often have a lack of meaningful eye contact, as the mother is often more focused on the outer environment. The young homeless child often experiences multiple adult caregivers who move into and out of their lives. These other caregivers can be the child's biological father living elsewhere, a new romantic relationship formed by the mother, or other friends or family members. For the intact families at SVdPV (approximately 10 percent), we still see this level of newly formed adult relationships moving in and out of the child's life. The impact of these ongoing kaleidoscopic scene changes on the child's developing attachment formations is not known.

Attachment Categories

Through careful observation of infant-parent interactions in the home, Ainsworth et al. (1978) created a laboratory paradigm called the Strange Situation to measure the quality of attachment in 12- to 18-month-old infants. Consisting of eight approximately three-minute episodes where the mother and a stranger enter and leave the room while the infant plays, the Strange Situation paradigm determines the nature of the child's attachment to the caregiver by coding the child's behavior when reuniting with the mother. On two occasions, the mother leaves the room for a brief separation and the reunion behavior is coded. Different reunion patterns were observed and coded. Infants coded secure gave great protest to mother's absence but easily soothed upon her return and returned to exploration with the toys. Ambivalent/resistant infants continued to be upset upon the mother's return, often escalating into tantruming anger and did not return to exploration. The avoidant child simply continued playing with the toys, avoiding the mother upon return. Ainsworth considered the secure and two insecure (ambivalent and avoidant) categories to be organized and predictable strategies a child used to approach his or her mother and that these reunion strategies reflected the child's ongoing experience with the caregiver. A fourth disorganized strategy, however, was suggested by Main and Solomon (1990) for those children showing bizarre behaviors when approaching the mother. This category is associated with child maltreatment in general and frightening behavior in the parent in specific (Main and Hesse 1990).

During our developmental assessments of young homeless children, we find that the child's interaction with the parent during the assessment is suggestive of the attachment strategy. Children who appear to us to be on the secure spectrum with their mothers seem to use their mother as a secure base throughout the testing. For example, these children commonly enter the testing room, stay close to their mother until comfortable, and then easily begin to explore the testing toys. They often laugh or smile with the parent and have good eye contact with both parent and examiner. They interact easily with the examiner, use focused, "studied" attention to tasks, are proud of themselves when the task is accomplished, and want to present their accomplishments to their mother. Children who appear to us to be on the ambivalent spectrum tend to stay close to their mother throughout the testing and superficially explore the testing toys. They are fussy, have little eye contact with the parent, do not easily smile, and never seem to settle throughout the testing. They have poor attention to tasks, and become increasingly frustrated with their mothers, often resulting in angry tantruming including flinging their body, arching their back, and/or kicking or biting the parent. Children who appear to us to be on the avoidant attachment spectrum generally enter the room and directly approach the examiner with the toys. These children minimally-to-never approach the parent, do not present their accomplishments to the parent, nor do they have eye contact, smiling, or any other interactions with the parent. Their attention to testing, however, is often good.

Any disorganized behavior seen in our developmental assessments is coded. Some of the disorganized behaviors seen to date (which would code on the disorganization scales if seen in the Strange Situation) are startles, apprehension of parent, freezing, stilling, complete body collapses, stereotypies or bizarre behavioral routines or postures, grimaces, dissociative stares, moving toward parent with startling speed when called, organized age-appropriate language regressing to incomprehensible speech or babble, and/or following a member of the testing team out of the room or asking a team member for a pick-up. Children who display disorganized behaviors in the development assessments are immediately given a referral for therapy. We found that 43 percent of the preschool children assessed (N=161) appear to us to be using avoidant strategies. Likewise we have found high rates of disorganization in toddlers age 18 to 35 months (20 percent). Of the infants age birth to 11 months, 41 percent appear to us to have caregivers who lack attunement significant enough to put the attachment bond at risk.

Attachment Outcomes

In the Sroufe et al. (2005) longitudinal study, secure children were found to be less dependent, more flexible, cooperative, and enthusiastic about learning than insecure children from preschool through high school. Secure children handled frustration easier, were more socially competent, had more friends, and increased their effort when they believed they were failing, unlike insecure children. Conversely, children found to have avoidant and ambivalent attachments were less socially competent, more dependent, and less persistent on tasks. Avoidant children also tended to be more aggressive, often bullying, while ambivalent children were often the victims of bullying. Avoidant attachment leading to childhood aggression has been found in multiple studies (Lyons-Ruth, Alpern, and Repacholi 1993; NICHD 2004). Disorganized behaviors greatly vary per child, but what is common is the breakdown of an organized strategy to approach a caregiver. High rates of disorganized attachment have been found in maltreatment samples, with one study reporting 82 percent of the children from maltreating parents were disorganized (Carlson et al. 1989). Attachment disorganization has been associated with serious adult pathology including borderline personality disorder, dissociative disorders, and violent offenders (Carlson 1998; Karr-Morse and Wiley 1997).

Affect Regulation

Early parent-child relationships are found to impact a child's developing nervous system, specifically the ability to regulate affect (Cirulli, Berry, and Alleva 2003; Schore 1994, 2000). In fact, Schore (1994, 1996, 1997, 2001a, 2001b) has powerfully shown that the maturation of the right hemisphere in particular is experience-dependent upon sensitive and attuned caregiving. Parental attunement to their young child's needs affects the neurochemistry of the brain and is associated with neuronal growth and connectivity. During the first year of life, neurons proliferate based upon the richness of experience and connect the vital brain systems associated with emotional regulation. Specifically, connections to the orbitofrontal cortex in the right hemisphere can override the reactivity of the flight/fight subcortical survival centers. Because the right hemisphere is dominant for growth and development during the first three years of life (Chiron et al. 1997), insensitive parenting and certainly maltreatment and neglect affect these critical connections. Furthermore, the right hemisphere has connections into the autonomic nervous system where the sympathetic and parasympathetic nervous systems are entrained through experience. Therefore, children who are chronically dysregulated have high sympathetic nervous system activation (as seen in the ambivalent attachment strategies), which can affect learning and attention. Although children presenting with avoidant strategies appear not to be activated, their nervous system is equally activated (Spangler and Grossmann 1993).

Furthermore, many of the disorganized behaviors are triggering survival responses originating from a subcortical structure called the amygdala. This system is evolutionarily old and responds primarily to threat. The unpredictable environments of maltreated children heighten the entrainment of the amygdala, which is chronically responding to threat at the expense of higher cortical connections to areas that can override this system. Threat often triggers freeze, stilling, and body collapses in children quite incapable of fight or flight. These freezing behaviors are under the control of the parasympathetic nervous system, which reduces heart rate and respiration in a feigned death reaction used for survival. When the parent cannot provide enough sensitivity and attunement to initiate positive affect while regulating negative affect, the child's own body will attempt to regulate high arousal through rapid switches in the autonomic nervous system.

Attachment security then implies that there is good-enough coregulation in the parent who is sensitive and attuned enough to the child's inner state. Reading children's internal cues is critical to this process. Self-regulation emerges from the caregiver's ability to regulate negative while enhancing positive affect within an attuned, loving, and affectionate relationship. In fact, Schore (1996) suggests that the attuned caregiver's regulation of negative while enhancing positive arousal entrains a balance between the sympathetic and parasympathetic branches of the infant's autonomic nervous system, thus creating optimal arousal ranges associated with focused attention. Early dyadic experiences then are imprinted into the implicit memory of the infant's right brain (Mancia 2006; Schore 1994), which "presides over the learning of various skills" (Mancia 2006, 84). Since flexible attention and affect regulation are critical to the exploration and learning needed to successfully master future stages of development, the inflexible use of attentional resources in the service of basic emotional regulation has profound implications for the success and opportunities of the developing child. In all but secure strategies, learning and exploration will likely be compromised.

Given the importance of caregiver-infant synchrony needed for secure relationships, affect regulation, and brain development, it is hard to fathom the emotional resources available to a homeless mother for this important work. The mother's own security, however, is likely to be a critical factor. Some mothers do appear to us to fit a secure category and do appear to provide a secure base for their children despite being homeless. We often find, however, that these impressions come from mothers who have been housed, and this is their first episode of homelessness. We find that only 10 percent of the mothers of children evaluated fit this category. All other mothers have moved from 2 to 10 times prior to the evaluation of their young child. The role these contextual variables play in the lives of homeless mothers raising young children awaits future research. However, the child's biologically encoded drive to form an attachment to the mother is considered beyond culture, although shaped by it (Bowlby 1969; van IJzendoorn and Kroonenberg 1988). The attachment bond to the mother is likely even more critical to a homeless child to ensure survival.

Is it possible that the impact of homelessness on a mother with a young child is so extreme that it distorts the biological attachment system of the child and all that this might mean? Stress in general increases arousal ranges. How a parent's own nervous system is entrained will affect how the parent expresses stress. In homeless mothers, we often find narrow ranges of arousal regulation that move quickly from anxiety to angry and hostile expressions that interact with ongoing depression and/or other mental health issues. Many mothers have trauma histories, further increasing their reactivity. Since trauma in the mother is known to be a significant risk factor for the young child if the trauma is unresolved (Hesse and Main 2000; Main 1996; van IJzendoorn 1995) and violence is associated with poverty (Payne et al. 2001), the role of unresolved trauma in the homeless mother needs further research. When we looked at a subset of children evaluated, we found that both infants and toddlers had lower mean behavioral scores on the Bayley Scales of Infant Development, 2nd edition (1993) than the normal distribution. Interestingly, the preschoolers tested within the age range for the Bayley were within expected ranges. Yet when we analyzed by our attachment impressions into secure versus not secure (avoidant, ambivalent, and disorganized), the behavioral scores were dramatically lower for the not-secure group (62 percent vs. 43 percent).

Homelessness

Homelessness is known to have a multisystem impact on development, especially on the young developing homeless child under five years of age. Significantly below average receptive language and visuomotor development has been found in homeless compared with housed preschoolers (Rescorla, Parker, and Stolley 1991). Bassuk and Rubin (1987) found that 47 percent of 81 homeless children under five years of age had at least one development delay with an additional 33 percent showing two or more developmental delays. In the Fox et al. (1990) survey of 50 homeless children age 4 to 10 housed with their mothers in New York hotels, 61 percent had language functioning at the 1st percentile and 29 percent had psychomotor functioning at the 5th percentile.

Studies assessing development in the homeless infant and toddler are underrepresented, yet may be the most illuminating due to the ontogenetic nature of development. The impact of homelessness on a preverbal child is further complicated by the dyadic nature of development. The developmental risk of homelessness therefore, may not clearly *show* itself when comparing task demands commonly assessed on developmental tests. García Coll et al. (1998) studied housed versus homeless infants and toddlers age 4 to 30 months using the Bayley Scales of Infant Development and the Vineland Screener. They found no significant differences between homeless and housed infants and toddlers for cognitive or motor development. When they collapsed the groups and analyzed by age, however, the younger children (≤18 months) had higher cognitive scores on the Bayley Mental Scale than did the older children (García Coll et al. 1998). We also find significant declines (p=.003) in the Mental Developmental Index of the Bayley Scales for toddlers and preschoolers compared with the majority of the homeless infants (≤18 months) evaluated. Significant increases in emotional and behavioral problems have also been found in studies assessing homeless preschoolers (Bassuk and Rubin 1987; Bassuk et al. 1997; Fox et al. 1990; Rescorla, Parker, and Stolley 1991). Thus, the impact of homelessness on the preschool child may have a greater negative impact on development because of tightly wound variables associated with the homelessness of the mother, including her emotional availability and sensitivity.

Payne, DeVol, and Dreussi Smith (2001) suggest that there is a *culture of poverty* where mothers play a different role than found in middle-class family systems. Specifically, these authors suggest that generational poverty is matriarchal in structure, with mothers holding the most powerful position in the family. These authors suggest that there are "hidden rules" in generational poverty (at least two generations) that are different from situational poverty created by a particular event. The hidden rules are embedded into belief systems and values that are not easily seen nor understood by middle-class care systems. If this is true, some homeless mothers may have unique beliefs about themselves and their children that are contrary to middle-class belief systems. Future research on homeless families controlling for these differences would be greatly helpful in designing interventions for homeless families.

DYADIC THERAPY INTERVENTION PROCEDURES

At SVdPV, dyadic play therapy interventions for homeless children and their mothers are provided by supervised training interns in psychology and marriage and family therapy. Interns are formally trained in attachment and affect regulation theories as a part of their internship experience. All interns are required to attend a two-hour-per-week formal developmental evaluation where one team tests and the other team observes through the one-way mirror (with parent consent). The supervisor is present in all developmental assessments and guides the integration of testing data, observation, and history at the end of the session. At that time, ranges of the child's cognitive, language, motor, and socioemotional development are known. We also have a sense of the parent-child relationship.

First Level of Intervention: Developmental Assessments

Briefly, all families entering SVdPV with children under five are required to have a development screening using Ages and Stages Questionnaires (ASQ; Bricker and Squires 1999) and Ages and Stages Questionnaires—Social Emotional (ASQ-SE; Squires, Bricker, and Twombly 2002). Teachers from the on-site childcare program fill out the ASQ after two weeks of childcare. If any of these questionnaires are in the delayed range, a formal evaluation is scheduled.

Formal evaluations begin with two five-minute parent-child interactions in a structured task and free play. If the parent consents for videoing this segment of the developmental screening, the video is rated using the Early Relational Assessment on 29 parent, 28 infant, and 8 dyadic variables (Clark 1985). After the ERA segment, a testing team enters the room, consisting of an examiner, an interviewer, and an observer. The supervisor serves as the interviewer. For children age 1 to 42 months, the Bayley Scales of Infant Development, 2nd edition (1993) is administered in the presence of the mother. The observer chronicles all mother-child and child-team interactions throughout the assessment. Specifically, the observer records all child vocalizations, words, smiles, quality of attention, approaches to parent, approaches to team members, and parent initiations and responses to child. The interviewer gathers information about the child's developmental milestones, quality of pregnancy and birth, medical concerns, number of moves made since the birth of the child, other children, location of father, foster placements, Child Protective Services involvement, health and well-being of the mother, and any trauma that the mother believes the child has had. Prior to the formal evaluation, mothers are asked to fill out a brief questionnaire assessing any concerns they might have about their child's development using the Parents' Evaluation of Developmental Status (PEDS; Glascoe 2006), which is reviewed with the mother by the interviewer. Additionally, mothers in the first postpartum year are given the Edinburgh Postnatal Scale (Cox, Holden, and Sagorsky 1987).

The formal evaluation is often the first in-depth look at the child's development and the issues involved in the family. At the end of the assessment, a book and a stuffed animal are given to the child. We begin showing the mother how to point out colors while she reads to the child to support learning and language. We also mirror the vocalizations and words of the child during the gifting and comment to the mother about the strengths of the child.

Second Level of Intervention: Psychoeducational Classes

All parents with children age birth to five are referred to the educational component of SAFECHILD, which includes approximately 20 "Mommy and Me" classes, focused on increasing attunement to the child through play while providing information about child development. These classes are designed to strengthen language and motor development through play and are focused on increased knowledge about child development in general. Homeless children and their parents greatly enjoy the Baby Classes, as every class provides an experiential playtime for both. We learned early on that many homeless mothers have not had enough play themselves, as they would split off interactions with their child during dyadic therapy to play. This prompted us to design Baby Classes to provide ways both mother and child can play together while we focus on their relationship, fun ways to support a child's development, bonding with other mothers for support, and interesting activities that can be used in their rooms. Baby Classes were also designed to correspond to developmental periods so that a mother with an infant might choose to attend Bonding with Baby, Infant Massage, and/or Baby Signs, whereas a mother with a toddler or preschooler could select classes appropriate to that age of development. Parents are also required to complete a tailored-to-homeless 0–5 Parenting Education class based upon information presented in videos about child development. We use the video series developed by the First 5 Commission of California. When disorganization, aggression, withdrawal, and/or misattuned parent/child interactions are seen in the developmental assessment, on the childcare site, or in the Baby Classes, referrals are made for dyadic therapy.

Third Level of Intervention: Dyadic Therapy

The second and third levels of intervention tend to occur simultaneously. When a referral for dyadic therapy is made, it is given to a training intern who schedules the initial interview with the parent/child. Because we are aware of the stated referring issue in all cases, we determine whether or not it is appropriate to have a toddler or preschooler present during the first interview based upon the information we have. All young infants (≤12 months) accompany the parent to the first interview.

Scheduling the First Interview

A meeting is scheduled by letter, with copies sent to the parent's staff contact or case manager. This allows the residential and case management staff to support the appointment, thereby reducing the possibility of a no-show. Ruby Payne and colleagues (2001) have commented that the concept of time is different for homeless persons, suggesting that the homeless respond more to activities in the present moment in contrast to plans or appointments made in the future. We find this to be true when scheduling appointments with our residents, as often it will take two or more attempts to schedule the first appointment. The reader may want to know that at SVdPV, all residents entering the Village sign a Release of Confidentiality to communicate with other in-house staff on a *need to know* basis. In this way, all critical departments help coordinate the care of the resident, thereby increasing the likelihood that they will attend their appointment.

The First Interview

During the first meeting, the intern begins to establish a rapport with the parent and child and explains the consent process, including limits of confidentiality. The intern will also ask for consent to video and explain that the videos will be used for both supervision and treatment. Although there are additional tasks in the first session, which might include other clinical scales such as the Child Behavioral Check List for 18-month- to 5-year-olds (Achenbach and Rescorla 2000), the intern is deeply listening to the mother's concerns and beginning to introduce preliminary goals for intervention. The intern is also assessing for what other treatment modalities might be needed (i.e., individual therapy) to support the mother, reduce her stress, and build her confidence. Through eye contact, smiling, and/or an occasional reflective comment, the intern also acknowledges and begins to establish a rapport with the child while observing how mother and child interact. At the end of the first session, we like to have agreed upon preliminary goals of where to begin by integrating our observations with the mother's identification of the problem and rating it on a scale of 1 to 10.

Establishing a point to begin, however, can be quite complicated, as the mother may experience her child as noncompliant and want us to *fix the child.* However, we may see that the mother is too distant, harsh, and authoritative for the child to develop optimally. Or a mother is surprised by a referral from the childcare program because a six-month-old infant can't be put down on the floor without crying inconsolably. Yet during the initial interview we learn that the mother has lost three children to Child Protective Services and wants desperately to do a good job with this child, so she never puts her down. The first mother consented for treatment when we asked if she would be willing to work with us for three sessions on a behavioral plan that included playing with her child. This mother did not consent to the use of video for intervention or supervision at this session. We often suggest to resistant parents a short-term plan that can be reevaluated and further extended once the parent feels more comfortable with us and the therapy process. For this parent, we decided to use a structured behavioral dyadic therapy (Parent-Child Interaction Therapy, Eyberg 1988) that would offer the most success in the shortest period of time. We find that using the Child-Directed Interaction of Parent-Child Interaction Therapy is particularly effective when working with homeless dyads. As she could see that her child was happier and more compliant, this mother consented for video as an intervention and greatly enjoyed reviewing her sessions with the therapist.

The second mother consented for treatment after we assured her that her daughter was developing normally (we knew this from the developmental assessment), yet the therapy could teach her *additional tips* to support her daughter's growth. This mother also consented for the use of video as an intervention so that she could see herself interacting with her baby. This therapy was done completely on the floor with the therapist highlighting the baby's return to mother after gradually moving away to explore toys. When mother saw herself on tape, she began to have the awareness of the connection between her own anxiety and not putting the child down to explore. This mother was entraining a level of anxiety in her child that gave the child the feeling that any place but mother's arms was dangerous.

In general, we receive referrals for dyadic play therapy for reunification issues; child compliance; feeding conflicts; withdrawn or unresponsive children; tantrums; aggression; biting; children exposed to domestic violence; children who have lost a parent, siblings, or loved relatives; developmental delays or arrests; and/or disorganization, parental insensitivity, and parental lack of knowledge about child development. If all goes well, the first session ends with signed consents and a rapport sufficiently built for a return.

Initial Stages of Treatment

The second session generally introduces the active treatment. We commonly see mothers and infants in our observation room where we can put down mats with blankets over them and infant toys. Dyadic play therapy for older toddlers and preschoolers is done in a play therapy room that is equipped with a variety of toys. In general, we have toy families of all ethnic backgrounds, animal families, musical instruments, dress-up clothes, a doctor kit, a variety of puppets with stage, drawing and coloring materials, play dough, books to read, stuffed animals, a sand tray, balls, toy basketball and net, army men, child table and chairs, toy trucks, a construction set, legos, blocks, toy kitchen with play food, toy phone, worker dolls (i.e., a chef, mailman, doctor), and various games (e.g., Candyland, Chutes and Ladders, Clue Jr.).

For infant therapies, we ask the mother to put the baby on the mat, inviting her to sit on the floor with the therapist. The mother may begin talking about the baby or her week while the therapist begins nonverbally introducing interesting objects for the infant to play with and then handing them off to mother. As the infant begins to interact with the mother's play, the therapist may comment on the infant's affect as she sees changes in facial tone, eye contact, gestures, and smiles. The therapist will begin using different voicing with the infant, including increased exaggerated facial expressions, and highlight the infant's response to the mother. In this way, the therapist teaches the mother about infant affect that signals when to play and when to disengage from play.

We find that many homeless mothers struggle to understand infant signals, particularly when the infant signals for disengagement from stimulation. For example, one mother reviewing a video of her infant and herself in dyadic therapy, felt excited and reached for her sleeping infant. The mother began kissing him on the neck and tried to play with him until he awoke. The infant, however, was asleep and not in the mood for play so became fussy and irritable. The mother now felt frustrated and began using a harsher voice saying, "What's the matter with you?" The therapist quickly said to the mother, "You probably wanted to hold him because of how cute you both looked on the video." The mother paused, yet nodded. "And he was asleep and not ready to play yet." In general, all infant dyadic therapies highlight the child's internal state to improve parent sensitivity and attunement. We also actively highlight the mother's own voice prosody, helping her find the voice range that her infant responds to. We also highlight the mother's face-to-face positive eye contact and how this affects her child. All dyadic therapies focus on reading the child's body communications, increasing positive affect while regulating negative affect, helping the mother identify different cries, and improving the mother's responsiveness.

For toddlers, we may start the therapy commenting on what toys the child selects. We again comment on the toddler's interests. We also encourage the mother to sit on the floor with the toddler. One mother followed the toddler around the room. She was very close to him the majority of the time. At one point, the toddler appeared backed up in a corner with the mother looming over him. As it turned out, the mother secretly felt her child never wanted to be around her. What was clear to us was that her pursuit of him likely kept him moving away. The therapist wondered out loud if he would show her his toys if she stayed in one location. Within the same session, the child presented a toy to his mother who was now seated in one spot. The mother's face showed her joy. This moment became a turning point in this therapy. The mother learned that she didn't need to work so hard to experience her child's love. Her child continued to present toys and soon began to invite her into his play.

Final Stages of Treatment

For us termination is almost never under our control. Often the family will spontaneously leave the Village for other opportunities. Furthermore, we find that very few homeless families are able to handle termination sessions. Instead, a therapist who has worked closely with a family may need to process the sudden termination with her supervisor. We have developed a rule of thumb to help with this seemingly uncontrollable aspect of working with homeless people: We try to give something in each session that the parent can use, because we never truly know if we are going to see the family again. We also set this goal for ourselves as therapists to help process feelings often created by sudden terminations. As it turns out, though, some families return to the Village a second time, only this time with a greater determination to succeed. In these cases, we simply reopen the file and pick up where we left off.

EMPIRICAL SUPPORT

Infant/Parent Psychotherapy

In general, there are three therapies we have found work well with homeless mothers and children. The first is the traditional infant/parent psychotherapy (IPP) advanced by Selma Fraiberg, Alicia Lieberman, and others. This treatment is sensitive to working with the parent's projections of her own early history onto the child. Fraiberg, Adelson, and Shapiro (1975) eloquently refer to this psychodynamic process as the *ghosts in the nursery*. Lieberman and colleagues (2005), however, rightly point out that many traumatized parents have at least some positive memories of their childhood experiences that can be drawn upon and used with their own child. IPP is completely compatible with attachment and affect regulation theories, as it assumes that the mother's own internal working model will be triggered when interacting with her child. In the world of affect regulation, Schore (1994) points out that the mother's internal working model based upon her own early dyadic experiences is encoded within implicit memory of her right hemisphere. Because children under three years of age are right hemisphere–dominant for development (Chiron et al. 1997), the mother's projections of her own early experiences will be encoded into the child's own right hemisphere. Changing the mother's maladaptive perceptions of her infant, then, will critically affect the intergenerational transmission of maladaptive behavior.

There are multiple studies showing the effectiveness of IPP, particularly when it is used within programs designed for specific populations. The original Child Development Project in Michigan (Fraiberg 1980); the Child Trauma Research Project in San Francisco (Lieberman 1997); the Steps Towards Effective, Enjoyable Parenting (STEEP; Erickson, Korfmacher, and Egeland 1992) in Minnesota; the Infant/Parent program at Mount Hope Family Center in Rochester, New York (Cicchetti and Toth 1987, 1995); and the New Orleans program for maltreated infants and toddlers in foster care (Larrieu and Zeanah 1998) all use IPP as a base intervention (for a more complete review see Lieberman and Zeanah 1999). Other infant/parent programs like the Watch, Wait, and Wonder program in Ontario, Canada (Cohen et al. 1999); the Attachment and Biobehavioral Catch-up for young children in foster care in Delaware (Dozier, Dozier, and Manni 2002); the Circle of Security project for preschoolers in Virginia (Marvin et al. 2002); and the Seattle parent training program (Speltz 1990), include other interventions such as parent education, behavioral coaching, and video feedback on a foundation of attachment theory.

Recently, an important treatment intervention study randomized 137 12-month-old maltreated infants to either weekly IPP therapy or Psycho-educational Parenting Intervention (PPI) for one year given by master-level clinicians. When compared with standard Child Protective Services community resources and a nonmaltreating normal control group, both the IPP and PPI interventions increased attachment security as measured by the Strange Situation (Cicchetti, Rogosch, and Toth 2006). Furthermore, interventions that focus only on increasing parent sensitivity have been found to be more effective in reducing childhood disorganization than interventions targeting multiple goals (Bakersmans-Kranenburg, van IJzendoorn, and Juffer 2005).

Use of Video in Dyadic Therapy

The use of video as an intervention is now common to a number of young child interventions. Bob Marvin and colleagues (2002) make extensive use of video as an intervention tool that is reviewed within a small group of parents. This 20-week group-based program called the Circle of Security strives to increase parent sensitivity by developing improved observational skills, reflection, and empathy toward their children within a safe "holding" environment for the parent. From Weeks 3 to 8, four segments of one parent/child video are reviewed within a small group of parents. Each parent has the opportunity to have segments from their own parent/child interaction shown in the group. The segments selected reflect (1) the child's need of the parent, (2) the parent responding with competency, (3) the parent struggling to find competency, and (4) a moment to celebrate the parent/child relationship. During Weeks 10 to 15, a second phase of video review occurs that focuses more on the feelings the parent has when viewing a segment reflecting a parent/child struggle. This group reports a 40 percent increase in *ordered* attachment patterns post intervention (Marvin et al. 2002).

Clark (1985) also recommends clinician/parent review of videoed structured and free play interactions used for the Early Relational Assessment. Parent sensitivity is increased by the clinician "wondering" with the parent what she is thinking and feeling during particular segments. Bakersmans-Kranenburg, Juffer, and van IJzendoorn (1998) found that video feedback was particularly effective for insecure-dismissive mothers. Insecure-preoccupied mothers also found the video feedback useful within a group setting.

Use of Behavioral Techniques in Dyadic Therapy

Various forms of behavioral therapy have been successfully used in dyadic therapies. In a meta-analysis of 88 interventions, Bakersmans-Kranenburg, van IJzendoorn, and Juffer (2003) conclude that a shorter-term behavioral focus on a specific issue associated with increasing parent sensitivity improves attachment security. In the Circle of Security project, Marvin and colleagues (2002) attempt to identify one "linchpin" issue that would make a real difference in the attachment relationship if changed.

Parent-Child Interaction Therapy (Eyberg 1988) is a behavioral therapy for young children age three to six that focuses on improving child compliance. Treatment duration is not fixed. The therapy has two stages: (1) Child Directed Interaction (CDI) and (2) Parent Directed Interaction (PDI). Mothers have rules to follow for both CDI and PDI and are encouraged to practice during the week. For CDI, mothers are taught to not give commands, not ask questions, and not criticize when playing with their child. Instead, they are encouraged to describe, imitate, reflect, praise, and be enthusiastic while following the child's lead. In the PDI, mothers are taught to give clear direct commands that are age-appropriate, which include praise when the child complies. Mothers are also taught to use calm but firm positive voices when giving commands. PDI helps parents to tell the child what to do instead of giving a "stop" command to change behavior. There is also a time-out procedure if the child continues in noncompliance. Traditional PCIT uses a microphone in the mother's ear with a clinician observing the play behind a one-way mirror. Five minutes of each new session are rated to track improvement in the mother's mastery on using praises, descriptions, and reflections. Preliminary data comparing PCIT-treated dyads with a wait list control showed significant decreases in child oppositional behavior and parental stress four months postintervention (Schuhmann et al. 1998).

CASE ILLUSTRATION

Referral

Jimmy was a handsome little 19-month-old boy referred for a dyadic play therapy with his homeless mother, who has two other children under 5 years of age. The family became homeless when Jimmy's father lost his job. Referrals came from three departments. The childcare program was concerned about Jimmy's speech development and his aggression with other children. The referral from the residential program was for extreme verbal abuse by the mother, which resulted in Child Protective Service reporting. The third referral was generated from his formal evaluation.

Formal Evaluation

The ERA taken at the beginning of the formal evaluation showed a mother who handed her son puzzle pieces using a firm yet pleasing voice.

She named the colors of the pieces for her son and praised him when he made a close approximation. Jimmy once said "No green" when the mother identified an orange piece. In the free play with a construction set that the mother set up, Jimmy made *zoom* vocalizations with a truck while the mother played out a scene herself. Jimmy did not join the mother's play and no other vocalizations were heard during the ERA. During both five-minute episodes, Jimmy glanced at his mother once, and the mother appeared to focus her eyes above Jimmy's head. We found no other eye contact between mother and child, and the child did not smile throughout.

On the PEDS, the mother indicated that her only developmental concern was Jimmy's speech and language development. When the evaluation team entered the room, Jimmy joined the examiner immediately without looking at his mother. Jimmy had a runny nose throughout, and his mother stated that he tends to get a lot of colds. The mother stated he was due for his shots and that she had made his well-child appointment. Birth and developmental milestones were within normal ranges. Jimmy often used the testing materials as play toys despite instructions; however, he was able to perform enough of the tasks to achieve basal levels on the Bayley. Several times he left the table to explore the room. Jimmy had very little eye contact with the examiner but did show a half smile to the interviewer when given a book to take with him. Only two words were heard during the testing. The observer noted that the mother looked at Jimmy twice during the testing. Jimmy went to his mother once and put his head in her lap. She rubbed his head without looking or speaking to him; he returned to the testing. Upon completion, Jimmy easily left the room walking behind his mother. Jimmy's scores for cognitive and language development were in the delayed range. His motor development was in expected ranges. Referrals were made for a medical evaluation, hearing test, speech and language therapy, speech enhancement group on the childcare site, dyadic play therapy, Baby Classes, and the 0–5 Parenting Education class. An individual therapy referral was also made for his mother.

Preintervention Case Conceptualization Based upon All Assessments

Jimmy's speech and language development was below expected ranges as seen in multiple settings, including the Speech Enhancement Group for toddlers given by our speech and language therapist. The team expected his biting and aggression on the childcare site to improve with more developed speech and more attunement from his mother. The mother-child relationship had some strengths, in that Jimmy received affection from his mother when he went to her to reestablish contact. The mother also did a good job scaffolding the puzzle task for Jimmy by highlighting color concepts and praising approximations.

Given the reports of the mother's emotional dysregulation seen by the residential staff, we hypothesized that the mother's own emotional dysregulation was likely traumatizing Jimmy, who presented to us as a very gentle little boy. The mother's reactivity was likely contributing to Jimmy's avoidant-appearing strategy and negatively impacting his cognitive and language development. We also suspected that Jimmy did not get much time alone with his mother due to the needs of the other children and felt that a play therapy with his mother would be beneficial to support his development. We believed that increased support for the mother in an individual therapy and focus on increased attunement to Jimmy's internal world in the dyadic therapy, would provide the greatest overall benefit to the dyad and Jimmy's development.

Primary Intervention Goals

For the mother:

1. Improve observation and reflection of natural movement of the child to explore and return to the mother for refueling through review of video
2. Increase eye contact, positive affect, pleasant voicing, and face-to-face interactions with the child
3. Increase praise, imitation, and reflection of the child's play
4. Increase enjoyment in the child's play

For the child:

1. Increase vocalizations in play
2. Increase the child's exploration of toys
3. Increase the child's eye contact
4. Increase smiling

Dyadic Play Therapy
(11 sessions over 5 months, 45-minute sessions)

Session 1: The first session of this dyadic play therapy was focused on reviewing the mother's concerns and goals, suggesting preliminary treatment goals, signing consents, and discussing the use of video as an intervention. The therapist discussed the mother's parenting strengths as seen in the ERA and how increasing Jimmy's positive affect, mirroring his language, and improving his eye contact would likely help his social interactions. Jimmy was also simultaneously in speech and language therapy at the time of this dyadic play therapy. The mother agreed with the above preliminary intervention goals and signed consent forms to video.

Session 2: Jimmy explored the playroom while his mother Joann sat in the chair talking with the therapist. He went to the toy kitchen set, made a sandwich with the play food, and handed it to the therapist. Wanting to join the mother into his play, the therapist said, "Thank you, Jimmy. Maybe Mom wants a sandwich, too," and encouraged Joann to sit on the floor with Jimmy. Jimmy seemed delighted to see his mother on the floor and promptly made another sandwich and handed it to her. Throughout this session, Joann tried to play with Jimmy by asking questions and using a teaching voice. The therapist, also sitting on the floor beside Joann, made reflective comments about Jimmy's play. "He seems to really like to play with the kitchen set." Joann stated, "Yes, he'll probably be a chef!" Joann then started to talk about her other children and how frustrated she was with her oldest child. Jimmy reached for the guitar and began strumming on it. Joann appeared irritated with the sound and used a firm voice telling Jimmy to find another toy. The therapist opened some of the toy bins for Jimmy so he could see all the other toys. Jimmy saw a ball, said, "Ball," and threw it to the therapist. The therapist said, "Ball . . . You would like to play ball?" and held the ball up for a throw to Joann. Joann received the ball and tossed it to Jimmy. Several rounds of ball were played. Jimmy lost interest in the ball and brought a book to his mother, wanting to sit in her lap. Joann received him and began looking at the book with him.

Session 3: Joann was invited to view the video of the first session. The therapist selected several clips where Joann and Jimmy were looking at each other. The therapist "wondered" with Joann what stood out to her in these clips. Joann struggled with a response, eventually saying, "He seems to like the kitchen set." This was similar to a comment the therapist had made in the session, which helped the therapist see that Joann needed help *seeing* what her son's communications mean. The therapist said, "Let's look at this again," and backed up the tape. "See, he is finished making the sandwich and what does he do before he hands it to you?" Joann saw that Jimmy looked at her first before handing her the sandwich. "Now look at your own face when he hands you the sandwich." Joann saw that she was smiling and then Jimmy smiled in return. This sequence was very important for Joann as she could see that her son was clearly smiling because she was. The therapist wondered with Joann if Jimmy's smiling would increase through her smiles. The therapist also had a wonderful videoclip to highlight for Joann how Jimmy needed to explore the room but when he was tired he needed to return to her for soothing. Joann appeared to understand that Jimmy bringing her the book was not so much his need to read as his need to be soothed.

Session 4: Jimmy entered the playroom and headed for the kitchen set and started to make another sandwich. Joann said, "Are you making me a sandwich? I'm hungry." Jimmy turned and looked at her. Joann was smiling; Jimmy gave a half smile. Jimmy handed her the sandwich and pulled out the animal families. He began to put all of the families together by species. The therapist reflected, "There are a lot of animals here." Joann reached for a mother bear and moved it like it was walking. Jimmy ignored her, and she retreated. Jimmy took several child animals and put them in a group, then took a father animal and stomped all over the children. He then threw the animal family against the bookshelf. Joann commented to the therapist that this was what he was doing in childcare. Jimmy found a puppet and began to put the puppet in Joann's face. He was rough, and Joann didn't like this play. Using a very angry voice that surprised the therapist, Joann said, "I'm not going to play with you anymore," and left the floor to sit in the chair. Jimmy turned away from Joann and began pulling toys out of the toy box.

Session 5: Because Joann had an open Child Protective Services file for verbal abuse of her young children, the therapist elected to do a video review of the last session. There is no set schedule for video reviews. Instead, the therapist clinically determines what would be beneficial to the therapy. In this case, she wanted to work with Joann around how angry she felt with Jimmy. The therapist first showed a clip of Joann's positive interaction with Jimmy in the first part of the session and how Jimmy responded to her smiles. When the interaction with the puppet was shown, the therapist asked what she was experiencing. Joann said, "I hate when someone gets in my face." The therapist was beginning to see how Joann's past trauma was triggered by her child. The therapist wondered if this happened to her often, which eventually led to Joann having some awareness that she was overreacting to her child.

By Session 6, all of the initial goals were actively in the play therapy and by Session 11, Jimmy's affect had greatly improved. Joann made considerable gains in her own emotional regulation, particularly with the coordinated support of her individual therapy. The dyad continued to use their looking at a book together as their special intimate time. Jimmy's speech was also improving with both individual and group speech and language sessions. Although the CPS file was closed, Joann continued to have some incidences of losing verbal control, but staff saw her as improving. The family spontaneously left the Village after a seven-month stay; we were told they moved to another location.

CONCLUSIONS AND FUTURE DIRECTIONS

The mother's *state of mind* with regard to her own attachment experiences has been found to predict infant attachment classification as measured by the Adult Attachment Interview (AAI; George, Kaplan, and Main 1996) with

75 percent correspondence (van IJzendoorn and Bakersmans-Kranenburg 1996). The AAI categories of Secure/Autonomous, Dismissing, Preoccupied, and Unresolved for loss or trauma correspond to the infant categories of Secure, Avoidant, Ambivalent, and Disorganized respectively. Increases in Dismissing and Unresolved categories have been found in mothers with low socioeconomic status (van IJzendoorn and Bakersmans-Kranenburg 1996). Given our high rates of avoidant impressions in the preschoolers and the trauma histories often found in our homeless mothers, controlled research studies are needed to begin to understand the multiple factors associated with the homeless mother.

A homeless mother's attachment experiences from her own childhood are too often heavily laden with trauma and grief that are quietly lived with, generally without treatment or support. High levels of emotional reactivity, depression and anxiety, drug and alcohol use, histories of trauma, domestic violence, low educational levels, and/or other mental health conditions are commonly found in our homeless mothers. Interventions targeting homeless mothers with young children are urgently needed to impact the generational turnover of conditions associated with homelessness. Future studies controlling for IQ, educational level, and attachment status in homeless mothers would begin to illuminate the factors underlying homelessness.

Given that infant attachment classifications have been found to significantly diverge from expected rates when maternal problems are identified (van IJzendoorn et al. 1992) and that quality of attachment has been associated with cognitive development in general and language development in particular (van IJzendoorn, Dijkstra, and Bus 1995), greater focus on homeless maternal attributes and resources is warranted. Specifically, the negative sequelae associated with affect dysregulation appear to impact cognitive development in general, with studies finding lower cognitive scores in children with insecure and disorganized attachments (Erickson, Sroufe, and Egeland 1985; Lyons-Ruth, Easterbrooks, and Cibelli 1997; NICHD, 2004; van IJzendoorn, Dijkstra, and Bus 1995). When we analyzed our attachment impressions on children for whom we had complete Bayley scores, we found that insecure (avoidant, ambivalent, and disorganized) children had significantly lower cognitive and behavioral scores on the Bayley than the children who appeared secure ($p = .002$ and $p = .03$ respectively).

Fluctuations in attention and/or behavioral dysregulation can affect learning. In fact, Main (2000) notes that attention can be compromised by the underlying working model in insecure attachments, e.g., the avoidant child's need to harness attention away from attachment needs and the preoccupied attention found in the ambivalent child for when the parent might be available. The often primitive strategies that desperately focus attention on survival mechanisms have been found in the disorganized child

(Hesse and Main 2000). When a large portion of a child's attention is in the service of attachment strategies, it is not difficult to understand the connection between security and learning in general.

Dyadic play therapy can be successfully used to help stabilize the critically important dyadic relationship needed for growth and development in a young child. Dyadic play therapy is especially effective for homeless dyads within programs providing wrap-around services that can support and reinforce the mother's new dyadic skills. Intervention goals focused on improving the mother's sensitivity, attunement, and ability to follow a child's lead in play help stabilize the child's needed attachment to her. The one study we found that measured attachment in homeless children found no differences in attachment security between homeless and housed children; however, both were rated low on attachment security (Easterbrooks and Graham 1999).

Working with homeless families is challenging. Yet we find that clinicians clear in purpose and intervention goals can advance the health of a child despite the numerous cancellations and no-show appointments. Seeing a withering child suddenly bloom because we have helped her mother understand her needs makes it all worth it!

REFERENCES

Achenbach, T. M., and L. A. Rescorla. 2000. *Manual for ASEBA Preschool Forms and Profiles.* Burlington: University of Vermont, Research Center for Children, Youth, and Families.

Ainsworth, M. D. S., M. C. Blehar, E. Waters, and S. Wall. 1978. *Patterns of attachment: A psychological study of the Strange Situation.* Hillsdale, NJ: Erlbaum.

Bakersmans-Kranenburg, M. J., F. Juffer, and M. H. van IJzendoorn. 1998. Interventions with video feedback and attachment discussions: Does type of maternal insecurity make a difference? *Infant Mental Health Journal* 19 (2): 202–219.

Bakersmans-Kranenburg, M. J., M. H. van IJzendoorn, and F. Juffer. 2003. Less is more: Meta-analyses of sensitivity and attachment interventions in early childhood. *Psychological Bulletin* 129 (2): 195–215.

———. 2005. Disorganized infant attachment and preventive interventions: A review and meta-analysis. *Infant Mental Health Journal* 26:191–216.

Bassuk, E., and L. Rubin. 1987. Homeless children: A neglected population. *American Journal of Orthopsychiatry* 57 (2): 279–286.

Bassuk, E. L., L. F. Weinreb, J. Dawson, J. N. Perloff, and J. C. Buckner. 1997. Determinants of behavior in homeless and low-income housed preschool children. *Pediatrics* 100 (1): 92–100.

Bayley Scales of Infant Development. 2nd ed. 1993. New York: Harcourt Brace.

Bowlby, J. 1969. *Attachment and loss,* vol. 1, *Attachment.* New York: Basic.

———. 1988. *A secure base: Parent-child attachment and healthy human development.* New York: Basic.

Bricker, D., and J. Squires. 1999. *Ages and Stages Questionnaires: A parent-completed, child-monitoring system.* 2nd ed. Baltimore: Brookes.

Carlson, E. A. 1998. A prospective longitudinal study of attachment disorganization/ disorientation. *Child Development* 69 (4): 1107–1128.

Carlson, V., D. Cicchetti, D. Barnett, and K. Braunwald. 1989. Disorganized/ disoriented attachment relationships in maltreated infants. *Developmental Psychology* 25 (4): 525–531.

Chiron, C., I. Jambaque, R. Nabbout, R. Lounes, A. Syrota, and O. Dulac. 1997. The right brain hemisphere is dominant in human infants. *Brain* 120:1057–1065.

Cicchetti, D., F. A. Rogosch, and S. L. Toth. 2006. Fostering secure attachment in infants in maltreating families through preventive interventions. *Development and Psychopathology* 18:623–649.

Cicchetti, D., and S. L. Toth. 1987. The application of a transactional risk model to intervention with multi-risk maltreating families. *Zero to Three: Bulletin of the National Center for Clinical Infant Programs* 7:1–8.

———. 1995. Child maltreatment and attachment organization: Implications of intervention. In *Attachment theory: Social, developmental, and clinical perspectives,* ed. S. Goldberg, R. Muir, and J. Kerr. Hillsdale, NJ: Analytic Press.

Cirulli, F., A. Berry, and E. Alleva. 2003. Early disruption of the mother-infant relationship: Effects on brain plasticity and implications for psychopathology. *Neuroscience and Biobehavioral Reviews* 27:73–82.

Clark, R. 1985. The Parent-Child Early Relational Assessment. Unpublished instrument. Department of Psychiatry, University of Wisconsin, Madison.

Cohen, M. J., E. Muir, M. Lojkasek, R. Muir, C. J. Parker, M. Barwick, and M. Brown. 1999. Watch, Wait, and Wonder: Testing the effectiveness of a new approach to mother-infant psychotherapy. *Infant Mental Health Journal* 20 (4): 429–451.

Cox, J., J. Holden, and R. Sagorsky. 1987. Detection of postnatal depression: Development of the Edinburgh Postnatal Depression Scale. *British Journal of Psychiatry* 150:782–786.

Dozier, M., D. Dozier, and M. Manni. 2002. Attachment and biobehavioral catch-up: The ABCs of helping infants in foster care cope with early adversity. *Zero to Three,* April–May, 7–13.

Easterbrooks, M. A., and C. A. Graham. 1999. Security of attachment and parenting: Homeless and low-income housed mothers and infants. *American Journal of Orthopsychiatry* 69 (3): 337–346.

Erickson, M. F., J. Korfmacher, and B. Egeland. 1992. Attachments past and present: Implications for the therapeutic intervention with mother-infant dyads. *Development and Psychopathology* 4:495–507.

Erickson, M. F., L. A. Sroufe, and B. Egeland. 1985. The relationship between quality of attachment and behavior problems in preschool in a high-risk sample. *Monographs of the Society for Research in Child Development* 50 (1–2, Serial No. 209).

Eyberg, S. 1988. Parent-Child Interaction Therapy: Integration of traditional and behavioral concerns. *Child and Family Behavior Therapy* 10 (1): 33–46.

Fox, S. J., J. Barrnett, M. Davies, and H. R. Bird. 1990. Psychopathology and developmental delay in homeless children: A pilot study. *Journal of the American Academy of Child and Adolescent Psychiatry* 29 (5): 732–735.

Fraiberg, S. 1980. *Clinical studies in infant mental health: The first year of life.* New York: Basic.

Fraiberg, S., E. Adelson, and V. Shapiro. 1975. Ghosts in the nursery: A psychoanalytic approach to impaired infant-mother relationships. *Journal of the American Academy of Child Psychiatry* 14:1387–1422.

García Coll, C., J. C. Buckner, M. G. Brooks, L. F. Weinreb, and E. L. Bassuk. 1998. The developmental status and adaptive behavior of homeless and low-income housed infants and toddlers. *American Journal of Public Health* 88 (9): 1371–1374.

George, C., N. Kaplan, and M. Main. 1996. Adult Attachment Interview. 3rd ed. Manuscript, Department of Psychology, University of California, Berkeley.

Glascoe, F. P. 2006. *Parents' evaluation of developmental status.* Nashville, TN: Ellsworth & Vandermeer Press.

Hesse, E., and M. Main. 2000. Disorganized infant, child, and adult attachment: Collapse in behavioral and attentional strategies. *Journal of the American Psychoanalytic Association* 48 (4): 1097–1127.

Karr-Morse, R., and M. S. Wiley. 1997. *Ghosts from the nursery: Tracing the roots of violence.* New York: Atlantic Monthly Press.

Larrieu, J., and C. H. Zeanah. 1998. An intensive intervention for infants and toddlers in foster care. *Child and Adolescent Psychiatric Clinics of North America* 7:357–391.

Lieberman, A., E. Padron, P. Van Horn, and W. W. Harris. 2005. Angels in the nursery: The intergenerational transmission of benevolent parental influences. *Infant Mental Health Journal* 26 (6): 504–520.

Lieberman, A. F. 1997. Toddlers' internalization of maternal attributions as a factor in quality of attachment. In *Attachment and psychopathology,* ed. L. Atkinson and K. Zucker. New York: Guilford.

Lieberman, A. F., and C. H. Zeanah. 1999. Contributions of attachment theory to infant-parent psychotherapy and other interventions with infants and young children. In *Handbook of attachment,* ed. J. Cassidy and P. R. Shaver. New York: Guilford.

Lyons-Ruth, K., L. Alpern, and B. Repacholi. 1993. Disorganized infant attachment classification and maternal psychosocial problems as predictors of hostile-aggressive behavior in the preschool classroom. *Child Development* 64:572–585.

Lyons-Ruth, K., M. A. Easterbrooks, and C. D. Cibelli. 1997. Infant attachment strategies, infant mental lag, and maternal depressive symptoms: Predictors of internalizing and externalizing problems at age seven. *Developmental Psychology* 33 (4): 681–692.

Main, M. 1996. Introduction to the special section on attachment and psychopathology: Overview of the field of attachment. *Journal of Consulting and Clinical Psychology* 64 (2): 237–243.

———. 2000. The organized categories of infant, child, and adult attachment: Flexible vs. inflexible attention under attachment-related stress. *Journal of the American Psychoanalytic Association* 48 (4): 1055–1096.

Main, M., and E. Hesse. 1990. Parents' unresolved traumatic experiences are related to infant disorganized attachment status: Is frightened or frightening parental

behavior the linking mechanism? In *Attachment in the preschool years,* ed. M. Greenberg, D. Cicchetti, and E. M. Cummings. Chicago: University of Chicago Press.

Main, M., and J. Solomon. 1990. Procedures for identifying infants as disorganized/
disoriented during the Ainsworth Strange Situation. In *Attachment in the preschool
years: Theory, research and intervention,* ed. M. Greenberg, D. Cicchetti, and E. M.
Cummings, 121–160. Chicago: University of Chicago Press.

Mancia, M. 2006. Implicit memory and early unrepressed unconscious: Their role in
the therapeutic process; How the neurosciences can contribute to psychoanalysis.
International Journal of Psychoanalysis 87:83–103.

Marvin, R., G. Cooper, K. Hoffman, and B. Powell. 2002. The Circle of Security
project: Attachment-based intervention with caregiver–preschool child dyads. *Attachment and Human Development* 4 (1): 107–124.

NICHD Early Child Care Research Network. 2004. Affect dysregulation in the
mother-child relationship in the toddler years: Antecedents and consequences.
Development and Psychopathology 16:43–68.

Payne, R. K., P. DeVol, and T. Dreussi Smith. 2001. *Bridges out of poverty: Strategies
for professionals and communities.* Highlands, TX: aha! Process, Inc.

Rescorla, L., R. Parker, and P. Stolley. 1991. Ability, achievement, and adjustment in
homeless children. *American Journal of Orthopsychiatry* 61 (2): 210–220.

Schore, A. N. 1994. *Affect regulation and the origin of the self: The neurobiology of emotional development.* Mahwah, NJ: Erlbaum.

——. 1996. The experience-dependent maturation of a regulatory system in the
orbital prefrontal cortex and the origin of developmental psychopathology. *Development and Psychopathology* 8:59–87.

——. 1997. Early organization of the nonlinear right brain and development
of a predisposition to psychiatric disorders. *Development and Psychopathology*
9:595–631.

——. 2000. Attachment and the regulation of the right brain. *Attachment and Human Development* 2 (1): 23–47.

——. 2001a. Effects of a secure attachment relationship on right brain development, affect regulation, and infant mental health. *Infant Mental Health Journal* 22
(1–2): 7–66.

——. 2001b. The effects of early relational trauma on right brain development,
affect regulation, and infant mental health. *Infant Mental Health Journal* 22 (1–2):
201–269.

Schuhmann, E. M., R. C. Foote, S. M. Eyberg, S. R. Boggs, and J. Algina. 1998. Efficacy of parent-child interaction therapy: Interim report of a randomized trail with
short-term maintenance. *Journal of Clinical Child Psychology* 27 (1): 34–45.

Spangler, G., and K. E. Grossmann. 1993. Biobehavioral organization in securely
and insecurely attached infants. *Child Development* 64:1439–1450.

Speltz, M. 1990. The treatment of preschool conduct problems: An integration of
behavioral and attachment concepts. In *Attachment in the preschool years: Theory,
research, and intervention,* ed. M. T. Greenberg, D. Ciccheti, and M. Cummings.
Chicago: University of Chicago Press.

Squires, J., D. Bricker, and E. Twombly. 2002. *Ages and Stages Questionnaires: Social
Emotional. A parent-completed, child-monitoring system for social emotional behaviors.*
Baltimore: Brookes.

Sroufe, L. A., B. Egeland, E. A. Carlson, and W. A. Collins. 2005. *The development of the person: The Minnesota study of risk and adaptation from birth to adulthood.* New York: Guilford.

van IJzendoorn, M. H. 1995. Adult attachment representations, parental responsiveness, and infant attachment: A meta-analysis on the predictive validity of the adult attachment interview. *Psychological Bulletin* 117 (3): 387–403.

van IJzendoorn, M. H., and M. J. Bakersmans-Kranenburg. 1996. Attachment representations in mothers, fathers, adolescents, and clinical groups: A meta-analytic search for normative data. *Journal of Consulting and Clinical Psychology* 64 (1): 8–21.

van IJzendoorn, M. H., J. Dijkstra, and A. G. Bus. 1995. Attachment, intelligence, and language. A meta-analysis. *Social Development* 4:115–128.

van IJzendoorn, M. H., S. Goldberg, P. M. Kroonenberg, and O. J. Frenkel. 1992. The relative effects of maternal and child problems on the quality of attachment: A meta-analysis of attachment in clinical samples. *Child Development* 63:840–858.

van IJzendoorn, M. H., and P. M. Kroonenberg. 1988. Cross-cultural patterns of attachment: A meta-analysis of the Strange Situation. *Child Development* 59:147–156.

14

Developmental Play Therapy for Very Young Children

Glenda F. Lester Short

BASIC RATIONALE AND THEORY

Dr. Viola Brody provides a theory and structured program for developmental play which she is credited with founding. Dr. Brody was influenced by the teachings of three people, A. Des Lauriers (1962), Janet Adler (1981), and Martin Buber (1958). At different times in her life, she experienced their teaching and incorporated some of their concepts into Developmental Play Therapy (DPT) (Brody 1978, 1997a).

Attachment and the bonding process are at the core of the theory of DPT. This process between a parent and a child is essential to the emotional quality between the parent and the child (Brody 1978, 1997a). When this emotional process has not occurred, the child is often emotionally needy and seeks attention through withdrawn or aggressive behaviors to obtain the bonding relationship. In this relationship, the child learns about the world and himself or herself. Attachment is believed to be formed when a close personal relationship using play and physical touch with an adult to and from a child is achieved (Ainsworth and Bell 1970; Bell 1970; Bowlby 1969; Spitz 1965). This attachment and subsequent bonding is believed to be necessary for a child to learn to relate to others in a productive manner. Developmental play therapy gives a child an opportunity to form new, healthier bonds with an adult so that other satisfying relationships will follow (Brody 1978, 1997a; Burt and Myrick 1980; Mitchem 1987).

Des Lauriers and Carlson (1969) speak of the relationship between a mother and child in early development phases, stating the assumption that some sort of communication exists between these two persons. They posit that the communication is of a different type where the baby has some type of expressive sound and body movement and the mother responds in an alert and attentive way with direct contact. It is critical to the child's development to have this persistent and consistent presence in a stable and predictable way. This is the beginning of development of the primary socialization process in the child (Des Lauriers and Carlson, 1969; Spitz 1965).

Use of the theory drives the goal of DPT. The goal states clearly that DPT assists the child to become a separate and differentiated person by first becoming attached and then separated. In the process of attachment, a motion of separation begins. Becoming aware of the feelings in these processes is paramount to successful attachment and separation. Attaining this attachment and separation allows for the child to attach and separate from others, helping the child to be less fearful and more familiar with her or his ability to attach and separate effectively. Additionally, using this process and training adults to use this process helps adults who have not attached and separated well in the past to become skillful with this process, thus allowing their children to become successful (Brody 1978, 1997a; Brody, Fenderson, and Stephenson 1976).

Children That Benefit from DPT

DPT has been used with a wide range of very disturbed children, including autistic and psychotic children (Brody 1997a, 1997b; Des Lauriers 1962). The video *Developmental Play Therapy Techniques* (Short and Center for Drug-Free Living 1996) demonstrates DPT being used with substance-exposed infants and children. Others have used DPT to work with sexually molested infants and children (Brody 1997a, 1997b; Short 1996a, 1996b; Mitchum 1987). Children who have learning difficulties and emotional handicaps, as well as introverted or hyperactive children, are candidates for DPT (Brody, 1978, 1997a, 1997b; Burt and Myrick 1980). Brody (1997a, 1997b) makes a point to describe the "child that kills" as a prime participant for DPT. She describes this child as one who is destructively acting out and having no core self. These children are impulsive and act out in destructive ways that hurt themselves and others. She believes that these children lack the most basic need: that of caring touch. Often these children are labeled with a diagnosis of Reactive Attachment Disorder.

Dr. Brody (1997a, 1997b) has discussed touch and children who have experienced abuse. She surmises that because of their abuse, these children do not own their bodies. Relationships with the young child begin with touch; there must be a relationship in order for the child to tell her or his story. When a child experiences "bad touch," it does not mean that he or she should not learn to experience caring touch. DPT offers the sexually abused child the opportunity to experience caring touch.

Dr. Brody asserts that most young children welcome caring touch if the adult is present and sensitive. Further, these children have a tremendous longing to be touched in a caring way. Cradling a child of abuse has a healing effect. This touch will help the child to talk about the abuse when she or he is ready to do so. The adult must find ways to make the touch acceptable for the child in appropriate ways. Brody (1997a, 1997b) insists that DPT is against all pain-producing stimuli as a therapeutic method in the treatment of children. Emotional pain may occur, but it will help the child to experience caring touch that will eventually heal the wounds and open up ways for the child to relate to adults who do not abuse.

Principles of Developmental Play Therapy

There are several courses of action that are used in DPT. The first is Dr. Brody's six guiding principles for the interactions between an adult and a child in developmental play therapy sessions (Brody 1997a, 1997b).

1. *A child who experiences herself or himself as touched develops a sense of self.* Brody (1997a, 1997b) explained that the child who is touched is enabled to recognize that she or he is a person. This causes the child to be able to recognize her and others for whom she has feelings and can interact with. The child can accept the touch or reject the touch; either response is an interaction. It offers relationship, and this is a way a child can grow.

2. *In order for a child to experience himself or herself touched, a capable adult must touch the child.* When talking about a capable adult, Brody (1997a, 1997b) says that this adult must have had experience in being touched and know how to provide the relationship needed for a child to feel touched. A child will know if the adult is able to provide this vital aspect of DPT.

3. *In order to be a Toucher, the adult must first be willing to learn to be the One Touched.* Brody (1997a, 1997b) was clear in her assertion that it is not easy to allow yourself to be touched, no matter what if your role is the therapist, the teacher, or the parent. She says, "The skin never forgets." When touched, people experience all their touches from the past; it opens up childhood memories, which involve both good and bad touch for most people.

4. *In order to feel touched, a child has to allow herself or himself to be touched.* Especially children who have been abused may not allow themselves to be touched. It may be too painful. This child may turn or push away or remain unresponsive. However, Brody (1997a, 1997b) assures that if the person involved in DPT remains steadfastly present, the child will begin to experience her or his bodily self. Slowly, the child allows the needed touch to begin the relationship.

5. *A child feels seen first through touch.* Brody (1997a, 1997b) discusses a child first experiencing being real through being seen at birth. She emphasizes that

this experience is allowed to occur when the child is touched by an adult, particularly the parents. She goes on to say that for humans, touch is a complex way of relating and is a higher-order way of relating. Touch is used to help a child feel touched and acknowledge his or her own body signals and experience a relationship to the person touching them.

6. *To provide the relationship the child needs to feel touched; the adult controls the activities that take place in a Developmental Play Therapy session.* The adult is the initiator and the person who takes charge in the sessions. This creates a safe experience for the child who is out of control and unable to relate because of past experiences. In order for the therapeutic relationship to become a possibility, the adult must be able to touch the child in ways that the child feels touched (Brody 1997a, 1997b).

The second action that Dr. Brody sets forth is the four broad initiatives that are exclusive of category but can be an ongoing interchange within each session. Those categories encompass the DPT therapist or caregiver actually noticing the child, touching the child, and responding to the child. Additionally, the DPT therapist or caregiver must work in such a way that the child cannot deny the therapist's or caregiver's presence and the fact that he or she is there to meet the child's needs (Brody 1997a, 1997b).

PLAY INTERVENTION PROCEDURES

Structure of the Overall Program

The program needs to incorporate at least two areas of structure (Brody 1978, 1997a, 1997b; Short 1996a, 1996b; Mitchum 1987; Burt and Myrick 1980). The first element is a training program for the parent or caregiver. Generally four weeks of training is given, with two hours each session. This training is held for the parent and/or caregiver without the children present. This training is to review developmental and parenting issues, for participants to learn to be comfortable with touch, and to learn the games used in this type of play therapy. The second element is that of groups with children and adults. These groups will be from 12 to 16 weeks in length, with a commitment of two hours each session. Sessions have also ranged from 16 weeks to 6 months or more, depending on the program and the play therapist's goals. A third element can be included and has been used in some programs: The home visit can be incorporated to help parents and/ or caregivers receive support at home to use the developmental play time throughout the week, instead of just in the weekly sessions. Home visits may also be used after the 16-week sessions for follow-up and continued support of the family. Ultimately, when a program is developed, the overall needs of the population giving and receiving this program service must be determined and the program set accordingly.

Session Structure

Each session incorporates greeting time, individual time, small group time, and treat time. The individual sessions include each therapist and/or caregiver with child working together in the room, which is set up with dyads of other therapists and/or caregivers and children. The dyads are with only six to eight children and their therapists and/or caregivers. The caregivers have been screened and trained to complete the sessions successfully. With very small children (infant to four years), the group meets only for an hour each week. The first twenty minutes is used to complete the one-on-one child-adult play. The next 20 minutes is called Circle Time, where the children and parent or parent figure all play in a large group. The last 15 minutes is used for juice time and departure.

Evaluation of Sessions

The evaluation of sessions is very important to incorporate into a program. The stress for the therapist and/or caregivers is high. DPT is not an easy type of play therapy for the child or the leaders. The physical and emotional strain is draining. A time before and after each session is sometimes used to help the therapist and/or caregiver to process what will be happening or what has happened in each session. Capturing the results of each session by using a video or audio device and journaling information is often helpful. These techniques allow for the leaders to see the progress made and understand how they are acting and interacting with the child. Techniques for improvement may be seen in the videos. Another helpful tool is the Attachment-to-Adult-Scale, which can be used with each session to determine the actual interactions that the child does. This tool can also be used as a pre and post test. Brody (1997a, 1997b) discussed the evaluation of the trainees, the children, the parent-child relationship, and the agency. This evaluation was completed by asking a series of questions and/or asking for their reactions to the sessions. Other evaluation techniques can be used as they fit for the program that is developed.

Methods and Techniques Used in DPT

The methods and techniques used in DPT structure the session so that it allows for the therapist and/or caregiver to provide for the child to be touched in healthy and productive ways. There are a variety of items needed to promote the individual sessions with the child. Brody (1997a, 1997b) states that she usually uses a rug (big enough for two to sit on) or a rocking chair and a table and chair. She also uses paper, crayons, pencil, and a bottle of skin lotion. Privacy is needed or a place away from the group in the individual session so that the child and adult are able to create a space for themselves. Toys are not in the room and are not a focus of DPT sessions.

One of the most used techniques is that of cradling the child. The adult holds the child in a nursing position so that eye contact is easy and a soft voice can be heard. The child is rocked while the adult sings or chants to the child. Cradling the child helps the child to feel safe and relaxed. There are times that children do not want to be cradled. Brody (1997a, 1997b) made a distinct note in her book regarding "holding" verses "cradling." If a child resists cradling, the adult stops the cradling and touches in a different way to make her or his presence felt. Sometimes the child sucks his or her thumb or wants to suck a bottle while being cradled. The DPT adult takes charge but does not force the child to do anything. The DPT adult never tickles the child. Remember, the touching is communication, a two-way street. Most children accept and want the cradling and enjoy this technique (Brody 1997a, 1997b).

Another technique used is a combination of hugging, kissing, speaking, and singing. Brody (1997a, 1997b) describes often asking a child if they have any kissable parts of their body. Children respond in different ways, but often the tone is set for playfulness and acceptance. The adult's attitude about touching is one of delight and sincerity. Letting this delight and sincerity show helps the child to begin to trust and feel safe. These techniques are spontaneous and fit to the child. The DPT adult can make up songs regarding the child's features or personality. These techniques are also used in group work with the children and DPT adults. Brody (1997a) describes specific use of hugging, kissing, speaking, and singing activities in her book *The Dialogue of Touch: Developmental Play Therapy.*

Touching and chanting body parts is a fun technique that makes the child aware of her or his body. It is an undeniable way for the child to experience herself or himself. Chanting or saying, "Where is your nose? Where is your nose?" or whatever body part the adult wishes to use, helps the child to identify the body part. Children delight in telling the adult where the body part is located and inviting the adult to touch that body part. Manipulating toes and fingers or arms or legs is another part of touching and chanting body parts (Brody 1997a, 1997b).

Setting limits is a major method used in DPT. According to Brody (1997a, 1997b), setting limits for children helps them to mature as they recognize they are not all-powerful. The child does not control the DPT sessions, the adult does. When limits are set the child learns to be an individual and experience his or her own *self.* A child will learn that the adult is in charge of the child and the child does not need to take care of himself or herself. Eventually, this knowledge will transfer to the child that the child is able to take care of himself or herself as he or she grows and matures. Children learn the "I—thou" (Buber 1958) relationship when limits are set (Brody 1997a, 1997b).

The techniques and methods used in DPT can be used in the individual and the group sessions with the children. Games are often a part of the group portion of the DPT session. The group sessions offer more opportunity for group fun. One such game is that of the "Train Going Somewhere" (Short 1993a, 1993b). Each adult and child dyad is hooked together by the conductor as they sit on the floor with their legs out in front of them. The child is sitting in the adult's lap or on the floor directly in front of the adult. The conductor blows the whistle and the train starts to move as the adults and children (when able) move their legs forward, scooting across the floor. The adult and child each take a turn saying what they see out the window or what place they are headed. This group activity allows for participation from all and solidifies group cohesion and interaction.

Stages of DPT

Brody, Fenderson, and Stephenson (1976) addresses four stages of DPT and gives sample activities for each of these stages. The first stage is the *Honeymoon Stage*, where the child and the adult both have fantasies of positive emotional involvement, getting their needs met, and feeling the warmth from one another. This stage is short-lived but pleasant for the adult and the child. The second stage is called the *Painful Stage*. In this stage, the child and adult come to know that there is no ideal relationship and certain negative feelings can be felt. These feelings range from hurt and rejection to anger. *Separation and Love* is the third stage. The child will experience the adult as a separate self. The child will be able in this stage to show caring for the adult through touch, questions, and sharing feelings. The fourth and final stage, *Preparation for Termination*, is a sadder time as the adult and child begin to plan for termination of the sessions. Feelings such as anxiety and loss are felt. It is noted that these stages and activities are used for individual and circle time for the children and adult.

EMPIRICAL SUPPORT

An Attachment-to-Adult-Scale was developed by Dr. Brody for the use in documenting the child's advancement toward being able to relate to adults with the use of DPT sessions. This scale has been used in various programs over the years to quantify and detail the usefulness of DPT. On it are several benchmarks of child-adult interaction, such as plays peek-a-boo, plays hide and seek, chase, running to be caught, hits, bites, cries with tears and sobs, cries with tears silently, greets adult, shows sadness, anger, crying, touches or hugs adult, plays with face of adult, and so on (Brody 1993). With this scale, a journal of their experience is kept by the therapist or caregiver. Programs and DPT therapists have videoed each session to show the obvious improvement of the child and evolving relationship with the therapist or caregiver (Short 1996a, 1996b; Brody 1993, 1997a, 1997b).

Very few empirical research reports have been disseminated on this scale or on developmental play therapy. One post-DPT group research study was completed on 19 children. Interviews were completed on the elementary-age children in first, second, and third grades in a Southern state. Students were asked to recall some of the DPT experiences so that researchers knew the students were recalling the correct experience. Then, a set of eight yes/no questions were asked of the students. Results were that 100 percent enjoyed the DPT group and all reported having friends. Additionally, 89 percent of the students reported that they had made new friends, and 61 percent currently were playing DPT games with their friends. The children's thoughts about their adult partners continued to be high (79 percent). These children did not have their parents in the DPT sessions and stated (37 percent yes and 63 percent no) that they did not perceive any different treatment from their parents. Fifty-six percent of the students noted they believed their adult DPT partners to be different than other adults (Burt and Myrick 1980).

DPT has been researched by using the Wechsler Intelligence Scale for Children (WISC). Children who participated scored an average of seven points higher on the full scale. The scores of nonparticipants declined slightly. The performance scale on the WISC of these children was significantly higher than the nonparticipating group (Brody, Fenderson, and Stephenson 1976). Anecdotal information was given by teachers and by the college students who served as adult partners to the children. This information was overwhelmingly positive.

Anecdotal research has been completed and published by several researchers (Brody 1978, 1997a, 1997b; Short 1996a, 1996b; Mitchum 1987; Burt and Myrick 1980). Videos have been developed by various therapists and programs to show the effectiveness of developmental play therapy (Brody 1997b; Short and Center for Drug-Free Living 1996).

CASE ILLUSTRATION

Hosea

The case of Hosea illustrates developmental play therapy with a child who experienced physical and sexual abuse, as well as neglect. When Hosea first presented to DPT he was 22 months old, he was mute, did not smile, and was not present in his body. He complied with all requests but stared into space, not acknowledging the adults or the other children's presence in the room. Hosea also stiffened to touch of any kind. He was unable to provide any structure or accept any structure to the session time. It was as if this child was not a part of the world and did not exist and the therapist did not exist as well. Hosea had lost his family, his father and mother who abused him sexually and physically. His younger sister and older brother had been removed from the home at the same time as Hosea. They were sent to relatives living in the same state. Hosea was sent to live with a distant maternal cousin in a state that was far away from his biological family. Hosea's parents were eventually sent to prison for their crimes against children and their dealing in drugs. His mother and father were both alcoholic and used cocaine on a regular basis (Short 1993a).

Hosea's defective bond with his biological parents left him with the inability to relate to anyone. He needed someone to provide conditions for him to be able to experience a relationship beginning with caring touch. Hosea was admitted to the DPT program. He also was included in the Therapeutic Day Care program. This day care program accepted children who were abused or children of drug and/or alcoholic parents. There was a consistent and structured program of activities for the children. Some parenting programs were established and some of the caregivers or parents were trained to provide DPT under the supervision of a qualified professional.

The first through the sixth session, Hosea lay limp in the therapist's arms, not responding. His big brown eyes were empty and open wide, focusing on the ceiling. There were no interactions or acknowledgement of his being there. During circle time, Hosea remained quiet and nonresponsive, electively mute. The therapist would hold his limp arm up and wave good-bye during the last song. He would also sit by himself and quietly drink his juice and eat his snack during these first six sessions.

In the seventh session, he interacted with the therapist by looking at her in the eye and placing his little hand on her cheek. Later in that individual session, he smiled at her and offered her his foot to take off his shoes so they could play with his toes. From that session on, slowly Hosea came back to life. He was given additional treatment with individual play therapy sessions with the same therapist. Hosea continued the DPT sessions and the day care. Within weeks, Hosea was able to relate and interact in normal ways. After the initial 16-week DPT session, his foster parents were trained in DPT and completed full sessions with him over several months. Hosea was eventually adopted by his foster family (Short 1993a).

Therapist's View of Hosea and DPT

The therapist kept a daily log of her work with Hosea. In this log was an account of her feelings and actual activities that Hosea was able to complete.

The journal shows that the first six weeks were very difficult for the therapist as the "child was absent from his body and the world. Hosea's eyes are vacant. He does not respond but allows me to take over his body. I am sad for Hosea. I hope I can help him with appropriate touch and caring." Later, her journal showed that Hosea was beginning to respond on the seventh session. "I cannot tell you how happy I am or what it felt like when he touched me back. It brought tears to my eye when he looked at me for the first time. When he offered me to take off his shoes to play, it was then I knew he would make it and do well. I am so happy for Hosea" (Short 1993a).

The therapist chronicled the changes in Hosea in all sessions. Her final entry showed that Hosea was able to relate to her and others as he talked now, smiled, touched appropriately, communicated his needs, and played with other children well. He also was able to begin relating to his foster parents as they came to several sessions of the later DPT sessions to watch the interactions and begin to learn how to work with Hosea in these sessions (Short 1993a).

CONCLUSION AND FUTURE RESEARCH

While some research may have been completed, much of it has not been disseminated to the professional public. Working with DPT has convinced several professionals and families that DPT works when it is instituted as Dr. Brody designed and intended. Future research agendas need to be formalized and be completed on various populations of children who are known to benefit from DPT and those who are not known to benefit, to include "normal" children and their parents. Research also needs to be completed on the DPT therapist and caregivers who work with the different populations of children. Exploration of ethnicities and cultural aspects of populations need to be better defined with quantitative and qualitative data. Information needs to be gathered to see if DPT would be helpful in work with adults or older children who are recovering from childhood trauma. These future studies can come in the form of basic informative studies, adding intervention studies when the base is better established.

REFERENCES

Adler, J. 1981. Who is the witness? Unpublished paper. Authentic Movement Institute, San Francisco, CA.

Ainsworth, M. D. S., and S. M. Bell. 1970. Attachment, exploration, and separation: Illustrated by the behavior of one-year-olds in a strange situation. *Child Development* 41:49–67.

Bell, S. M. 1970. The development of the concept of object as related to infant-mother attachment. *Child Development* 41:291–311.

Bowlby, J. 1969. *Attachment and loss.* 3 vols. New York: Basic.

Brody, V. A. 1978. Developmental play: A relationship-focused program for children. *Child Welfare* 57 (9): 591–599.

———. 1993. Attachment-to-adult scale. Unpublished paper.

———. 1997a. *The dialogue of touch: Developmental play therapy.* Northvale, NJ: Jason Aronson.

———. 1997b. *Developmental play therapy sessions: A clinical session.* Denton: Center for Play Therapy, University of North Texas.

Brody, V. A., C. Fenderson, and S. Stephenson. 1976. *Sourcebook for finding your way to helping young children through developmental play.* Tallahassee: State of Florida, Department of State.

Buber, M. 1958. *I and thou.* New York: Scribner.

Burt, M. A., and R. D. Myrick. 1980. Developmental play: What's it all about? *Elementary School Guidance and Counseling,* October, 14–21.

Des Lauriers, A. 1962. *The experience of reality in childhood schizophrenia.* New York: International Universities Press.

Des Lauriers, A., and C. F. Carlson. 1969. *Your child is asleep: Early infantile autism.* Homewood, IL: Dorsey.

Mitchum, N. T. 1987. Developmental play therapy: A treatment approach for child victims of sexual molestation. *Journal of Counseling and Development,* 65:320–321.

Short, G. F. 1993a. Developmental play therapy: A case study. Unpublished paper.

———. 1993b. Games to play with children using DPT. Unpublished paper.

———. 1996a. *Developmental play therapy session.* Hospital Video Productions, Orange County Memorial, Orlando, Florida.

———. 1996b. Play therapy interventions for substance-exposed infants and toddlers. *The Source* 6 (1): 8–10.

Short, G. F., and Center for Drug-Free Living. 1996. Video. *Developmental play therapy techniques with substance-exposed infants and toddlers.* Hospital Video Productions, Orange County Memorial, Orlando, Florida.

Spitz, R. A. 1965. *The first year of life.* New York: International Universities Press.

15

Play-Based Intervention for Very Young Children with Autism: The PLAY Project

Richard Solomon

INTRODUCTION AND OVERVIEW

Children with autism do not play very well with others. In fact, these children typically avoid people altogether, spending their time alone over-focusing on their favorite activities: opening and closing doors, turning on and off light switches, flipping through the pages of the same book, or putting their Thomas the Tank Engine trains in a row. While typical children seek novelty through play, *children with autism want to keep the world the same through repetition.* So it may seem paradoxical to use play as a primary modality for intervention with young children (age 15 months to 6 years) with autism. Can you really "teach" a child with autism to play?

In fact, you can. In this chapter on play-based intervention for very young children with autism, I will present an innovative model program called the Play and Language for Autistic Youngsters (PLAY) Project. *The PLAY Project systematically trains parents and professionals to use play principles, strategies, methods, and techniques with very young children with autism in a cost-effective manner. It is primarily designed to help parents be their child's best play partner.* The project has research evidence to support its methods (Solomon et al. 2007), has recently received an NIH grant to do a controlled study of the model, and has been successfully disseminated in the United States, strongly suggesting that it is not only theoretically sound but practical as well.

First though, I'd like to set the stage by briefly describing what autism is both diagnostically and neurologically; why there has been such a dramatic increase in prevalence (now affecting 1 in every 88 boys!) (MMWR 2007); and what the National Research Council recommends we do for intervention (Lord, Bristol-Power, and Cafierol 2001). After that, I'll describe how the PLAY Project model addresses the national need for a play-based parent-training approach for the very young child with autism. I'll present a case study and conclude with a review of the research evidence for social pragmatic (i.e., play-based) approaches.

BACKGROUND, THEORY, AND RATIONALE

Autism is a neuro-genetic condition characterized, according to the DSM IV (the official psychiatric Diagnostic and Statistical Manual) by three primary features and an age-related criterion:

1. Qualitative impairment in social interaction
2. Qualitative impairment in communication/language
3. Restricted repetitive and stereotyped patterns of behavior, interests, and activities
4. Delays or abnormal functioning must occur prior to age three years

Officially, children with these difficulties are considered to have a pervasive developmental disorder (PDD). In common usage we say the child has an "autistic spectrum disorder." Indeed, the impairments do range across a spectrum from severe (i.e., no language, very self-isolating and dominating behaviors that preclude engagement); to moderate (i.e., fair language skills though not normal, some desire to socialize but inability to do so, and dominating interests that are symbolic [trains, cars, dinosaurs, etc.], also known as "pervasive developmental disorder not otherwise specified" [PDD NOS]); to very mild (i.e., normal language, a little "odd" socially, and dominating intellectual interests), known as Asperger's syndrome.

Because of this spectrum of severity, we are identifying children with milder cases. Because of public awareness, early intervention programs, and better screening instruments, we are also finding these children earlier. Recent studies indicate that autism can be identified as early as 14 months (Landa and Garrett-Mayer 2006). As a result, autism is increasingly being recognized in young children. It affects 1 in every 150 children (MMWR 2007), with boys being four times more affected than girls. In Michigan, the number has risen from 250 identified children in 1983 to over 7,000 in 2006! The U.S. Census Bureau estimated the number of children with autism in 2002 as 200,000, with predicted increases up to 550,000 by 2008. Some have called this trend an epidemic. But is autism really increasing?

In addition to better identification and broader diagnostic criteria, there does appear to be an absolute increase in the prevalence. Suspicions are centering on genetics *and* in utero exposures to neurotoxins (Houlihan et al. 2005). Immunizations and mercury exposure *after* birth have been ruled out as primary causes. According to one neuroscientist: "Although yet to be identified environmental factors likely contribute to the development of autism, heritability studies suggest that the impact of those factors must be imposed upon individuals genetically predisposed to the disorder" (Minshew 2006). In fact, several "autism genes" have been identified (Geschwind et al. 2001; Szatmari et al. 2007), and studies have shown that many parents of children with autism have autistic-like traits though not the condition (Silverman et al. 2002).

Whether due to genetics and/or the environment, the impact of autism on children's brains is becoming increasingly clear. Thanks to national scientific collaboratives, neuroscientists have been able to study autopsied brains of children with autism. They have discovered that, fundamentally, autism is a disorder of brain complexity (Just et al. 2006). Studies from multiple sources (Williams, Goldstein, and Minshew 2006) suggest abnormalities of neuronal development and poor connectivity between brain structures leading to functional abnormalities in the most complex activities, namely, language, social skills, and higher order thinking. The brain of the child with autism is like a net that cannot catch the complexity of the world in its web.

There is one saving grace: brain plasticity. Brain plasticity is the ability of the brain to reshape itself from the outside in. In others words, experience changes brain structures (viz., neurons). In recognition of this, the National Academy of Sciences/National Research Council convened a group of experts to recommend guidelines for the education of young children with autism (Lord, Bristol-Power, and Cafierol 2001). Here in a nutshell is what they recommended:

- Start intervention early (*14 months to 5 years of age*) . . .
- Provide *25 hours/week* of direct intervention . . .
- That is *engaging* . . .
- *Individualized* (1:1 or 1:2 teacher-to-student ratio) . . .
- And has a *strategic direction* (language, social skills, academic skills, etc.)

By providing this type of intensive intervention, the hope is that children with autism will be able to achieve the goals of personal independence and social responsibility.

It wasn't long ago that professionals believed that " . . . therapeutic intervention . . . has little beneficial effect for autistic children, except to prevent further deterioration" (Standard Psychiatry Textbook 1989). The research literature soundly contradicts this view and agrees with the NRC recommendations: intensive intervention, especially when provided when the child is young, probably reshapes brain connections and certainly can change the course of the child's life.

Among the intensive therapeutic approaches two broad types of interventions—behavioral and social-pragmatic/play-based—are typical (Prizant and Wetherby 1998). Though the approaches differ deeply in their fundamental theoretical underpinnings, they share the key elements recommended by the NRC. In behavioral approaches (Howard et al. 2005; Lovaas et al. 1973; Lovaas 1987; Sallows and Graupner 2005; Simpson 2005; Smith 1999), the children are typically drilled using an operant learning (Skinnerian) paradigm to increase language, social, and cognitive skills. These drill-based methods have been carefully evaluated and repeatedly shown to be effective in improving IQ and language skills. Their impact on social skills is less certain (Shea 2004).

In the social pragmatic/play-based approaches, drill and techniques are secondary to following the child's lead and promoting joint attention and contingent interactions through having fun. The motto of the PLAY Project is: "When you do what the child loves, he will love being with you." The PLAY Project uses Stanley Greenspan's Developmental Individual-Differences, Relationship-Based (DIR) framework to inform its structured play-based approach (Greenspan and Wieder 1997a; Greenspan and Wieder 1997b; Wieder 2005). While social pragmatic approaches are more difficult to quantify compared to behavioral approaches, scientific support for them is steadily growing (Aldred, Green, and Adams 2004; Drew et al. 2002; Greespan and Wieder 1997b; Ingersoll et al. 2005; Mahoney and Perales 2004; McConachie et al. 2005; Rogers and Delalla 1991; Solomon et al. 2007; Tannock, Girolametto, and Siegal 1992).

Intensive interventions are usually implemented over two to four years, until the child is six years old. The cost of these interventions *when delivered by professionals* is very expensive, ranging between $25,000 and $60,000 per year. Because of this, they are often not provided in the large majority of financially strapped state departments of education, and they are well out of financial reach for most families to obtain privately. With the increasing numbers of children being identified nationally, the cost of intensive intervention so high, and the benefits so great, there is an urgent national need for cost-effective interventions for young children with autistic spectrum disorders. Training parents to be the child's first interventionist has been recognized as the most practical way to deliver initial services (Diggle, McConachie, and Randle 2005). The PLAY Project parent-training model has the potential to address this national need. Its approach is consistent with the National Research Council recommendations. It has been pilot tested (Solomon et al. 2007) and it has been implemented successfully in real-world settings in 17 states.

THE PLAY PROJECT MODEL

Program Description

Over the last seven years, under my direction as a developmental/ behavioral pediatrician, The PLAY Project (www.playproject.org) has established itself as "a community-based/regional autism training and early intervention center dedicated to empowering parents and professionals to implement intensive, developmental interventions for young children with autism in the most effective and efficient way" (from the project's vision statement).

The DIR Theoretical Framework. The PLAY Project's theoretical framework, as mentioned above, is derived from the DIR model of Stanley Greenspan, as detailed in the Clinical Guidelines of the Interdisciplinary Council on Learning Disorders (Greenspan 1992; Greenspan and Wieder 1997a). The DIR model focuses on social reciprocity, affect (the feeling life of the child), and social communication. Greenspan's six functional developmental levels (FDLs) are like a "developmental ladder" that describe the course by which children typically gain the ability to relate to others. These are

- Self-regulation and shared attention (FDL 1) (birth to 4 months)
- Engagement (FDL 2) (4–9 months)
- Two-way communication (FDL 3) (9–15 months)
- Complex two-way communication (FDL 4) (15–24 months)
- Shared meanings and symbolic play (FDL 5) (2–3 years)
- Emotional thinking (FDL 6) (3–5 years)

In infancy, babies learn to regulate themselves to stay in a calm, attentive state for longer and longer periods of time (FDL 1). By 4 to 9 months of age, this shared attention extends to full engagement (FDL 2) in games such as peek-a-boo and patty-cake. A key element of Greenspan's theory is the importance of interactional "circles"—that is, the back-and-forth contingent reciprocal exchange of communication. At each FDL, the number and complexity of circles increases. Soon, then, infants as young as 9 to 15 months begin two-way communication as partners in the relationship (e.g., chase, catch, etc.) and can sustain playful back-and-forth interactions (FDL 3) that become increasingly complex. By 15 to 24 months, toddlers are using a combination of gestures and words; simple pretend play (e.g., feeding dollies, phone to ear, etc.) is emerging; and back-and-forth interactions take on the quality of simple conversations (FDL 4). By age two, communication becomes progressively more meaningful and symbolic, allowing young children to understand routines, one- and two-step commands, and so on (FDL 5). From age three to five, children become amazingly sophisticated in their ability to think emotionally. They talk in complex sentences and

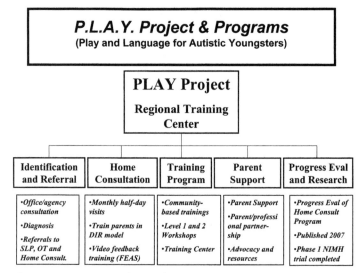

Figure 15.1.   PLAY Project and Programs

bridge ideas such that rich imaginative play becomes the hallmark of their functional communication (FDL 6).

In our program, Greenspan's theoretical framework has been transformed into a train-the-trainer model that makes his theory practical for professionals and parents. Let's turn now to the key components of the PLAY Project model (see figure 15.1).

Identification and Referral (Michigan). The PLAY Project has been disseminated to over 50 agencies in over 17 states nationally. I operate one of these centers in southeast Michigan, where The PLAY Project serves as a regional resource to help families obtain a diagnosis of and referrals for their children with autism. Experience gained through the "laboratory" in Michigan has helped the PLAY Project staff learn about the networking process in communities and the importance of community in helping families no matter where they live.

I make the diagnosis of ASD and follow hundreds of children on the spectrum. I work in collaboration with community-based referral sources that provide medical services, special education, speech and language therapy, occupational therapy, and behavioral-developmental interventions. The goal is to help families obtain services that are consistent with the National Research Council. (This is not easy to do for families. In Michigan, as in the large majority of states, there are no publicly funded services that routinely and consistently provide 25 hours of intensive intervention for these children.) Altogether there are 15 PLAY Projects in Michigan that, in total, serve nearly 15 percent of all young (14 months to 5 years old) children with autism in the state. I also serve on the Autism Committee of the Michigan Chapter of the American Academy of Pediatrics, and I educate pediatricians about the importance of early identification, referral, and intervention (that is, *don't* "wait and see how the child does." Refer to intervention right away!). This local, regional, and statewide experience has served to disseminate the model in other states and regions where difficulties with diagnosis, referral, and intervention are widespread.

The PLAY Project Home Consultation (PPHC) Program. The centerpiece of the PLAY Project model is the home consultation program, which is designed to train parents to be their child's best play partner.

The home consultants, who have degrees in child development fields (occupational therapy, speech/language pathology, early childhood education, social work, recreational therapy, child psychology), receive structured, intensive, year-long training in the model (see Training below). A full-time consultant can take care of 25 new families, though most consultants are part-time and will serve 10 to 15 families. Families typically receive 10 half-day (three-hour) home visits per year. Between home visits, families get written feedback and suggestions for ways to improve their playful engagement. Families are expected to provide 15 hours per week of engaging PLAY-based intervention. Consultants may travel up to an hour radius from the service/home base to serve families. Thus, large regions of a state can be served by a small group of PPHC providers. Most of the PPHC programs are located in private agencies that charge families directly for services. The cost on average is $3,500 to $4,000 per year (10 visits). When intensive intervention is provided by professionals instead of parents, the costs can range between $25,000 and $60,000 per year, making the PLAY Project a very reasonable alternative. Some agencies provide the services free through grants, while others (rarely) can cover the costs through health or mental health insurance.

The PLAY Project is outcomes-oriented. During the *first visit*, home consultants collect baseline information that not only informs clinical judgment but can be used to evaluate outcomes (see appendix 15-A for a list of evaluation instruments). In subsequent visits, home consultants train/ coach parents to play with their child by teaching them to use *The PLAY Project Skill Sequence* (see figure 15.2 below) as their main training tool.

The Skill Sequence introduces the parents to the PLAY Project's *key principles*. These include (1) the importance of affect (the feeling life) in the context of relationship (i.e., the importance of have fun with people); (2) playing at the right developmental level (not over their heads); and (3) providing the right dose (i.e., two hours per day of on-the-floor, engaging intervention).

We familiarize parents with the key concepts of *comfort zone, sensory/motor profile,* and *functional developmental levels.*

PLAY Skill Sequence: Summary

1. List principles and strategies based on comfort zone (CZ), sensory profile (SP), and functional developmental level (FDL).

2. Assess child's unique: CZ activities, SP, and FDL.

3. Define daily and weekly curriculum/activities.

4. Follow child's cues, lead, and intent to increase circles.

5. Create menu of specific techniques.

6. Videotape and critically review interactions and progress.

7. Refine curriculum, methods, and techniques.

Figure 15.2.   PLAY Skill Sequence: Summary

- The child's *comfort zone* is defined as "what the child will do when you let the child do whatever he or she wants to do." Comfort zone activities are repetitive, stereotyped, dominating interests.
- *Sensory-motor profile* is the child's unique set of responses to the world based on her or his perceptions. Some children are overreactive to the world, sensitive to noises, sights, and so on; others are underreactive and will lie around and be hard to engage or arouse. Some children, for example, become over-focused on visually stimulating objects and will watch spinning toys over and over. Many have poor auditory processing abilities and will act as if they are deaf and not turn to their names. Most children with autism love deep pressure. So it makes sense that, if we want to engage children, we will limit the modes that bother or absorb children and focus on the sensory modes that engage them.
- Greenspan's Functional Developmental Levels are described above. How these levels are used to help children climb the developmental ladder will be detailed in the case study below.

The Skill Sequence guides the home consultant in accurately *assessing the child's unique developmental profile,* developing a *curriculum of activities* for the parents and teaching them the methods that promote contingent reciprocal interactions (i.e., *following their lead and intention to increase circles*). It also provides families with dozens of *specific techniques* that help them implement the approach. Video feedback offers parents the perfect blend of theoretical and concrete specifics. They can see themselves in interaction which can be analyzed to improve their approach. As the child (hopefully) makes progress, the curriculum must be refined. So the sequence starts all over again in this iterative developmental process.

Two other educational tools are used to orient parents to the The PLAY Project. These include *The PLAY Project CD-ROM* and *Parent Training Manual*. Both are built around the Skill Sequence. The CD-ROM is a replica of the one-day workshop (see below) and explains the Skill Sequence by showing over 30 videoclips of parents playing with their children.

Each half-day/three-hour home visit uses *modeling, coaching, video feedback*, and *written feedback* to help implement and then refine the skill sequence. *Modeling* involves the consultant's actually demonstrating for parents how to use the strategies, methods, and techniques of the Skill Sequence; *coaching* involves observing the parents as they play with their child and giving them positive feedback about their performance; *video feedback* involves analyzing a 15-minute segment of film taken at the home visit. Often the home consultant will review, explore, and discuss this segment with the parent in an open-ended way to see how the parents' perceptions match that of the home consultant. The video is reviewed back at the office and subsequently used to give *written feedback*. Written feedback happens twice. At the end of the home visit, parents are given three written suggestions that can be used immediately to help PLAY. Then home consultants review the videotape session and send the parents written recommendations based on their observations.

Community Training Programs. Key to the PLAY Project's mission is educating communities about the science of autism, the importance of the National Research Council recommendations, and the PLAY Project model. *Community-based trainings* include grand rounds presentations for medical professionals and community lectures and workshops. The basic and advanced workshops introduce professionals and parents to the PLAY Project methods for lower and higher functioning children with autism, respectively. Over the last five years, dozens of communities in 17 states have been served, with thousands of parents and professionals attending community-based trainings. Evaluations of lectures and workshops have been very positive.

A replica of the basic PLAY Project workshop is available on DVD. Like the workshop, it follows the Skill Sequence. The unique feature of the DVD is that it shows dozens of videoclips of parents playing engagingly with their young child with ASD. Thus, parents can model strategies, methods, and techniques after watching other parents do it. This makes the basic educational materials readily available to the community and extends the service delivery system.

Finally, in terms of community resources, a new component of the PLAY Project refers parents to an online site called Relate Now (www.relatenow .com), which connects parents to PLAY Project professionals, other PLAY Project parents, information on autism, and national and local support organizations. Relate Now has an intelligent interactive technology that allows parents to type in keywords that describe their child and the site will find videos and resources that match the child's profile. For instance, parents can watch archived footage of parents playing with a child who is like their own child. Relate Now also provides online tools to track and assess children's progress, serving as a centralized therapeutic chart that can be shared (only with parents' permission) with the interdisciplinary team (SLP, OT, MD).

Agency Training Programs. Agency training programs are much more intensive and extensive than the community trainings. Over 50 agencies (private rehab services, schools/preschools/early intervention programs, hospitals and community mental health agencies) in 17 states have been trained to provide the home consultation program in their communities (see www.playproject.org for a listing).

Agency trainings occur in two phases. First, agency personnel come to Ann Arbor, Michigan, for four days of intensive training, where future home consultants are taught to use the PLAY Project model, the Skill Sequence, and the nuts and bolts of setting up a home consultation program within their agencies. In the second phase, when they return to their agencies, they start making home consultation visits and send the videos of home visits to PLAY Project supervisors who give them *audiotape* feedback on their videotapes. This use of video and audiotape allows for efficient, effective long-distance supervision. Agency personnel can, with good planning, start serving families within a month of being trained.

The PLAY Project supervisors, who have at least two years of experience in the model, review the consultant's ability to teach the parents the PLAY Project/DIR methods. Supervision is provided for 12 to 18 months, at which time agency staff may (if they are evaluated positively) be certified by the PLAY Project. Cost of the year-long training ranges from $4,500 to $5,500 per year, depending on the number of personnel trained per agency.

Community Outreach. As PLAY Project agencies start up their community-based programs, the PLAY Project helps them develop a community-wide network by bringing project workshops to the community, connecting them to physician/referral sources, and by offering technical assistance (letters, brochures, fact sheets, flyers, media packages, TV and radio interviews, etc.). Recently, the PLAY Project has established a close working relationship with Easter Seals National and is disseminating home consultation programs through their national affiliates all over the United States.

Program Evaluation. As mentioned, the PLAY Project is outcomes oriented. Baseline and repeated measures are built into the clinical model so a child's progress can be evaluated objectively (see case study). An evaluation of the PLAY Project Home Consulting program has been peer reviewed and published by the journal *Autism* (Solomon et al. 2007) (see empirical support below). And the project has received an NIMH grant to implement a controlled trial of the PLAY Project versus standard community services.

CASE STUDY

Our hopes and dreams are that Logan[1] will live a typical life . . . The PLAY Project has helped us to relate to our son at a level we were never able to before.

Mother of four-year-old Logan

I remember the first time I met Logan. He did not make eye contact with me, nor interact with me. I sat next to Logan at his train table for at least 20 minutes, simply copying his actions. Logan did not look up from what he was doing or even acknowledge that I was there. Just recently, on my 13th PLAY visit to Logan's home, he greeted me at the door, gave me a hug, and said, "Hi, Ms. Jennifer—are you ready to play with me?" Logan has a sense of humor now: He actually teases his mother and me. He comes up with many different play themes, and he is getting much better at reasoning and problem solving.

Logan's PLAY Project home consultant

When Logan, who was almost three years old, first came to my office it was, sadly, easy to see that he had the triad of autistic characteristics: delays in language; problems with social interaction; and dominating, repetitive interests. A beautiful, chubby little boy with black curly hair that framed a pixie face, he had 15–20 single words (a substantial delay) that reflected his interests: book, up, out, (1-2-3) go, juice, train, Barney, and so on. He seemed to understand routines but couldn't follow a simple command, such as "Get that train and give it to me." When his parents called him, he turned to his name so seldom that they had his hearing tested. His hearing was not the problem. He, like all children with autism, lived in his "neurological comfort zone" to avoid the chaos that was life, and spent much of his time looking through books or lining up trains, cars, and trucks; he "would watch videos all day long if you let him."

I made the diagnosis of *mild* autistic disorder because I saw something in Logan that suggested he had potential. He could be engaged, especially around sensory-motor play, and once engaged he could sustain a few interactions that made him laugh. This was a good prognostic sign. He had some expressive language before age three, no dysmorphic physical features (i.e., he looked "normal"), evidence of intelligence (his interests were symbolic—books, trains, Barney, etc.), relatively easy engageability, and a solid family. And he had a good sense of humor. His parents, Ann and Tom, were married. He had an older six-year-old brother, Drew, who loved to engage his brother. Tom was an engineer who made a good living and Ann was a stay-at-home mom who could put in the time for PLAY. In fact, Logan had all the good prognostic signs except one—response to intensive intervention. Currently his only service had been the public special education preschool, which did not provide much intensity.

So I referred him to the PLAY Project Home Consulting Program nearest to the family home. Jennifer, an occupational therapist trained in the PLAY Project methods, began her once-a-month, half-day home visits. She mod-

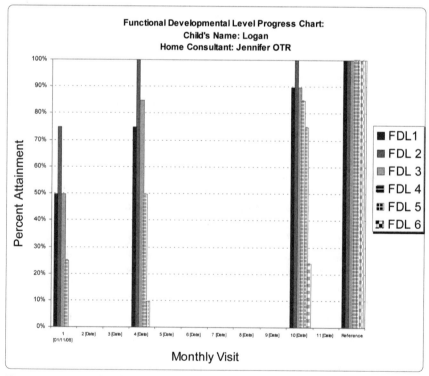

Figure 15.3. Functional Developmental Level Progress Chart

eled, coached, and gave video feedback (see program description above). Logan's initial profile is shown in figure 15.3, visit 1.

He was, according to Greenspan's developmental profile (see FDLs above), a child who was only fairly well regulated—for example, he threw a lot of "fits" when things didn't go his way and he spent about half of his time in his comfort zone, absorbed in lining up cars and ignoring his family (FDL 1: Attention and Self-Regulation). Thus, his Level 1 on the bar graph was rated, in a rough clinical estimate, as only 50 percent of what would be typical for a child his age (figure 15.3, visit 1). While playing trains, for instance, Logan would turn his back and not let his parents into his play. He would lie down on the floor and run the trains in front of his eyes. He was not that hard to engage (FDL 2: Engagement) (75 percent of typical). He did not often initiate interactions on his own. When children reach a solid 100 percent FDL 3 (Two-Way Communication), they will not leave you alone. This was our goal for Logan, but he was far from it (thus, 50 percent at Level 3). We gave him a little credit for FDL 4 (25 percent) because he showed intelligence by doing some problem solving (push a chair over to the cupboard to get food); he could open and close several circles of interaction when roughhousing with his dad; and he had a little pretend play (he would make car sounds)—all of which are characteristic for FDL 4.

After the first play session, Jennifer developed a curriculum of activities for Logan (Step 3 in the Skill Sequence) that included especially rough-and-tumble play, chase, jumping on the bed, being swung in a blanket, water play, and some simple pretend activities (animal sounds, feeding a baby, etc.)—all designed to get him having fun with people. His parents limited "train time," TV, computer, and videos. They put in about two hours per day, in multiple 15- to 20-minute play sessions, trying to engage him.

In the second and third (figure 15.3, visits 2 and 3) sessions, Jennifer taught the family to get more and more circles of interaction (Step 4 in the Skill Sequence). A *circle*, by definition, is a contingent, reciprocal interaction that is at the center of play. "Opening a circle" means initiating an interaction (the first volley). "Closing a circle" means responding contingently. Perhaps most important is Greenspan's idea of the "affect diathesis hypothesis," a technical way of saying that it is *feeling* that drives development. So it is a key principle in the PLAY Project that parents must promote *play with people* in a way that is *not* teaching/drilling but in a way that is fun (i.e., engages *affect*) for the child. This sounds simple but, in actual experience, children with autism don't come out and tell you what fun is for them. They act as if to say, "I'd rather be alone, thank you."

So we must teach parents to woo their children into interaction by recognizing subtle cues or following their child's lead in order to read their intentions moment to moment (see Step 4 in the Skill Sequence). This ability to engage in subtle, moment-to-moment interaction—the dance of relationship (more like riding a bucking bronco!)—is at the core of early play. We teach techniques like "taffy pulling" (i.e., stretching out interactions to get more circles); "theme and variation" to keep games from being repetitive; and "suspense and surprise" to heighten anticipation and increase affect and circles (Skill Sequence Step 5). The PLAY Project has more than 50 techniques that help parents, once they have their child engaged, answer the question: What do I do next?

By his fourth visit, already his profile had changed (see figure 15.3). His parents could see his progress and were thrilled. Logan's parents were good players. They did what he loved and now he loved being with them. In fact, he would not leave them alone. We had created an attention-seeking "monster." He was more regulated and available (FDL 1= 75%), always engageable (FDL 2 = 100%), and frequently initiating (FDL 3 = 85%). As connectedness increased, words became more meaningful and Logan's words started pouring out. We introduced songs and song games (e.g., "Ring around the Rosie," "Wheels on the Bus," etc.), which he loved. He now had over 100 words and, more importantly, he could follow spontaneous one- and two-step commands: "Logan (he would turn to his name consistently), go get the trains in your bedroom and bring them to me." He was using gestures along with words to communicate more complex intentions, which is the hallmark of FDL 4 and he was playing simple pretend (e.g., Daddy would pretend to be asleep, Logan would wake him up, and Daddy would tickle him and say, in mock anger, *"Don't* wake up *Daddy*!!" which Logan totally got.) His receptive language was growing. He understood longer and longer sentences ("Let's get ready. We're going to visit Grandma and Grandpa") (FDL 5 = 10%). This was major progress. See his profile at visit 4 on figure 15.3.

This was a boy on the move. Over the next four visits, Jennifer worked on FDL 4 and 5 activities: pretend play with puppets, cars (even trains could now be played with interactively), and little dolls in a dollhouse. Logan loved sword fighting with cardboard tubes from wrapping paper. He was enjoying hide-and-seek. And, more importantly, he was solid, *with* us, easily engaged and fluid in his interactions. The core deficits of autism were being addressed with this play-based intervention.

When he went to visit relatives, everyone noticed the new Logan. He no longer sought out isolation (unless it was really noisy and chaotic). He could join his cousins in simple chase games and wanted to be around other children. His social skills were still not those of an average 3-and-a-half-year-old, but he was no longer falling behind. He had made almost a year's progress in six months. This was not all our doing but was, in good part, due to his untapped potential. Not all children will make this kind of progress, but many do because the PLAY Project will find—through play—their potential, wherever it is.

At about the nine-month mark, despite Logan's wonderful progress, Jennifer noticed that Logan's mother, Ann, was looking weary and overwhelmed. In addition to doing the PLAY Project, she was also taking him to speech and language therapy, occupational therapy, horseback riding, and swimming. Almost none of the therapies were covered under insurance, which was putting financial strain on the family which was really stressing Tom, Logan's father. On top of everything, as Logan made progress, he was becoming more demanding and developing behavioral problems with frequent temper tantrums and even aggression like spitting, hitting, screaming, and throwing things. Logan's older brother, Drew, was beginning to complain: "No one is paying as much attention to me as they are to Logan!" Mom and Dad hadn't had time away together in they couldn't remember how long. Things were starting to fall apart.

A recent study on stress and children with disabilities showed that families with children with autism have more stress symptoms than families who have a child with some other kind of disability (Schieve et al. 2007). The demands that children with autism make on the family system—the intensive therapy, the multiple therapies, the often difficult behavior, the cost to the family budget, the emotional demands on the family—are enormous. Divorce rates in families with a child with autism are at 88 percent. The PLAY Project trains home consultants to be very sensitive to the emotional challenges of a family raising a child with autism. Jennifer recognized and supported Logan's mother's feelings. She referred the family to me for a counseling visit. I gave some behavioral advice, convinced Ann and Tom to allow the extended family to give them a long weekend to catch their breath, recharge their batteries, and give them some perspective. Ann started going out once a week with "the girls." Dad had a weekly fun day with Drew to alleviate a growing jealousy and the family, for the time being, got back on track emotionally.

With renewed energy, the family was able to support Logan as he marched up the developmental ladder. Our strategies and methods continued to focus on lots of circles and paying attention to his attention and intentions, but we were also making more and more demands on him for longer and more meaningful interactions. Jennifer introduced the important Wh-type questions like "Logan, *what* are you doing?" Our focus was on actions, ideas, feelings, and pretend dramas. We could model language and Logan would imitate it. A very important technique is "Speaking for the Child." When Logan gestured, we would articulate his gesture verbally. For instance, when he would cry about having to stop doing something, we would teach him to recognize his own feelings and negotiate:

"Logan, you don't want to stop playing."

He would stop crying and shake his head no.

"You want to watch a little more TV."

A smile would shine through his tears.

"OK. A little more TV?"

And he would ask, "More TV?" his little voice rising in request.

"OK. A little more. Just 5 more minutes."

In this way, Logan was learning about time, how to negotiate, and how to deal with his negative emotions. In other words, he was now able to understand abstract experiences (FDL 5 and emerging 6). Using the PLAY Project strategies, methods, and techniques in day-to-day interactions increased the "dose" of interaction throughout the day and, as an addition to on-the-floor-play (aka "floortime," Greenspan and Wieder 1997a), was a rich a source of developmental stimulation for Logan.

By home visit 10, Logan was continuing his climb up the functional developmental levels while maintaining integrity at the lower FDLs. His attention and self-regulation were almost solid; his engagement was 100 percent. He initiated all the time and could sustain long, multi-interactional sequences in a continuous flow with his play partners (see figure 15.3, visit 10). His play grew truly imaginative, as his fixation on lining up trains evolved into dramas about trains crashing and then needing help from the "train doctor." Other trains worried about him and so modeled empathy. This is the beginning of FDL 6 (see figure 15.3, visit 10).

When PLAY Project methods are used properly, the child will not feel put upon to perform. Following the child's lead ensures this. You know when the play is at the right level: The play is fun and interesting for both parent and child. At the same time, we trained Logan's parents to woo him upward in development by gradually introducing new twists to the play, little problems and quandaries, demands for consideration of others, and so forth. In these ways, we challenged Logan to be a creative, problem-solving boy. He was developing empathy and taking others' perspectives, all of which will serve him well in his interaction with peers as Logan heads toward kindergarten.

When we reviewed Logan and his parents' last videos in a group at my office, many of the therapists there questioned Logan's diagnosis. Indeed, to an outsider, play at FDL 6 would look like typical play with any child. This is a far cry from where Logan had started. Stuck as he was initially, Logan, with the help of his family, was able to follow the long and winding road out of his isolation through the allure of play.

EMPIRICAL SUPPORT

Logan's success was not unique. Clinically, most of the children in the PLAY Project make good to excellent progress. In this last section of the chapter I would like to share the empirical support for the so called social-pragmatic (play-based) approaches in general and research evidence for the PLAY Project (Solomon et al. 2007) in particular.

Despite clinical acceptance, the scientific evidence for social-pragmatic approaches has been limited (Dawson and Galpert 1990; Rogers 2000; Siller and Sigman 2002). These approaches are more difficult to operationalize and quantify compared to behavioral approaches (Rogers 2000). Nonetheless, evidence that social-pragmatic approaches can help young children with autism is growing (Aldred, Green, and Adams 2004; Drew et al. 2002; Greenspan and Wieder 1997b; Ingersoll et al. 2005; Mahoney and Perales 2004; McConachie et al. 2005; Rogers and Delalla 1991; Solomon et al. 2007; Tannock, Girolametto, and Siegal 1992).

The prototypical *social-pragmatic approach* is, as mentioned, represented by the work of Greenspan and his developmental, individualized, and relationship-oriented (DIR) model (Greenspan 1992; Greenspan and Wieder 1997a, 1997b). Joint attention and the promotion of contingent interaction are at the methodological core of all social-pragmatic models. Greenspan's case series (Greenspan and Wieder 1997b) involved a cohort of 200 children. This sample had a highly motivated, middle- to upper-income parent population. It can only be considered as an observational study, as there were no controls and no detailed description of the specific intervention protocols used. Nonetheless, after two years of intervention, 58 percent of treated children showed improvements and no longer met the criteria for autistic disorder on key measures (e.g., CARS).

Four other recent studies are of interest here. In a fascinating longitudinal study, Siller and Sigman found that certain behaviors of parents predicted subsequent development of the children's communication skills. In particular, caregivers who synchronized their behaviors to their children's attention and activities helped children with autism develop superior joint attention and language when compared to parents who were less contingent or synchronized. In short, parents appear to be able to learn various methods of intervention to help them effectively interact with their young children with autism (Siller and Sigman 2002). Mahoney and Perales (2005) used a controlled design and a parent-training model very similar in hours and methods to the PLAY Project. His group found highly significant improvements in the intervention group (N = 20 children with PDD) on social reciprocity and language measures compared to the control group (N = 30 children with other types of developmental delays). In another controlled trial, McConachie et al. studied the Canadian Hanen model. Parents of 51 children age 24 to 48 months received either immediate intervention or delayed access to the course. Outcome was measured seven months after recruitment in parents' use of facilitative strategies, stress, and adaptation to the child, and in children's vocabulary size, behavior problems, and social communication skills. A significant advantage was found for the intervention group in parents' observed use of facilitative strategies and in children's vocabulary size. The training course was well received by parents and has a measurable effect on both parents' and children's communication skills (McConachie et al. 2005). And finally, Aldred, Green, and Adams (2004), in a randomized controlled trial of parent training that used a social communication intervention methodology, showed statistical and clinical improvement compared with controls on the ADOS (Autsim Diagnostic Observation Scale) total score, particularly in reciprocal social interaction.

Evidence for the PLAY Project. In our study entitled "Pilot Study of a Parent-Training Program for Young Children with Autism: The PLAY Project Home Consultation Program" (Solomon et al. 2007), 74 children referred to the University of Michigan Developmental and Behavioral Pediatrics Clinic from October 2000 to February 2002 who were diagnosed as having autistic spectrum disorders were enrolled. None of the children participated in any other intensive intervention. Sixty-eight children had pre and post data available. Children were evaluated using a pre/post design at the start and at the end of the first year of enrollment in the PLAY Project Home Consultation Program (for a description of the program see above). Baseline demographic characteristics were obtained. While several measures were administered before and after intervention, I will review here briefly the most important outcome measure—the FEAS.

The FEAS (Greenspan, DiGangi, and Wieder 2001) is a valid and reliable, age-normed, clinical rating scale that can be applied to videotaped interactions between children with autism and their caregivers. It separately measures (1) changes in caregiver nurturing and contingent reciprocal interaction and (2) children's functional development (i.e., Greenspan's six FDLs). To establish inter-rater reliability for the FEAS, two raters, blind to the caregiver and the child's clinical status, were trained to reliability using a selection of 20 training tapes of children with autism who ranged in severity across FDLs. Both raters rated all tapes before and after intervention and they agreed with each other in a highly statistically significant way

In terms of the types of children studied, there was approximately equal representation between mildly, moderately, and severely affected individuals. On average, children were 3-and-a-half-years old at enrollment, with a range of 2 to 6 years. There were 51 boys and 15 girls. Approximately 70 percent of mothers and 70 percent of fathers had bachelor's degrees or above.

Child FEAS scores showed a highly statistically significant increase over the 12 months of the project ($p \leq 0.0001$). When FEAS scored were translated clinically, 45.5 percent of children made good to very good clinical gains. It didn't matter how severely affected the children were to start with, as no statistical relationship was found between initial ASD severity and FEAS scores. We also rated the children clinically, to compare our judgments to the FEAS scores. Based on these clinical ratings, 52 percent of children made very good (1.5 FDLs or better) clinical progress over the study period, with 14 percent making good progress (1.0 FDL). In terms of the "dose" of intensity, there was a trend (p = .09) suggesting that the more hours a parent put in playing, the better the child did on the FEAS scores.

This study is the first evidence for a programmatic approach that uses Greenspan's DIR theory. On the more conservative FEAS ratings, 45.5 percent of the children participating in the project made good to very good functional developmental gains. Clinically, 66 percent of the children rated made good to very good gains. FEAS scores and the clinical scores were highly statistically significant pre to post. When a child moves from an FDL 2 to an FDL 4, for instance, this represents the difference between being self-isolating versus being able to consistently communicate in a two-way interactive fashion. This represents an advance of more than a year in development. Thus, nearly half of the children made clinically significant developmental gains, with most making very good (i.e., greater than 1.5 FDL of progress) clinical gains.

Without a control group, it is not possible to say that changes in post-FEAS scores are directly attributable to the home-based training. The current controlled study funded by the National Institutes of Mental Health (NIMH) plans to address this important issue. It could be argued that, since most children were participating in special education programs, these programs confound the outcomes. But even when children are given up to 10 hours of intensive intervention, it does not substantially affect the course of their development (Lovaas 1987). Also, the development of children with autism who do not receive substantial intervention is poor (Rutter 1970). Thus our results cannot be explained easily on the basis of a natural course of improvement. More in-depth, repeated, and objective measures of development (i.e., language, IQ, etc.) will need to be added to future studies to improve the robustness of the outcomes. Such measures are planned in the current NIMH study.

CONCLUSION AND FUTURE DIRECTIONS

"Play is so important to optimal child development that it has been recognized by the United Nations High Commission for Human Rights as a right of every child" (Ginsburg 2007). For children with autism this birthright is denied twice over. First, there are not enough resources given for the appropriate services for children with autism. The National Research Council recommends 25 hours per week of intensive intervention services. The vast majority of states don't offer these types of services and insurance companies don't pay for them. Secondly, children with autism thwart our efforts to play with them because they prefer self-isolation as a fundamental aspect of their neuro-genetic condition.

For communities in our country, then, the challenge is to create options for parents that meet the NRC guidelines. The PLAY Project offers a cost-effective option for states and communities. Through its community-based trainings, Internet resources, train-the-trainer agency and school programs, and home consultation model, it can be disseminated broadly and efficiently.

For parents, the experience of having a child with autism begins with the experience of loss. Their child cannot engage, let alone play, with them. Parents are haunted by the big questions: Will he go to a regular school, be able to hold a job, get married, have a normal life, be independent? The grief of not having the expected, typically developing child gives way to an even more immediate and intimate grief, peculiar to autism—not being able to interact with your own child, not having your child call you mommy or daddy. Parents are at a loss as to what to do. They show up at my developmental/behavioral pediatric practice seeking direction, support, help—and hope. After I make the diagnosis, I can honestly give them hope.

While I educate parents about all their intervention options, it is my firm belief that parents should be their child's first and best play partners, especially if their child has autism. So, I introduce them to the PLAY Project. I tell them that autism is a genetic condition—not the fault of their parenting—that responds to intensive play-based intervention most of the time. I explain that the brain of the child with autism is like a loose net that cannot capture the complexity of the world in its web, and it is our job to tighten that net through rich, playful, engaging interventions. As a pediatric professional, it is a relief to be able to refer families to an evidence-based program in their community that can help. And it is the great satisfaction of my work to hear parents say that for the first time they feel connected to their child and their child feels connected to them through play.

APPENDIX 15-A
THE PLAY PROJECT EVALUATION MEASURES

- Gilliam Autism Rating Scale (GARS) (diagnostic confirmation of autism)
- Greenspan Social-Emotional Growth Chart (a parent report of their child's functional development)
- Functional Emotional Assessment Scale (FEAS) (a videotaped observation measure of the parents' nurturing interactions and sensitivity to child cues as well as child's functional developmental level)

- FDL progress chart (see case study)
- REEL-3 (a parent report language measure)
- Sensory Profile (Dunn) (a parent report of sensory/motor issues)
- Satisfaction Surveys (at three months and one year)

NOTE

1. Names have been changed to protect privacy.

REFERENCES

Aldred, C., J. Green, and C. Adams. 2004. A new social communication intervention for children with autism: Pilot randomized controlled treatment study suggesting effectiveness. *Journal of Child Psychology and Psychiatry and Allied Disciplines* 45 (8): 1420–1430.

Dawson, G., and L. Galpert. 1990. Mothers' use of imitative play for facilitating social responsiveness and toy play in young autistic children. *Development and Psychopathology* 2:151–162.

Diggle, R., H. McConachie, and V. Randle. 2005. Parent-mediated early intervention for young children with autism spectrum disorder. *Cochrane Database of Systematic Reviews* 2 (2002).

Drew, A., G. Baird, S. Baron-Cohen, A. Cox, V. Slonim, S. Wheelwright, J. Swettenham, B. Berry, and T. Charman. 2002. A pilot randomized control trial of parent-training intervention for preschool children with autism. *European Child and Adolescent Psychiatry* 11: 266–272.

Dunn, W. 1999. *The Sensory Profile manual.* San Antonio, TX: The Psychological Corporation.

Geschwind, D. H., J. Sowinski, C. Lord, P. Iversen, J. Shestack, P. Jones, L. Ducat, and S. Spence. 2001. The autism genetic resource exchange: A resource for the study of autism and related neuropsychiatric conditions. *American Journal of Human Genetics* 69 (2): 463–466.

Ginsberg, K. R. 2007. The importance of play in promoting healthy child development and maintaining strong parent-child bonds. *Pediatrics* 119 (1): 182–191.

Greenspan, S., G. DeGangi, and S. Wieder. 2001. *Functional emotional assessment scale: Clinical and research applications.* Bethesda, MD: Interdisciplinary Council on Developmental and Learning Disorders.

Greenspan, S. I. 1992. *Infancy and early childhood: The practice of clinical assessment and intervention with emotional and developmental challenges.* Madison, CT: International Universities Press.

Greenspan, S. I., and S. Wieder. 1997a. An integrated developmental approach to interventions for young children with severe difficulties in relating and communicating. *Zero to Three: National Center for Infants, Toddlers, and Families* 15, no. 5.

———. 1997b. Developmental patterns and outcomes in infants and children with disorders in relating and communication: A chart review of 200 cases of children with autistic spectrum disorders. *Journal of Developmental and Learning Disorders* 1 (1): 87–141.

Greenspan, S. I. 2004. Greenspan social emotional growth chart. Psychological Corporation of America.

Houlihan, J., T. Kropp, R. Wiles, S. Gray, and C. Campbell. 2005. BodyBurden: The pollution in newborns. Environmental Working Group 14, July.

Howard, J. S., C. Sparkman, H. Cohen, G. Green, and H. Stanislaw. 2005. A comparison of intensive behavior analytic and eclectic treatments for young children with autism. *Research in Developmental Disabilities* 26:359–383.

Ingersoll, B., A. Dvortcsak, C. Whalen, and D. Sikora. 2005. The effects of a developmental, social-pragmatic language intervention on rate of expressive language production in young children with autistic spectrum disorders. *Focus of Autism and Other Developmental Disorders* 20:213–222.

Just, M., V. Cherkassky, T. Keller, R. Kana, and N. Minshew. 2006. Functional and anatomical cortical underconnectivity in autism: Evidence from an fMRI study of an executive function task and corpus callosum morphometry. *Cerebral Cortex* 16, no. 7.

Landa, R., and E. Garrett-Mayer. 2006. Development in infants with autism spectrum disorders: A prospective study. *Journal of Child Psychology and Psychiatry* 47:629–638.

Lord, C., M. Bristol-Power, and J. Cafierol. 2001. *Educating children with autism.* Washington, DC: National Academy Press.

Lord, C., and J. P. McGee, eds. 2001. *Educating young children with autism.* Washington, DC: National Academy Press.

Lovaas, O. I. 1987. Behavioral treatment and normal educational and intellectual functioning of young autistic children. *Journal of Consulting and Clinical Psychology* 55:3–9.

Lovaas, O. I., R. Koegel, J. Q. Simmons, and J. S. Long. 1973. Some generalizations and follow-up measures on autistic children in behavior therapy. *Journal of Applied Behavior Analysis* 6:131–166.

Mahoney, G., and F. Perales. 2004. Relationship-focused early intervention with children with pervasive developmental disorders and other disabilities: A comparative study. *Journal of Developmental and Behavioral Pediatrics* 26:77–85.

McConachie, H., V. Randle, D. Hammal, and A. Le Couteur. 2005. A controlled trial of a training course for parents of children with suspected autism spectrum disorder. *Journal of Pediatrics* 147:335–340.

McEachin, J., T. Smith, and I. Lovaas. 1993. Long-term outcome for children with autism who received early intensive behavioral treatment. *American Journal on Mental Retardation* 97 (4): 359–372.

Minshew, N. J. 2006. Interdisciplinary Council for Developmental and Learning Disorders, (ICDL) annual conference. MacClean, VA.

MMWR Morbidity and Mortality Weekly Report 56, no. SS-1 (February 2007).

Prizant, B., and A. Wetherby. 1998. Understanding the continuum of discrete-trial traditional behavioral to social-pragmatic developmental approaches in communication enhancement for young children with autism/PDD. *Seminars in Speech and Language* 19:329–351.

Rogers, S., and D. Delalla. 1991. A comparative study of the effects of a developmentally based instructional model on young children with autism and young children with other disorders of behavior and development. *Topics in Early Childhood Special Education* 11:29–47.

Rogers, S. J. 2000. Interventions that facilitate socialization in children with autism. *Journal of Autism and Developmental Disorders* 30 (5): 399–409.

Rutter, M. 1970. Autistic children: Infancy to adulthood. *Seminars in Psychiatry* 2:435–450.

Sallows, G. O., and T. Graupner. 2005. Intensive behavioral treatment for children with autism: Four-year outcome and predictors. *American Journal on Mental Retardation* 110 (6): 415–438.

Schieve, L., S. Blumberg, C. Rice, S. N. Visser, and C. Boyle. 2007. The relationship between autism and parenting stress. *Pediatrics* 119:S114–S121.

Shea, V. 2004. A perspective on the research literature related to early intensive behavioral intervention for young children with autism. *Autism* 8 (4): 349–367.

Siller, M., M. Sigman. 2002. The behaviors of parents of children with autism predict the subsequent development of their children's communication. *Journal of Autism and Developmental Disorders* 32 (2): 77–89.

Silverman, J. M., C. Smith, J. Schmeidler, E. Hollander, B. Lawlor, M. Fitzgerald, J. Buxbaum, K. Delaney, and P. Galvin. 2002. Symptom domains in autism and related conditions: Evidence for familiality; Autism Genetic Research Exchange Consortium. *American Journal of Medical Genetics* 114 (1): 64–73.

Simpson, R. 2005. Evidence-based practices and students with autism spectrum disorders. *Focus on Autism and Other Developmental Disabilities* 20 (3): 140–149.

Smith, T. 1999. Outcome of early intervention for children with autism. *Clinical Psychology: Science and Practice* 6:33–49.

Solomon, R., J. Necheles, C. Ferch, and D. Bruckman. 2007. Pilot study of a parent-training program for young children with autism: The PLAY Project Home Consultation Program. *Autism* 11 (3): 205–224.

Szatmari, P., A. D. Paterson, L. Zwaigenbaum, et al. 2007. Mapping autism risk loci using genetic linkage and chromosomal rearrangements. *Nature Genetics* 39:319–328.

Tannock, R., L. Girolametto, and L. Siegal. 1992. Language intervention with children who have developmental delays: Effects of an interactive approach. *American Journal on Mental Retardation* 97:145–160.

Wieder, S., and S. Greenspan. 2005. Can children with autism master the core deficits and become empathetic, creative, and reflective? A ten- to fifteen-year follow-up of a subgroup of children with autism spectrum disorders (ASD) who received a comprehensive developmental, individual-difference, relationship-based (DIR) approach. *Journal of Developmental and Learning Disorders* 9:1–29.

Williams, D. L., G. Goldstein, and N. J. Minshew. 2006. Neuropsychologic functioning in children with autism: Further evidence for disordered complex information-processing. *Child Neuropsychology* 12:279–298.

Index

About the Editors and Contributors

EDITORS

Sophronia Kelly-Zion has been a practicing play therapist for 12 years, providing services in residential treatment settings, schools, and public mental health centers. She is a licensed clinical social work supervisor and a registered play therapist supervisor. Currently she is employed with Judson Independent School District in San Antonio, Texas, where she works with elementary-age at-risk students. In addition to adjunct teaching of play therapy courses at the university level, she has been actively involved in the Texas Association for Play Therapy (TAPT) as a board member at the chapter and the state level and has been the editor of the TAPT newsletter.

Judith McCormick is a play therapist for the Health Services Executive in Limerick, Ireland. She is also involved in training and consulting in play therapy. Ms. McCormick is a licensed clinical professional counselor and a registered play therapist supervisor and holds a certificate in infant and toddler studies from the Erikson Institute in Chicago. She is the past president of the Illinois Association for Play Therapy and coedited the *International Handbook of Play Therapy* with Dr. Charles Schaefer and Dr. Akiko Ohnogi.

Akiko Ohnogi is a clinical psychologist and play therapist in private practice in Tokyo who specializes in treating children, adolescents, families, parent education, and multicultural issues. Dr. Ohnogi is also adjunct faculty of International Christian University. She is one of the cofounders and board director of the Japan Association for Play Therapy, and a board member of the International Mental Health Professionals Japan and Nana's Children

Mental Health Foundation in the United States. Dr. Ohnogi provided direct psychological assistance to Sri Lankan tsunami orphans through Operation USA and the Association for Play Therapy (USA), and she was also responsible for training hospital staff at the Niigata Prefectural Mental Health Medical Center regarding response and treatment to the Chuetsu earthquake. Her publications include several Japanese journal publications and coediting, with Dr. Charles Schaefer and Ms. Judith McCormick, the *International Handbook of Play Therapy.*

Charles E. Schaefer is professor of psychology at Fairleigh Dickinson University in Teaneck, New Jersey. He is cofounder and director emeritus of the Association for Play Therapy. Dr. Schaefer has authored or edited over 60 books on play therapy, child therapy, and effective parenting. In 2006, he received the Lifetime Achievement Award from the Association for Play Therapy. He maintains a private practice focusing on children and families in Teaneck, New Jersey.

CONTRIBUTORS

Sue Ammen, PhD, RPT-S, Alliant International University, Sacramento, California, and Aurora Mental Health, Aurora, Colorado. E-mail: sammen@ alliant.edu.

Helen E. Benedict, PhD, RPT-S, Department of Psychology and Neuroscience, Baylor University, Waco, Texas. E-mail: Helen_Benedict@baylor .edu.

Sue Bratton, PhD, LPC, RPT-S, Center for Play Therapy, University of North Texas, Denton, Texas. E-mail: Sue.Bratton@unt.edu.

Nancy J. Cohen, PhD, CPsych, Hincks-Dellcrest Centre; Department of Psychiatry, University of Toronto; and Department of Human Development and Applied Psychology, OISE/UT, and Department of Psychology, York University. E-mail: nancy.cohen@utoronto.ca.

Stefan C. Dombrowski, PhD, School Psychology Program, Rider University, Lawrenceville, New Jersey. E-mail: sdombrowski@rider.edu.

Theodore J. Gaensbauer, MD, University of Colorado Health Sciences Center; Irving Harris Program in Child Development and Infant Mental Health, Division of Child Psychiatry; and private practice, Denver, Colorado. E-mail: Tgaensbauer@aol.com.

Hilda R. Glazer, EdD, RPT-S, School of Psychology, Capella University; Mount Carmel Hospice and Palliative Care; and private practice, Columbus, Ohio. E-mail: hglazer@sbcglobal.net.

Joy Goldberger, MS, CCLS, Child Life Education Coordinator, Johns Hopkins Children's Center, Baltimore. E-mail: JGoldbergr@aol.com.

Roxanne Grobbel, JD, LCSW, associate director, All 'Bout Children, West Palm Beach, Florida. E-mail: ROXINFL@aol.com.

Steve Harvey, PhD, RPT-S, ADTR, Child and Adolescent Mental Health Service, Taranaki District Health Board, New Plymouth, New Zealand. E-mail: Steve-connor@xtra.co.nz.

Kim Kelsay, MD, assistant professor, Department of Psychiatry, University of Colorado Health Sciences Center; codirector, Pediatric Day Treatment Program, National Jewish Medical and Research Center, Denver, Colorado.

Beth Limberg, PhD, RPT-S, California School of Professional Psychology, Alliant International University, Sacramento, California; and Zero to Three DC: 0–3R Training Task Force, Washington, D.C.

Keri Linas, MA, doctoral candidate, University of Denver.

Toni W. Linder, EdD, Child, Family, and School Psychology Program, Morgridge College of Education, University of Denver. E-mail: toni.linder@gmail.com.

Mirek Lojkasek, PhD, CPsych, Hincks-Dellcrest Institute; Department of Psychiatry, Faculty of Medicine, University of Toronto; and private practice, Toronto. E-mail: mlojkasek@hincksdellcrest.org.

Anne Luebering Mohl, PhD, CCLS, Johns Hopkins Children's Center, Baltimore.

Elisabeth Muir, private practice, Christchurch, New Zealand.

Evangeline Munns, PhD, CPsych, RPT-S, Munns Psychological Consultant Services, King City, Ontario. E-mail: emunns@sympatico.ca.

Ruth P. Newton, PhD, psychology supervisor, Child and Family Mental Health Services, St. Vincent de Paul Village, San Diego, California. E-mail: ruth.newton@neighbor.org.

Jane Robinson, LMHC, RPT/S, executive director, All 'Bout Children, West Palm Beach, Florida. E-mail: Ejanerob@aol.com.

Virginia Ryan, PhD, CPsych, MBAPT, Social Policy and Social Work Department, University of York, York, England. E-mail: vryan@personal.karoo .co.uk.

Glenda F. Lester Short, LCSW, PhD, Sociology and Social Work Department, Appalachian State University, Boone, North Carolina. E-mail: GlendaShort@MissouriState.edu.

Richard Solomon, MD, medical director, The PLAY Project, The Ann Arbor Center for Developmental and Behavioral Pediatrics, Ann Arbor, Michigan. E-mail: drrick@aacenter.org.

Kim Stokka, MA, RPT-S, LPC, LMFT, doctoral candidate, University of Denver.

Susan G. Timmer, PhD, Child and Adolescent Resource and Evaluation Center, University of California at Davis Children's Hospital; Human Development Graduate Group; and School of Medicine, University of California, Davis.

Nancy Zebell, PhD, Child and Adolescent Resource and Evaluation Center, University of California at Davis Children's Hospital, Davis, California.